POSTCOLONIAL

WHITENESS

POSTCOLONIAL

WHITENESS

A Critical Reader
on Race and Empire

EDITED BY

ALFRED J. LÓPEZ

STATE UNIVERSITY OF NEW YORK PRESS

Published by
STATE UNIVERSITY OF NEW YORK PRESS, ALBANY

© 2005 State University of New York

For information, address the State University of New York Press,
90 State Street, Suite 700, Albany, NY 12207

Production, Laurie D. Searl
Marketing, Anne M. Valentine

Library of Congress Cataloging-in-Publication Data

Postcolonial whiteness : a critical reader on race and empire / edited by
Alfred J. López.
    p. cm.
  Includes bibliographical references and index.
  ISBN 0-7914-6361-3 (alk. paper) — ISBN 0-7914-6362-1 (pbk. : alk. paper)
    1. Indigenous peoples. 2. Postcolonialism. 3. Racism. 4. Whites—Race
identity. I. López, Alfred J., 1962–

JV305.P67 2005
305.809—dc22   2004045399

10 9 8 7 6 5 4 3 2 1

To Susan López, wife and partner;

and to Sofia and Diego, our beautiful Latino babies

(who, like their daddy, look white but aren't)

CONTENTS

PREFACE AND ACKNOWLEDGMENTS

This book began life in April 2000, as a panel at the Seventh International Caribbean Women Writers and Scholars Conference, Universidad de Puerto Rico, Mayaguez. My fellow panelists, Lisa Blansett and Linda Strong-Leek, were also my colleagues at Florida International University, where we were all assistant professors. A third FIU colleague, Ryan Trimm, had planned to join us but finally could not attend. The success of our panel, entitled "Whiteness, Colonialism, and Caribbean Women," energized us as we conspired to produce an edited volume based on the understudied theoretical intersection of whiteness and postcoloniality.

Nearly five years later, now that the product of our Puerto Rican daydream is finally coming into the world as a book, much has changed. I regret that this book appears without the contributions of my former FIU colleagues. Happily, if paradoxically, Ryan Trimm's fine essay on Caryl Phillips's *Cambridge* does appear in these pages; I am grateful that at least one link remains to the volume's original conception. I am thankful to Lisa Blansett and Linda Strong-Leek, good colleagues then and now, for their help during the crucial first stages of this project, and to Donald Watson, then Chair of English at FIU, for his support of both the panel and the book in the early stages.

At The University of Mississippi, I have also received generous support from my chair, Joseph Urgo, and have enjoyed a wonderful rapport with colleagues in English and elsewhere who share my interest in whiteness studies and postcoloniality. A special debt of thanks goes to Sharrón Sarthou, who painstakingly converted the manuscript to conform to Chicago style (from MLA style—no small task, that) and compiled the index. I am also deeply grateful to my wife, Susan López, both for her careful and insightful reading of the proofs and for contributing her art, which is prominently featured on the cover.

I am utterly indebted to my editor at SUNY Press, Jane Bunker, who remained steadfast and loyal to this project throughout. Laurie Searl has been an invaluable ally as the production editor, as has copyeditor Alan Hewat. An earlier version of my chapter on whiteness and psychoanalysis appears in *Psychoanalysis, Culture, and Society* in 2004, under the title "Who's Afraid of the Big White Wolf? Whiteness, Counter-transcendence, and Freud's Wolfman." I am grateful to *PCS's* editor, Lynne Layton, for all her help with the Freud chapter. And I am especially thankful to all the contributors, who have stuck with me through a lengthy and not always predictable process. I hope that they find the final product worthy of all their hard work and patience. Some very fine scholars have contributed to this volume, and I hope that I have done them and their work justice.

Finally, the world is obviously a very different place today than it was when I began work on this book. George W. Bush was not yet president of the United States. The events of September 11 had not yet happened. The meaning of whiteness itself, as a signifier of global hegemony and imperialism, was somehow more abstract than it is for me today. September 11 does appear occasionally in this volume, beginning with my own introduction. Yet the shadow of September 11 also hangs over the book as a whole. As you read these chapters you may find yourself wondering whether a different kind of postcolonial whiteness could have prevented the attacks of September 11, by rendering impossible the kind of entrenched, implacable hatred that inspired them. I have wondered that myself as I read these pages over. I wonder whether the Bush administration's rhetoric of "freedom" and the "liberation" of Iraq isn't just the latest version of the colonial civilizing mission: the advanced white society once again presuming to teach other civilizations how to live (even as the soldiers we send to enforce our *neo-colonial* imperatives are disproportionately black and Latino).

I rushed home from that Mayaguez conference to witness the birth of my daughter Sofia, who was born with her mother's white skin and my dark hair and eyes. My son Diego, born almost four years later, is even paler and a redhead to boot (like his mother). I can only wonder what sorts of complications the appearance of white, redheaded, green-eyed, Mississippi-born Cuban Americans will have on the concept of whiteness as we know it today. Perhaps the whole idea of race will become irrelevant in my children's lifetime and books such as this one will become obsolete, or at best quaint historical documents. Perhaps the best a book such as this can hope for is paradoxically to contribute to a future in which it will no longer be necessary. One can hope.

ONE

INTRODUCTION:
WHITENESS AFTER EMPIRE

ALFRED J. LÓPEZ

In a sentence: the past half century or so has been the first time since the dawn of modernity, since the rise of capitalism and the knitting together of the globe in one unified "system," that white supremacy has been called seriously into question on a world-historical scale.

—Howard Winant, "White Racial Projects"

[T]o apply the colour white to white people is to ascribe a visible property to a group that thrives also on invisibility.

—Richard Dyer, *White*

The Negro is not. Any more than the white man.

—Frantz Fanon, *Black Skin White Masks*

THE PERSISTENCE OF WHITENESS

WHITENESS IS NOT, yet we continue for many reasons to act as though it is. It would seem a simple enough assumption that the end of colonialism ushers in the end of whiteness, or at least of its unrivaled ascendancy. Yet the cultural residues of whiteness linger in the postcolonial world as an ideal, often latently, sometimes not. Although the state of being demonstrably

1

white remains, as Richard Dyer deftly puts it, "a passport to privilege" (Dyer 1997, 44), and despite the obvious role that the visibility of whiteness—what Satya Mohanty calls the "white man as spectacle" (315)—has played in the colonial context, whiteness itself remains a largely unexamined category. Despite the efforts of scholars such as Henry Louis Gates and Kwame Appiah to portray race generally as a kind of malignant fiction,[1] and calls from Dyer, Ross Chambers, and others to bring greater scrutiny to bear on whiteness as a tacit norm,[2] whiteness in the postcolonial moment continues to retain much of its status and desirability, if not its overt colonial-era power. Although the two groups approach race from different, and arguably incompatible, directions— the former wishing to do away with race as a category entirely, the latter to render whiteness visible as one racial category among others—they neverthe- less share the aims of critiquing the privilege and power associated with white- ness, and exposing the ways in which whiteness has historically used its normative power to suppress and marginalize its others.[3] Howard Winant, whose eloquent state-of-the-discipline statement begins this chapter, dates the move to critique white hegemony on a global scale to the period "since World War II, and particularly since the 1960s" during which "*the world has undergone a profound shift in the global logic of race or . . . racial formation*" (Winant 2001, 99), the most significant challenge to global white supremacy since Columbus. But even this globalized challenge, Winant admits, "could not dislodge, but only somewhat weaken, that ferocious tradition of white supremacist world rule" (99). However passionate Fanon's declarations to the contrary, it seems that rumors of whiteness's demise have been greatly exaggerated.

Fanon is emphatic in his desire to be seen (and assumedly, read) as "a man, nothing but a man" (Fanon [1952] 1967, 113); yet the impossibil- ity of such a raceless *rapprochement* with the white colonial Other recurs throughout *Black Skin White Masks*. The famous statement in the epigraph, which would apparently disavow both whiteness and its racial other, is framed on the one hand by Fanon's reference to himself as "the man of color" and on the other by an imperative that both whites and blacks "turn their backs on the inhuman voices which were those of their respective ancestors" (231). The apparent ambivalence of Fanon's vacillation between the negation and affirmation of race exemplifies a dialectic of race con- sciousness that has lingered within postcolonial studies into the present moment: on the one hand the humanist impulse to, as Fanon himself puts it, "discover and to love man, wherever he may be" (231) and on the other the drive toward reparations, equity, payback—what elsewhere in *Black Skin White Masks* Fanon calls the former slave's desire to "*make himself recognized*" (217) through conflict specifically with the erstwhile white master.[4] In this context, then, it is not merely freedom that the black slave wants, but more specifically a freedom-*from* its subjection to white colonial power—a psychological and ontological freedom that mere national inde- pendence does not necessarily bring.

Homi Bhabha recognizes this "sense of division" and "uncertain dark" in Fanon's writings, and in *Black Skin White Masks* specifically, as the mark of a "transgressive, transitional truth" (Bhabha 1994, 40). Fanon's foundational postcolonial manifesto proves to be transitional for the same reason that it is so transgressive: the articulation of a particular moment in the dialectic of erstwhile masters and former slaves that exposes both the continuing privilege of whiteness and the hollow sham of the promise of true integration. Bhabha carries over this reading of Fanon into his own theorizations of race and ethnicity, most pointedly in his definition of colonial mimicry as "the desire for . . . *the subject of a difference that is almost the same, but not quite. . . . almost the same but not white*" (Bhabha 86–89).

With the notable exception of Bhabha and a few others, however, postcolonial studies has generally shied away from explicit discussions of race such as those found in Fanon and Bhabha.[5] Curiously, even those texts that address Fanon's and/or Bhabha's writings seldom focus on race. This apparent avoidance of race may stem from the poststructuralist sensibility of much postcolonial writing, with its accompanying aversion to any seemingly oppositional logic and affinity for linguistic and literary, as opposed to sociological, critique. Conversely, the undertheorization of colonial whiteness may be the product of a simple conflation; that is, whiteness in this context may be so closely associated with colonial domination that no further distinction seems necessary or desirable. (Such analyses overlook, of course, the key role of nonwhite colonial elites in consolidating and maintaining colonial and neocolonial power.)[6] Whatever the reason, postcolonial studies has to date produced relatively little scholarship exploring the relations between race and power, and specifically between whiteness and the consolidation and maintenance of colonial power. Perhaps the most pointed example of this curious "race-blindness" in postcolonial studies appears in Routledge's *The Post-colonial Studies Reader*, arguably the single most comprehensive and widely read survey in the field; in a nearly five hundred-page anthology featuring excerpts from more than eighty texts, the word *race* emerges in only five essays for a total of eight appearances, one in conjunction with *ethnicity* (which merits its own dozen mentions in the volume).[7]

In the United States, however, whiteness studies has emerged within the last ten years as a field that does address relations between race and power within an American studies setting. Very little of this work, however, has focused on the United States in a specifically colonial or postcolonial context, having opted instead for a broader approach to race and ethnicity. Arguably the founding text of American whiteness studies, Toni Morrison's *Playing in the Dark* focuses on the ways in which white cultural discourses reduce representations of blackness to the level of function, as tropes employed in the construction of white identity. Richard Dyer's *White* refines and develops this iconographic approach to whiteness, and has emerged as an *ur*-text that has generated much commentary and discussion as well as subsequent studies;

certainly it is, with the possible exception of Morrison's text, the most widely cited book-length study in the field. Neither text, however, features any sustained discussion of colonial and/or postcolonial contexts, with the exception of Dyer's very fine chapter on the BBC television serial *The Jewel in the Crown*.[8]

The influence of these canonical texts upon subsequent scholarship has tended on the one hand toward a critical approach that focuses on representation and iconographies of whiteness, in both literary and visual contexts. On the other hand, the ascendance of Dyer's and Morrison's writings has meant that relatively little scholarship has moved beyond representations of whiteness in Anglo-American culture to the more salient question of how the representational power of whiteness has historically operated in the service of colonial and neocolonial regimes, and has specifically served such regimes in the domination of their nonwhite others.

It is precisely these missing elements in postcolonial and whiteness studies, respectively, that the present volume seeks to address. This collection of essays examines the interrelations between whiteness and the history of European colonialism, as well as the status of whiteness in the contemporary postcolonial world. Together the essays present a range of critical and theoretical responses to two fundamental questions. First: *What happens to whiteness after empire?* What transformations, for example, does the nation's self-image undergo when former colonial subjects return to London or Paris as citizens of the erstwhile "Mother Country"? How do those cultural processes resemble—and how do they diverge from—those experienced by whites of the former oppressing class in South Africa who remain behind in the post-apartheid state, to live and work alongside the newly empowered black majority? How does class impact the ability of white populations to receive their new fellow citizens and subjects?[9] What happens to whiteness, in other words, after it loses its colonial privileges?

The volume's second central question is perhaps more poignant and difficult: *To what extent do white cultural norms or imperatives remain embedded in the postcolonial or postindependence state as part—acknowledged or not—of the colonial legacy?* Here we may think of any number of colonial-era discourses and practices, from the adoption of the erstwhile mother tongue (whether English, Spanish, French, or some other) as the new national language, to the persistence of color-based socioeconomic caste structures in former colonies such as Jamaica and the Dominican Republic. These examples and many others point to the stubborn persistence of whiteness as a cultural norm in many of the postcolonial world's official and unofficial cultural practices. Further, what emerges in the relation between former colonizers and colonized, now fellow citizens in a postindependence state, is their common dependence upon—and complicity with—the ideology of whiteness, or more specifically of white (hence Western) superiority. Each must now face the unpleasant truth of their own complicity in telling, and believing in, the cultural lie of colonial whiteness. Such a bitter epiphany, I would argue, is indispensable for the future health of the postindependence state in particular and the postcolonial world as a whole. Such a facing-down of colonial ghosts is crucial to the task of constructing an integrated postcolonial subject.

Whiteness thus represents not only the contents of the colonial unconscious, but the very agent of its own repression: it is that which would simultaneously recast everything else in its own image and banish the scene of the recasting into an originary myth. Thus does the colonizing process displace or "bleach" the precolonial past and replace it with its own cultural imperatives. Each of the volume's contributors will approach and examine some aspect of these two central questions: on the one hand, whiteness's radically altered status in the postcolonial world, and on the other its lingering (if not always acknowledged) influence. While there is a great deal of scholarship in postcolonial and whiteness studies individually, relatively little addresses the particular intersections of race and power that help fuel colonialism at every stage. Further, there is currently no book-length text that focuses on this very fertile ground for scholarly study; it is indeed remarkable that none of the best-known postcolonial scholars have attempted such a work. One important task for the present volume, then, is to make a thorough assessment of this undertheorized convergence of postcoloniality and whiteness as an important and burgeoning field of study.

It is telling that whiteness studies has concentrated its efforts mostly on the United States, with a few exceptions (most notably Dyer's work), making it seem something of an opposite number to postcolonialism. While the latter has recently come under criticism precisely for its collective myopia regarding U.S. involvement in historical colonialisms and the neocolonial relationship it maintains today with many of its minority populations,[10] whiteness studies has for the most part declined to explore its various and significant points of convergence with the postcolonial. Given the growth of whiteness studies in the past decade, and the proliferation of published studies examining whiteness across a remarkable range of cultural contexts, it is both significant and curious that European colonial whiteness—arguably whiteness at its apex, in its most ascendant and global powerful form—has not loomed large in these analyses. One may rightly wonder whether, to introduce a variation on a concept I have introduced elsewhere, whiteness and its lingering, if somewhat latent, hegemonic influence over much of the world does not occupy some as-yet-unexamined corner of the "colonial unconscious": a continuing malaise that many postcolonial whites (and nonwhites) intuit but few are willing to address.[11]

A converse but equally instructive absence arises in postcolonial studies: although so much postcolonial criticism and theory thematizes its counterhegemonic writings in terms of the marginalized racial, ethnic, and cultural identities of the colonized, relatively little space has been devoted to the dominant colonial cultures *as* racial and ethnic imperatives—and specifically to whiteness itself as a cultural imperative functioning in the service of empire. The signifier *whiteness*, then, functions in this sense as the marker or index of the traces of colonial legacies that yet lie latent (but not dormant) in the postcolonial world's own "colonial unconscious," which it owes to itself to uncover and interrogate. I suspect that much of postcolonial studies' inability to address whiteness as a subject position stems from the race-based meta-opposition that grounds much of its thinking: white as colonizing, colonial/nonwhite as colonized, postcolonial.[12]

Such a founding principle, left unexamined, can and does fuel much of the misguided critical polemic over what or who is or is not authentically postcolonial. That European colonialism was a white, implicitly and explicitly racist undertaking should by now be beyond argument. What is just as obvious, yet too often overlooked, is that whiteness continues to play a role in the postcolonial world, that there are white subjects, cultural groups, who think of themselves as postcolonial. The point is that there remains in the early twenty-first century a *postcolonial* whiteness struggling to come into being, or rather a number of post-empire, post-mastery whitenesses attempting to examine themselves in relation to histories of oppression and hegemony of their others in order to learn the difficult, never-mastered skill that Heidegger used to call *Mitsein*: Being-with. It is this learning of a postcolonial *Mitsein*, this being-with others after the fact of domination, abuse, and outright murder of them, that constitutes the ground of the most important negotiation between erstwhile colonizers and colonized that postcolonial studies can offer. One philosophy for the white subject wishing to escape from the necessity of referring to a "universal" privileged white—that is, how to distinguish the new antiracist white subject from its erstwhile racist "self"— is to work through the relation to nonwhiteness phenomenologically, as an intersubjective relation. Thus my own recourse here and in my previous work[13] to the Heideggerian *Mitsein*, a "being-with" that undoes white solipsism and escapes the ontological dead end of colonialism by changing the script of the Hegelian Lordship-Bondage relation, or at least its outcome.

It is in the interest of helping foster precisely this spirit of intersubjectivity and mutual recognition between postcolonial whiteness and its others—once slaves and colonial subjects, now peers and fellow citizens— that I have assembled the present volume. In uncovering hegemonic whiteness not only in its historical colonial forms but in its contemporary neo- and postcolonial traces, I and the other contributors to this book hope to contribute not to an undoing or annihilation of whiteness, as some would have it,[14] which in any case would be as impossible as any other such project of cultural "purification" (as our century of failed ethnic cleansings and "final solutions" has amply taught us), but the inscription of a new script or narrative of whiteness: a post-mastery whiteness that would be empowered to enter into this relation of *Mitsein* with its others in an barely glimpsed, emergent postcolonial world.

WHITENESS AND THE POSTCOLONIAL

If postcolonialism can be said to represent any single principle or embrace any single critical project, it would be a critique of the West's historical domination of its others, the corresponding assumption of its cultural superiority over those others, and especially the discourses that enable both. This definition is undeniably broad and allows for all kinds of divergences among methods, ideologies, even competing literary and critical canons.[15] Yet for all the irregularities and inconsistencies that often surface among any gathering of texts under the heading *postcolonial*, the category itself emerges from a particular institutional history: namely, the grouping of writers and writings in English departments under the term "Commonwealth" (Mukherjee 1996, 5–6). As I have pointed out elsewhere, aside from the continuation of England as a conceptual center in such a curriculum, such a framework also willy-nilly maintains the oppositional structure of the old colonialism: England as center/metropolis, the "Commonwealth" as margin or province always read in the context (if not the shadow) of the erstwhile mother country.[16]

But we must distinguish here among the various approaches and methodologies—among postcolonialisms, as it were—currently existing somewhat incongruously under the heading *postcolonial*. There has been no shortage of critics who find the term too overdetermined, too ubiquitous to be useful; Aijaz Ahmad, to cite my favorite example, considers "postcolonialism" a term that "designates far too many things, all at once" (Ahmad 1995, 9). The term *postcolonial* paradoxically suffers from the very flexibility that has rendered it useful in such a variety of historical and cultural contexts. The very overdetermination of the term, in other words, its very inflation as a signifier, comes as a quite mimetic consequence of its efficacy; it fits so many contexts, I would argue, precisely because there are so few places on the globe where European colonialism did not leave its mark. Nevertheless, for present purposes it would be useful to have a roadmap of the various theoretical "camps" that make up this unwieldy field of study, in order to better indicate the particular forms of postcolonial scholarship I am interested in engaging here.

Several postcolonial scholars have attempted within the last few years to "speak for" the field to the extent of naming its referent; or put another way, postcolonial studies has now itself enough of a history for a number of scholars to attempt to write something resembling a poetics of the field, its primary texts, practices, and methods. It is instructive of the difficulty of this task, however, that the two most prominent such attempts—from eminent postcolonialists Gayatri Spivak and Robert Young—approach it from almost diametrically opposed directions. Spivak's epic *Critique of Postcolonial Reason* is explicitly indebted and clearly committed to a typically (for Spivak) eclectic poststructuralist approach to postcolonialism, yet its chapter headings examine the field in the broadest possible terms: "Philosophy," "Literature,"

"History," "Culture." Spivak's *Critique* constitutes an attempt to engage these established, broadly defined disciplines while defending the continued efficacy of deconstruction in the service of postcolonial goals, aims, and concerns.[17] On the other hand, Young's more recent *Postcolonialism: An Historical Introduction* aims to do precisely what its subtitle suggests: offer a more conventional, linear exposition of postcolonialism as an epistemologically discreet category unto itself, with a specific history, ideology, and so on.[18] The only exceptions to this approach appear in the book's final section on theoretical formation, which displays a certain eclecticism even as it attempts to define an overarching theoretical matrix for postcolonial theory, and in the more personal preface and epilogue that frame the volume.[19]

But it is not only methodology that distinguishes these two texts, but the very object of their disparate analyses. Young's historicist approach unambiguously defines postcolonialism as the culmination of a third world Marxism born of anticolonial struggle, and thus focuses its attention on explicitly revolutionary figures such as Fanon, Che Guevara, and Mao Zedong. Conversely, Spivak's tireless (and exhausting) deconstruction of postcolonialism and the field's customary understanding of itself never settles for such a comprehensive or straightforward formulation (indeed the book's subtitle, "Toward a History of the Vanishing Present," provides an early hint as to its approach), favoring instead a close analysis of a handful of key texts. Also, in marked contrast to Young's predilection for third world anticolonials Spivak opts to interrogate the continental philosophical canon—Kant, Hegel, Marx, whom she reads not as ancestors or founders of postcolonialism but as "remote discursive precursors"—as well as a diverse group of literary texts running from Bronte and Jean Rhys to Baudelaire and Kipling to J. M. Coetzee. Even Spivak's historical analysis (in a chapter entitled, somewhat misleadingly, "History") resists the kind of historicized account that Young's book seems to strive for; the chapter seems more preoccupied with placing postcolonial India within a larger global context than with offering any broader history of postcolonial thought itself as an object, as Young's text is at pains to do.

Although the two volumes cannot avoid mentioning some of the same names (most notably Marx, Foucault, and Derrida), they take divergent approaches to these apparently shared interests. Although space will not allow an exhaustive study of these interests and their presentation in the Young and Spivak, we can briefly examine each text's presentation of Derrida and deconstruction. Aside from a doggedly poststructuralist approach within the main text, Spivak's appendix "The Setting to Work of Deconstruction" concludes the book with a concise genealogy of deconstruction as a critical practice with special attention to the "ethical turn" in Derrida, or what Spivak calls "affirmative deconstruction," whose originary movement Spivak traces back to 1968 and "The Ends of Man" (Spivak 425–26). This brief appendix or ghost limb to Spivak's text seems to function as a defense of the ethical efficacy and "responsible action" (428) of deconstruction in the act of its "setting to work" (427, 431). Conversely, Young's study treats Derrida very much as a historical subject and even as an acquaintance of the author; parts of it seem written to Derrida himself, and refer to him in the second person. The chapter subtitled "Derrida in Algeria," in fact, focuses squarely on Derrida's personal history as an Algerian-born Jew, a fact that Spivak's more text-centered analysis refers to only fleetingly and only at the end of her appendix, as if an afterthought.[20] Although both texts seek to demonstrate poststructuralism's relevance for anticolonial struggle, Young's chapter makes it a particular point to portray poststructuralism itself as "one echo of the violence of Algeria playing itself out in an insurrection against the calm philosophical and political certainties of the metropolis" (Young 2001, 412), thus historicizing the entire enterprise of deconstruction by positing the founder's personal subalterity and "experience" of anticolonial struggle as its very precondition—not a particularly Derridean critical move, and certainly not one that the deconstructivist Spivak would be likely to make herself.[21]

The point here is to demonstrate how even texts that seek to represent some sort of conclusive or overarching picture of postcolonialism as a discrete field of study cannot be reconciled to a single set of critical practices or assumptions, or even a canon of readings. If two of postcolonialism's leading critics can't even agree on a canon of key texts in their respective poetics of the field, then any critical enterprise calling itself "postcolonial whiteness studies" would be well advised to remain wary of the dangers inherent to relying on general references to "the postcolonial" or assumptions about its contents, or of glossing over the very heterogeneous nature of what has always been a contentious field of study. One common result of such overgeneralizations has been a tendency to cast postcolonialism in terms of an anglocentric model, which maintains and even reinforces England's place at the center of the post-empire on which the sun apparently never sets. As I have argued elsewhere at some length, one of postcolonial studies' ongoing flaws has been a prevalent notion of the field that congratulates itself on its "cultural diversity" while its arguably most widely read critical anthology continues to define its object of study as "those literatures written in English in formerly colonized societies" (Ashcroft 1995, 1). A study of postcolonial whiteness that accepts this definition of postcolonialism would itself be guilty of uncritically privileging whitenesses that speak English, and even of reinforcing the grim fact of English as the world's preeminent white language.[22]

Even the more commendable efforts toward an encapsulating theory or poetics of the postcolonial, culminating in Young's and Spivak's recent efforts, have had to contend with three areas of significant theoretical difficulty: questions of *epistemology*, *agency*, and *hybridity and hegemony*. I have discussed these issues in some detail elsewhere under slightly different headings;[23] here I will limit myself to a brief summary of each general problem. Each of these objections, as we will see, carries over to different degrees and in varying forms into whiteness studies, and thus any commingling of whiteness and postcoloniality will need to maintain an awareness of them.

The objections to the term *postcolonial* as constituting a discrete epistemological category do not only center on questions of semantics and historicity (when this "post-" is supposed to begin, what distinguishes it from its root word "-colonial," and so on).[24] More importantly, epistemological critiques of the postcolonial focus on the larger question of the field's self-definition and its apparent inability to produce its referent as a stable object for its study. What such critiques, most famously Ella Shohat's, emphasize is what they see as an unresolved tension between an abstracted philosophical distinction and a more temporally concrete historical one. Postcolonialism seeks to encompass a generalized condition of colonization and its aftermath yet also wants to engage in specific but disparate historical and cultural contexts, from the Algerian War of Independence to the Cuban Revolution to cultural practices such as Indian *sati*; even Bhabha's most rarefied theoretical interventions attempt such engagements, albeit in ways that critics such as Shohat would still consider problematic.

Critiques of the status of agency in postcolonial studies, or rather of some postcolonial critics' formulation of the subaltern and its possibilities for agency, take a more pointedly ideological form. The most virulent of these critiques have accused postcolonialism broadly (too broadly, given the diversity of the actual field) of producing a discourse that privileges cultural and linguistic differences over the concrete historical and economic conditions of colonization and its aftermath, thus ignoring what Benita Parry calls "the voice of the native" in her struggles against oppression and reducing actual anticolonial struggles to a theoretical *techne*, or what Parry dismisses as mere "devices circumventing and interrogating colonial authority" (Parry 1987, 43). Parry and others assert that such critical practices actually work *against* the agency of subaltern groups and the emergence of their "voice," and further Western hegemony, by privileging the discourses of third world elite academics such as Bhabha and Spivak and their specious "representation" of the subaltern. It is characteristic of the epistemological paradoxes I have just described as immanent to postcolonialism that the very inclusion of critiques such as Parry's and Kwame Appiah's in so many discussions of the postcolonial actually undermine their railings against what E. San Juan Jr. calls "postcolonial doctrine" (San Juan 1998, 6), or at least co-opts them by demonstrating both the significance of the subject to have attracted such a range of critical studies and its flexibility in accommodating them—in short, of the diversity of argument and critical method that can and does exist under the banner of "postcolonial studies."[25]

Finally, the critique of "hybridity" as a privileged, even celebrated concept within postcolonial studies has argued that such approaches diminish the field's efficacy as an oppositional anticolonial discourse. Such critiques argue that the emphasis on hybridity, syncretism, and ambivalence in postcolonial studies constitutes an implicit rejection of oppositional narratives of resistance and liberation, most prominently third world Marxism, and an embrace of the concepts and language of poststructuralism and postmodernism. (Of course, this critique is also part of the larger polemic over the political efficacy of deconstruction that appears in Spivak and to a lesser extent Young.) Of course this objection does not equally apply to all postcolonial discourses; Bhabha's deconstructivist approach is more susceptible to this kind of critique than the more apparently politically committed stance of, say, Edward Said.[26] Nevertheless, what is at stake in this critique is whether the questions that a certain type of postcolonial theory has raised—about difference and hybridity, about both colonizing and colonized subject positions in relation to hegemonic colonial discourses of power and their various neocolonial manifestations—contribute to anticolonial struggle or distract from it. According to this type of general objection, the writing of theory does not necessarily constitute an adequate form of "resistance" (a point that Bhabha pointedly denies in "The Commitment to Theory").[27] Consequently, this privileging of theoretical difference over "actual" resistance and struggle belies postcolonial studies' own shortcomings as an anti-colonial praxis.

Notwithstanding the flaws that these general critiques have exposed within postcolonialism, the turn toward what we now recognize as postcolonial studies has sought to break the literary, cultural, and ideological hegemony that white English and other European literatures have historically maintained over their nonwhite and near-white others. Taking its cue from poststructuralist theories, much postcolonial scholarship seeks to undo the binary thinking of "colonizer/colonized" and other such essentialized oppositional categories—including the concept of "race" itself—and expose the ways they function to perpetuate the cultural dominance of the West and the marginality of its colonized and once-colonized others. Further, as I have argued elsewhere, in the most general sense postcolonial studies seeks to both interrogate the colonial discourses of the past and provide analyses or articulations of the diasporic, migratory condition that is perhaps the most salient characteristic of the postcolonial world.[28] Even given the theoretical difficulties that critiques of the postcolonial have indicated, postcolonial studies even in its present form remains a body of work that strives to move beyond the limitations of an economic or historicist approach to encompass issues of class, gender, race, ethnicity, language, and geographical location— in short, all of the tangible and intangible factors that constitute the shaping and maintenance of nations and peoples. Marxist critiques tend to miss the crucial point that domination is not only about economic subjugation but also penetrates the minds and bodies of the oppressed, a point that both San Juan's book and, in whiteness studies, David Roediger's class-centered critique fail to grasp.[29]

Further, postcolonialism doesn't neatly or without violence fit any dialectical model of humanist progress; it is thus inaccurate to treat the field as a form of idealism, because it is possible only in the most general terms to identify the multitudinous discourses existing under the banner of the "postcolonial" as a single, easily summarized ideal or essential horizon of expectations. To dismiss the postcolonial as another failed "end of either history or ideology," as San Juan does (San Juan 14), or reduce it to a grouping of underdeveloped "national allegories" that lag behind "first-world cultural development," as Fredric Jameson so notoriously does (Jameson 1986, 65, 69) is to forget that postcolonial studies draws much of its strength from the critique, largely learned from poststructuralist thought, of precisely such categories of social and cultural development. The most compelling writings in whiteness studies, from Dyer's *White* to Frankenberg's writings to Wray and Newitz's *White Trash* volume, exemplify this resistance to totalized notions of race and ethnicity and tendency toward what Michel Foucault has called "an autonomous, non-centralized kind of theoretical production,"[30] a critical orientation largely derived from the same theoretical precursors that inform much postcolonial criticism.

Finally it is worth pointing out, if only in brief, that the by-now familiar criticism of theoretical interventions informed by structuralist and poststructuralist approaches—which have been somewhat pejoratively called "constructionist" approaches—does not form an automatic or necessary opposition with criticisms that claim a more overt historical or activist engagement. Deconstructivist approaches to postcolonialism, or to whiteness, do not automatically or necessarily represent an evasion of the world in their analyses of colonial discourses, although the danger of a sort of solipsism is always present. The choice is not, as Robyn Wiegman's recent critique of whiteness studies would have it, between agency and constructivism. Although Wiegman sees what she calls "an emphasis on agency that situates a theoretically humanist subject at the center of social constructionist analysis" as a "contradictory" effect of current approaches to whiteness studies (Wiegman 1999, 135), I see no necessary contradiction in theorizing a subject that is aware of its own constructedness in terms of constitutive discursive influences yet wishes to project itself as a human agent in what is, after all, a human struggle played out on the level not only of state and collectivity but also (and especially) of individuals.[31] Thus, it is not necessarily or automatically a contradiction in terms to argue for the social constructedness of whiteness as a colonial imperative while positing a subject—who is after all, the concrete focus of such imperatives—as a human agent who must contend with and strive to overthrow them. Such a subject and agent necessarily acts out of a sense of historical and cultural specificity, and both postcolonial and whiteness studies are unavoidably historiographic enterprises to the extent that they are concerned with hegemonic discourses and their effects on subjects.

To the extent that postcolonial critiques, however well intentioned, eliminate race as an object of inquiry, they neglect a crucial dimension of the colonial ideology. One does not make whiteness as a malignant colonial ideology go away by simply showing how it deconstructs itself, any more than one can do away with the concept of the subject itself by such maneuverings. One can and should, however, strive to show both how whiteness does not essentially, irrevocably come with the kinds of privileges that it now enjoys, and how the privileges of being white have always come at the expense of those who are not. The point is not to undo or "abolish" or destroy whiteness, as the "race traitor" school of whiteness studies argues, since this sort of ethnic self-cleansing (literal or otherwise) is neither desirable nor possible.[32] John Brown, a favorite "race traitor" example, never renounced his whiteness, symbolically or otherwise. Neither has Breyten Breytenbach, the self-identifying "Albino Terrorist" who has written so eloquently about his years in prison for fighting against the Apartheid regime in South Africa.[33] There is no need to resort to the self-sacrificing, self-destructing white male rebel as a trope of the new postcolonial whiteness, a paradoxically self-serving figure who would allow whites to retain their central status as "emancipators" (à la Lawrence of Arabia, dancing across the traintops) and thus their power and privilege.

On the other hand, one effective way to administer the desired privilege-ectomy to the white subject is to show how its position within the colonial society is neither uniformly dominant nor stable, but contingent upon a performance of white power. The reflection on this point offered by George Orwell, as a ruminative colonist in "Shooting an Elephant," is instructive: "A sahib has got to act like a sahib. . . . He wears a mask, and his face grows to fit it" (Orwell [1936] 1970, 269). Here Orwell reveals the fictiveness of white dominance precisely as a performance, an act that must constantly be kept up (here again is Mohanty's "white man as spectacle"), as Orwell's colonial policeman is compelled to murder the elephant in question for no other reason than to make a show of white decisiveness and authority in front of the natives (271). Once the authority and superiority of whiteness reveals itself to be a fiction, the revoking of its privileges cannot be far behind.

The postcolonial critique of whiteness cannot end with the defrocking of the latter, however, for the simple reason that whiteness remains as part of the postcolonial world. White settlers in the United States, Australia, South Africa, Canada, and other areas not only did not disappear or leave upon the establishment of these nations, but were in each instance instrumental to their founding. Such situations do not fit Fanon's infamous description of anti-colonial revolutions as "a total, complete, and absolute substitution" (Fanon 1963, 35), because whiteness remains behind in the new postcolonial state, in the form of both actual white subjects (former colonizers turned citizens) and the cultural and ideological apparatuses that continue to reflect the values of the colonial regime—a national language or religion, educational system, government infrastructure, and so on. The postcolonial critique of whiteness must thus move beyond narrow anticolonialism or reverse racism to ask whether a new relation to whiteness is possible after empire—to construct, in effect, a whiteness without privilege, while still acknowledging the lingering traces of white normativity that remains more or less latent in the postcolonial world as an irreducible part of the colonial legacy.

WHITENESS AND AMERICAN STUDIES

Whiteness studies in the American studies context begins precisely with this premise of exposing or undoing whiteness as a tacitly privileged subject position. This movement toward rendering whiteness both visible and subject to critique—that is, to challenge both its invisibility and its (unspoken) claims to an essential superiority—characterizes what Mike Hill calls the "'first wave' of white critique" (Hill 1997, 2). This whiteness made ethnic or "strange,"[34] a whiteness thus rendered "examinable," as Chambers might put it, marks the success of this first wave of whiteness studies at forcing a moment of reckoning upon its once-invisible object. If the movement that Toni Morrison has described as "a serious intellectual effort to see what racial ideology does to the mind, imagination, and behavior of masters" (Morrison 1992, 12) has succeeded in bringing unprecedented attention to the lingering presence of white privilege, it has also made it necessary to up the critical ante. If whiteness has been made to see itself—or more accurately, to see itself as others see it, have seen it—it has now reached a moment of crisis. No longer able to portray itself as either benign or "normal" (in the sense of constituting a norm), whiteness must now reckon with its own history of aggression and hegemony.

Hill's introduction to his edited collection on whiteness focuses on the new whiteness as a "terror," and invokes the Oklahoma City bombings among other examples to illustrate the ways in which late twentieth-century whiteness has tried to distance itself from its more extreme articulations.[35] Hill sees this emergence of a " 'terrifyingly' ordinary" whiteness—that is, the tension between the extremity of white supremacist actions and the paradoxical recourse to a sort of populist ordinariness (or in other words, the claim to whiteness *as* the claim to normalcy, and vice versa) as characteristic of a "second wave" of whiteness studies (3). Yet to grasp the full extent of the impact that the first wave of whiteness scholars has made, it is necessary to move beyond individual acts of white terrorism (Hill also discusses the bombing at the 1996 Summer Olympics in Atlanta) to a more broadly ontological analysis. What will happen to normative whiteness now that it has begun to gauge the horrors it has perpetrated on its others, and begins to terrorize even itself? This is a moment of reckoning whose full impact has been postponed by the nearly incomprehensible horror of 9/11. Now whiteness has a new, nonwhite threat to rally itself against, and thus the question of its own implication in and responsibility for helping to create the global political conditions that brought the attack about is deferred, as is the question of why the United States has enemies in the first place. Although the 9/11 attacks were not directly about race, and American whiteness not the target—had it been so the terrorists would surely not have chosen New York, arguably the United States' most multicultural city—certainly the rise in violence directed at Arab Americans, as well as much of our public policy, especially that of racial profiling, would indicate that both the American government and a significant portion of its population do see the attack and subsequent conflict in racial terms.[36]

The effect of this shift in focus, from the white terrorists within to the Arab ones without (and within) has the effect, I think, of deferring white America's inevitable moment(s) of reckoning with itself and its historically wronged others. By rallying around the flag and defending "freedom," whites in America can indulge in the temporary distraction allowed by a specious patriotic "color-blindness"; anyone introducing the least divisive issue, including questions about race, into the post-9/11 public arena is accused of being unpatriotic or worse.[37] Whiteness thus attempts to generate its own *différance* by projection or sleight-of-hand—the matter of why America was singled out for such an attack is both deferred and made different, and the specter of white terror, both at home and abroad, temporarily fades. Yet now that the critique of whiteness has rendered it visible, and thus subject to critique, the question of "What now?"—what we might call the question of the question of whiteness—is irrevocable.

If then, as Gregory Jay asserts, whiteness studies is the "ghost haunting multiculturalism and critical race studies" (Jay 2002, 1), it has also brought Euro-American whiteness to what we might provisionally call a crisis of recognition. For perhaps the first time since its invention some few hundred years ago,[38] whiteness finds itself to some extent caught in the other's gaze; it has come to be aware of itself as a race-object among other race-objects, or at least as an entity that can be and is apprehended that way by the other's gaze. This new and uncomfortable condition—what, borrowing from Sartre, we might call a "whiteness for-itself"—also begins to form an uneasy state of being-with (*Mitsein*) as it learns to be looked at by its others. This *Mitsein*, which is half of Martin Heidegger's famous distinction in *Being and Time* between Being-with and Dasein-with (*Mitsein und Mitdasein*), emphasizes both the interdependence of subjectivities and the indispensability of this intersubjective relation for being. Heidegger's division of "Being-in-the-world" into three distinct moments, the third of which, "being," is the being-with, makes clear that the fundamental characteristic of being is precisely its being *with* others.[39] This dependence upon the other for the subject's being makes this relation both fluid and radically contingent. For if what constitutes whiteness is in fact a transcendental relation to its others—if, to put it in another context, as Morrison claims, it is possible "to discover, through a closer look at literary 'blackness,' the nature—even the cause—of literary 'whiteness' " (9)—then clearly the truly intersubjective encounter with the Other must constitute a moment of reckoning and of accountability. As Vron Ware explains in her analysis of post-empire England, "The postwar migration of workers and their families from the former colonies involved a reckoning with ideas about "race" and history and culture derived from the past" (Ware 2001, 208). Certainly such moments as Ware describes are in the end always partial and localized. The question of whiteness itself, whiteness qua whiteness, is never the immediate issue, thus rendering all such moments, whether billed as *rapprochement*, Truth and Reconciliation, War Crimes Tribunals, etc., part of the series of *tuchés*—in Lacanian terms, one in the string of missed encounters with the Real that nevertheless keep the subject locked into a dialectic of desire and demand with the Other.[40] Nevertheless, as Sartre observes in his writings on the Heideggerian *Mitsein*,

> The Other is the *ex-centric limit* which contributes to the constitution of my being. He [sic] is the test of my being inasmuch as he throws me outside of myself toward structures which at once both escape me and define me; it is this test which originally reveals the Other to me. (Sartre [1947] 1956, 244–45)

Learning to see a whiteness that, in Sartrean terms, is suddenly externalized and thrown "outside of itself" toward others who would both "escape and define" it—or in other words rendering whiteness visible (and thus strange) and subject to critique—is only the first step, as Hill correctly sees. The real action is not in bringing whiteness to reckoning, but in what happens next. And what happens to whiteness next, especially in the postcolonial moment, is what this book is all about.

POSTCOLONIAL WHITENESS

In my previous work I have outlined certain categories or conditions under which such a postcolonial critique of whiteness might proceed: the concept of whiteness respectively as cultural aesthetic, ontological relation, and cultural history.[41] For present purposes, however, it may be more useful to address specific points of convergence between postcolonial and whiteness studies. Given that neither of these fields of study can be glossed in any meaningful way as a stable or homogeneous entity, we can still identify certain problems or questions that various forms of these disciplines hold in common. For the purposes of the present study, we may identify at least four such points of convergence: (1) the concept of whiteness as a cultural hegemon, (2) the history of the spread of hegemonic whiteness through colonialism, (3) a broadening of the comparative focus of the debate on whiteness beyond a strictly U.S. model, and (4) a growing awareness within postcolonial studies of the United States itself as an imperial power.

Although what Wiegman calls "the use of class as the transfer point between looking white and believing you are white" (135) is not universally applicable, as she argues in her critique of class-based whiteness studies, it is undoubtedly an effective point of departure for deconstructing white cultural imperatives—especially as they manifest in nonwhite bourgeois communities, of which there are no shortage in the postcolonial world: Cuban Americans, Indian Brahmins, Afro-Jamaican bourgeoisie—the list goes on.[42] What these and other such groups share is an investment in whiteness to some degree or other as an indispensable component of their own upward mobility within their respective societies, which each group retains as part of its own particular legacy of colonialism. This is arguably the most apparent point of convergence, and perhaps the most poignant, between whiteness and postcolonial studies: the example of nonwhites not "looking white" but nevertheless "believing [they] are white," claiming superiority by virtue of their relative whiteness and establishing economic and cultural hegemony over other less-privileged groups on racial grounds.

Thus, to cite just one example from personal experience, the Cuban American professor who some years ago at my dissertation defense objected to my reading Cuban literature and culture in opposition to "the West," arguing that Latin Americans were as "Western" as any North American. Antonio Gramsci has pointed out in a different context that while terms such as "East" and "West" are "arbitrary and conventional, that is historical constructions," the terms have nevertheless "finished up indicating specific relations between different cultural complexes" (Gramsci 447). The crystallization of "East" and "West" as terms in a fixed opposition of essences comes for Gramsci out of "the point of view of the European cultured classes, who, as a result of their world-wide hegemony have caused them to be accepted everywhere" (447). So while my former professor's argument may be geographically true, it strikes me today as a bit ingenuous: Being "Western" in this context has less to do with where one sits on the map than with one's relation to a colonial history in which "Western-ness" is bound up with both colonial dominance *and* whiteness.

Over the last two decades, however, under the assault of postcolonial and more recently whiteness studies, this *concept of whiteness as a cultural hegemon* has found itself increasingly subject to interrogation. The idea of whiteness as a cultural aesthetic norm combines with the idea of whiteness as a desirable and even necessary trait for colonized subjects who wish to achieve class mobility and financial success in a colonized (or formerly colonized) society. This tandem of whiteness as both aesthetically desirable and pragmatically necessary begins to be exposed as a product of the so-called civilizing mission of colonialism. The effect of the colonial sham on the individual level is a subject who simultaneously identifies with the white ideal and is radically alienated from it; this is the essence of Bhabha's formulation of the colonial subject who is *"almost but not quite . . . almost but not white"* (Bhabha 89). The collective result in the colonial context is a hegemonic cultural inscription that would systematically suppress and marginalize the cultural values of the colonized population. Under this scenario, assimilation to the colonizer's cultural world becomes essential for any colonized subject who hopes for any social or material advancement. As I point out elsewhere, to gain access in this scenario to the social, economic, and political power of the colonial or neocolonial state requires that the colonized subject suppress his or her own cultural practices and beliefs and learn to live "like a white man."[43] As Fanon, Bhabha, and others have pointed out, however, even those subjects who most successfully internalize the white ideal, no matter how skilled the mimicry or complete the performance, can never attain their goal. It is Fanon who best describes the existential double bind of the colonized subject of color: "[T]he educated Negro suddenly discovers that he is rejected by a civilization which he has none the less assimilated" (*Black* 93). Once the white lie of assimilation becomes clear, there is no reason for whiteness's others to continue the sham.

From its beginnings in the sixteenth and seventeenth centuries, the *spread of hegemonic whiteness through colonialism* has not necessarily meant that all whites enjoyed the same privileges by simple virtue of race identification. Whiteness certainly produces differently classed subjects, as "White Trash" whiteness scholars such as Matt Wray and Annalee Newitz have persuasively demonstrated.[44] However, this focus on economically disempowered and/or culturally marginalized whitenesses within domestic contexts, generating what Wiegman aptly calls "minoritized white subjects," by its attention to particularized white subjects elides the extent to which whiteness *as a concept* remains wedded to cultural imperatives that have historically been complicit in the oppression, colonization, and outright genocide of nonwhite peoples the world over.

Certainly the contributors to this volume would recognize along with Wray and Newitz that whiteness is not a monolithic construct and does not hold the same level of power and prestige in all its embodiments. Individual white subjects are no doubt "internally differentiated," allowing for the fact that some groups of whites "also experience deprivation, stigmatization, and subjugation";[45] one very fruitful topic for a postcolonial approach to whiteness has been precisely the Irish, whom the English regard as "uncivilized" and therefore "not white," a rationale the latter employed to justify more than two centuries of colonization (three, if you count Northern Ireland).[46] But the example of colonized or otherwise oppressed whites in whatever context does not change the historical ascendancy of a certain kind of whiteness—let's call it a bourgeois imperial whiteness. And certainly this dominant form of whiteness did and does come with all sorts of privilege and has had all manner of atrocities committed in its name. Not for nothing does

bell hooks associate whiteness with violence and terror, nor does a prominent group of whiteness scholars collectively classify whiteness as "THE
INSTITUTIONALIZATION OF EUROPEAN COLONIALISM."[47] As this
volume tries to demonstrate, the best way for a specifically *postcolonial* approach to whiteness to demonstrate its heterogeneity is to examine whitenesses
"marginalized" by virtue of geography and/or relative cultural distance from
dominant colonial histories. Or as Ruth Frankenberg puts it, the rise of
global whiteness "is linked to imperial and colonial expansion, simultaneous
with the making of (white dominant) nation states" (Frankenberg 1997, 8).
Thus the emphasis in the pietes to follow on whitenesses across a variety of
geographic and cultural contexts, few of which can be categorized as mainstream Anglo-American whiteness (and even this categorization can be
deceiving, as Roberts's chapter on Princess Diana amply illustrates).

Through such a transnational approach to whiteness across a range of
geographic and cultural incarnations, the concept of whiteness itself as a
form of hegemony historically linked to colonialism clashes in the postcolonial
moment with new, competing narratives of national histories, most of which
aim to reinscribe all that colonial historical narratives had suppressed in the
name of "education" (think Macauley's Minute here)[48] or "management" or
"maintaining order"—categories that, at least in the colonial context, share
many intentions and effects in common.[49] In the postcolonial or postindependence moment, such repressed histories tend to surface with a vengeance in the form of embarrassing, painful events from the nation's colonial
history to be confronted and worked through. More than merely pointing
out such moments in the history of colonial whiteness, the new nation's job
is one of remembrance and of mourning, of repentance (or defiance) and
forgiveness (or punishment). This process in fact constitutes an examination,
if not a construction and a founding, of the new nation's collective *conscience*: The salient questions are not just about what has happened, but
about what to do about it and how to move on as a nation. How smoothly
the process of what in South Africa is known officially as "Truth and Reconciliation" moves forward will largely determine the fate of the nation and
its citizens, white or not.

Beyond the status of whiteness within a single nation's borders, however, this volume argues for *a broadening of the comparative focus of the debate
on whiteness beyond a strictly U.S. model*—that is, beyond a United States–
centered model that allows American studies to duck postcolonial issues and
lets the United States off the hook for its own imperialist history and current
colonial practices[50] and toward an awareness of what Vron Ware and Les
Back call "the transnational relationships within the cultures of racism
and . . . the histories of specific local and national arenas in which racial
power is forged" (Ware, Vron, and Back 2002, 13–14). Likewise, the Editorial Collective that compiled *The Making and Unmaking of Whiteness* prom-
isingly asks "how whiteness circulates as an axis of power and identity around

the world" (Brander Rasmussen 2001, 3), thus implicitly bringing whiteness out of American studies and potentially into the postcolonial realm. Nothing else in their book explicitly pursues this task, however; even Ware's essay in the same volume, despite its opening claim that "whiteness needs to be understood as an interconnected global system, having different inflections and implications depending on where and when it has been produced" (Ware 2001, 185), is more about domestic English race and class issues than how the current situation grows out of a history of colonialism and slavery. Thus, even texts that gesture toward such a transnational approach to whiteness studies in their introductions, such as *The Making and Unmaking of Whiteness* and Ware and Back's *Out of Whiteness*, invariably revert to a domestic Anglo-American focus for the remainder of the book, treating the occasional foray into English domestic issues as "international."[51] Such an examination of the relations between whiteness, national identity, and individual subjects, which until now has remained a mostly missed opportunity, is precisely what the present volume seeks to perform or at least initiate.

WRITINGS ON RACE AND EMPIRE

I have not organized the chapters in this volume under any particular headings or subdivisions, although I have grouped together essays that explore similar areas or take similar approaches. Generally then, the first four essays all address whiteness in the postcolonial moment as an ideal or norm that its others either aspire to or resist. The essays in this section explore whiteness as the cultural imperative masquerading as an aesthetic ideal, and examine the ways in which postcolonial whiteness manages to retain much of the privilege and prestige it held at the height of colonialism. This notion of whiteness as an explicit and implicit cultural ideal—of beauty, desirability, virtue, purity—lingers in the postcolonial world in surprising ways, and presents a formidable obstacle for both subjects of color and whites who find themselves marginalized in some other way (by nationality, ethnicity, gender, sexuality, etc.), who either strive for an unattainable ideal (Bhabha's "*almost but not quite. . . .*") or must learn to assert their own cultural difference in the face of the universalized white norm.

Diane Roberts's "The Body of the Princess" examines the legacy of Princess Diana and what she represented as the most visible symbol of a white England greatly diminished from its erstwhile role as the preeminent colonial power and clinging to what little remains of its Victorian-era glory. John Hawley's, Anikó Imre's, and Gerry Turcotte's chapters each approach this lingering mystique of whiteness from the perspective of various marginalized white and nonwhite groups. Hawley's "Lavender Ain't White" explores the relation of black and Latino drag-queen cultures to the glamorous whiteness of "the (white) soap operas" to which they aspire, and examines the extent to which normative feminine whiteness retains a significant influence over the queens' aspirations and desires. Anikó Imre's "Whiteness in Post-Socialist Eastern Europe" focuses on Hungarian Gypsy (Romani) culture in its struggle for self-assertion in the face of a hegemonic Euro-whiteness that has historically sought to dominate and even destroy it. Gerry Turcotte's "Vampiric Decolonization" continues with an exploration of another localized, hybrid discourse: Mudrooroo's appropriation of the Gothic vampire novel as a postcolonial narrative that critiques "the way Indigenous identity, mythology, spirituality and values have been fed on by European invaders" and "suggest[s] how Indigenous writers might conceivably bite back."

The middle three chapters, taken as a whole, explore the vagaries of postcolonial whiteness in its sociological, psychological, and ontological dimensions, and the ways in which the demise of colonialism has served to destabilize not only white supremacy on the collective level but the very notion of what it means to "be white" as an individual. The crisis of whiteness arguably begins at precisely the point at which the colonized subject of color can see through it. Once the hollow sham of maintaining the old tired hegemonic relations in the name of a specious "assimilation" becomes clear, whiteness must begin to surrender its position of mastery and move toward an intersubjective relation of recognition (*Anerkennen*) between subjects. Obviously this does not mean that all of the inequalities of the old system disappear in one fell swoop. Colonial cultural norms worked their way into the colonized mind over the course of a long, patient, systematic process, and there is no reason to believe that Fanon's "total, complete, and absolute substitution " (Fanon 1963, 35) ever occurs as suddenly or as thoroughly as his formulation of an anticolonial "*tabula rasa* which characterizes at the outset all decolonization"(35) would initially appear. But it is on the level of individuals, of daily interactions on the streets and in the towns of the formerly colonized nation, in the workplaces, in restaurants and bars, where the former colony begins the transformation to the postcolonial nation. The chapters by Melissa Steyn, Cheryl Herr, and myself each address this crisis of the postcolonial white subject, as well as the compensating mechanisms by which whiteness manages to reassess and reinvent itself in forms that continue to assert its privilege and prestige.

Steyn's 'White Talk' demonstrates how white South Africans now living under black majority rule, in need of new strategies to help shore up their identities and guard their privilege as whites, are drawing on the resources available to them through the prestige and power still inherent in less discredited forms of Western whiteness, which allow them to maintain a measure of hegemony in post-apartheid South Africa by virtue of their association with them. The next two chapters, Herr's "The Color of Schizophrenia" and my own "The Gaze of the White Wolf," explore different mental health discourses in their respective efforts to uncover how white cultural imperatives penetrate into the health sciences on both collective and individual levels—that is, in the form of both universalizing diagnostic tendencies and hegemony in the analyst-patient relation. Herr's chapter calls for a multidisciplinary approach to postcolonial mental illness that is attuned to both cultural difference and the ways in which colonial racialization have historically contributed to higher rates of psychoses in both Ireland and the Caribbean. My own chapter focuses on Freud's landmark case study of "The Wolfman" to argue for psychoanalysis as a discourse that retains the capacity of remaining open to the endless calculation of cultural difference, while also remaining vigilant to its own history of complicity with normative male European whiteness.

The volume's final three chapters explore the ways in which the constructions of reality inherent in discourses of colonial history function to authorize and maintain whiteness as the norm, while disguising their own constructedness behind what Ashcroft et al. call the myth of "a value free, 'scientific' view of the past" (355). In this context, history as a discipline emerges as a crucial tool for the domination of the colonized, but also one that postcolonial writings have employed strategically. Postcolonial studies has sought not simply to reject or reverse the narratives known collectively as "colonial history," but to explore the conditions of its narrativization, of its construction in response to the political and rhetorical exigencies of colonialism. With this task in mind, each of the last three chapters seeks to engage its chosen colonial history as narrative—that is, not as a transparent continuum of events that are simply recorded, but as a discourse and a rhetoric that has functioned in the service of colonial whiteness and must now be revised and rewritten by its others.

Frances Singh's "Motley's the Only Wear" locates a literary prototype of the new and globally aware postcolonial whiteness in the most unlikely of historical places: Conrad's "Harlequin" from *Heart of Darkness*, the white Russian sailor whom Marlow describes as a "fabulous . . . insoluble problem" (Conrad 54) and whose multilingual, multinational qualities make him a much-overlooked model of an ex-centric whiteness that could eschew mastery and learn to live intersubjectively with its others. Christopher Kelen's "Hymns for and from White Australia" offers a study of Australia's foundational white mythology as reflected in the ambiguities and anxieties of its national anthems: the official "Advance Australia Fair" and the *un*-official "Waltzing Matilda." In "The Times of Whiteness," Ryan Trimm tracks whiteness in Caryl Phillips's *Cambridge* as the signifier of a normalizing, authorizing discourse operating in a sort of temporal schism, a constant deferral of reference through which whiteness establishes itself as an originary nonidentity that positions all other identities as raced, thus rendering whiteness both invisible and atemporal, or "out of time."

THE FUTURE OF WHITENESS

In the conclusion of *White*, Dyer warns of the danger of white subjects distancing themselves, not only temporally but representationally and politically, from both neo-Nazi and other white supremacist groups of the present moment and colonial histories and other past forms of "extreme" whiteness (of which, as we have seen, Hitler's is only the most famous example). This distancing mechanism allows whiteness to continue to see itself as "non-particularity, the space of ordinariness" (Dyer 223), a collective willed blind-ness essential to both the maintenance of white cultural hegemony and the avoidance of accountability. In the more crass, blatant forms of this phenom-enon by which "normal" everyday whites comfort themselves by this psychic distancing mechanism, we may witness Jerry Springer's and other daytime talk shows in which foul-mouthed, hostile white supremacist groups are pit-ted against self-righteous studio audiences. On a more subtle, dissimulating level, however, are self-congratulatory films such as *Schindler's List* in which we see a noble white man combat the evils of "extreme" whiteness. Thus, everyday whiteness can distance itself from its most virulent manifestations *while maintaining its cultural privileges.*

Such a distancing also allows for what Dyer calls the "exquisite agony" (206) of white liberal guilt, which likewise seeks to appease and appeal to the other's capacity for orderly dissent while surrendering little of its own entrenched privilege.[52] White liberal guilt at its most performative has the additional effect of diverting attention from the facts of white racism and oppression to how badly the Enlightened White Liberal feels about it. Ulti-mately exercises such as Les Back's self-loathing ruminations after a series of interviews with a white supremacist leader, which he describes as a "reflexive interpretive reading of whiteness" (Ware and Back 45), serve as more self-portrayals of the earnest white ethnographer trying his Levinasian best to dialogue with the other. The fact that Back winds up hating himself for allowing the white supremacists to get too chummy with him—the fact that he feels so *guilty* about it all—does more to illustrate the dangers of white liberal guilt than all of the book's earlier questions about whether whites should study whiteness, and unwittingly serves as a strong argument *against* such self-representation.[53] I concur wholeheartedly with Back's later assess-ment that "if the interrogation of whiteness is to possess ethical integrity, it must accept this ambivalence" (57). Self-reflexive moments are not offensive in themselves, as long as the critic doesn't languish there—self-flagellation, which we all know is ultimately self-serving, should not be the point. Such white guilt has been both the enabling condition of postcolonial studies and its worst enemy. Or put another way: White guilt has been the prevalent condition blocking postcolonial studies from any careful examination of precisely *how* whiteness has managed all the damage it has inflicted on its others and what other forms a postcolonial whiteness might take.

Thus, postcolonial studies must be able and willing to respond to cer-tain foreseeable problems or risks in turning its focus to the analysis of colonial whiteness. The emergence of postcolonial whiteness as an object of study means that those of us who undertake it must vigilantly guard against those who view it as an opportunity to (1) construct an apologist narrative for whiteness, either in terms of a revisionist history or a distancing from what we now know whiteness to have been; (2) reinstate whiteness as a landmark or standard of reference in cultural or literary studies; and perhaps most insidiously, (3) settle for elaborate expressions of guilt as a substitute for or excuse from the most minute and rigorous analysis of what exactly whiteness has been and continues to be today. As Dyer points out, white guilt can paradoxically function as a validation of white liberal superiority as a more sensitized, and thus morally refined, whiteness: "We may lacerate ourselves with admission of our guilt, but that bears witness to the fineness of a moral spirit that can feel such guilt—the display of our guilt is our calvary" (11).

The turn to postcolonial whiteness thus presents itself as an opportunity to *dislocate* it, to shift the focus from uncritical representations of subaltern others to an emphasis on the conditions of white colonial production of such representations of both others and itself, and the extent to which it has historically done so in the name of extending and maintaining colonial power. As Winant explains, the task before us is to

> think, finally, of what it means to acknowledge that the half-millennium of domination of the globe by Europe and its U.S. inheritors is the historical context in which racial concepts of human difference have attained their present, and still relatively unquestioned, foundational status. (Winant 107–108)

The chapters in this volume not only "think" this acknowledgment, but embrace it as the necessary precondition to any critique of whiteness, postcolonial or not. The point of such an "acknowledgment" would thus be to disrupt the production of the text of whiteness precisely by asking the questions that it has eluded for so long. The task of a postcolonial critique of whiteness must finally be, as Anthony O'Brien suggests, "to ask new questions of old histories," thus allowing us to "move on from solipsism and myths of centrality" (O'Brien 55) that have maintained whiteness in its position as the invisible, omnipotent arbiter of world culture for far too long.

NOTES

1. See Gates, 2–15 and Appiah, 28–46.
2. See Dyer, especially 1–4, and Chambers.
3. In this context, the recent arguments in the United States by conservative thinkers for a more "race-blind" society must be viewed with suspicion, as a cynical attempt to deploy the language of equality as a ruse to return whiteness to its place as unacknowledged, invisible norm. For a recent and widely read example of this sort of argument, see D'Souza.
4. This is a conflict that Fanon's later writings pointedly resolve in favor of the latter tendency. See for example Fanon, *Wretched*.

5. For examples of others who do take on the issue of race within colonial and/or postcolonial contexts, see Trinh 1991; Hall; and Davies 1995.

6. Fanon certainly does not overlook this dimension of colonial relations, nor does his work neglect the relations of what he variously calls the "national middle class" and "national bourgeoisie" with the colonizing regime and its legacy on the one hand and the national working classes on the other. Indeed, in Fanon's view the national bourgeoisie welcomes independence from the colonial regime as an opportunity to effect "the transfer into native hands of those unfair advantages which are a legacy of the colonial period" (*Wretched*, 152). See also Fanon, *Wretched*, 149–54 and 175–76.

7. See Ashcroft 1995, 518, 524.

8. See Dyer, 184–206.

9. For some very good sociological analyses of this downsized, even defensive working-class whiteness in postcolonial England, Ware, "Perfidious" and *Out*, 33–59, 99–110, and 196–226.

10. For some pointed critiques of postcolonial studies for its failure to address U.S. "internal colonization" of Native Americans and inner-city Latinos and African Americans, as well the United States' role in the spread of global capitalism as a form of economic and cultural imperialism, see San Juan; Chun; Cherniavsky. See also Trías Monge for a study of the United States' continued "protection" of Puerto Rico and other such properties.

11. See López, *Posts*, 85–119.

12. One admirable exception to this tendency in postcolonial studies is Ashcroft et al.'s *Post-colonial Reader*. Both the editors' introduction to the section entitled "Ethnicity and Indigeneity" and the contributors' essays they include in it generally eschew the binary oppositions of race and colonial power that I am critiquing here. See Ashcroft, 213–45.

13. See López, *Posts*, 224–25.

14. See Garvey 1997.

15. For a lengthier discussion on this point that I pursue elsewhere, see López, *Posts*, 121.

16. See López, *Posts*, 3.

17. See Spivak, especially 423–31, an appendix entitled "The Setting to Work of Deconstruction."

18. See Young *Postcolonialism*, 2001, especially 15–69, in which Young argues for a neat division between "periods" leading up to the present postcolonial moment.

19. See Young, *Postcolonialism*, 337–426, vii–xi, and 427–28 respectively.

20. For Spivak, "Derrida's own position as a Franco-Maghrebian" does not necessarily lead one away from deconstruction as an efficacious critical activity, nor does Derrida's own discussion of "his early years in Algeria." Spivak does not elaborate on or further discuss these remarks, which appear in the book's final paragraph. See Spivak, 431.

21. Young actually goes farther along this line of thought in a previous book, in which he seeks to place poststructuralism's originary beginnings as "not May 1968 but rather the Algerian War of Independence." See Young 1990, 1.

22. See López, *Posts*, 40, 219n.

23. See López, *Posts*, 10–14.

24. For a particularly thorough and widely read critique of just this type, see Shohat.

25. Excerpts from both Parry's and Appiah's attacks on postcolonialism appear in Ashcroft et al.'s *The Post-colonial Studies Reader*, the best-known such anthology, and have been anthologized in a number of other such readers. Both of these texts thus paradoxically enter the realm of "postcolonial studies" even as they would disavow their own status as "postcolonial" writings and attack the field itself. See Ashcroft, 36–44 and 119–24 respectively.

26. For examples of Said's more strident political writings, see Said, *After* and *Question*.

27. See Bhabha, 19–39.

28. See López, *Posts*, 6–7.

29. All of the essays in this collection share with Roediger, as do I, the "desire to produce an antiracist white (or postwhite) subject, one whose political commitments can be disaffiliated from the deployments of white supremacy." I part company with Roediger's notion of a class solidarity that transcends race and ethnic identity, however, because it represents a throwback to outdated theorizations of the transcendental Marxist proletariat subject, a model that has historically ignored differences of gender, race, and ethnicity to its own eventual chagrin. Such a class-constituted postwhite subject does indeed fall prey to the dangers Wiegman sees of "reconfirm[ing] a universalist narcissistic white logic" that ultimately serves only to reinvent whiteness as antiracist while allowing it to keep (and shore up) its privilege and power. See Roediger, 8–13; Wiegman, 123. For a concise but theoretically indispensable account of Marxism's difficulties in maintaining the fantasy of the transcendental proletariat subject, see Laclau, especially 47–91.

30. See Foucault 1980, 81.

31. This tension between human agency and social constructedness—or put another way, between the subject and the social environment that hails or interpellates it—is at least as old as the Platonic dialogues. For present purposes we need only go back as far as Marx's famous claim that "social being" determines consciousness, and Engels's more nuanced qualification of this point in a letter to Joseph Bloch, to see the ambivalence that has historically existed between these competing but not irreconcilable terms. See Marx, 11–12 and Engels, 760–62 respectively.

32. I emphatically disagree with Wiegman's claim that "[t]he abolition of whiteness reclaims the democratic possibility of human society." On the contrary, the "abolition" or ethnic cleansing, literal or otherwise, of whiteness or anything else perpetuates the oppositional logic of hegemony by simply reversing it. The task of undoing whiteness from within must necessarily challenge postcolonial whites across the spectrum of nationalities and subject positions to "disinvest" themselves from their own whiteness and enter more fully into a relation of postcolonial *Mitsein* with their others. For postcolonial whites this means the end of seeing this disinvestment as a unilateral move, a self-congratulatory gesture that allows whites, as Annalee Newitz puts it, "to critique themselves before anyone else does." White self-flagellation is not the point here; an honest reckoning in good faith, and a willingness on all sides to work through painful histories (and presents) and *move on*, is. See Wiegman, 143; Newitz, 149.

33. Breytenbach's memoir tells of his "undercover" work against the apartheid regime, his capture and interrogation, imprisonment, and eventual release. See Breytenbach.

34. Dyer's word—specifically, in the introduction to *White* he describes his own goal as "the project of 'making whiteness strange.'" See Dyer, 4.

35. See Hill.

36. A U.S. Dept. of Justice memo written shortly after 9/11 alerts law enforcement agencies to the Department's concern over the growing number of incidents of violence against Arab Americans and anyone else who looks "like a terrorist"—that is, anyone with remotely Middle Eastern features. At the same time, CNN reports that Arab Americans can expect to be targets of racial profiling at airports and other public places in the United States. See Daniels; "Arab."

37. As an example from my hometown, take the three Miami-Dade firefighters—all three African American—who allegedly refused to ride in a fire truck that had a U.S. flag draped over it. Given the atmosphere of post-9/11 media hype and controversy, it should perhaps not be surprising that the Miami-Dade Fire Dept. placed the three men on "administrative leave," or that they have become the targets of a barrage of harsh, even threatening e-mails. Yet it is remarkable how quickly white America turns on its citizens of color when they refuse to toe the (color) line during a national crisis. See Olkon; White.

38. For more on the construction of the white race as a kind of political fiction and how it comes to be constituted out of a scattering of national identities, see Allen; Roediger; Ignatiev.

39. See Heidegger [1933] 1962, 149–68.

40. For more on the *tuché* generally and how Lacan himself applies the term, see Lacan [1973] 1998, 53–64.

41. See López, *Posts*, 93–96.

42. For more thorough discussion of each of these communities, see López, "*Patria*"; Figuera; and Cliff respectively.

43. See López, *Posts*, 94–95.

44. See Wray and Newitz, 1–12.

45. See Birgit Rasmussen, 8.

46. See Ignatiev 1995.

47. See hooks, 165–79 and Birgit Rasmussen, 13.

48. For the text of Macaulay's infamous "Minute on Indian Education," see Macaulay.

49. For a useful book-length discussion of how colonial education functions in the service of establishing and maintaining colonial power (in this case English), see Viswanathan.

50. See San Juan; Chun; Cherniavsky; and Trías Monge.

51. See Ware, "Perfidious" and *Out*; Brander Rasmussen et al.

52. Dyer is specifically talking about white women in the cited passage; but certainly that shoe fits men just as well, imagery aside. For the full discussion of Dyer's analysis of the representation of white women in association with the "demise" of colonialism, see Dyer, 184–206.

53. For the full text of Back's article, see Ware, *Out*, 33–59.

REFERENCES

Ahmad, Aijaz. 1995. The politics of literary postcoloniality. *Race and Class* 36, no. 3:1–20.

Allen, Theodore W. 1994. *The invention of the white race, vol. 1*. London: Verso.

Appiah, Kwame Anthony. 1992. *In my father's house: Africa in the philosophy of culture*. New York: Oxford University Press.

Arab-looking fliers expect scrutiny, try to lessen shame. August 28, 2002. *CNN.com*. *http://asia.cnn.com/2002/travel/news/08/28/flying.behavior.ap.ap/*. August 30, 2002.

Ashcroft, Bill, Gareth Griffiths, and Helen Tiffin, eds. 1995. *The post-colonial studies reader*. London: Routledge.

Bhabha, Homi K. 1994. *The location of culture*. London: Routledge.

Brander Rasmussen, Birgit, Eric Klingenberg, Irene J. Nexica, and Matt Wray, eds. 2001. *The making and unmaking of whiteness*. Durham: Duke University Press.

Breytenbach, Breyten. 1985. *The true confessions of an albino terrorist*. New York: Farrar, Straus and Giroux.

Chambers, Ross. 1997. The unexamined. In *Whiteness: A critical reader*, ed. Mike Hill, 187–203. New York: New York University Press.

Cherniavsky, Eva. 1996. Subaltern studies in a U.S. frame. *boundary 2—An International Journal of Literature and Culture* 23, no. 2:85–110.

Chun, Allen. 1996. Fuck Chineseness: On the ambiguity of ethnicity as culture as identity. *boundary 2—An International Journal of Literature and Culture* 23, no. 2:111–38.

Cliff, Michelle. 1990. Object into subject: Some thoughts on the work of black women artists. In *Making Face, making soul/haciendo caras: Creative and critical perspectives by feminists of color*, ed. Gloria Anzaldúa, 271–90. Boston: Aunt Lute.

Conrad, Joseph. [1899] 1988. *Heart of darkness* . Ed. Robert Kimbrough. Reprint. New York: W. W. Norton.

Daniels, Deborah J., and Ralph F. Boyd Jr. November 5, 2001. Response to violence, threats, and discrimination against Arab-Americans and other Americans of Middle Eastern and South Asian descent. U. S. Department of Justice memorandum. *http://www.ojp.usdoj.gov/ocr/memo1128.htm*. August 16, 2002.

Davies, Carole Boyce. 1995. *Black women, writing, and identity*. New York: Routledge.

D'Souza, Dinesh. 1995. *The end of racism*. New York: Free Press.

Dyer, Richard. 1997. *White*. London: Routledge.

Elphick, Richard, and Hermann Giliomee, eds. 1989. *The shaping of South African society, 1652–1840*. 2nd ed. Middletown, CT: Wesleyan University Press.

Engels, Friedrich. [1890] 1978. Letter to Joseph Bloch (1890). *The Marx-Engels reader, second edition*. Ed. Robert C. Tucker. Reprint. New York: W. W. Norton.

Fanon, Frantz. [1952] 1967. *Black skin white masks*. Trans. Charles Lam Markmann. New York: Grove Weidenfeld.

———. *The wretched of the Earth*. Preface Jean-Paul Sartre. Trans. Constance Farrington. New York: Grove, 1963.

Figueira, Dorothy M. 2002. *Aryans, Jews, Brahmins: Theorizing authority through myths of identity*. Albany: State University of New York Press.

Foucault, Michel. 1980. *Power/knowledge: Selected interviews and other writings 1972–1977*. Ed. and Trans. Colin Gordon. New York: Pantheon.

Frankenberg, Ruth, ed. 1997. *Displacing whiteness: Essays in social and cultural criticism*. Durham: Duke University Press.

Garvey, John, and Noel Ignatiev. 1997. Toward a new abolitionism: A *Race traitor* manifesto." In *Whiteness: A critical reader*, ed. Mike Hill, 346–49. New York: New York University Press.

Gates Jr., Henry Louis, ed. 1986. *"Race," writing, and difference*. Chicago: University of Chicago Press.

Hall, Stuart. 1995. "New Ethnicities." In *The post-colonial studies reader*, ed. Bill Ashcroft, Gareth Griffiths, and Helen Tiffin, 223–27. London: Routledge.

Hamner, Robert, ed. 1990. *Joseph Conrad: Third world perspectives*. Washington, DC: Three Continents.

Heidegger, Martin. [1933] 1962. *Being and time* . Trans. John Macquarrie and Edward Robinson. San Francisco: Harper Collins.

Hill, Mike. 1997. Introduction: Vipers in Shangri-la: Whiteness, writing, and other ordinary terrors. In *Whiteness: A critical reader*, ed. Mike Hill, 1–18. New York: New York University Press.

hooks, bell. 1992. Representing whiteness in the black imagination. In *Displacing whiteness: Essays in social and cultural criticism*, ed. Ruth Frankenberg, 165–79. Durham: Duke University Press.

Ignatiev, Noel. 1995. *How the Irish became white*. London: Routledge.

Jameson, Fredric. 1986. Third world literature in the era of multinational capital. *Social Text* 15(Fall): 65–88.

Jay, Gregory. August 19, 2002. Whiteness studies: Deconstructing (the) race. *http://www.uwm.edu/%7Egjay/Whiteness/index.html*.

Jolly, Rosemary. 1995. Rehearsals of liberation: Contemporary postcolonial discourse in the new South Africa. *PMLA: Publications of the Modern Language Association* 110(January), no. 1:17–29.

Keegan, Timothy J. 1996. *Colonial South Africa and the origins of the racist order*. Charlottesville: University Press of Virginia.

Lacan, Jacques. [1973] 1998. *The seminar of Jacques Lacan, book XI: The four fundamental concepts of psychoanalysis* (1973). Ed. Jacques-Alain Miller. Trans. Alan Sheridan. Reprint. New York: W. W. Norton.

López, Alfred J. 2001. *Posts and pasts: A theory of postcolonialism*. Albany: State University of New York Press.

———. 2002. *La patria y el tirano*: José Martí and the role of literature in the formation of Cuban nationalisms. *Cuban Studies* 33:137–55.

Macauley, Thomas. [1835] 1995. Minute on Indian education. In 1995. *The post-colonial studies reader*, ed. Bill Ashcroft, Gareth Griffiths, and Helen Tiffin, 428–30. London: Routledge.

Marx, Karl. [1859] 1904. *A contribution to the critique of political economy*. Trans. N. I. Stone. Chicago: Charles H. Kerr.

———. 1972. *The Marx-Engels reader*. Trans. Robert C. Tucker. New York: Norton.

Mohanty, Satya P. 1991. "Drawing the color line: Kipling and the culture of colonial rule. In *The bounds of race: Perspectives on hegemony and resistance*, ed. Dominick LaCapra, 311–43. Ithaca: Cornell University Press.

Morrison, Toni. 1992. *Playing in the dark: Whiteness and the literary imagination*. Cambridge: Harvard University Press.

Mukherjee, Meenakshi. 1996. Interrogating post-colonialism. In *Interrogating post-colonialism: Theory, text, and context*, ed. Harish Trivedi and Meenakshi Mukherjee, 3–11. Shimla: Indian Institute of Advanced Study.

O'Brien, Anthony. 1994. Staging whiteness: Beckett, Havel, Maponya. *Theatre Journal* 46:45–61.

Olkon, Sara, and Nicole White. September 22, 2001. Flag flap is overblown, firefighters say. *Miami Herald*, 3B.

Orwell, George. [1936] 1970. Shooting an elephant. *The collected essays, journalism, and letters of George Orwell, volume 1: An age like this 1920–1940*, ed. Sonia Orwell and Ian Angus, 265–72. New York: Penguin Books.

Parry, Benita. 1987. Problems in current theories of colonial discourse. *Oxford Literary Review* 9:27–58.

Roediger, David. 1991. *The wages of whiteness*. London: Verso.

Said, Edward W. 1998. *After the last sky*. New York: Columbia University Press.

———. 1992. *The question of Palestine*. New York: Vintage.

San Juan Jr., E. 1998. *Beyond postcolonial theory*. New York: St. Martin's Press.

Sartre, Jean-Paul. [1947] 1956. *Being and Nothingness* (1947). Trans. and intro. Hazel E. Barnes. Reprint. New York: Philosophical Library.

Shohat, Ella. 1992. Notes on the 'post-colonial.' *Social Text* 31, no. 32:103–27.

Spivak, Gayatri Chakravorty. 1999. *A critique of postcolonial reason: Toward a history of the vanishing present*. Cambridge: Harvard University Press.

Trías Monge, José. 1997. *Puerto Rico: The trials of the oldest colony in the world*. New Haven: Yale University Press.

Trinh T. Minh-ha. 1991. *When the moon waxes red: Representation, gender, and cultural politics*. New York: Routledge.

Viswanathan, Gauri. 1989. *Masks of conquest: Literary study and British rule in India*. New York: Columbia University Press.

Ware, Vron. 2001. Perfidious Albion: Whiteness and the international imagination. In *The making and unmaking of whiteness*, ed. Birgit Brander Rasmussen, Eric Klingenberg, Irene J. Nexica, and Matt Wray, 184–213. Durham: Duke University Press.

Ware, Vron, and Les Back. 2002. *Out of whiteness: Color, politics, and culture*. Chicago: University of Chicago Press.

White, Nicole. October 24, 2001. 3 who removed U.S. flag remain on leave. *Miami Herald*, 1B.

Wiegman, Robyn. 1999. Whiteness studies and the paradox of particularity. *boundary 2—An International Journal of Literature and Culture* 26 no. 3(Fall): 115–50.

Winant, Howard. 2001. White racial projects. In *The making and unmaking of whiteness*, ed. Birgit Brander Rasmussen, Eric Klingenberg, Irene J. Nexica, and Matt Wray, 97–112. Durham: Duke University Press.

Wray, Matt, and Annalee Newitz, eds. and intro. 1997. *White trash: Race and class in America*. New York: Routledge.

Young, Robert J. C. 1990. *White mythologies: Writing history and the West*. London: Routledge.

———. 2001. *Postcolonialism: An historical introduction*. London: Blackwell.

TWO

THE BODY OF THE PRINCESS

DIANE ROBERTS

MOST CULTURES FROWN ON NECROPHILIA. In America and Britain we actively encourage it. When Diana, Princess of Wales, was alive, we desired her; we fantasized about touching her, consuming her, even if at the passive distance of a television screen or newspaper page. In the likeness first used clumsily by her brother Lord Spencer, then more elegantly by editorial writers and poets, she became Diana the Huntress hunted down and destroyed by her own hounds. Now that she's dead, we still devour her; we feed on her dead body. Not a pretty picture.

But maybe it's not necrophilia, after all. Maybe it's not sexual but religious, the beginning of a hagiography for the new millennium. We live in an age when observant faith, for those who have it, has become stripped-down, almost ritual-free, drive-in McChurch divorced from mystery. Royalty still has some threads of mystique clinging to it, some irrational but powerful sense of the numinous. And Princess Diana, even more than the consecrated monarch, Queen Elizabeth II, came to embody royalty. Althorp, Diana's family home, has already become a place of pilgrimage. The princess, her real body now invisible, lying in her tomb on a flower-strewn island, will take to performing miracles like St. Catherine of Alexandria, another golden-haired royal martyr.[1] She will become the patroness of the poor and downtrodden like Evita, another smart dresser. She will be the icon of a generation like Marilyn Monroe, another disappointed bride. Later she will be resurrected. She is already a trinity: "Born a Lady, became a Princess, died a Saint," read one of the handwritten tributes stuck with the bouquets in the gilded gates of Kensington Palace.[2]

31

Diana incorporates not just an elevated feminine whiteness but a reinscribed one, a representation of the cultural and affective power of the West. Royalty has always been produced to reify not just power but an idealized racial image. The pale-skinned, white-haired, pearl-draped Queen Victoria, her image reproduced on stamps, money, biscuit tins, postcards and her portrait hung in colonial offices all over the British Empire served to make white rule of the nonwhite seem normative. Even now after the British Empire has shrunk to a few rocky island colonies in the Atlantic, and the British queen only a half-remembered head of state in modern democratic Commonwealth nations, the idea of royalty is still an effective symbol of how the imperial is irreducibly white. As Anne McClintock argues, "[I]mperialism and the invention of race were fundamental aspects of Western, industrial modernity" (McClintock 1995, 5). If, as the narrator of Michelle Cliff's *Abeng* avers, Victoria is "[the] whitest woman in the world" (Cliff [1984] 1991, 5), then Diana to a large extent represents and embodies that Victorian legacy, albeit paradoxically, as the most visible symbol of a Britain far removed from its Victorian pinnacle of imperial power. Diana as "white goddess" thus emerges as postcolonial Britain's best last best hope of retaining its sense of continued relevance and consequence in the world. As Gwendolyn Audrey Foster has observed, this iconography of Diana is symptomatic of

> a deep nostalgia for a white class that had been based on royal birth and marriage. Diana, Princess of Wales, is emblematic of the good-white female of class and nobility. Though her marriage to Prince Charles was a disaster, the media portrays her as the beneficent, long-suffering good-white mother, who seemingly gave up her party-girl ways to make sure that her sons kept their whitened royal stature. (Foster 2003, 125).

To the Elizabethans, Britain's first empire-builders, the female body, except for the interdict, anointed, and authoritatively virgin body of Elizabeth I, was "naturally grotesque" and out of control, things always going into and coming out of it (Stallybrass 1986, 126). The vigilance that the early modern British and their descendants felt the female body required finally paid off in Victorian ladyhood, when a woman could be read simultaneously as chaste and the producer of children: Queen Victoria herself had nine. We've been living with that Cult-of-True-Womanhood hangover ever since, negotiating a way for women to be mothers and yet asexual, fruitful wombs yet without genitals, the madonna who never behaves like, well, Madonna.[3]

The extremes of the emblematic royal feminine were captured for contemporary culture by Princess Diana and her symbolic opposite (and sister-in-law), Sarah, Duchess of York. Both struggled with their bodies in public.[4] Diana's precipitous (read originally by the press as "glamorous") weight loss owing to bulimia, getting thinner and thinner, signaled a wish to erase her body altogether, to achieve the perfection of invisibility even as her "fashionable" slimness guaranteed that she would be photographed more and more. Sarah's contrasting weight gain (and occasional diet-driven losses), mercilessly chronicled in the tabloids, showed another side of eating disorders. Her current American job as spokesperson for Weight Watchers underlines her position as a woman whose flesh is out of control, in need of an addiction-recovery plan to subdue the buttocks and thighs and breasts and stomach that rendered her too visible, too corporeal, and too close to some color other than whiteness for both royal dignity and rigid contemporary definitions of female attractiveness.

If Diana is the inheritor of the Victorian mantel of white womanhood—frail, delicate, sexually pure—Sarah's slide toward a scandalous fleshiness places her by contrast dangerously close to the stereotype of the "Woman of Color," a trope Ruth Frankenberg defines by her "apparently excessive appetites," both epicurean and sexual (Frankenberg 1997, 12). Blonde Diana corresponded to the elevated fairy princess/movie star late twentieth-century audiences demand for their heroines, while Sarah with her red hair (traditionally the color of fallen women, from Mary Magdalene onward) corresponded to the approachable goodtime girl whose "appetites" always get her into trouble. Or, to use Bahktin's model, Diana inhabited the "classical body": single, ethereal, sanctioned, and official:

> an entirely finished, completed, strictly limited body, which is shown from the outside as something individual. That which protrudes, bulges, sprouts, or branches off (when a body transgresses its limits and a new one begins) is eliminated, hidden or moderated. All orifices of the body are closed. (Bakhtin 1984, 320)

Sarah, on the other hand, is figured by the "grotesque body":

> multiple, bulging, over-or under-sized, protuberant and incomplete. The openings and orifices of this carnival body are emphasized, not its closure and finish. It is an image of impure corporeal bulk with its orifices (mouth, flared nostrils, anus) yawning wide and its lower regions (belly, legs, feet, buttocks and genitals) given priority over its upper regions (head, "spirit," reason). (Stallybrass and White 1986, 9)

Sarah, thinner and soberer, lives on. Diana is dead. Yet representations of her still feed our insistence on the binary of high and low, pure and impure. Had she lived, married Dodi Fayed, a decidedly "dark" man, her place on the pedestal would hardly have been assured. Her body was entering the public domain; because of the publication of intimate tapes and memoirs, the princess who once could act almost as if her children came about through parthenogenesis was beginning to be seen as a *sexual* being. The classical, closed body of royalty becomes—not quite grotesque or "open" to all—but nevertheless a producer of desire. The princess-as-icon still functions in our culture, but her body is also subject to invasion. This happens to modern princesses: the Duchess of York explains the virtues of cranberry juice on American television (beneficial to the urinary tract), nude photos of Jacqueline Kennedy appear, and the body of Eva Peron, embalmed and practically sanctified, was the victim of sexual molestation some years after her death. Interfering with a princess is no longer a treasonable offense. What all of these examples illustrate, to invoke Frankenberg's schema once more, is how within white colonial/neocolonial societies "White Woman's" place in the hierarchy, although certainly more privileged, is no more secure than that of the "Woman of Color"; even the white princess is "advantaged only conditionally on her acceptance of the terms of the contract. This includes especially her sexual practices, for the trope-ical family is strictly heterosexual and monoracial in its coupling" (Frankenberg 12). Once Diana began to violate these terms, most pointedly in her affair with Dodi Fayed, her place within the imperial hierarchy was no longer secure.

This chapter will undoubtedly raise more questions than it answers about a woman whose face is still as familiar to us as our own, yet whom most of us never saw in real life. She is an unresolvable paradox. "Diana Studies" is upon us as an academic discipline. There has been a conference at the University of Kent where specialists in feminism, art history, psychology, media studies, history, and sociology analyzed the reaction to Diana's death. Mythologizing is rampant: at the Kent conference, a psychotherapist was quoted saying of the fine warm weather: "It seems right, because summer ended when she died and now it's spring again."[5]

But who is Diana for us? Which Diana do we worship? Which do we commodify? It's impossible to know who she was as a human being with a real body, real desires. But as an idealization, especially a racial and gender idealization, we can learn a great deal about our anxieties and aspirations by exploring her vertiginous movements from fairy-tale princess to tragic heroine to madwoman in the palace to martyr. As Marina Warner reminds us, "A symbolized female presence both gives and takes value and meaning in relation to actual women" (Warner [1985] 1987, xx).

Who was Diana? Who knows? In a way it does not matter. We made her up. We use princesses—Dianas, Graces, Jackies—to preside over our system of both rewarding and punishing women for the extremes of purity and pollution our impulse to binarism creates. We use princesses to produce femininity and race, marking boundaries, high and low.

PRODUCING THE PRINCESS

Royalty is a construction. It always was, from the Egyptian Pharaohs, sculpted monumentally as if they were giants, to Elizabeth I, whose portraits in dresses heavy with pearls and rubies, both erase her body and celebrate its virginity (always figured as white), depicting her at once as the Fairy Queen (a supernatural being) and a tough, worldly, almost genderless ruler. Male members of royal families operate within a certain set of images having to do with military and sexual potency; post-Victorian female royals are represented as sexually forbidden, their bodies suppressed, yet nonetheless exhibited to the public.

The princess' body corresponds to Bakhtin's "classical" body, which elevated "entirely finished, completed, strictly limited" form (Bakhtin 320). At the state opening of Parliament, Queen Elizabeth II stands in a stiff, pale, gem-encrusted dress and long white gloves. She wears diamonds mined in South Africa, rubies "given" by Indian maharajahs and sapphires taken from Burma—the spoils of Empire. She is the feminine *embodiment* of the state. America may not have a monarch but it has its own, self-generated royalty in the Kennedy family, its own aristocrats in the New England Brahmins, the Ivy Leaguers, the fourth- and fifth-generation rich. We create our own consecrated bodies in actors, sporting figures, and politicians (of course, this also happens in the U.K.), people to whom we, symbolically, bend the knee, bodies we cannot touch but long to gaze upon.

In the United States we invent or borrow princesses. Princesses Grace, Caroline, Margaret, and Diana have been so ubiquitous in the American media over the last fifty years you'd think they were our own (Princess Grace, of course, used to be). On a smaller scale there are the legions of young women given the title of princess or queen in local or national beauty pageants, allegorical representations of a region or a product. There is something psychically necessary to Americans about a girl in a long white dress and a tiara, whether she is the Peanut Queen, Miss America, or Princess Diana. Yet even now, when Miss America has been a black woman and black women become local beauty queens, the overwhelming majority of America's homegrown "royalty" is very white. In this context the body of the princess constitutes a catalogue or perhaps a map of desire, revealing the power relations of a given society:

> The social formation of the body is the more effective because it extorts the essential while seeming to demand the insignificant: in obtaining the respect for form and forms of respect which constitute the most visible and at the same time the best hidden (because most "natural") manifestation of submission to the established order. (Bourdieu 1977, 95)

The princess, whether crowned in cheap diamante by the local mayor or wearing ancestral jewels, is the repository of cleanliness, of virtue, the designated work of art of her culture. Her closed and statue-like body is to be looked up to. It goes without saying that she will be beautiful (or collectively declared to be beautiful); it goes without saying she will be young (or collectively declared to be young-looking); it goes without saying she will be white. The princess is a commodity, created and sanctioned by those who buy her image, a fiction written to feed those who "read" her. The story of any princess—Jacqueline Kennedy, Miss America, or Diana Spencer—is deeply satisfying to us archetypally, emotionally. We are hard-wired to be interested in princesses because they represent the unattainable, the numinous, the exalted. We revel in the distance between the princess and us, the high and the low, even as we simultaneously celebrate the moments when the princess seems weak or vulnerable, *just like us*. We fit the princess into the story we want told: there is a good reason fairy tales do not star lawyers, bankers, or social workers but are about princesses, or about cinder-girls or goose girls who become princesses. This is both political and sexual: "[P]aradoxically the normative 'Woman' could become the emblem of the perfect and impermeable container, and hence a map of the integrity of the state. The state, like the virgin, was a *hortus conclusus*, an enclosed garden walled off from enemies" (Stallybrass 129). Elizabeth II represents an inviolate state: Diana and Sarah, her sometime-daughters-in-law, represent that purity, that *whiteness*, to lesser and greater degrees endangered.

VEILS OF ROYALTY

The British establishment and the Royal Family have always been quite good at the marketing of princesses. In 1863, when the Prince of Wales (later Edward VII) married Alexandra of Denmark, her image was reproduced over and over again in magazines and newspapers.[6] The court was still in mourning for Prince Albert, who had died in 1861, yet the wedding of the high-living prince to the long-necked, fair-haired nineteen-year-old princess was cause for national rejoicing. When the Duke of York (later George VI) married Lady Elizabeth Bowes-Lyon in 1923, they broke with the tradition that royal weddings, unlike coronations, were essentially private affairs, and had the ceremony in Westminster Abbey. Ever since then, the Royal Family has used royal weddings as occasions to advertise themselves *as* a family, to provide glitter and ritual and to be the ideal image for the society they officially reign over.

As Michael Rogin explains, "Spectacle is about forgetting. . . . The historicizing concept of amnesia suggests that the forgotten link in political spectacle is the visible tie to the past" (Rogin 1993, 508). The nations of the old Empire could be reminded of the white family in their palace thousands of miles away through pageantry that both invokes a glorious, if vague, past and suppresses the real history of colonization. The wedding of Princess Elizabeth to Prince Philip of Greece in 1947 was a reminder of white leadership of the Empire/Commonwealth, even though the Mother Country was exhausted, poor, and on postwar rationing. Likewise, the iconography of Diana as "England's rose" speaks to the continuing relevance of class.

"A family on the throne is an interesting idea," wrote Bagehot. "And a Royal Family sweetens politics by the seasonable addition of nice and pretty events." The Royal Family is supposed to be both an ideal and a reflection of society as a whole. Writing of the Stuarts, Jonathan Goldberg says:

> The family functioned in the Renaissance to reproduce society. This is not so simple as it sounds. On the one hand, family structures mirror the largest structures of society. But, on the other hand, procreation is not merely reproductive in a biological sense. Biology is transformed, and the family serves to reproduce society. The body is inscribed in a social system. (Goldberg 1986, 8–9)

This is no less true now. Gender roles have shifted in society as a whole, but not as radically in the symbol-saturated world of royalty. In the late twentieth century, photographs of the Royal Family, plastered on newspaper fronts, in magazines, and on souvenirs, and the television pictures of the 1981 wedding of Charles and Diana, underline both a "romantic" ideal of love and traditional patriarchy. Indeed, as has often been noted, the story seemed just like one of Lady Diana's step-grandmother Barbara Cartland's gooey novels: the dashing, yet brooding, prince is won over by the innocent charm of the ingénue. The photo of the Prince of Wales and Lady Diana, taken the day they announced their engagement, shows them at Buckingham Palace, the tall bride-to-be standing two steps below her fiancé so that he, the man, could tower over her. An official portrait by Snowdon shows the prince smiling into the camera, his arm around Lady Diana, who is wearing a frilly white blouse. Her cheek is against his shoulder (again, to perpetuate the fiction that he was taller) and her left hand, showing off her sapphire and diamond engagement ring, clings to his lapel. His position is commanding, "masculine"; hers is dependent, "feminine."

Representations of the couple reinforce this conformist gender and, covertly, racial ideal. The public had already been primed for the "fairy tale" by endless pictures of the very young Lady Diana, peering out shyly (like Disney's cartoon deer, Bambi) from under her blonde fringe and accepting bouquets from pink-cheeked children. Even when tabloid snappers caught her at her job at the Young England Kindergarten, wearing a thin skirt and no petticoat (and thus treating the world to a look at her long legs), she remained the pale English Rose, the woman without a past—except several hundred years of aristocratic ancestors. Horrified columns by feminists decrying the alleged medical examination Lady Diana underwent to certify her a *virgo intacta*, and condemning the way the Royal Family sold the youth and inexperience of the bride as an asset to the marriage rather than a danger, only served to strengthen the symbolic narrative. The endless photographs of Diana from this time often backlight her, making a halo of her golden hair. As Richard Dyer points out, "[I]dealized white women are bathed in and permeated by light. It streams through them and falls on to them from above. In short, they glow" (Dyer 1997, 122).

This idealization was reinforced further by the wedding. "Weddings are the privileged moment of heterosexuality, that is, (racial) reproduction, and also of women since they are glorified on what is seen as their day" (Dyer 124). The whiteness of the wedding dress amplifies the "glow" that certifies the white woman as the privileged body. Diana's dress seemed to envelope her in a cloud of ivory and lace ruffles over an enormous crinoline. It was the most "feminine" dress possible, all curves and bows with a very long veil that sometimes covered her completely; it was also a body-obscuring dress, hiding Diana's legs, breasts, touching her waist but not tight, obscuring even her feet.[7] Here was the certified white virgin almost formless, in a dress that emphasized less of her figure than any royal bride in recent memory.[8] Like the ideal of the lady or belle in the American South, signified by the hoop skirt that gives her, as William Faulkner said, the appearance of floating, not walking, the huge skirt hides the disruptive area of the body, the forbidden genitals.[9] The coveted body, which would simultaneously be pure and produce heirs to the kingdom, is both present and absent.

If Lady Diana in her huge meringue of a dress is all softness and femininity, the Prince of Wales in his dark naval uniform is all hardness and masculinity. He even wears the phallic cliché of a sword. In one famous wedding photo by Patrick Lichfield, the prince stands very erect in the throne room at Buckingham Palace, one foot resting on the top step of the dais; the new princess sits at his feet, her acres of dress spread out. She almost looks as though she is curtseying to him, leaning slightly forward. Yet she is also the center of the photograph: the eye is drawn to her face, her hair, and the Spencer tiara on her head. She appears in a compelling oval of whiteness: dress, face, fair hair crowned with diamonds. She functions both as gender emblem and racial signifier.

The Royal Family has always reproduced itself in pictures: coins, statues, paintings, photographs, and now television, reiterating its symbolic identification with the nation. Elizabeth I had herself painted over and over again in allegorical modes emphasizing how her body is the equivalent of the state. The Ditchley portrait shows her standing on a map of England, a colossus in a stiff court gown (Strong 1963, 75–76). She is Gloriana, Astraea, Albion, Mary, even Christ. In one portrait she wears a pendant of a pelican, an emblem of Christian self-sacrifice. She often appeared in person in clothes that exposed her breasts, sometimes her belly. Louis Montrose suggests that this signifies both her virginity *and* her status as the "selfless and bountiful mother" (Montrose 1986, 67).[10] But Elizabeth also, both in representations of her and evidently in real life, took pains to emphasize her very pale skin, even painting it lighter. Presiding over a nation solidifying its hold on Ireland (where the native Celtic population were not accorded the same level of whiteness as the English), reigning over a nation that was increasingly cosmopolitan in its racial mix (there were a number of black Africans living in London), and colonizing America, with its native population, Elizabeth underscored her difference, her elevation, in whiteness.[11] By contrast with Elizabeth's display of feminity aligned with white power, Diana's iconography of whiteness underscores the anxiety of Thatcher's Britain. Diana the white goddess stands as the paramount symbol of an empire in decline, of a Britain far removed from the apex of Victorian (or even Elizabethan) power and a postcolonial Britain struggling to come to terms with its own burgeoning racial and ethnic mixed-ness. As Vron Ware points out, in today's "post-Empire, post-decolonization" Britain, "the content of Englishness, like whiteness itself, appears to be of a volatile nature, easily evaporating when put under pressure" (Ware 192). And under pressure it certainly is: In the wake of festivities surrounding the fiftieth anniversary of the arrival of the SS *Empire Windrush*, "[t]he question of where the new generations of British-born black inhabitants fit in" (Ware 192) is overshadowed, I would argue, by the larger question of whether and to what extent the nation remains (or can even be imagined) as racially and ethnically homogeneous. Diana as an icon of postcolonial English whiteness, even or especially after her death, provides a perfect image upon which a nation displaces its longing for better days, days of white English beauty, glamor, and power. The fact that the Great White Hope in this instance is dead only makes her image that much more canonizable, that much less troublesome to manage.

The Stuarts, under whom the slave trade flourished and Atlantic plantation wealth burgeoned, also practiced symbolic representation, but with the emphasis on the family as figuring the state. Roy Strong points out that Charles I and the French princess Henrietta Maria "are the first English royal couple to be glorified in the domestic sense" (Strong 1972, 70). Through numerous portraits as husband and wife, then as mother and father of many princes and princesses, representations of Charles and Henrietta Maria elevate the domestic sphere while embodying the mystic nature of monarchy, politicizing the private. Jonathan Goldberg notes the white angel presiding over their betrothal portrait and the later portrait by Van Dyck which "domesticate[s] the mythological energies of Mars and Venus" in the way the king and queen hand each other the gods' attributes of laurel and olive (Goldberg 15).

If the current Charles had been pictured exchanging laurel and olive with Diana, no one would understand. Those are no longer our emblems. But we do understand the uniform, the sword, juxtaposed with her ruffled necklines and swirling skirts. The "intimate" honeymoon photos of Charles and

Diana holding hands, kissing after polo matches, and dancing are unprecedented in the history of royal representation. Charles and Diana presented not merely an allegory of union, of simultaneous domesticity and regality, but a romance lived via newspapers and television. When Diana became pregnant, her swollen body was not hidden (as had been the case with previous royal women) but much photographed, with and without her permission (there were some notorious photos of her in a bathing suit). With the birth of Prince William not quite a year after the wedding, it is easy to see just how mystified—and controlled—the careful imagery of the reproducing Royal Family can be. Diana slips easily from fairy princess to madonna, her youth and beauty intact yet now with a sense of her having been useful in upholding the ideological construct of hereditary (white) monarchy. She appears in pastel colors holding her baby, a perfect Christmas card image. Her virginity appears to have renewed itself: in a twenty-first birthday picture taken for *Vogue*, she wears a ruffled, lacy, high-necked white Victorian blouse, reminiscent of her engagement portraits. Like Elizabeth I, she was both impenetrable and the mother of the nation.

THE GHOST PRINCESS

In producing two sons, Diana's body served the national narrative of royal fruitfulness. Like Henrietta Maria, she is celebrated for acting out the most feminine of roles. And yet, as she later revealed, she was at war with her own body during this period, suffering from postnatal depression and bulimia. After Prince Harry's birth in 1984, she appears gaunt, her fresh young face drawn and strained, her fingers so thin that her rings no longer fit her. In the portraits by Snowdon, she again wears white, but now it hangs loose on her bones. Here Diana approaches a sort of death-in-life that has itself functioned as an icon of white Victorian beauty. Both Susan Sontag and Mario Praz have in different contexts examined both the "beauty" of white death and its function as a trope of sublimity in much nineteenth-century poetry.[12] Diana's "sublime pallor" in these portraits continues her representation as a neo-Victorian icon, albeit in an unforeseen and ominous way.

Whiteness here confronts us as an object of both beauty and purity on the one hand and "a certain nameless terror," as the narrator of *Moby Dick* puts it, on the other. What is suppressed, one might say latent, in this emaciated, even (in retrospect) morbid Diana is what Dyer calls the "association of whiteness with the bringing of death," specifically with such groups and events as the Ku Klux Klan, Nazis and the Holocaust, and the colonization of most of the world. What remains is Diana as victim, as suffering martyr. Thus, her depression and bulimia paradoxically work to further entrench her image as secular saint: the beautiful, good, pure, suffering princess.[13] Or as Foster explains it: "Portrayed as a saint, Diana epitomizes the relationship between white motherhood and blondeness and lightness, which is itself a marker of saintliness and religious deity" (Foster 2003, 125).

By the mid-1980s, Diana had acquired an advantageous opposite. Sarah Ferguson was big, loud, and animated, photographed bursting out of tight bodices, thighs revealed in windblown skirts, mouth perpetually open. In contrast, Diana seemed to recede, become more distant and more ethereal. Sarah's plump body was "not separated from the world by clearly defined boundaries" (Bakhtin, 26, 27). She was criticized for talking too much, a traditional sign of the "loose woman."[14] Her volubility kept her in constant trouble: In an interview with glossy American television reporter Diane Sawyer, she referred to herself and Diana as the "Thelma and Louise of Buckingham Palace," and claimed that her wild overspending was not as bad as Diana's depressions, addictions, and eating disorders (Spoto 1997, 101). By the late 1980s, grainy tabloid shots of her topless finished her marriage, and she was consigned to the margins of royalty.

Diana, on the other hand, *appeared* to become still more disembodied. In 1989, she was pictured on magazine covers and newspaper fronts as distant, perfect. Much was made of the photos of her dressed for the state opening of Parliament in long white gloves, a stiff, white, lace-overlaid Edwardian-looking dress and a great pearl-and-diamond diadem, worn by Queen Alexandra (another royal blonde). However, these calculatedly regal images were competing with reports that the princess was having an affair with gin heir James Gilbey and had become obsessed with Oliver Hoare, an art dealer. The Prince of Wales' continuing relationship with Camilla Parker-Bowles was, by this time, old news. By the time the "Squidgygate" tapes (sexually suggestive conversations intercepted from a cell phone between Diana and Gilbey) broke later in 1989, Diana's position on the national pedestal had become decidedly shaky. She was now the subject of sexual speculation, "open," in ways she had never been before. The classical, closed white body was in danger of slipping down into grotesquerie: Diana's position in the race-and-class hierarchy was now open to challenge.

There was an interesting attempt in 1991 by the Royal Family to reconstruct the unity of the Prince and Princess of Wales by releasing a portrait by Snowdon, himself a divorced ex-member of the Royal Family. It shows the prince and princess with their sons at Highgrove, the prince's country house. Diana sits on a rustic (but expensive-looking) bench uncharacteristically dressed in riding boots and breeches with Prince William at her feet. Charles stands behind her in "county" gear, one hand on her shoulder, one hand on Prince Harry's. Prince Harry holds the bridle of a handsome horse. On a table next to them and in a picnic basket at Diana's side you see beautifully colored, beautifully arranged fruit. In the background is a large old oak.

The picture carefully echoes Gainsborough's *Mr. and Mrs. Andrews*, country gentry parked in the middle of a romantic English landscape. It also recalls Daniel Mytens's portrait of Charles I and Henrietta Maria in which the couple appear with dogs instead of children, but dressed for hunting with a tree and a horse in the background (Goldberg 1986, 15–16). The fruit signifies the "harvest" of the union, their two sons, while the oak tree behind Charles is both a witty reminder of his namesake, Charles II, who legendarily hid in an oak tree to avoid being captured by Cromwellian forces, and an ancient evocation of mythic kingship, dating back to the Romans. Portraying Charles and Diana simultaneously as the kind of upper-middle-class family popularly held to inhabit large houses with stables in the English countryside, reproduced in portraits by Reynolds and Lawrence, *and* as the embodiment of the state, Heir Apparent and mother of a future king, was supposed to stabilize the image going out to the world, falling back on the old symbols of the nation to glue the family back together. But the ideological thrust of the image could not compete with the information in possession of the very media the Royal Family relied on to transmit the cohesive fiction of calm and plenty.

ICON UNDER PRESSURE

In the last three years of her life, representations of Diana careened all over the iconographical map. Her racial, even her class position, could now be challenged.[15] There was Diana the sufferer, undermined by a sinister Court, assailed by *tabloidistas* hoping to catch her still-forbidden body in pictures with a bit of breast or thigh as she wept or ran from them; there was Diana the saintly, photographed striding bravely (in nice Gap khakis and a blinding white shirt) into a landmine area in Angola at the behest of the HALO Trust (a name that evoked Diana in her white angel/goddess aspect) or holding Mother Theresa's hand; there was Diana the Modern Mother, pictured hanging out with her children in jeans and baseball caps, taking them to amusement parks or fast-food restaurants; there was Diana the '90s Babe, no longer distanced by a tiara, a hat or gloves, wearing even more glamorous designer clothes to charity balls and society weddings; and there was Diana the cut-loose single girl, photographed (often surreptitiously) with one of the transgressive men she went out with—the English rugby star, or, even more shockingly, the Asian doctor. Finally, it was images of the princess with Dodi Fayed, the dark-skinned Muslim playboy, the forbidden lover, which came to dominate Diana iconography.[16] Even the "vulgar" Sarah Ferguson had at least stuck to white men:

> Inter-racial heterosexuality threatens the power of whiteness be
> cause it breaks the legitimation of whiteness with reference to the
> white body. For all the appeal to spirit, still, if white bodies are no
> longer indubitably white bodies, if they can no longer guarantee
> their own reproduction as white, then the "natural" basis of their
> dominion is no longer credible. (Dyer 25)

When Diana was a guest on Mohammed Fayed's yacht in July 1997, she borrowed a motor launch and "visited" the huge contingent of long-lensed photographers who had been following her around. The journalists report that she was simultaneously playful and pleading, wishing to be left alone yet soliciting pictures, wearing a leopard-print bathing suit. Of course she was not left alone: a short while later, high-powered lenses captured her (in a blue bathing suit this time) with Fayed's son Dodi, sunning herself and, at one point, appearing to kiss him.[17]

These images, which seemed to "prove" that Diana and Dodi Fayed were having an affair, are strangely reminiscent of the paparazzi photographs taken of Elizabeth Taylor and Richard Burton on an Italian beach in 1962 when they were filming Joseph Mankiewicz's Cleopatra. Burton and Taylor are shown embracing while sunbathing: in a couple of shots, the straps of her bathing suit are down as she tans her back. These pictures alerted a salivating world that Taylor and Burton—although married to other people at the time—were an item.[18] In the yacht photos of Diana and Dodi Fayed, she appears at one point with her straps undone—the same image of intimacy that invites the viewer to fantasize about their sexual relationship.[19]

But what is shocking to the racial economy here is that Diana (even with a tan) is very white, while Fayed almost crudely embodies the dark rapist, the despoiler out of racist fictions from Thomas Dixon's The Clansman to Valentino's The Sheik to the television miniseries The Jewel in the Crown, first shown in 1984 and repeatedly subsequently.[20] Dyer argues for the series as a prototypical example of white women associated with the end of empire, and thus viewed as endangering the civilizing mission of empire precisely by introducing the element of (hetero) sexuality: "[U]nwittingly, [women] enflamed the already overheated desires of native men; they sapped their own men's energies or, as already noted, were liable to wind up betraying them" (Dyer 186). Further, the presence of white women in the colonies has historically meant a renewed questioning of the conduct of empire and its treatment of the colonized. I would argue that it is precisely some latent or unresolved trace of these archaic fears left over from the end of empire that fueled much of the Diana backlash in her final days, as she became associated through her relationship with Fayed with Victorian-Edwardian women as both "the conscience of empire [and] the cause of its decline" (Dyer 186).

It's not as if Diana did not complicate representations of herself quite calculatedly. Indeed, she proved herself a master of category confusion. One of the most reproduced photos to appear in newspapers or on television was of Diana in Pakistan (part of a former colony) in July 1997 at the Shukat Khanum Memorial Cancer Hospital, a facility set up by cricketer-turned-conservative politician Imran Khan (who had also married a white English woman, Jemima Goldsmith, a point not lost on the media). Diana holds a sick child, the child's hair almost gone (one assumes from cancer treatment), her large brown eyes turned up to Diana's face. Diana wears sky blue and a white diaphanous scarf as she gazes down at the child, one pale hand around the shoulder of the child, one holding the child's dark hand.

The resonance with images of the Virgin Mary as *Mater Amabilis* could not be stronger. The composition resembles a number of paintings, including one by Murillo in the Leuchtenberg Gallery, a woodcut of 1513 by Albrecht Dürer, and the *Virgin and Child with St. John* by Titian. The gold of Diana's hair and the blue and white she wears are the colors of the Virgin, seen in endless Annunciations, Immaculate Conceptions, Nativities, and Holy Families. The white signifies the Virgin's purity, the gold the stars of the sky, and the blue the sky itself—or perhaps the sea. Marina Warner suggests a connection with older goddesses of the heavens and life-giving water (Warner [1976] 1985, xx, 266). But the clothes Diana wears are not Western, but Eastern, Muslim, the *shalwar kameez,* and the child this madonna holds is brown. The dark skin of the child simultaneously underscores Diana's image as race-spanning mother to all children, and as white, her glow contrasted with the child's darkness: a Mary both traditional and revisionist, who plays up the saintliness but eschews, seemingly playfully, the "relationship between white motherhood and blondeness and lightness" upon which so much of the Diana iconography depends for its coherence (Foster 2003, 125).

Diana's sexual, religious, and racial cross-dressing was a clear assault on historical white hegemony, on imperialism itself:

> The processes of imperialism express, in representation, white identities. They are forged from the roles and functions of white people in imperialism and the qualities of character that performing them is held to require and call forth. . . . The white male spirit achieves and maintains empire; the white female soul is associated with its demise. (Dyer 184)

Maybe more important than the "white female soul" is the white female body. In her last days, Diana had become subversive. The magazines and newspapers that marketed her image could not sell a coherent Diana: there were too many Dianas. Her body had become a paradox, encompassing the incongruous extremes of madonna and harlot, empedestalled white woman and a woman "polluted" by her association with a man of color. It would be putting it too strongly to say that Diana embodied *both* Bakhtin's classical and grotesque bodies, because despite the display of her more obvious flesh, she retained status as an elevated being, albeit one in peril of slippage. Yet it is clear that Diana was a long way from the sanctified virginity she represented as a bride in 1981. She was sexualized yet adored, almost as if she contained the potential to in herself destroy the debilitating binaries that still imprisoned women. But, of course, a woman of privilege, by her very nature unique, separated from the mass of women, does not really tear down the walls for anyone, *even* herself. We, the voyeurs, still watch through the veil of our social constructions; we still read with the vocabulary of the old stories: Cleopatra, the queen who died for love of a foreigner; St. Catherine, who died a martyr to intolerance; Evita, who died beloved by the masses yet disliked by the elite.

DIANA VICTRIX

Everything changed when Diana died. Her sexual body was suppressed, her celestial body reasserted. She was *transfigured*—I use this word in the sense the church uses it, to mean the transformation of a body from normal flesh to something more.[21] Mark 9 tells how Peter, James, and John watched Jesus become "transfigured before them, and His raiment became shining, exceeding white as snow," as Elijah and Moses appeared out of heaven with him and God spoke, saying "THIS IS MY BELOVED SON" (Mark 9: 2–4, 7).[22] In 1380, Wyclif explained transfiguration as a body "turnyng into glorious forme." Transfiguration is the sign that Christ is not only human as the rest of us are human but divine at the same time. Luminosity and whiteness are associated with transfiguration—they are often associated with Diana as well, with her white dresses and the representations of her as saint or madonna. In the week between her death and funeral, the images of her that appeared on television and in British and American newspapers heavily underscored this. The Diana of bulimia, depression, of unsuitable romantic liaisons, even the Diana of clinging black cocktail dresses, was largely suppressed in favor of Diana in her wedding dress, Diana tiara-ed in one of the pearl-decked state-occasion dresses, or Diana with children or the sick or the old.[23] In other words, a firmly *white* Diana. A column in *The Evening Standard* on 6 September, the day of the funeral, ran with two photos, one of her with her two sons, and one taken by Patrick Demarchelier for *Vogue* of her in close-up, her champagne-gold hair and glowing white face and hands against a dark sweater. The headline reads, "At the Height of Her Beauty, She will be Forever Thus" (Spencer 1997, 19).

I cannot begin to account for the strange outpouring of grief that led people in Britain and America to cover every nonmoving surface with bunches of flowers. The Dianologists are, no doubt, already at work on the mechanics of public grief, displaced feeling for celebrities, etc. But what is clear is that the representations of her—and of other members of the Royal Family—served to bring the narrative of her life back into line, giving her story the coherence it almost lost when she moved vertiginously between races and religions. Images of Dodi Fayed who, obviously, also died in the Paris crash, were almost impossible to find in the newspapers or on television. Diana was hoisted back onto her pedestal, back into the realm of the closed classical body, her whiteness, her class elevation, and her untouchability underlined once more:

The angelically glowing white woman is an extreme representation, precisely because it is an idealisation. It reached its apogee towards the end of the nineteenth century and especially in three situations of heightened perceived threat to the hegemony of whiteness. British ideological investment in race categories increased in response to spectacular resistance to its empire, notably the Indian Mutiny of 1857 and the Jamaican revolt of 1865. . . . The Southern US ideal of womanhood intensified . . . after the Civil War, with the defeat of official racism and slavery. (Dyer 127)

I won't contend that Diana's romance with Dodi Fayed is anything like equivalent to the fear generated by the Indian Mutiny, or the hysteria produced by the implied racial threat of the presence of freed slaves amongst white women after 1865. And it is true that one of the remarkable things about the mourning for Diana in Britain, at least, was the great many people of color who kept vigil at Kensington Palace or spent the night before the funeral in St. James' Park. Nonetheless, the packaging of Diana as a very white Our Lady continued the whole week between her death and burial. The pictures of her in diamond tiaras evokes *Maria Regina*, crowned queen of heaven; the photos of her with her sons (one of whom will be king and, unless disestablishment finally takes place, Defender of the Faith) evokes the *Virgo Dei Genetrix*, and the sad-eyed Diana, photographed jewel-less on one of her missions of mercy, evokes the *Mater Dolorosa*. As if somehow responding to a long-repressed Roman Catholicism—or even paganism—in their souls, the hundreds of thousands in the streets of London made shrines of candles and garlands that would not have looked out of place in Mexico City on the Day of the Dead or Seville during the Virgin's *Feria*. Diana's appellation as "England's Rose," given to her by Elton John, echoes a title of the Virgin—the Rose of Sharon, the Rosa Mundi.

The story of Diana resumed as myth, overwhelming all other stories in Britain and America, including the death of Mother Theresa. It seemed for a while that Diana as goddess or martyr would overtake and destabilize the monarchy—the last, greatest remnant of imperialism itself. The tabloids demanded that the Royal Family show themselves in London, in other words, be photographed and filmed, preferably in displays of grief that suited the national narrative of "tragedy." The queen eventually acquiesced, going on television in black, allowing photos of the princes holding hands and looking at their mother's floral tributes with their ashen-faced father. And when, at the funeral, Diana's brother, Lord Spencer, appeared to blast the Royal Family for the "bizarre" life they forced his sister to lead, then had himself photographed the next day, a poignant, lone figure amongst the flowers on her grave at Althrop, it almost seemed that the defining story of the British monarchy was about to be rewritten. Some commentators (David Cannadine and Elaine Showalter in the 6 September *Guard-*

ian, for example)[24] sensed a major paradigm shift, perhaps even the fall of the House of Windsor and a sweeping away of the old patterns for a new model army of a "feeling" Britain without protocol or hierarchy. A new dawn for an old nation, ideas encouraged by the Labour Prime Minister, Tony Blair, who coined the term "People's Princess."

DIANA CONTAINED

It didn't happen, of course. The old patterns and the old representations reemerged about the time the flowers, now rotting, were being cleared from in front of the palaces.[25] The conspiracy theories that arose as soon as word of Diana's death was spread only underscored the importance of royalty. Even the idea that somehow the queen and MI6 had Diana murdered so that she would not "disgrace" the Royal Family by marrying a Muslim and bearing a "brown baby" only displays the public sense of the queen's power, and the need, filled by all conspiracy theories, that an important or visible person not be able to die in a mere accident, like any of us, but must be killed by larger, more organized, more important and conscious forces. Lord Spencer's attacks on the Royal Family, read in America (somehow) as the righteous anger of an ordinary man whose beloved sister was done to death partly by the rich and remote Windsors, and read more accurately in Britain as the disdain of the ancient aristocracy for the parvenu "German" monarchy, were almost instantly discredited.[26] Lord Spencer pledged that he would struggle to see that "Diana's boys" were brought up "normally," then had to go through a divorce action involving drugs, adultery, betrayal, lying, and a very great deal of money.

Everybody wins in Diana's canonization—everybody white, anyway. Her once potentially disruptive body is now frozen in photographs and dispersed like pieces of the True Cross, powerful but controlled. Her deified name appears on tea towels and tubs of Flora margarine—so appropriate since in death she also became the goddess of flowers, or at least flower sellers. Her image is also found in the face of her son, Prince William. If nothing else, the resemblance might ensure the future of the monarchy: who better to be king than the son of a goddess-saint? In death, Diana has regained the elevation and whiteness she endangered in life. Dodi Fayed is gone, vanished as if the empire never dared strike back. Diana is a triumph of mystic capitalism: the sacrosanct body sold and resold yet never felt to be tainted. In Britain, there was a little bit of dissent: *Granta* ran a section entitled "Those Who Felt Differently," people not caught up in Diana hysteria. *Private Eye* generated howls of rage with its black-bordered cover and "Media to Blame" headline over a shot of crowds in front of Buckingham Palace saying, "The papers are a disgrace. I couldn't get one anywhere," and another person saying "Borrow mine—It's got a picture of the car."[27] In America, her apotheosis is unchallenged. Diana dolls are sold in the pages of *Parade* and exhibitions of her dresses draw large crowds. The marketing of her image is merging with the marketing of other celestial bodies—she has become part of the "angel" boom, a phenomenon that sells books and calendars with accounts of angels who often seem to look like Diana—blonde, tall, blue-eyed, and crowned with diamonds.

Now we have the pale-skinned, Christian world pitted (despite what George W. Bush might say) against the dark-skinned Muslims, the perpetrators of terrorism. We are not surprised: it would be those people. As we see in the case of Diana—especially in her sanitized afterlife as "England's Rose"—the pure white body, as Foster argues, is defined precisely in contrast to "the insistent prevalence of images of an/other. . . . 'Whiteness,' as a category, is maintained by a constant supply of Colonialist imagery" (Foster 1999, 5). So if there's no longer a Diana to embody that Western, hegemonic whiteness for us, we still know what the idea is. Diana collapses the categories of princess, mother, virgin, and victim into an incandescent picture on a commemorative plate. We are still worshipping white goddesses, whatever names we give them.

NOTES

I am grateful to Alfred López for his excellent suggestions and help with this chapter.

1. St. Catherine of Alexandria was one of the most popular saints of the Middle Ages, especially in Britain. She is usually pictured in the rich robes of royalty and wearing a crown, holding a book or a palm frond and a sword with a spiked wheel (the instrument used to torture her) behind her. She supposedly lived in the fourth century, a remarkable scholar who refused to disavow her Christianity and was martyred by Emperor Maximinus II. St. Catherine appears to be largely fictional; indeed, the Roman Catholic Church removed her from its official calendar of saints in 1969. But her legends have produced many churches and paintings, such as Raphael's "Mystic Marriage of St. Catherine" in which the grown-up saint is shown with the Virgin and Infant Christ who is placing a wedding ring on her finger. The wheel, often depicted as a sort of stylized sun, has led some scholars to speculate she is really a Christianized version of a "pagan" goddess. Her feast day, 25 November, is still in the Anglican calendar.

2. The Princess' ghost has already been seen by people waiting in the queue to sign books of condolence at St. James' Palace in the first few days after her death. She supposedly appeared smiling mysteriously in a dark corner of a portrait of Charles II.

3. Madonna herself has now reinvented herself as a mother rather than as a Material Girl with her daughter Lourdes, named after the place in the Pyrenees where Bernadette Soubirous saw the Virgin eighteen times.

4. For the sake of clarity and brevity, not the usual American ignorance of protocol, I will mostly not accord Diana, Princess of Wales and Sarah, Duchess of York their full titles but use their Christian names. Like many other women who have achieved mythic status (Madonna, Evita, Cher) they are quite recognizable with just one name.

5. As reported by Alex Renton in *The Evening Standard*. Renton also quotes the wonderfully named Dr. Margaret Mitchell, reader in psychology at Glasgow Caledonian, as saying that Diana's potential as an academic subject is endless: "Her cultural meaning in life and how that was thrown into perspective by her sudden death. It fits into death studies. It fits into cultural studies—the Diana package fits into so many other disciplines." Renton reports as well that Sydney University will soon publish a volume of essays called Planet Diana. Of course, a story such as this in a popular newspaper serves both to underscore Diana's continuing fascination while making populist fun of academics. Renton quotes Dr. Jude Davis of Winchester in predictably jargon-filled mode: "I will outline a history of the Diana sign whereby its transition from a magical synthesis of binary oppositions to a focus of argument and inspiration has opened up possibilities for unpacking the knot of meanings around royalty, patriarchy, class, imperialism and ethnicity." See Renton, 8–9.

An article by Clare Garner (less sneering at academics) also tells how The Free University in Berlin ran a series of thirteen lectures called "Myths and Politics from Princess of Wales to Queen of Hearts," and the Universities of Lancaster and East London have held psychoanalytic and media studies symposia on the princess. See Garner.

6. This is, to some extent, true of all royal weddings beginning in the Middle Ages, especially the wedding of the heir to the throne. The body of the sovereign or the sovereign-to-be was identified with the nation itself and so any alliance was necessarily symbolic of the country as a whole.

7. Apparently Diana lost weight from stress right before the wedding, and so the dress was actually a size too big for her.

8. Princess Anne's wedding dress had been high-necked but tight-waisted; the present queen's had been positively sexy with its deep V-neck. Even Queen Victoria's daughters often wore low-cut, nipped-waist wedding dresses to show off their corseted hour-glass figures.

9. See Roberts *Faulkner*, especially ch. I.

10. As late as the early 1970s, emblems of virginity show up in portraits of royal ladies; there's one of Princess Anne in a white dress with a unicorn cavorting on a peculiarly lunar landscape in the background.

11. For more on this royal iconography of whiteness, see Gerzina and Walvin.

12. See Sontag; Praz.

13. We should of course not overlook here the association with the suffering white princess in so many fairy tales: Cinderella, Sleeping Beauty, Snow White et al.

14. See Stallybrass, 127 and Roberts, *Myth*, 9–19 and 80–85.

15. In 1995, she gave an interview to the BBC's *Panorama* program, in which she dressed in black and wept beautifully. It was as if she was attempting to reclaim victim status in the face of her husband's blatant infidelity with another blonde, Camilla Parker-Bowles. And at the time, much was made of the fact that she chose an interviewer of Asian background, Martin Bashir.

16. Fayed's father Mohammed had been involved in a spat with the previous Conservative British government over his citizenship for years and was so a constant staple for the tabloids. Nonetheless, commentators focused on Diana rather than the Harrods owner in expressing distaste. Few were overtly racist, but many mentioned her blonder hair (either lightened in the sun or in the salon) and her rounder stomach. Diana was thirty-six years old and no longer the bulimic waif she had been;

the media who produced her image seemed caught by surprise by evidence of her body's maturing.

17. At least one of the British tabloids that got these pictures computer-enhanced them so as emphasize the embrace—if that's what it was.

18. See Hughes-Hallett, 329–50.

19. Since World War II, there seems to be one royal woman designated as the Bad Girl at any given time. Princess Margaret, who almost married a divorcé (unthinkable in the 1950s and early 1960s), stayed unmarried until she was thirty, conspicuously smoked, drank, and night-clubbed, then was the first to get divorced, used to have the field all to herself. Then Princess Michael of Kent came along to draw the fire, then Sarah Ferguson, and finally, to some extent, Diana herself.

20. See Dixon; Sheik; and Jewel respectively.

21. The Feast of the Transfiguration is celebrated on 6 August, just a few weeks before Diana's death date—a day that has already taken on its own quasi-religious significance.

22. For full citation, see Holy.

23. The survey I did of these papers and television reports was not scientific. I looked at *The Guardian, The Independent, The Times, The Daily Mirror, The Daily Mail,* and *The Sun* in Britain, and *The New York Times, The Washington Post, USA Today,* and *The Atlanta Constitution* in the United States. I watched CNN and BBC television news. Anecdotal evidence strongly suggests that piety over the dead and an impulse on both sides of the Atlantic to mythologize her acted on almost all the mainstream media.

24. See Cannadine.

25. The Royal Family have even found themselves a new blonde, Sophie Rhys-Jones, now married to Prince Edward, Earl of Wessex. Sophie looks oddly like Diana (if not quite so "pretty," according to royal watchers), wears dashing hats and chic clothes. And then there's Princess Anne's hipster daughter Zara (also a blonde) and the young princesses Eugenie and Beatrix. The Windsors know how to manufacture princesses for the new millennium.

26. The narratives of Diana as produced in America during the month or so after her death merit a full-length study of their own. As many of the books produced to hit the market as soon as possible after the funeral (at least in time for Christmas) suggested, Americans largely chose to read Diana as an "ordinary" girl kidnapped Grimm-like by the gothic British monarchy which proceeded to drive her crazy (or at least into eating disorders). The suppression of Diana's actual background, and lack of understanding of the British class system, allowed Americans to claim her—as we often do with British princesses (the last one we "claimed" was Princess Margaret who, with her racy ways in the 1960s, was thought to be "more American"). Diana was also called American: veteran CBS newsman Dan Rather explained in a piece in *The Evening Standard* of 6 September, and on his broadcasts to the United States, that Diana was like "us" because she was "vulnerable and talked about it." But her privileged background (Diana was an aristocrat, brought up in large houses, given a trust fund at eighteen—not exactly "ordinary") is uncomfortable for the American victim story so it is deemphasized.

27. *Private Eye* further compounded its satirical sins by running a column reading: "In recent weeks (not to mention the last ten years) we at the Daily Gnome, in common with all other newspapers may have inadvertently conveyed the impres-

sion that the late Princess of Wales was in some way a neurotic, irresponsible and manipulative troublemaker. . . . We now realise as of Sunday morning that the Princess of Hearts was in fact the most saintly woman who has ever lived. . . ."

In the States, Diana humor was confined to *Spy* magazine, in which the princess made the "100 Worst" list at number two. Diana jokes appeared on the Internet within hours of her death (along with "respectful" websites) and a rock 'n' roll band called The Iron Johns in Tuscaloosa, Alabama, wrote a series of songs as a "tribute" called "Princess in the Wind." Numbers include "My My Princess Di" (sung to the tune of Neil Young's "Hey Hey My My") and "Tumbling Di." Otherwise, laughs at the princess' expense are few and far between.

REFERENCES

Bakhtin, Mikhail. 1984. *Rabelais and his world* (1965). Trans. Helene Iswolsky. Bloomington: Indiana University Press.

Bourdieu, Pierre. 1977. *Outline of a theory of practice*. Trans. Richard Nice. Cambridge: Cambridge University Press.

Cannadine, David. 6 September 1997. The making of the myth of Saint Diana. *Guardian*, 6: 12.

Cliff, Michelle. [1984] 1991. *Abeng*. Reprint. New York: Penguin Books.

Dixon, Thomas. 1905. *The clansman; An historical romance of the Ku Klux Klan*. Ill. Arthur I. Keller. New York: Doubleday.

Dyer, Richard. 1997. *White*. London: Routledge.

Foster, Gwendolyn Audrey. 1999. *Captive bodies: Postcolonial subjectivity in cinema*. Albany: State University of New York Press.

———. 2003. *Performing whiteness: Postmodern re/constructions in the cinema*. Albany: State University of New York Press.

Frankenberg, Ruth, ed. 1997. *Displacing whiteness: Essays in social and cultural criticism*. Durham: Duke University Press.

Garner, Clare. 9 February 1998. Myths and politics from Princess of Wales to Queen of Hearts. *Independent*, 3.

Gerzina, Gretchen. 1995. *Black London*. New Brunswick: Rutgers University Press.

Goldberg, Jonathan. 1986. Fatherly authority: The politics of Stuart family images. In *Rewriting the Renaissance*, ed. Margaret Ferguson, Maureen Quilligan, and Nancy J. Vickers, 3–32. Chicago: University of Chicago Press.

Holy Bible: 21st Century King James Version. 1994. Ed. William D. Prindle. 21st C King James.

Hughes-Hallett, Lucy. 1991. *Cleopatra: Histories, dreams, and distortions*. New York: Vintage.

Jewel in the Crown, The. 1984. Christopher Morahan and Jim O'Brien, directors. London: Granada Television of England.

Lawson, Mark. 6 September 1997. A new divine cult starts here. *Guardian*, 13.

Jack, Ian. 1997. Those who felt differently. *Granta* 60 (Winter): 9–35.

McClintock, Anne. 1995. *Imperial leather: Race, gender and sexuality in the colonial context*. London: Routledge.

Media to Blame. 5 September 1997. *Private Eye*, 932.

Montrose, Louis. 1986. "A Midsummer Night's Dream" and the shaping fantasies of Elizabethan culture: Gender, power, form." In *Rewriting the Renaissance*, 65–87.

Praz, Mario. 1933. *The romantic agony*. Oxford: Oxford University Press.

Renton, Alex. 16 March 1998. Turning Diana into an ology. *Evening Standard*, 8–9.

Roberts, Diane. 1995. *Faulkner and Southern womanhood*. Athens: University of Georgia Press.

———. 1995. *The myth of Aunt Jemima*. London: Routledge.

Rogin, Michael, 1993. 'Make my day!' Spectacle in imperial politics. In *Cultures of United States Imperialism*, ed. Amy Kaplan and Donald E. Pease, 499–529. Durham: Duke University Press.

Sheik, The. 1921. George Melford, director. Hollywood: Paramount.

Sontag, Susan. 1979. *Illness as metaphor*. New York: Vintage.

Spencer, Mimi. 6 September 1997. At the height of her beauty she will be forever thus. *Evening Standard*, 19.

Spoto, Donald. 1997. *Diana: The last year*. New York: Harmony.

Stallybrass, Peter. 1986. Patriarchal territories: The body enclosed. In *Rewriting the Renaissance*, 123–42.

Stallybrass, Peter, and Allon White. 1986. *The politics and poetics of transgression*. London: Methuen.

Strong, Roy. 1963. *Portraits of Queen Elizabeth I*. London: Clarendon.

———. 1972. *Van Dyck: Charles I on Horseback*. London: Penguin.

Walvin, James. 1971. *The black presence: A documentary history of the negro in England, 1555–1860*. London: Orbach and Chambers.

Warner, Marina. [1976]1985. *Alone of all her sex: The myth and cult of the Virgin Mary*. Reprint. London: Picador.

———. [1985] 1987. *Monuments and maidens: The allegory of the female form*. Reprint. London: Picador.

THREE

LAVENDER AIN'T WHITE:
EMERGING QUEER SELF-EXPRESSION
IN ITS BROADER CONTEXT

JOHN C. HAWLEY

> If whites expect to be able to say anything relevant to the self-determination of the black community, it will be necessary to them to destroy their whiteness by becoming members of an oppressed community.
>
> —James H. Cone, *A Black Theology of Liberation*

THEORIZING WHITE OMISSIONS

RICHARD DELGADO AND JEAN STEFANCIC'S edited collection entitled *Critical White Studies: Looking Behind the Mirror*, is fascinating on a number of levels, and apparently rather comprehensive—with sections dealing with the question of how whites see themselves and see others; how history, biology, gender, law, and culture have played their roles in shaping the issue; how one might approach the question of multiracial people and of "white consciousness"; and finally how whites who wish might become part of the solution.[1] But in none of the lengthy volume's 114 essays is the topic of queerness discussed at any length, as if it were as invisible to the editors as "whiteness" appears to be to so many in the United States and western Europe. Robyn Wiegman elsewhere surveys the field of white studies and points to certain "omissions" in its interests, and notes that "whiteness studies tends to be described as a project devoted to dismantling whiteness from a white perspective, which disturbingly disassociates scholarship from the various ethnic studies areas as being part of the scholarly archive on the social construction of whiteness" (Wiegman 1999, 122). She goes on to suggest that "early feminist work . . . is also jettisoned from the new multidisciplinary scheme," and concludes that "these moves reconvene the logic of white masculinity as the generic subject even as the ideological hold of that subject is supposed to be under abolition" (122). In the present chapter I hope to take a few steps to counter this oversight, briefly turning the reader's attention to those who are not only "nonwhite," but also "non-straight." Why should we want to do this? The two questions Alfred J. López seeks to address in this collection ("What happens to whiteness after it loses its colonial privileges?" and "To what extent do white cultural norms or imperatives remain imbedded in the postcolonial or post-independence state as a part—acknowledged or not—of the colonial legacy?") are interesting in their own right, but they use a more complete palette when questions of gender and sexuality are included. This is especially true when queer theory becomes the prism through which those colors fan out, since, as becomes increasingly clear, queer theory and postcolonial theory have a great deal to say to each other[2]—and, by impli-cation, to whiteness studies.

As Peter McLaren notes, "It's not that whiteness signifies preferen-tially one pole of the white-nonwhite binarism. Rather, whiteness seduces the subject to accept the idea of polarity as the limit-text of identity, as the constitutive foundation of subjectivity" (McLaren 1998, 68). Queer theory seeks to overcome binarisms of this sort and to subvert the power structures that sustain them. The binary system generally benefits those who are white, who generally do not make much of their race and see it as the normal condition from which all other races diverge. Complicit with this naivete are the claims of Western humanism. As Richard Dyer writes in his seminal study *White*, "The claim to power is the claim to speak for the commonality of humanity. Raced people can't do that—they can only speak for their race" (Dyer 1997, 2). Thus, to "race" white people is to destabilize their claim to speak for humanity in general. This also suggests why universalism is a contentious topic in postcolonial studies, often seen as a form of Eurocentric cultural imperialism.[3] Similarly, to "sexualize" men and women, as queer theory seeks to do, interrogates the binary sys-tem that implicitly excludes or marginalizes the "non-straight" or queer. As Dyer suggests,

> We may be on our way to genuine hybridity, multiplicity without
> (white) hegemony, and it may be where we want to get to—but we
> aren't there yet, and we won't get there until we see whiteness, see

its power, its particularity and limitedness, put it in its place and end its rule. (3–4)[4]

But a true decolonization would see still more, and would interrogate the "normalcy" of a binary sexual code.

An application of queer theory (which purposely blurs borders that may otherwise seem natural) to questions of race and to "whiteness" potentially opens up new avenues for research in such fields as film studies.[5] As Chris Straayer observes, queer theory can approach the topic from a fresh angle: "With the recognition of homosexual negotiations, gender-specific viewer allocations are fractured, and the theorized viewer is freed for a more complex, multipositioned, undetermined engagement with film" (Strayer 1996, 3). Fortunately for film studies with a postcolonial focus, recent scholarship from India and elsewhere has begun to do the same thing,[6] although other books that might have taken the opportunity to broaden their definitions have instead chosen to pass over in silence recent transgressive films.[7] It is crucial that these voices gain an audience in the West because, as Dyer observes,

> Against the flowering of a myriad postmodern voices, we must also see the countervailing dominance of US news dissemination, popular TV programmes and Hollywood movies. Postmodern multiculturalism may have genuinely opened up a space for the voices of the other, challenging the authority of the white West, but it may also simultaneously function as a side-show for white people who look on with delight at all the differences that surround them. (Dyer 3)

Regarding postcolonial theory itself: The same concerns that postcolonial theorists traditionally bring to studies of the British Commonwealth, the former French colonies, etc.—"the controlling power of representation in colonized societies, . . . the discursive operations of empire, the subtleties of subject construction in colonial discourse and the resistance of those subjects, and . . . the differing responses to such incursions" (Ashcroft, Griffiths, and Tiffin 2000, 186–87)—all these should also be addressed to the communities in the United States fixed by whites as ethnic.[8]

Through the lens of whiteness studies this chapter begins with the application of postcolonial and queer theory to the United States, and moves then to "the rest" of the world, seeking to demonstrate that monochromatic Euro-American humanism would benefit from closer examination. This is obviously not to obliterate the Renaissance ideal of making human beings the proper objects of human study, but to follow Edward Said's lead and seek a humanism that will transcend the dominant Enlightenment philosophy of "man" and its hegemonic notions of civilization.

THE AMERICAN EMPIRE WRITES BACK

> This is white America. Every other nationality not of the white set
> knows it and accepts it to the day they die. That is everybody's dream
> and ambition as a minority, to live and look as well as a white person.
>
> —Willi Ninja, *Paris Is Burning*

Jennie Livingston's 1991 film *Paris Is Burning*, a documentary on "voguing"
and the drag balls of Harlem, met with generally favorable reviews and eight
major awards, including prizes from the New York Film Critics, the Los
Angeles Film Critics, and the Grand Jury Prize from the Sundance Film
Festival, but received a scathing review from bell hooks. We will return to
hooks's emotional reading of the film, but first consider Roger Ebert's point
that this is more than a portrayal of traditional drag:

> Once such events would have been known as drag balls, and the
> competitors would have been called drag queens. But now look at
> what they've mutated into: What are we to make of this young
> military school student, the spotlights glistening on his sword and
> scabbard, or the sleek business executive in a Brooks Brothers suit?
> If the drag balls of years past demonstrated a kind of yearning among
> men who wanted to look like women, the balls in *Paris Is Burning*
> exhibit an even more poignant longing. The models compete to see
> who could pass in worlds that are almost completely closed to gays
> and blacks—especially, gay blacks.[9]

The exclusive worlds mimicked in the film are those of business, "the horsey
set," the private schoolboy/girl, as well as the more expected categories of
haute couture, both from Paris and from the less haute *All My Children*. It
is true that one might ask whom Ebert's "we" may refer to here, since the live
spectators in the contests portrayed in Livingston's film may not share much
in common with the white film critic and are clearly well acquainted with
the various judging categories that surprise Ebert.

Ebert's observation regarding the "mutation" of these balls, however, is
in fact echoed by Dorian Corey, one of the "mothers" in the documentary.
These older heads of voguing "houses," mirroring the House of Dior or the
House of Chanel, describe each of their "families" as "a gay street gang," some
members of which live lives of not-so-quiet desperation, some in fact sleeping
on the piers in New York and stealing the clothes and accessories they need
to play their chosen roles as they strut their stuff on the makeshift catwalks of
Harlem. The mutation, sadly notes Corey, is on several levels. In his day folks
wanted to look like Marlene Dietrich (although, he confesses, he would have
preferred to look like Lena Horne—he never makes clear what stopped him
from doing so), and now they're wanting to look like Alexis or Crystal from

the (white) soap operas. Now, he says, it's no longer about what you can create, but about what you can acquire. Corey's tone is warm and sympathetic— "mothering," in fact, but nostalgic and a bit world-weary, as if his older generation's yearnings were somehow freer, perhaps more "successful" in imagining and creating a better place. Without using the terminology, his assessment of the current scene over which he presides embodies the worst fears of someone such as Frantz Fanon or Ngugi wa Thiong'o, whose assessments of the colonized mentality ring true in this film. These young people perform the selves they would most like to be, and, while there is the occasional category that valorizes aspects of the contemporary black scene—the "Banjee" boy or girl, for example—those aspects tend to emphasize the tough street hood. Here, as in all the categories of competition, the crucial point is to portray this bad boy or girl so convincingly that you would be mistaken as "real." An unnerving binarism is displayed here: the unreachable world of *Dynasty*, and the inescapable world of the street (and both "options" seemingly combined in the valorization of gangsta rap and concomitant violence, materialism, homophobia, and aggression toward women on Black Entertainment Television). Recognizing the inadequacy of the dream offered, "Octavia Saint Laurent" tells the filmmaker: "I don't think the world has been fair to me, not yet, anyway." "I'd like to be a spoiled rich white girl," says "Venus Xtravaganza." And Willi Ninja, heading another of the houses, suggests that "[w]hen it comes to a minority, especially blacks, we as a people for the past four hundred years, is the greatest example of behavior modification in the history of civilization. . . . We have to learn how to survive. . . . If you have captured the great white way of living or looking or dressing or speaking, you is a marvel."

Clearly, being a marvel is mainly the point of the whole thing. As Dorian Corey puts it, "It's a small fame, but a fame."[10] Some of the contestants dramatically announce that their goal is to be "legendary." And this, after all, is not simply a display but also a contest. The film begins with a voice announcing: "You have three strikes against you: black, male, and gay. If you're going to do this, you'll have to be stronger than you ever imagined." And one participant, "Kim Pendavis," puts it this way: "Competition makes me stronger, makes me want to come back and get them." Among the several paradoxes involved in voguing, therefore, is the conception that putting on a dress and parading before others is a sign of one's strength, not one's alienation, because the contestants themselves have created the rules of the game. Another paradox is the goal of "realness," which translates for many in the film as "being able to blend," being effective enough in the transformation that one can leave the ballroom in costume, get on the subway, and apparently fool the "normal" people whose rules one is now *choosing* to transgress, in trickster fashion—when, out of costume, one transgresses them willy-nilly because there is no entry point for inclusion. The idea reverberates in the viewer long after the film has ended: enter the world of the other (in this case, the white male world) as if one were a member of the empowered.

Not least among the ironies is the adopted name of another of the house mothers: Pepper Labeija, as if the move from black to a "softer" tone would bring with it the sophistication implied in all things French. (And if the salt—or peppa—loses its tang . . . ?)

The film is fascinating from start to finish. bell hooks thinks it is too, but strongly objects to the film on a number of points. Her review, in truth, seems more an angry response both to the (mostly white) audience with whom she viewed it ("Several times I yelled out in the dark: 'What is so funny about this scene? Why are you laughing?' " [hooks 1996, 223]) and, sadly, to the white lesbian director. hooks does everything but state outright that Jennie Livingston had no right to show this to the (straight) white world because a white director inevitably turns such "rituals" into "spectacles" (223).[11] The depths at which hooks identifies with the portrayal on the screen is revealed in her diary, from which she quotes. There, she reveals that a similar discomforting of the white world was precisely why she herself occasionally dressed as a man: "I'll make it real, keep them guessing, do it in such a way that they will never know for sure" (214).

On one hand, hooks takes steady aim against the colonization interpellated in the aspirations of these drag balls, but then angrily attacks the director who had the audacity to document the fact. No one could deny the power of her observation of the underlying poignancy of the contests. She writes, for example, that

> in many ways the film was a graphic documentary portrait of the way in which colonized black people (in this case black gay brothers, some of whom were drag queens) worship at the throne of whiteness, even when such worship demands that we live in perpetual self-hate, steal, lie, go hungry, and even die in its pursuit. The "we" evoked here is all of us, black people/people of color, who are daily bombarded by a powerful colonizing whiteness that seduces us away from ourselves, that negates that there is beauty to be found in any form of blackness that is not imitation whiteness. The whiteness celebrated in *Paris Is Burning* is not just any old brand of whiteness but rather that brutal imperial ruling-class capitalist patriarchal whiteness that presents itself—its way of life—as the only meaningful life there is. (hooks 218)

Perhaps, but one must ask who it is that is doing the celebrating here—and the first obvious answer would be: the participants, not Livingston's (white, upper-middle-class?) audience, many of whom feel an outrage similar to that recorded by bell hooks. One might consider whether the colonization here is not a race, but class, issue—shared by Eminem's hip hop wannabe white followers as fully as by Pepper Labeija and friends. Where do these aspirations come from if not from Madison Avenue?

Like hooks, I also found Dorian Corey's seasoned estimation of the mutation of the balls very informative and not only nostalgic but also implicitly critical. As hooks incisively remarks, Dorian Corey "emphasizes the way consumer capitalism undermines the subversive power of the drag balls, subordinating ritual to spectacle, removing the will to display unique imaginative costumes and the purchased image. Carey [sic] speaks profoundly about the redemptive power of the imagination in black life, that drag balls were traditionally a place where the aesthetics of the image in relation to black gay life could be explored with complexity and grace" (hooks 225). But hooks herself overlooks the Hispanic element of the drag ball scene (the House of Extravaganza, for example, seems predominantly Puerto Rican), and she sounds fairly matriarchal in her regret that other reviewers celebrated the film "as though [Livingston] did this marginalized black gay subculture a favor by bringing their experience to a wider public" (223). Were the members of this subculture to speak for themselves, there seems little doubt that they would delight in seeing their moment in the spotlight announced with such fanfare. We can agree with hooks that this fact may be partly lamentable as a demonstration of the whitewashed notion of glamour, but that seems little reason to kill the messenger who brought the bad news, and still less reason to shove them back into the closet. The criticism hooks makes, in short, while seeming to valorize the drag balls by designating them rituals, seems in fact to be an agonized and angry dismissal of them (and their participants) as the detritus of a hegemonic white empire:[12]

> Just as white cultural imperialism informed and affirmed the adventurous journeys of colonizing whites into the countries and cultures of "dark others," it allows white audiences to applaud representations of black culture, if they are satisfied with the images and habits being represented. . . . [But] at no point in Livingston's film are the men asked to speak about their connections to a world of family and community beyond the drag ball. The cinematic narrative makes the ball the center of their lives. And yet who determines this? (hooks 223–24)

A very good question, with no simple answer. The participants, in stating they were willing to steal the gowns in which they will parade, suggest the importance they themselves assign to the event. And one cannot ignore the trangressive potential of mimicry that adds to the audience's engagement with these faux-*Dynasty* characterizations, etc. Yet, writes hooks, "had Livingston approached her subject with greater awareness of the way white supremacy shapes cultural production—determining not only what representations of blackness are deemed acceptable, marketable, as well as worthy of seeing—perhaps the film would not so easily have turned the black drag ball into a spectacle for the entertainment of those presumed to be on the outside of this experience looking in" (221–22). Again, a provocative and aggressive interpretation of the director's motives. But one cannot ignore hooks's suggestion that these drag balls are not "worthy of seeing," while musing over what an African American director such as Spike Lee might have done differently—and why he hasn't.[13]

If hooks arguably demonstrates white colonization of black consciousness on several levels, one might observe that the campy images in vogueing are more reliably interpreted as a desire to redefine oneself as an agent with choices. The implied critique embodied by these contestants is not just against the white society that cramps their lives, but also against the heterosexual African American and Hispanic societies that cramp their styles. Hybridity in the United States very slowly takes the place of race—and this clearly includes a hybridization of many people's sexuality.

How new is this? In fact, one of the defining texts of American (white?) culture, *Moby Dick*, has been analyzed as an arresting appeal to transracialization as the only meaningful answer to the wounds of the Civil War, slavery, and racism. In her interesting analysis of Melville's "deconstruction of the many myths of whiteness" in his chapter on "The Whiteness of the Whale" in *Moby Dick* (Babb 1998, 98), Valerie Babb discusses Ishmael's relationship with Queequeg, the "head-peddling purple rascal" (Melville [1988], 21), and directs our attention to such passages as that in which Ishmael sleeps in the same bed with Queequeg. Ishmael remarks the next morning: "I found Queequeg's arm thrown over me in the most loving and affectionate manner. You had almost thought I had been his wife" (25). Following Leslie Fiedler's lead, Babb remarks that

> the homoerotic cast to Ishmael and Queequeg's association is an instance in which sexuality deconstructs rather than constructs whiteness. . . . [Ishmael] enters into a homoerotic union with a "spouse" of another race, an act that defies both the championed heterosexual norm of white identity and the racial purity represented through the ideal of white femininity. (Babb 115)

Babb points out that Ishmael proceeds to cover his body with tattoos, becoming increasingly a mirror for Queequeg and in the process representing "a white identity proud not to be visibly 'pure' and unafraid of being marked as a hybrid of many racial and cultural influences" (116). Can it be that the white audiences are not participating in spectacle—but in fact are silent minimal participants in the *ritual* that hooks partially admires? Can it be that the laughter in the theater is a "safe" crossing-over, a verbal tattooing of oneself?

In any event, central though *Moby Dick* certainly is in defining some American aspirations, it offers no convincing threat to the self-perpetuating whiteness of American culture, nor does the fleeting marriage between white audiences and Livingston's subjects. This is obvious as that hegemony is reinscribed in less highbrow venues: popular horror films,[14] science fiction, and war stories. Eric Avila has documented the effects on the public of the on-slaught since the 1950s of cinematic portrayals of alien invasion as a threat to the American family. Avila writes that "[t]he many threats that preoccupied post-war Americans—Communists, homosexuals, racialized minorities—were viewed as dangers not so much to the individual or the society at large, but rather to the stability and coherence of the American family. The national culture, moreover, almost always coded the family as white" (Avila 2001, 63).[15] Richard Dyer notes how this also plays itself out as hypermasculine heroism in films such as *Rambo, Tarzan, Rocky, Conan the Barbarian*, etc. In his view, the psychology underpinning such films is both classist and racist:

> The built body is a wealthy body. It is well fed and enormous amounts of leisure time have been devoted to it. The huge, firm muscles of Gordon Scott, Steve Reeves or Arnold Schwarzenegger made the simplest contrast with the thin or slack bodies of the native peoples in their films. Such muscles are a product and sign of affluence. (Dyer 155)

He has a point, but this world of white hypermasculinity is even less acces-sible, in the eyes of the "houses" of Harlem, than are the worlds of *Dynasty* and the Champs Elysees—not because many of the contestants could not bulk up, but perhaps because some of them wish to escape the race memory of slavery that saw them *only* as hunks or studs. White muscles were never so overdetermined.

And even in films that ostensibly address the race issue in the United States and seem to offer the hope of a better future for all citizens, white assumptions and unacknowledged positioning at the center of reality gener-ally assert themselves.[16] Such films, write Sarah Projansky and Kent Ono, "construct people of color within otherwise culturally and racially flat, pri-marily white, contexts" (Projansky and Ono 1999, 153), thereby "obscur[ing] the centrality of whiteness by never directly addressing specifically what it means to be 'white'" (155). The central point is that these films position whites "within a Eurocentric/colonialist framework and African Americans within . . . an assimilationist framework" (171). Their self-congratulatory message seems to be: Look, they can be just like us! Or as Dyer puts it, "White power . . . reproduces itself regardless of intention, power differences and goodwill, and overwhelmingly because it is not seen as whiteness, but as normal" (Dyer 10). It may be that white filmmaker Livingston inadvertently plays into this scheme by implicitly assuring her (white) audience that, whatever their sexuality, they can tell themselves they are more "normal" than these contestants. But is this a question of race? How would a predomi-nantly black male audience respond to the film?

Normalcy understood as "Americanness" plays an increasingly important role in nonwhite cultural expressions, if only as something against which
to delineate one's singularity. Various branches of the Hispanic community
face this challenge in ways that can be both comic[17] and angry, especially if
questions of sexuality are added to the mix.[18]

And while sharing many of the African American community's ambiguous responses to "the" American dream, Hispanics also grapple with political
questions having to do with place of family origin. On a daily basis, for example, the Cuban American community deals with a complicated set of cultural questions. Karen Christian studies the Janus-like problem facing immigrant
gays and lesbians in this community: Flavio Risech, she writes, is a gay, politically progressive Cuban American who "observes that to exhibit leftism as a
Cuban-American in Miami, or queerness in Havana, can result in ostracism or
more violent repercussions" (Christian 1997, 55). And on the other hand, in
Elías Miguel Muñoz's *The Greatest Performance*, a lesbian teacher and a gay
artist in their interactions with American gay and lesbian communities

> discover that gaining acceptance into these Anglocentric commu-
> nities requires a sort of cultural whitewashing, which they achieve
> by downplaying or concealing their Latina/o roots. . . . By erasing
> visible evidence of his *cubanidad*—and by performing whiteness—
> [Mario] avoids the rejection that can accompany being identified as
> ethnic Other. . . . [and] in order to be culturally intelligible as an
> American lesbian—according to [her white lover's] racist standards—
> Rose must suppress the indicators that mark her as underdeveloped
> Other. (Christian 61–62)

In recent films such as *Before Night Falls* and *Strawberry and Chocolate* this
uncomfortable mix takes center stage, and the impression left by each of
these cultural works is that the issue of queerness in Cuban American (and
perhaps Hispanic American) communities remains a juggling act. It (generally?) requires a binary understanding of male and female roles, even in
same-sex relations—nothing queer about that, right?

In any case, many of these cross-cultural anxieties/prejudices fit the
schema outlined by Richard Dyer, who notes that

> the history of identity politics has . . . been marked by the increas-
> ingly strong and heard voices of, for instance, non-white and work-
> ing-class women, lesbians and gay men, who do not entirely recognize
> themselves in these "As a [gay man, working class person, etc.] . . ."
> claims. Many such claims have come to be seen as having been all
> along the claims of white women, the white working class, white
> lesbians and gay men. (Dyer 8)

In any case, the resulting complex self-expression can be a mind-blowing border blurring, a community redefining performance such as Guillermo Gomez-Peña's or Alina Troyano's. Chon Noreiga writes that in Alina Troyano's performance artistry in which she becomes "Carmelita Tropicana," "lesbian identity becomes the center of Cuban nationalism, even as it also struggles against the authoritarian state, *cubanidad*, and the U.S. blockade of Cuba!" (Troyano 2000, x). Some of Troyano's characters "witness to a past and memory that [they] never had–the *lo que tenía* (what I used to have [before the revolution]) of exilic memory" (xi). It can be an in-your-face assault on expectations, as in "Chicas 2000," in which Carmelita addresses the audience in these words:

> Look at us, we are all in the soup together. All complicit in this Chusmatic Casino ("*chusma*: loud, gross, tacky and excessive behavior, tasteless with attitude, similar to white trash, only people-of-color trash") (72). You, Igor, for pitting *chusma* against *chusma*, we *chusmas* for fighting one another, and you ladies and gentlemen for coming here to watch *chusmas* degrade themselves before your very eyes. Well, we have our dignity. We are proud of our bodies, our accents, our emotions. Igor, always a wanna-be *chusma*. It's time you accepted yourself for who you are. Sit and we'll dedicate to you this *dernier cri* [last cry] from a woman who gave us not Dada but mama art, a woman who made the magic real for little boys who dreamed of one day wearing eyelashes, sequins, and mascara, the one and only La Lupe. (Troyana 120)

Troyano does her own sort of voguing, dolling up to mock her audience's expectations, no matter what those may be, and in the process queering the line between the real and the possible.

And this may serve as our segue into the recent chusmatic-wannabe film *To Wong Foo, Thanks for Everything! Julie Newmar*. Three drag queens, played by John Leguizamo ("Chi Chi Rodriguez"), Wesley Snipes ("Noxeema Jackson"), and Patrick Swayze ("Vida Boheme")—a safe mix of races—set out from New York to Hollywood in a yellow Cadillac convertible, in the hope of being selected Miss Drag Queen America. Leguizamo is actually designated a drag princess by the older two, but, in Cinderfella-like fashion, ends up winning the Hollywood contest. The casting seems to intend to present the diversity of America, but Swayze (inevitably) gets the dominant role as doyenne for the other two. And Julie Newmar, whom the three admire for her "statuesque" qualities, makes a cameo appearance at the end to crown Leguizamo, who previously seemed a cross between Carmen Miranda and Rosie Perez, but now is dressed from head to toe in white—as if this Puerto Rican, having transformed himself into a *faux* virgin, has at the same time become *fully* American. Leguizamo jokes that "I wanted to come across like a Latino Sharon Stone. . . . Except that I kept my panties on." As in *Paris Is Burning*, emasculation provides a gateway into a make-believe acceptance by the white world.

And what do the white principals think of the world they've created? In his review of the film Randy Shulman describes it as "a kicky, fun-filled fantasy," and suggests that "the movie owes a debt to *The Wizard of Oz* and the feelgood films of Frank Capra and Preston Sturges; its warm, fuzzy message of believing in oneself is hokey yet appealingly sweet." Shulman goes on to quote several of the principals. "They're superhuman characters," says [screenplay writer] Beane, "They're wonder women who sprinkle love and move on." "*Priscilla [Queen of the Desert]* took itself too seriously," says Swayze. "It was much more of a character study into the lives and heads of its own drag queens as opposed to creating a movie anybody can identify with. *Wong Foo* doesn't take itself quite so seriously—and I think because of that, it's accessible to anyone. For me, it's a drag queen movie that reinstates family values."[19] Ronald Smith interviews Julie Newmar, who gives her reaction to the film:

> It's about time that we learned about the troubles and travails and secrets and private pains of the other. [Can it be she's taking the film too seriously for Swayze?] The three stars would show up to have their make-up done and they'd completely surrender in the chair for three hours. Now they know what it's like. They've gone through the physical experience; the high heels, the bazooms and tight waists, learning to keep your knees together when you walk. It's alarmingly, beguilingly, touchingly funny. (Newmar Interview 22 May 2002)

Newmar's assessment of the film as a study of "the other" echoes weirdly in the context of Leguizamo's joke about portraying Sharon Stone—the female equivalent of Sylvester Stallone, Arnold Schwarzenegger, Jean-Claude Van Damme, etc. The film, says Newmar, reminded her of her friendship with Candy Darling, the Harlow-esque drag queen who was part of Andy Warhol's underground. Newmar read the eulogy at Darling's funeral. "Darling's was an extraordinarily high achievement," she told Smith; "her skin was so flawless, her behavior not limpid but liquid, the movement of her hands exquisite." Again, imagining skin as an achievement is bizarre—"an extraordinarily high achievement."[20] Perhaps Newmar is voicing the aspirations of any "real" drag queen. As Elizabeth Arden has always known, surface is important—*that*, at least, we can work on.

The last two films under discussion in this section are Australian and French, but arguably find a comfortable fit within the American view of whiteness. The film to which Patrick Swayze referred (and to which anyone who has seen either film inevitably refers) is *The Adventures of Priscilla, Queen of the Desert*, released the year before *To Wong Foo*, and so similar to the American film that the coincidence seems more than remarkable. Swayze is certainly correct in his estimate of the Australian film as more serious—humorous and campy, but nonetheless intent on demonstrating that the central character (the Swayze character, if you will), here played by Terence Stamp, is facing a midlife crisis unlike any other portrayed in recent films. Against the backdrop of their trip from Sydney to Alice Springs, in the heart of aboriginal Australia, and moving to the rhythms of disco songs by Abba, the Village People, and Whitney Houston, Stamp's character ("Bernadette") parades around in various frocks, looking more like Freya Stark than Lawrence of Arabia, and yearning nostalgically for his earlier days as a founding member of "Les Girls," back when being a drag queen really meant something. In its mawkish closing scene, she (the Stamp character is a transsexual) finds true love. Previously, she and her two white companions have become stranded in various out-of-the-way spots, one of which is an aboriginal community. Here they put on a colorful performance, supported by the popular gay anthem "I Will Survive," and meet with happy acceptance. In fact, one of the aboriginals also puts on a dress and the disco music is accompanied by didgeridoos. This is really the only hint in the film, except for a comic but degrading bit involving a mail-order bride from Asia, that there is anything but a white world out there, gay or straight. Unlike the Swayze film, *Priscilla's* characters seem to be people, and not cartoons. But both films share the central positioning of a white character. His/her liberation makes the whole adventure worthwhile, it seems. The aboriginals provide a semi-comic backdrop, apparently living in the dark around campfires.

Finally, we can turn to the French film *Ma Vie en Rose* to see a hermetically sealed white world that threatens to stifle its principals with its colonizing notions of sexuality. In a marvelously affecting acting job, little seven-year-old Ludovic knows in his heart that he is really a girl, and that given time this will become obvious to the world around him. Ludovic's understanding and relatively free-spirited grandmother recommends that his parents allow him to "live his dream," and thereby "banalize" it. But it is not until he meets a girl "like him"—that is, a girl who knows she is a boy—that his essential insight into the needless borders of French life rings true. Somewhere out there will be a world large enough to include him. As his psychiatrist tells him, though, it may be that there are some secrets he will have to wait a few years before revealing to others. All of this washes over a white audience like so much bubble bath, but what is also striking is the "banality" of even the dream world into which Ludovic occasionally escapes, and where his mother finally also finds a kinder understanding of her son's challenging gender dilemma (but let us remember: *he* is a seven-year-old, and can be forgiven this escape). This is the film's "charming" cartoon-like soap opera World of Pam, presided over by a Barbie-like bleach-blonde fairy who sprinkles the world with pixie dust to make all manner of things well. The fairy could not be whiter; her happy world could not be more artificial and antiseptic—just the sort of "perfect" world that the rest of the film seems to be arguing against, and acceptable only if seen as the fantasy of a seven-year-old white boy who, while questioning his gender, has no doubts about his color in a world of privilege.

As López argues elsewhere, "Much of the process of psychic decolonization depends upon a sort of 'repigmentation' or 'unbleaching' of suppressed cultural histories to reflect both the precolonial past and the ugly truths of colonial violence and oppression" (López 2001, 89). In a world such as that in which Ludovic grows up, the very notion of one's own pigmentation as a white (or, as the tints in this film make quite clear, as a pink) must also be added to this decolonizing mix—"our racial particularity," as Richard Dyer puts it.[21] The white picket fence may well keep Ludovic's personal crisis well within the bounds of his extended family, but it also apparently keeps out the real world that is far more complex than his family is able to realize.

FEAR OF A QUEER PLANET

If your way is natural, my way is too. It's like liquids. They take the shape of their containers. . . . The enemy is out there. I have to load my guns and fight.

—Barbara, *Woubi Cheri*

And what of "the rest" of the world? In his essay "The United States in South Africa: (Post)Colonial Queer Theory," Ian Barnard argues that

[t]ogether with the trendy litany of minoritized identities that divides people into discrete categories of race, gender, and sexuality, and that thus cannot conceptualize queers of color, or white female queers, this conflation of gayness and whiteness erases the existence of queers of color in the United States, and in South Africa, where an imperialist U.S. gay teleology is already imposing its own models of identity, of queerness, and of queer progress onto the South African scene. (Barnard 2001, 135)

Barnard begins his demonstration of this thesis with an analysis of two gay male porn films, pointing out that "both *The Men of South Africa*, and its sequel, *The Men of South Africa II*, were made in the early 1990s in a South Africa still under formal apartheid, are 'all-white' and 'all-male,' and are distributed by a mail-order company in San Francisco specializing in 'exotic gay pornography' " (129). In the films, "black South Africans . . . are treated—like the animals—as props; they are accorded no individuality, agency, subjectivity, or humanity. Black people serve to enrich the locale with extra otherness and at the same time by counterpoint to emphasize the normalcy of the otherwise exoticized white characters" (131). As such commodification makes clear, the "enemy" that Barbara from *Woubi Cheri* refers to is not only those in his/her country that proscribe non-normative sexuality, but also the white colonizer—who may well be gay.

In his article "Out in Africa," Gaurav Desai argues for the right of African gays to tell different stories about themselves than has been possible heretofore. Desai demonstrates the high cost demanded of those who choose no longer to "pass" in a society that may seem interested in posing the same sort of question that queers feel a desire to answer, despite the imposed stigma of neocolonialism leveled against gays in Africa. Desai also contends intelligently with the limitations of Frantz Fanon's groundbreaking study of this issue. Fanon undoubtedly still resonates in any discussion of whiteness: "All around me the white man," he writes, "above the sky tears at its navel, the earth rasps under my feet, and there is a white song, a white song. All this whiteness that burns me" (Fanon [1952] 1991, 114). Less poetically, he angrily denounces the fact that

> for several years certain laboratories have been trying to produce a serum for "denegrification"; with all the earnestness in the world, laboratories have sterilized their test tubes, checked their scales, and embarked on researches that might make it possible for the miserable Negro to whiten himself and thus to throw off the burden of that corporeal malediction. (111)

Most importantly, Fanon addresses the black man first, proposing "nothing short of the liberation of the man of color from himself" (10). Desai agrees with Diana Fuss and others, however, who note an inescapable homophobia that limits Fanon's discourse (Desai 2001, 146–47). Fanon seems very much to concur with the common African perception of homosexuality as "La maladie des blancs."

As we turn to the response of Africans themselves to this sort of objectification, let us recall once more bell hooks's review of *Paris Is Burning*. hooks speaks principally of African Americans, but one of the points she makes takes on added importance against the backdrop of African self-expression:

> Gender bending and blending on the part of black males has always been a critique of phallocentric masculinity in traditional black experience. Yet the subversive power of those images is radically altered when the latter are informed by a racialized fictional construction of the "feminine" that suddenly makes the representation of whiteness as crucial to the experience of female impersonation as gender, that is to say, when the idealized notion of the female/ feminine is really a sexist idealization of white womanhood. (hooks 216–17)

It is worth taking a look at the recent Ivory Coast film *Woubi Cheri* in light of hooks's criticism, since it suggests possibilities for self-expression without the valorization of white (Western) role models. It is true that all involved in the film speak French and may be a very small (and how representative?) slice of life in Abidjan, but they nonetheless are there, making a statement, and saying some things reminiscent of sentiments expressed in *Paris Is Burning*—statements lacking in the commodification, desire for acquisition, and valorization of white divas that hooks (and Dorian Corey) find upsetting in the recent American voguing scene.

Woubi Cheri is an account of the founding of the Ivory Coast Transvestite Association in December 1997. "Barbara" is the most prominent spokesperson in the film and, like all the others, wears non-Western clothing throughout the film. He explains that "*woubi*" means gays who are not transvestites; "*yossis*" are their "husbands," generally bisexual, often married to women at the same time. "*Toussous*" are lesbians. "*Controus*" are males hostile to both "*woubis*" and "*yossis*."[22] We are presented with a series of couples: Vincent and Avelido, Laurent and Jean-Jacques. Along with Barbara, some mature voices are Bibiche and Tatiana. Like Dorian Corey, Barbara is nostalgic for the *yossis* of yesteryear, who seemed more sincere; today's husbands are more jaded somehow, more manipulative. And *woubis* back then were more subtle. Laurent shares the dissatisfaction: "Here in Africa you don't live love," he complains. "You only live shit, self-interest . . . I haven't yet met a man who can love a *woubi*, whereas a *woubi* can love a *yossi* to death." "People here think transvestites are nothing but gangsters," one of Barbara's friends adds. "But we're not. That's just how we're born. We didn't buy *woubia* in the marketplace. If so, no one would have chosen what we are today. . . . Without the right to be different, Africa is going nowhere."

Clearly, the filmmakers are editing their message as surely as Jennie Livingston (or any filmmaker) has done, and one cannot help but edit one's own response to what the film allows us to see. Nonetheless, *Woubi Cheri* is striking in its apparently straightforward expression of the difficulties of being a man who loves men and a woman who loves women in the Ivory Coast. At the same time, one is also struck by the frustrated but determined sense of being what one is, regardless of what African (or Western) society may demand. Barbara, in fact, seems called to a missionary zeal, as he tells the camera:

> I do better every day when I'm out and about. I spread my magic powder to change *controus* into *yossis* . . . [he laughs]. I promote *woubia*. I like that, the good and the bad all mixed up. Africa is a strange place. Like the Ivory Coast, it is my country. I need to be here to speak my own language. . . . So many towns in which to spread the word. It's like cleaning a house that's constantly dirty. You just have to keep cleaning.

Between the lines, one may hear the call of Paris, the suggestion that Barbara knows life would be easier in a Western culture. But in the party that his organization hosts at the film's conclusion, all the *woubis* wear bold blue African (female) outfits, and dance not disco, but a traditional circle dance from Senegal.

Dakan, a somewhat more disturbing exploration of the theme of coming out, is directed by Mohamed Camara and set in Guinea-Conakry. With the faint call of the *muezzin* in the background, the film shows the painful but persistent relationship between two adolescent men, Manga and Sori, both from families with some money (again, everyone speaks French), though Sori's is pointedly rich. This class distinction seems as much an issue as the burgeoning (and blatant) attraction the two men have for each other. Both sets of parents object to this expression of love, and both seem to rationalize their objections principally as one of obligation: their sons must provide them with grandchildren, and must take over the family business. Sori is coerced into abandoning Manga for a woman, whom he marries and with whom he sires a child. Manga is put through a lengthy and extensive African equivalent of aversion therapy, which disorients him but fails to "convert" him. Manga does try, however, and becomes engaged to a white woman, Oumou, who has been raised by her black nanny after her French parents die in her infancy. When this does not work as a deterrent to his attraction to Sori, Oumou angrily exclaims, "You promised you'd never wear a dress again." This is figurative; both Sori and Manga seem quite happy as otherwise traditional males, though Manga does express a desire to have Sori's child. After first rejecting her son after this reaffirmation of his orientation, Manga's mother blesses his inescapable choice of Sori. The film's ending, however, is remarkably disturbing and unrealistic (perhaps intended as either romantic or critical of the lack of options in such a society)—the two men, having abandoned Sori's wife and child without a word, drive off into the sunset and into no clear future except, it would seem, alienation from everybody else. Like it or not, *Thelma and Louise* comes to mind.

López writes that "one of the cultural residues left in the wake of empire is precisely [the] ideal of or aspiration to whiteness, what we might call a postcolonial 'will to whiteness' that lurks in the burgeoning state's national racial unconscious, as an unacknowledged, because unexamined, national aesthetic" (López 95). In an increasing number of films and novels around the developing world, however, a local queer community is finding ways to assert its own brand of queerness, one that is not overdetermined by San Francisco, London, Paris, etc.[23]

Nonetheless, the lack of true resolution in films such as *Dakan* suggests the ongoing truth of López's observations about the various narratives being produced by postcolonial writers, and in the context of this chapter points out the added complexity for writers and directors who are queer. López writes that in various postcolonial novelists, the protagonist's growth into a final and unproblematic identification with his culture, as the structure of the *bildungsroman* would require, is . . . frustrated or stunted. . . . [and such books (and films) thereby] unceasingly interrogate the very psychic machinery that works to suppress their most crucial insights, which produces a tactical resistance to the ascendance into consciousness of the most painful self-recriminations [for earlier co-optation by white colonial masters]. (99, 119)

The means that have had to be taken to gain access to the world of publication and filmmaking can complicate the "indigeneity" of the resultant product, adulterating the authority of the speaker. Thus, we have another twist on Gayatri Spivak's now-classic question "Can the subaltern speak?"[24] These writers and directors were really never part of the subaltern class of their various countries, but much of what the queer members of their coterie portray seeks to suggest a possible cross-class blurring of the borders that keep "subalterns" (of various sorts) in their place. The extent to which those who offer agency to these new voices have themselves been trained in the West cannot help but complicate their message and "authenticity," at least in the eyes of some of their countrymen and women. Thus, what López says of white colonial masters cannot help but resonate in the lives of some "non-white" others:

> [An] ongoing and unresolved tension (what Freud would call an "economy"), between what the colonial ego must banish from its sight for the sake of its functioning and the residues or memory-traces of an entire inventory of colonial acts of aggression, domination, violence, and so forth—between, in other words, manifest white denial and latent white guilt—continues to fuel the ambivalence of relations between whiteness and its others in the postcolonial world. (López 90)[25]

And this ambivalence seems inevitably to taint (or tint) the postcolonial writer and director, as well, who must grapple with the white skin that may lurk beneath more colorful masks, one's own or those of one's others.

The questions involved in coming out are painful in any culture, but films (and, of course, novels) are appearing with some rapidity throughout the world, investigating the possibilities of remaining in the emerging world, avoiding the lure of the West, and carving out a visible presence as queer. Ang Lee's *The Wedding Banquet*, while clearly embedded in American gay culture, nonetheless valorizes Chinese customs and points to the protagonist's reactive deracination as a retrievable loss. Deepa Mehta's moving film *Fire* has sparked scholars such as Ruth Vanita and Saleem Kidwai to "queer" India, unearthing evidence to counter arguments that suggest homosexual orientation was imported by the conqueror (whether Moghul or British). Vanita argues, in fact, that homophobia was structured in India "by masculinities that become normative in colonial and postcolonial nationalisms."[26]

QUEERS AS SUBALTERNS

In a 1987 interview with Angela Ingram, recorded after Gayatri Spivak's return from a visiting professorship at the Centre for Historical Studies at Jawaharlal Nehru University in New Delhi, the following exchange takes place:

Spivak: You know, I said a bit ago, that it really depends on what one does with being white which is much more interesting, because being white you have to do more if you really want to be politically correct. Whereas I can have an alibi, although, born a Brahmin, upper-class, senior academic in the United States, highly commodified distinguished professor, what do you want?

Ingram: "Highly commodified distinguished professor." That's good.

Spivak: Right. Not *as* commodified, let's say, as Hillis Miller or Stanley Fish, or Fredric Jameson, all my friends, but nonetheless, commodified. I still have an alibi. My skin. And you don't.

Ingram: I'm a lesbian, though. Can't I use that? No. I can't. It doesn't "show."

Spivak: Right. You have to wear a T-shirt. (Spivak *Postcolonial*, 86)

Spivak points out that, in India, her *class* also "shows," and she is deferred to on that basis; in Britain, less so; in the United States, not at all—there, she is simply brown, and a woman. In the United States, outside the academy, she would be forgiven for any views because they would be irrelevant in a white world of men. Ingram, on the other hand, is a woman, but white. In the United States she has no "alibi" for her opinions—unless, perhaps, she somehow announces her sexuality, in which case she is moved to another pigeonhole altogether. This is the brave new world of globalization—a world in which what "shows" may not reveal anything of importance, from the agent's point of view, although the gaze directed her way nonetheless interprets only those markers it is able to see.

In this light, Robyn Wiegman's assessment of the uncomfortable status of whiteness studies offers a provocative summary of the points this paper arguably exemplifies:

[Whiteness studies] begins to generate a range of contradictory, sometimes startling effects. The most critically important include: (1) an emphasis on agency that situates a theoretically humanist subject at the center of social constructionist analysis; (2) the use of class as the transfer point between looking white and believing you are white; (3) a focus on economically disempowered whites, both working class and poor, as minoritized white subjects; and (4) the production of a particularized and minoritized white subject as a vehicle for contemporary critical acts of transference and transcendence, which often produces a white masculine position as discursively minor. (Wiegman 136–37)

From a postcolonial perspective, read "third world" for "economically disempowered whites" and one hears echoes of the colonial desire to raise the "others" up to one's own level of civilization. From a queer perspective, read "sexually non-normative individual" for "a particularized and minoritized white subject" and one sees the purported difference between gays and lesbians who are First Worlders with an "alibi," and those of any color and nation who are, in fact, less comfortable with and in the world.

NOTES

1. See Delgado.

2. See for example Vanita; Hawley, *Theoretical* and *Theories*; Povinelli; Goldie; Harper.

3. See for example Viswanathan.

4. Wiegman, however, provocatively points to the limitations of Dyer's argument. "In assigning the power of white racial supremacy to its invisibility and hence universality," she writes, "Dyer and others underplay the contradictory formation of white power that has enabled its historical elasticity and contemporary transformations" (117). Wiegman attempts to "discuss the ways in which white power has reconstructed, and continued to reconstruct, itself in the context of the demise of segregation" (118). In Wiegman's view, "much of the force of contemporary white racial power arises from the hegemony of liberal whiteness" (121) that conceives of whiteness as a social construction. "On the one hand," writes Wiegman, "it responds to the contemporary leftist desire to produce an antiracist white (or postwhite) subject, one whose political commitments can be disaffiliated from the deployments of white supremacy and refunctioned as cross-race and cross-class struggle. In doing so, it encounters, on the other hand, the critical difficulty of that antiracist subject whose self-conscious and willful self-production can only reconfirm a universalist narcissistic white logic, mobilized now through the guise of an originary discursive blackness that simultaneously particularizes and dis-identifies with the political power of white skin." Wiegman then confirms George Lipsitz's assertion of "the impossibility of the anti-racist white subject" (123).

5. See for example Waugh; Hanson;Straayer; Bad Object-Choices; as well as the comprehensive catalog, *The Bent Lens*.

6. See for example Vanita.

7. See Mishra.

8. See Singh.

9. See Ebert.

10. And see Vorlicky on performance.

11. The complex dynamic of this engagement might be suggested by Kate Davy, who asked an African American lesbian why, in her opinion, so few black lesbians over the years have participated in the Women's One World (WOW) theatrical productions. "It's the same problem," the woman responded, "that black women and white women have had with each other for three hundred years" (205). Davy goes on to discuss the collation of whiteness and the politics of respectability, and remarks that "white womanhood needs to be theorized as an institution in the service of white control and supremacy in the same way that heterosexuality has been used as an institution in the service of patriarchy" (213).

12. See also Frankenburg on this point.

13. hooks's suspicion of Livingston's motives may carry the baggage of a good many encounters with whites who finally are judged to be too closely wedded to their race's hegemony. If one is to agree with the analysis of literary scholars such as Jane Davis, "according to the tradition of how [American] whites are understood by many [African American] black writers, whites are hypocritical, defensive, in denial, arrogant, ignorant, fake, crafty, passive-aggressive, cunning, sneaky, self-satisfied, backstabbing, silencing, and dishonest" (Davis 148).

14. Consider, in this regard, Thomas E. Wartenberg's interesting "Humanizing the Beast: King Kong and the Representation of Black Male Sexuality." "The film enables (White) viewers to see that their own reactions to difference are structured by assumptions about the significance of that difference that are, in fact, unfounded" (176).

15. See Hansen.

16. See note 9 above.

17. See for example Serros

18. Note for example Cherrie Moraga's account of her upbringing: "I was educated; but more than this, I was 'la güera': fair-skinned. Born with the features of my Chicana mother, but the skin of my Anglo father, I had it made. . . . [E]verything about my upbringing attempted to bleach me of what color I did have. . . . [But] the joys of looking like a white girl ain't so great since I realized I could be beaten on the street for being a dyke." See Moraga, 28–29.

19. See Shulman.

20. See Smith.

21. See also Scherzer.

22. I am told that various countries in Africa have terms with similar designations. Thus, in Swahili cultures: "mashoga" (pl), "shoga" (sing.) are effeminate men; "basha" (sing.) their straight husband.

23. See, for example, Drucker; Vanita; and my two collections of essays from 2001.

24. See Nelson, 271–313.

25. See also Lane and Young.

26. "Notwithstanding some scholars' discomfort with ascribing to colonialism the modern erasure of earlier homoeroticisms (and other eroticisms), evidence so far available indicates overwhelmingly that a major transition did indeed occur at that historical moment . . . [as exemplified by] the heterosexualization of the ghazal, the suppression of Rekhti, and the introduction of the antisodomy law. . . . Following Ashis Nandy's classic account, several scholars have analyzed

how anxieties around masculinity involve fear of the 'feminine' in women and in men. In the Fire debates that [Geeta] Patel and [Monica] Bachmann document, the fear emerges that female-female desire may undermine both masculinity and female homosociality. These gender-based anxieties are deeply intertwined with anxieties around religious, community, and national identities" (4, 8).

REFERENCES

Adventures of Priscilla, Queen of the Desert, The. 1994. Stephan Elliott, director. Polygram / Gramercy.

Ashcroft, Bill, Gareth Griffiths, and Helen Tiffin. 2000. *Post-colonial studies: The key concepts.* New York and London: Routledge.

Avila, Eric. 2001. White flight and the urban science fiction film in postwar America. In *Classic Hollywood, classic whiteness,* ed. Daniel Bernardi, 52–71. Minneapolis: University of Minnesota Press.

Babb, Valerie. 1998. *Whiteness visible: The meaning of whiteness in American literature and culture.* New York: New York University Press.

Bachmann, Monica. 2002. After the fire. In *Queering India: Same-sex love and eroticism in Indian culture and society,* ed. Ruth Vanita, 234–43. New York and London: Routledge.

Bad Object-Choices, ed. 1991. *How do I look?: Queer film and video.* Seattle: Bay Press.

Barnard, Ian. 2001. The United States in South Africa: (Post)colonial queer theory? In *Postcolonial and queer theories: Essays and intersections,* ed. John C. Hawley, 129–38. Westport: Greenwood Press.

Before Night Falls. 2000. Julian Schnabel, director. Fine Line.

Bernardi, Daniel, ed. 2001. *Classic Hollywood, classic whiteness.* Minneapolis: University of Minnesota Press.

Christian, Karen. 1997. *Show and tell: Identity as performance in U.S. Latina/o fiction.* Albuquerque: University of New Mexico Press.

Conan the Barbarian. 1982. John Milius, director. Universal.

Cone, James H. 1986. *A black theology of liberation.* New York: Orbis.

Dakan. 1997. Mohamed Camara, director. California Newsreel.

Davis, Jane. 2000. *The white image in the black mind: A study of African American literature.* Westport: Greenwood.

Davy, Kate. 1997. Outing whiteness: A feminist/lesbian project. In *Whiteness: A critical reader,* ed. Mike Hill, 204–25. New York: New York University Press.

Delgado, Richard, and Jean Stefancic, eds. 1997. *Critical white studies: Looking behind the mirror.* Philadelphia: Temple University Press.

Desai, Gaurav. 2001. Out in Africa. In *Postcolonial, queer: Theoretical intersections,* ed. John C. Hawley, 139–64. Albany: State University of New York Press.

Drucker, Peter, ed. 2001. *Different rainbows.* London: Millivres.

Dyer, Richard. 1997. *White.* London: Routledge.

Ebert, Roger. [9 August 1991] 22 May 2002. Paris is burning. *Chicago Sun Times.* http://www.suntimes.com/ebert/ebert_reviews/1991/08/664369.html.

Fanon, Frantz. [1952] 1991. *Black skin, white masks.* Trans. Charles Markmann. Reprint. London: Pluto.

Fire. 1996. Deepa Mehta, director. Zeitgeist.

Frankenberg, Ruth. 1993. *The social construction of whiteness: White women, race matters.* Minneapolis: University of Minnesota Press.

Goldie, Terry, ed. 1999. Introduction: Queerly postcolonial. Special issue of *ARIEL: A Review of International English Literature* 30, no. 2.

Greatest Performance, The. Elías Miguel Muñoz, director.

Hanson, Ellis, ed. 1999. *Out takes: Essays on queer theory and film.* Durham: Duke University Press.

Harper, Phillip Brian, Anne McClintock, José Esteban Muñoz, and Trish Rosen, eds. 1997. *Queer transexions of race, nation, and gender. Social Text* 52–53.

Hawley, John C., ed. 2001. *Postcolonial, queer: Theoretical intersections.* Albany: State University of New York Press.

———, ed. 2001. *Postcolonial and queer theories: Essays and intersections.* Westport: Greenwood Press.

Hill, Mike, ed. 1997. *Whiteness: A critical reader.* New York: New York University Press.

hooks, bell. 1996. *Reel to real: Race, sex, and class at the movies.* New York: Routledge.

Jackson, Claire, and Peter Tapp, eds. 1997. *The bent lens: A world guide to gay and lesbian film.* St. Kilda, Victoria, Australia: Australian Catalogue Company.

Kincheloe, Joe L., Shirley R. Steinberg, Nelson M. Rodriguez, and Ronald E. Chennault, eds. 1998. *White reign: Deploying whiteness in America.* New York: St. Martin's Press.

Lane, Christopher. *The ruling passion: British colonial allegory and the paradox of homosocial desire.* Durham: Duke University Press, 1995.

López, Alfred J. 2001. *Posts and pasts: A theory of postcolonialism.* Albany: State University of New York Press.

Ma Vie en Rose. 1997. Alain Berliner, director. Haut and Court/Sony.

McLaren, Peter. 1998. Whiteness is . . . the struggle for postcolonial hybridity. In *White reign: Deploying whiteness in America,* ed. Joe L. Kincheloe, Shirley R. Steinberg, Nelson M. Rodriquez, and Ronald E. Chennault, 63–76. New York: St. Martin's Press.

Melville, Herman. 1988. *Moby-Dick, or the whale.* Reprint. Evanston and Chicago: Northwestern University Press.

Men of South Africa, The. 1991. Kirsten Bjorn, director. Video. Trekker Productions-International Wavelength.

Men of South Africa, The. 1992. Boereseuns/ Boer Boys. Kirsten Bjorn, director. Video. Voortrekker Productions-International Wavelength.

Moraga, Cherrie. 1981. *The bridge called my back: Writings by radical women of color.* Boston: Persephone.

Nakayama, Thomas K., and Judith N. Martin. 1999. *Whiteness: The communication of social identity.* Thousand Oaks, CA: Sage.

Nakayama, Thomas K., and Robert L. Krizek. Whiteness as a strategic rhetoric. In *Whiteness: The communication of social identity,* ed. Thomas K. Nakayama and Judith N. Martin, 87–106. Thousand Oaks, CA: Sage.

Nelson, Cary, and Lawrence Grossberg, eds. 1988. *Marxism and the interpretation of culture.* London: Macmillan.

Paris Is Burning. 1991. Jennie Livingston, director. Off White Productions.

Patel, Geeta. 2002. On fie: Sexuality and its incitements. In *Queering India: Same-sex love and eroticism in Indian culture and society,* ed. Ruth Vanita, 222–33. New York and London: Routledge.

Povinelli, Elizabeth A., and George Chauncey, eds. 1999. *Thinking sexuality transnationally*. A special issue of *GLQ: A Journal of Lesbian and Gay Studies* 5, no. 4.

Projansky, Sarah, and Kent A. Ono. 1999. Strategic whiteness as cinematic racial politics, In *Whiteness: The communication of social identity*, ed. Thomas K. Nakayama and Judith N. Martin, 149–74. Thousand Oaks, CA: Sage.

Rambo III. 1988. Peter MacDonald, director. TriStar.

Rocky. 1976. John G. Avildsen, director. United Artists.

Rothenberg, Paula S. 2002. *White privilege: Essential readings on the other side of racism*. New York: Worth.

Said, Edward. 1993. *Culture and imperialism*. New York: Knopf.

Serros, Michelle. 2000. *How to be a Chicana role model*. New York: Riverhead.

Sherzer, Dina. 1996. *Cinema, colonialism, postcolonialism: Perspectives for the French and francophone world*. Austin: University of Texas Press.

Shulman, Randy. [31 August 1995] 22 May 2002. Review of "To Wong Foo, Thanks for Everything! Julie Newmar." *Metro* (Washington, DC). home.online.no/~jane1/towongf1.html.

Singh, Amritjit, Joseph T. Skerrett Jr., and Robert E. Hogan, eds. 1996. *Memory and cultural politics: New approaches to American ethnic literatures*. Boston: Northeastern University Press.

Smith, Ronald L. 22 May 2002. Interview with Julie Newmar. http://www.geocities.com/Hollywood/ Academy/8035/wong.html.

Spivak, Gayatri. 1988. Can the subaltern speak? In *Marxism and the interpretation of culture*, ed. Cary Nelson and Lawrence Grossberg, 271–313. London: Macmillan.

———. 1990. In *The post-colonial critic: Interviews, strategies, dialogues*. Ed. Sarah Harasym. New York: Routledge.

Strawberries and Chocolate. 1993. Tomás Gutiérrez Alea and Juan Carlos Tabío, directors. Sandrew Film.

Straayer, Chris. 1996. *Deviant eyes, deviant bodies: Sexual re-orientations in film and video*. New York: Columbia University Press.

Tarzan and the Amazons. 1945. Kurt Neumann, director. RKO.

To Wong Foo, Thanks for Everything! Julie Newmar. 1995. Beeban Kidron, director. Universal.

Troyano, Alina. 2000. *I, Carmelita Tropicana: Performing between cultures*. Boston: Beacon.

Vanita, Ruth, ed. 2002. *Queering India: Same-sex love and eroticism in Indian culture and society*. New York and London: Routledge.

Visnawathan, Gauri. 1989. *The masks of conquest: Literary study and British rule in India*. New York: Columbia University Press.

Vorlicky, Robert H. 1997. Performing men of color: Male autoperformance, highways performance space, the NEA, and the white Right. In *Whiteness: A critical reader*, ed. Mike Hill, 248–64. New York: New York University Press.

Wartenberg, Thomas E. 2001. Humanizing the beast: King Kong and the representation of black male sexuality. In *Classic Hollywood, classic whiteness*, ed. Daniel Bernardi, 157–77. Minneapolis: University of Minnesota Press.

Waugh, Thomas. 2000. *The fruit machine: Twenty years of writings on queer cinema*. Durham and London: Duke University Press.

Wedding Banquet, The. 1993. Ang Lee, director. Samuel Goldwyn.

Wiegman, Robyn. 1999. Whiteness studies and the paradox of particularity. *Boundary 2* 26, no. 3: 115–50.

Wizard of Oz, The. 1939. Victor Fleming, director. Blackhawk.

Woubi Cheri. 1998. Philip Brooks and Laurent Bocahut, directors. California Newsreel.

Young, Robert. 1995. *Colonial desire: Hybridity in theory, culture, and race.* New York: Routledge.

FOUR

WHITENESS IN POST-SOCIALIST EASTERN EUROPE: THE TIME OF THE GYPSIES, THE END OF RACE

ANIKÓ IMRE

WHITENESS AND NATIONALISM IN EASTERN EUROPE

"I BELIEVE AMERICA TAUGHT our son's killer to hate African-Americans." This is how Camille Cosby's controversial article starts in the July 8, 1998, issue of *USA Today* (Cosby, 15A). "Presumably," she continues, "Markhasev did not learn to hate black people in his native country, the Ukraine, where the black population was near zero. Nor was he likely to see America's intolerable, stereotypical movies and television programs about blacks, which were not shown in the Soviet Union before the killer and his family moved to America in the late 1980s" (15A). Cosby levels a passionate charge against the racist foundations of the American nation, a charge that "opened a real dialogue on race" (Cohen 1998, 26). However, her statement also echoes two highly debatable assumptions: that certain forms of racism are specific to particular groups and historical situations, and that film and media shape ethnic and racial identities in predictable ways.

bell hooks also addresses these assumptions when she recalls discussing Wim Wenders's film *Wings of Desire* (1988) with white friends:

> *Wings of Desire* evoked images of that imperialist colonizing whiteness that has dominated much of the planet. This image was reinforced by

the use of nonwhite people as colorful backdrop in the film, a gesture that was in no way subversive and undermining in that much
of the film was an attempt to represent white culture in a new light.
Encountering white friends raving about the magic of this film, I
would respond by saying it was just "too white." They would give
me that frustrated "no racism again, please" look that is so popular
these days and explain to me that, after all, Berlin is a white city.
(hooks 1991, 167)

hooks writes that this film made her think about "white culture" not
simply in terms of skin color, but rather "as a concept underlying racism,
colonization, and cultural imperialism" (166). This is a useful starting point,
but it ignores the fact that whiteness is far from being a monolithic concept.
Irish culture, for instance, contests the conflation of white and colonizer.
And there are predominantly white cultures that have not directly participated in historical processes of colonization and imperialism. In countries of
Eastern Europe, most people would probably still insist that issues of colonization and race are not relevant to the region, despite the fact that, similar
to Berlin, these places are much less "white" than they used to be. Since the
end of socialism, as a result of large-scale Eurasian migrations, a massive
onslaught of global media, and the fervor of the neo-fascist, racist persecu-
tion of Gypsies and racialized foreigners, a new awareness of racial difference
has emerged in the post-Soviet region. But, despite the variety of colors that
are now present on the streets and screens of Poland, Slovakia, the Czech
Republic, or Hungary, whiteness as a moral category has remained transparent. Its politics and aesthetics have remained beyond analysis.

In the following, I will first attempt to explain why this is so. I will
argue that white supremacy's function in the constitution of East European
national identities is rooted much deeper than either these nations' official
self-representations or the Western media portrayal of recent ethnic confrontations would suggest. Since the end of socialism, much of the struggle over
ethnic and racial representation has taken place in, and under the influence
of, films and other media, indigenous as well as imported. However, this has
happened without adequate analysis or even acknowledgment of the constitutive role that media representations have played in the shifting relationships of national, ethnic, and racial majorities and minorities. I will analyze
East European representations in which whiteness appears contested and
contestable, "as a process, not a "thing," as plural rather than singular in
nature" (Frankenberg 1997, 1). The changing situation of Gypsy, or Romani,
minorities within Eastern Europe provides a useful lens through which we
can examine how whiteness has been called upon to provide legitimacy to
the post-socialist nation-state. In the concluding part of this chapter, I will
point to new, transnational Gypsy self-representations that address the racial
foundations of East European nations and, at the same time, prompt us to ask

whether the postcolonial nation-state is the only relevant category in terms of which we should examine issues of whiteness.

THE RETURN OF THE RACIST REPRESSED

Judging by the recent racist outbursts of ethnic nationalism in Eastern Europe and the former Soviet Union, the question appears to be less whether discourses of colonization, race, and, in particular, whiteness, are relevant to the functioning of East European societies, but rather how such discourses have managed to stay submerged for so long. With the collapse of socialism, East Europeans have suddenly awakened from their relative imprisonment within the Soviet Bloc to find their national boundaries vulnerable to influences from a world that had moved on to an increasingly transnational order. They have been confronted with the possibility that identities are far from taken-for-granted, not the least because of the power of global communication and information networks. It is not surprising that, emerging from the discredited communist rhetoric of egalitarianism and internationalism, East Europeans have fallen back on nationalism as a "source of self-confidence, an ideological substitute for the vanished certainties of the communist era" (Tismaneanu 1994,102). As Vladimir Tismaneanu writes,

> Postcommunist nationalism is . . . a political and ideological phenomenon with a dual nature. As an expression of historical cleavage, it rejects the spurious internationalism of communist propaganda and emphasizes long-repressed national values. On the other hand, it is a mental construct rooted in and marked by Leninist authoritarian mentalities and habits. Its targets are primarily forces that champion pro-Western, pluralist orientations, but also individuals or groups perceived as alien, different, potentially destructive of a presumably homogeneous ethnic body (such as immigrant, Gypsy, or gay minorities). Nationalist discourse demonizes the West and insists on rejecting any attempts to turn postcommunist nations into "the external proletarian armies" of the capitalist metropolis. (106)

Dominant East European political groups have resorted to nationalist manipulation and mobilization in order to maintain their monopoly on power (105). The unquestionable goal of "preserving the nation" against alien influences has played out in terms of the preservation of national cultures, primarily in print and broadcast media. The call to save the national culture has often been issued in the name of a resistance to the demonic values conveyed by "cultural imperialism," associated with consumerism, global media homogenization, and multiculturalism. However, this does not mean the rejection of the West as a whole. Rather, the binary logic of nationalism has dictated that the West be split in two: authentic and false; old and new;

sophisticated and mass-oriented. Influences deemed "harmful" for the nation are associated with the United States, in opposition to good old "authentic" European values.

This dichotomy has several advantages for the political and cultural elite. First of all, the "return to Europe," which has become an indispensable slogan for East European political campaigns (Iordanova, "Balkans," 2000), allows discourses of imperialism and racism to remain unexamined within nationalism. East European nations' unspoken insistence on their whiteness is one of the most effective and least recognized means of asserting their Europeanness. The fact that racism has surfaced at the end of the cold war is, precisely, an indication that the Eurocentric, black-and-white self-image of East European nations is under contestation, along with concepts such as national destiny and national character. The "new-old nationalisms" of Eastern Europe (Eisenstein, *Hatreds*, 45), and the accompanying "new racisms" (Žižek, "Ez van"; "A Leftist Plea") betray the very insecurity of modernist nationalisms in their confrontations with the postmodern, transnational media and economy.

The insistence on the invisibility of whiteness, and on an absolute "color line" between white and nonwhite, provides the foundation for a series of rigid, hierarchical binary divisions in East European national ideologies: truth/lie, human/inhuman, high culture/mass culture, individual/collective, and scientific/superstitious. Of course, these dichotomies have been the very devices with which the West naturalized its hierarchical relationship to its colonies (Shohat and Stam 1994, 201). Indeed, in a sense, Eastern Europe has adopted racism and nationalism from the West: On the one hand, as the Bulgarian theorist Alexander Kiossev puts it, East European nations, "on the periphery of civilization," came into existence and have survived through a process of "self-colonization." These nations voluntarily accepted the superiority of European Enlightenment ideas of rationality, progress, and racial hierarchy (18). On the other hand, similar to its relationship to third world nations, "Europe" has been far from innocent of imposing its imperial master narratives on the populations of Eastern Europe: the "Other Europe" has provided a favorable, admiring mirror even after the end of actual imperial ventures to Asia and Africa. It has remained a resort for living out forbidden or unrealizable fantasies without taking full responsibility for them.

This process continues under the cover of liberal democracy, occasionally surfacing in such contradictions as the effective media "racialization" and subsequent abandonment of the Balkans, and the simultaneous, somewhat hypocritical Western diplomatic protests against the legal and political inequality of Gypsy minorities in Eastern Europe. In the first case, the Western media coverage of the war in Yugoslavia—one of the hotbeds of the "ethnic conflicts" that have burst into violence in postcommunist Eastern Europe since 1989—insisted on distancing the war from Western, rational frameworks of interpretation. The confrontations were represented as the results of ancient, internal and unresolvable tribal disagreements (Iordanova, "Balkans"; Ó Tuathail 1996, 191–95; Ravetto 1998, 47; Žižek, "Ez van"). In the second case, while the European Union has set future East European member states strict standards for improving the political and economic situation of ethnic minorities, the borders of "Europe" are increasingly protected from "alien invasion." There are "Gypsy ghettos" in Italy, and ethnic violence is on the rise in Austria and Germany.[1]

One of the primary difficulties of using Western theories of ethnicity, race, and colonialism to mark whiteness and contest ethnocentric nationalisms in Eastern Europe is that in East European languages, state politics, and in social scientific studies of Eastern Europe, the category of "race" has remained embedded within that of "ethnicity." Most studies of East European nationalisms continue to approach their subjects in terms such as "political" and "ethnic" (Kennedy 1994, 27). The failure—or refusal—to distinguish race from ethnicity deflates the state's violence and the social policies that accompany prejudices against a racialized group (Shohat and Stam, 183). Race and racism continue to be considered concepts that belong exclusively to discourses of coloniality and imperialism, from which Eastern Europe, the deceased "second world," continues to be excluded, and from which East European nationalisms are eager to exclude themselves. For instance, seeing my interest in the current racist backlash against the Roma, white Hungarians repeatedly anticipated my "American" reaction, and vehemently warned me not to set up an analogy between Gypsies in Eastern Europe and African Americans in the United States. I have been told not to confuse a racial minority, whose ancestors were forced into slavery, with an East European "historical," ethnic minority such as the Roma; not to force the "white guilt" that Americans "rightly" feel about the extinction of Native Americans on innocent East Europeans, for whom both colonization and whiteness are distant concepts; and not to hold up misguided American racial policies such as affirmative action as ideals for Eastern Europe, freshly liberated from the burden of censorship. At the same time, in Hungarian, it is perfectly acceptable to use the phrase "It's not for white people" to describe hard physical labor, and it is considered to be free of contradiction to say, "I hate Gypsies, but I am not a racist."

This point returns us to the questions of why Ennis Cosby's murderer did not need to see American media images to become a racist, and why Wim Wenders and other white European masters of high culture are held in so much critical regard throughout Eastern Europe. It is true that direct imperialism, and its necessary consequence, colonialism—understood in a narrower, historical sense as the forceful domination and economic exploitation of a distant land—bypassed East European cultures.[2] However, imperialism as the "theory, and the attitudes of a dominating metropolitan center ruling a distant territory" (Said 1993, 9) has thoroughly influenced the formation of East European nations. The latter came into existence by adopting the models of European national and imperial development. Models and symbols of imperial "Europeanness," which were imported by traveling intellectuals and disseminated primarily by schools and universities, have been in great demand in Eastern Europe for centuries (Kiossev 2000, 18). The concept of "cultural nationalism"[3] usefully describes this "eastern type of development," formulated as a desire to be European, demonstrating "an overwhelming concern for fictions and symbols" in the absence of the "proper," European political institutions of the nation state (Csepeli 1991, 328).

In a sense, of course, nationalism is always a product of colonization (Balibar 1991, 89), and racism has been both an ally and a product of the colonization process (Stam and Spence 1976, 35).[4] Edward Said explains that the cultural exchange between Europe and the "Orient"—India, Egypt, or the Ottoman world, for instance—was initially a mutual process. However, as imperial economic interests had gained in importance, it became necessary to justify Europe's natural superiority to colonized cultures along racial lines (Said and Burgmer,"Bevezetés," 2000). The subsequent institutionalization of racism became a crucial component of East European nationalisms, as well, the "Europeanness" of which was in question from the start.[5] Since Eastern Europe's participation in imperialism has been fantasmatic, rather than based on direct contact with others, it has operated by national consensus, unfettered by anticolonialist critique and white guilt.

Wimal Dissanayake sums up the relationship of nationalism to colonization: "Nationalism simultaneously extends the range and depth of colonialism, offers resistance to it, subverts its imperatives and determinants, and reproduces it in subtle and not so subtle ways" (Dissanayake 1994, ix). In Eastern Europe, these functions have been distributed along the geographical West-East division: the resistance to and the subversion of colonialism have been reserved for invasions from the East (the Tartars, the Ottoman Empire, the Soviets), while eager reproduction has characterized the self-colonizing relationship to Europe.[6] The United States has recently become a third player in this paradigm, standing for a simplified understanding of neocolonialism and media imperialism.

Whiteness has stayed unmarked, embedded in Hungarianness, Bulgarianness, and other nationalities. As Zillah Eisenstein writes in relation to recent events in Bosnia, nationalism in Eastern Europe functions as a form of racism (Hatreds, 48).[7] Unlike Frantz Fanon, Haile Gerima, or Edward Said, for whom watching Tarzan provoked a schizophrenic "crisis of identity" (Stam and Spence, 157), East Europeans have never had to doubt whom to cheer for, and never confused themselves with cannibals. Racism has remained, perhaps, the most poorly articulated factor in the relationship between official ideologies and people's fantasies during and since communism. Instead of theorizing the postcommunist transition in the context of (post)coloniality, discourses of market and democracy currently appropriate the rhetoric of public debates in Eastern Europe—further confirming the racialized/gendered/sexualized silences that are prerequisites to building and maintaining nation-states (Eisenstein, *Hatreds*, 43). As Eisenstein writes, "Democracy, when used on behalf of nationalist rhetoric, allows racism to flourish. In many of the east european post-communist nations, freedom of speech has allowed hatred toward jews, roma, and other ethnic minorities to be spoken openly" (49).

This is not to say, of course, that one should simply substitute "ethnicity" for "race." "Ethnicity" is useful in that, in contrast to "race," it implies the constructedness of the subjectivites and identities it describes (Hall 1997, 378). Ethnicity is "fictive" (Balibar 1991, 96) in the sense that it is continually crossed and reinvented by racial, linguistic, class, gender, sexual, religious, and other identities. However, as Stuart Hall argues, this constructedness is a double-edged sword. It can usefully shift a politics of race from the assumption of essentialist racial homogeneity to a politics of solidarity based on the recognition of differences within ethnic groups—as Hall's study of the emergent British "new ethnicities" demonstrates (Hall 1997, 378–79). However, in order to employ ethnicity in the interests of racialized minorities, the notion of ethnicity needs to be "decoupled" from the way it functions in the dominant discourses of the state, from "its equivalence with nationalism, imperialism, racism": discourses that have taken advantage of the flexibility of "ethnicity" in order to disavow the realities of racism (379).

In postimperial and postcolonial cultures of the third world, where the realities of racial difference and racism have been impossible to disavow in the long run, the shift in cultural politics from "natural" racial identities to provisional ethnic positionalities has been engaged and discussed for decades. In Eastern Europe and studies of Eastern Europe, however, where racism has survived fossilized under the surface of "ethnic" and "national" relations, a similar shift has not taken place. Therefore, in order for racialized minorities, most prominently the Roma, to decolonize the "ethnic" label imposed on them, and transform themselves into Hall-style "new ethnicities" on the non-innocent ground of differences within similarities, it seems necessary for them to come into representation first. Their status of the stereotyped other needs to be acknowledged and analyzed in terms of political and economic injustice, which has been carried on for centuries with the help of racist representations. And conversely, the invisibility of the dominant national minorities, grounded in the assumption of the absolute superiority of "whiteness," needs to be foregrounded within a wide range of cultural representations.

The dichotomies that sustain primordial nationalisms and perpetuate the hegemony and moral transparency of whiteness have begun to be eroded in the process of the transition from state socialism to global capitalism, from resistant nationalism to transnational neocolonialism, from the terror of European, white, male high culture to the terror of American popular culture. The cohesion of the nation-state and the validity of nationalism are under attack by transnational flows of immigrants and images. As elsewhere in the world, in Eastern Europe the "national genie" is becoming "increasingly unrestrained by ideas of spatial boundary and territorial sovereignty," where "key identities and identifications now only partially revolve around the realities and images of place" (Appadurai 1993, 413–14). This situation is bound to expose contradictions in the nation-state's claim to authenticity, and unsettle the unspoken racialized hierarchy of nationalism.

WHITENESS AND THE ROMANS

The most formidable challenge to the invisible support that whiteness has provided East European nationalisms has come from the changing situation of the Romani. The Romani, or Gypsies,[8] have come to play a complex role in the processes of the postcommunist transition. On the one hand, the insecurity of postauthoritarian societies has induced a search for scapegoats, often reviving dormant or unacknowledged racial prejudice (Pók 1998, 531–33). The Romani have made for perfect scapegoats: They have lived in East European states for centuries, maintaining their diverse diasporas and resisting nation-formation and assimilation to the majority nation[9] (Hancock 2001), while the majority of them lack economic and political power. Longing for pure, ethnocentrically based national identities (Salecl 1994, 20; Ravetto 1998, 43), post-socialist East European states have leveled unparalleled discrimination and violence against Gypsies.[10] In the general atmosphere of nationalist revival, the Roma communities' "transnational" character has continued to be stigmatized as nomadic and backward.[11] At the same time, the desired European Union membership and the relative accessibility of Roma-related state policies to foreign media make the East European state more vulnerable and accountable than it was before. It is clear that the serene, European, democratic national front that the state attempts to present is, precisely, a front, which covers up boiling racial tension within the nation.

The white, national majority's relationship with Romani minorities is fraught with contradictions that threaten to expose the unstable boundaries of East European nationalisms. The post-1989 backlash against East European Roma is a symptom of the inevitable realization that nationalism is becoming obsolete under the pressure of the transnational, and that its crucial component, racial purity, is an illusory construction. Violently distancing themselves from Gypsies is an effort by "true" East Europeans to deny their own impurity, the fact that they are often equated with Gypsies in the West.[12] Part of the reason why East Europeans treat the Roma as exoticized and pre-civilized creatures is that they are treated as "Gypsies" by the Western media.[13] At the same time, the Canadian authorities discovered in the early 1990s that "white" Hungarians were posing as Gypsies in order to be granted refugee status in Canada, which the Hungarian prime minister simply denied ("Hungarians" 2000). This is an utterly ironic proof of the fragility and even the reversibility of the rigid racial hierarchy that nationalism constructs, in the post–cold war era of global mobility.

Comparing Hungarian and Gypsy narratives of origin yields further, ironic proof that nations are not products of natural destinies rooted in language, race, soil, or religion (Appadurai, "Patriotism," 414). Both tribes derive from Asia, migrated westwards, mixed genes and languages with those of many other tribes along the way, and eventually settled in Eastern Europe. In addition, although some Gypsies have more distinctive ethnic features, many are physically indistinguishable from Hungarians. Some scholars maintain that, genetically, Gypsies today are predominantly European.[14] Hungarian nationalism, however, simply disavows these similarities and turns differences into evidences of two diametrically opposed kinds of national characters.

The precise details of the travels of the nomadic tribes who could be considered the ancestors of Hungarians—such as the site of the "ancient homeland" or the identity of linguistic relatives—are still a matter of myth and ongoing debate. Of course, the factual value of these arguments is not as important as the political profit that national elites can gain from the idea of such spectacular progress from Asia to Europe. As opposed to the *myth* of national origin, which is concerned with the long journey through Eurasia, the official *history* of the Hungarian nation as such begins "precisely" in AD 896, with the European settlement of the tribes. Hungarian historiography has focused on the European performance of Hungarians (see László 1981). The contrast between the pre-civilized Asian past and the progressive European past (and future) of the nation has been naturalized not only through the sexual division between active men and passive women, but also through a literal adoption of and insistence on what Anne McClintock calls the "Family Tree of Nations," an essential part of the ideological foundation of European imperialism:

> In the image of the Family Tree, evolutionary progress was represented as a series of anatomically distinct family types organized into a linear procession, from the "childhood" of "primitive" races to the enlightened "adulthood" of European imperial nationalism. . . . The merging of the racial evolutionary Tree and the gendered family into the Family Tree of Man provided scientific racism with a simultaneously gendered and racial image through which it could popularize the idea of linear national Progress. (McClintock 1995, 359)

Since national consciousness, throughout Eastern Europe, has been closely tied to the fate of the national language, the debates about the origins of the Hungarian language have been saturated with the racial politics of nationalism. An early historian of the language claimed that Hungarian "united the bold figurative character of the East with the sobriety of the West" (Sherwood 1996, 27). The "Turkish-Finnish war" of the late nineteenth century

divided intellectuals and the general public alike as to which linguistic kin-
ship would be more desirable to establish. The Finno-Ugric family of languages is frequently represented by a tree model that bears a conspicuous
similarity to the Family Tree of Man: It ranks related languages according to
the extent of their westward progress. The group that made it the farthest
from the Asian steppes are unquestionably the Hungarians, with the Finns
as second best (see Benkö and Imre 1972; Engel 1990, 27–49; László 1981).[15]
The "temporal anomaly" within nationalism—"veering between nostalgia for
the past and the impatient, progressive sloughing off of the past" (McClintock,
358–59) thus implies a sense of natural superiority to cultures to the east of
Hungary, which compensates for an equally strong sense of inferiority toward
cultures in Western Europe.

The "tribal," "nomadic," "Asian" part of the Hungarian national story
is represented, retroactively, as at once a mythical resource and a conscious
preparation for the founding event of the nation: the "Settlement." It was
territorial conquest that began the magical transformation of nomadic tribes
into a unified nation. The claiming and defending of the territory are precisely the acts that supposedly make all Hungarians inherently superior to all
Gypsies, since the latter have never had a serious interest in forming nation-
states. Since the Gypsies' plight was never glorified by the sacred act of
"settlement," which would have transformed them from "tribe" into "nation," they can only be represented in pejorative, deeply prejudiced ways in
the Eurocentric language of modern nationalisms. Since Hungarians and
Gypsies share vague, nomadic origins and the "trope of the tribe" (Appadurai,
"Patriotism," 422–23), Hungarian nationalism has to insist on the act of
territorial settlement as a distinctive event, and on locking Gypsies into
stereotypes that characterize them as "still" nomadic,[16] backward, and genetically averse to "progress." Furthermore, while Hungarian national ideology
regards the genetic heterogeneity of the nation as scientific proof of its
"strength," Gypsies' genetic and cultural heterogeneity is considered proof of
degeneration, inability to achieve collective stability.

THE ROMANS AS GYPSY

There is a special urgency to looking at the situation of Gypsies through the
lens of critical theories of representation. Even more than in the case of
other marginal or minority groups, the reality of Gypsy life is overshadowed
by stereotypes of Gypsies throughout the world. Gypsies exist for most people
as pickpockets, musicians, or fairy tale characters, invariably associated with
dark powers or, at best, a simple, easy life unfettered by the responsibilities
of the modern citizen. As Ian Hancock puts it,

> Just as no one would question the fear of trolls and goblins or argue
> for their rights, the fear of Gypsies likewise goes unchallenged. . . .
> [B]ecause of a history of exclusion of Roma from education and

because of cultural restrictions on greater integration of Roma in the mainstream, the Gypsy image has taken on a life of its own and Romani populations have been administered and studied through the filter of that image. (Hancock)

According to György Kerényi, in Hungary, "the half million Roma exist only as a people with a Gypsy existence and identity. Being a Gypsy is an exclusive and indelible mark, which allows no other role" (Kerényi 1999, 147). Nationalist and racist stereotypes of Gypsies in Eastern Europe—and elsewhere—are wrapped in the images of the subhuman, and thus manage to evade ideological critique. It is impossible to reestablish the often severed connections between the socioeconomic and the cultural spheres without taking seriously representations of Gypsies.

Postcommunist film and media have shown a revived interest in the image of the Gypsy.[17] In Hungary alone, since 1989, nineteen feature and documentary films have been produced with Gypsy-related topics, whereas during the three decades between 1960 and 1989 only nine were made altogether ("Roma-filmek" 1999). These films fall into two broad categories: one consists of documentaries of Gypsy life, which intend to "bring silenced voices to the center of the debate" (Portuges, 197) and wish to "correct the record" (Iordanova 2001, 3). András Salamon's *Városlakók* (1997), which depicts the ordeals of urban Gypsies within a white majority, or Tamás Almási's *Meddő* (1995) about helpless, unemployed Gypsy communities in the north of Hungary, are outstanding examples. However, the majority of these films have not been made by Romani filmmakers (Iordanova 2001, 3). Most of them unavoidably approach their subject with the questions, and often the answers, of the white majority. In a similar vein, even though issues of Romani minorities have recently had more exposure in the dominant news media than before, "the representation of Gypsies is dominated by conflicts: unemployment, crime, and other social problems" (Gyurkovics 1999, 22).

Representations in the second category revive the romanticized image of the free-spirited, childish Gypsy (Iordanova 2001, 3). Hancock notes the recent increase in the representation of the Gypsy as an illiterate, inarticulate buffoon on Bulgarian, Romanian, or Slovakian television screens. Like turn-of-the century black and white minstrels in America, such characters are played by white people, and they help maintain a status quo that invariably renders the Roma figures of fun (Hancock). The Gypsy as the "dancing slave" has been recently reinvented in Hungary as well. While Gypsy characters are indispensable to popular jokes and cabarets—mostly representing the simple-minded petty criminal—they have no part to play in soap operas, talk shows, or commercials, where dominant cultural values of the nation are reflected, created, and confirmed (Kerényi 1999, 147).

Most of the recent "Gypsy" films are populated by what Erzsébet Bori appropriately calls "screen Gypsies" (Bori 1998):

> Screen Gypsies—in contrast with real ones, who are as heteroge-
> neous in their language and history as in their lifestyles and val-
> ues—are quite alike all over the world: their souls are made of songs,
> and their hearts are made of gold; they live in picturesque and
> photogenic poverty, and survive on the surface of ice; they fear God
> and the police, because their passionate temperament and inde-
> structible vitality make them prone to violating the Ten Command-
> ments and state laws. (Bori 53)

Films about screen Gypsies draw on the international romantic stereotypes of "Gypsy freedom, music, flower-patterned skirts, wild emotions, and horses" (Rádai 1999, 21)—images that have very little to do with the recent past of actual East European Roma, and nothing to do with their present. The recent renaissance of the romanticized, vagrant Gypsy in Hungary is a mim-icry of Western stereotypes and a commercial attempt to market Hungarian cultural products.

However, instead of distinguishing Gypsy and non-Gypsy cultures, images of "screen Gypsies" further confuse the two in the eyes of the West. This is especially true in Hungary, where the Roma constitute more than 5 percent of the population (Barany 1998, 322). Gypsy music is a touristic emblem of Hungarian culture, and the Western media portray the "Wild East" as Hungarians portray Gypsies (Portuges, 198).[18]

The film *Romani kris* (*Gypsy Law*) (dir. Bence Gyöngyössy, 1997), made in German-Hungarian-Bulgarian co-production, received Hungary's feature film nomination for the Oscar, and was awarded a First Film Prize at the 1997 Montreal Film Festival. With a shrewdly calculated marketing strategy, it combines Gypsy romanticism with the captivating story and the high cul-tural credentials of *King Lear*. It takes place within a Roma community somewhere in Hungary, at an undefined time during the last fifty years. Most of the story unfolds in retrospect, as remembered by the aging Gypsy patri-arch Lovér/Lear, played by Djoko Rosic. Lovér is an exile in the present, wondering around with his faithful companion Tamáska, the sensitive and musically-inclined village fool, looking for his youngest daughter to ask for her forgiveness before he dies. The retrospective narrative begins in an idyl-lic extended family environment that does not resemble any actual Gypsy community during communism. Gypsies are one with nature; the music never stops, and grandfather is full of fantastic stories to tell the children. The trouble starts when a "white man from town" arrives with the order that, in the name of modernization, the Gypsies need to move into town. In a moment of collective passion, "typical" of hot-blooded Gypsies, Lovér murders the urban messenger. The crime is temporarily covered up, but the murderer is tortured by his own conscience, which is embodied in his youngest and most honest daughter, Sarolta, a stunning "Gypsy beauty" with long dark hair and a natural talent for dancing. Sarolta refuses to dance for her father at his birthday party—a drawn-out, fully exoticized Gypsy celebration—foreshadowing the troubles that will inevitably strike as a result of breaking the law. And so the story continues until the father has been punished enough to be redeemed, and to be reunited with the "good" Sarolta. As a Hungarian review says, *Romani kris* is a not-too-original fairy tale at its best, and kitsch at its worst: "What does it have to do with Gypsies, what does it want from them, and what does it want to say about, or through them? (And to whom?) It is not a good enough reason that this is what the world is interested in right now" (Bori, 53).

Even more interesting are those films that romanticize Gypsy characters to continue a tradition in which Gypsies are used as allegorical expressions of the nation. In this case, although allegory is intended to set up a barrier between Gypsies and the "real" nation, the analogical connection still calls attention to the similarities between the two groups and leaves these films open to deconstructive critique. One of the seminal texts of this tradition is the epic allegorical poem "A nagyidai cigányok" ("The Gypsies of Nagyida"), written by cherished nineteenth-century poet János Arany. The poem satirically commemorates the failed revolution of 1848, venting a bitter disappointment about the humiliated ideas of national independence, which many leading intellectuals of the times shared. While the poem blames Hungarians themselves for the failure of nationalism, the guilt is projected into Gypsy characters. They are full of high ideals, but action remains limited to talking about dreams and to satisfying bodily needs. The critical revival of "A nagyidai cigányok" in the 1990s cannot be a coincidence, considering the current and similarly frustrated transitional moment. Both moments call for Gypsy characters to carry the disavowed, undesirable features of the Hungarian nation, and, thereby symbolically purify "real," that is, white, Hungarians. In a recent Hungarian deconstructionist conference, devoted entirely to the interpretation of "A nagyidai cigányok," several papers hinted at the historical parallel, but none of them reflected on the political implications of inventing and appropriating images of a racialized ethnic group in order to achieve an intellectual-national catharsis.[19]

A number of recent Hungarian films cast Gypsy or other racialized characters in order to reflect on the changing portrait of the nation or the changing role of the national intellectual. Livia Szederkényi's award-winning feature film, *Paramicha* (1993) is an avowedly "intellectual" film. Szederkényi explains how she searched for years to find the right protagonist, who could be the filmmaker's, or, in general, the intellectual's, mirror. Szederkényi says she had tried to find somebody through whom she could "understand herself":

And, suddenly, it occurred to me that [this character] must be Chinese. Because I needed someone who is just there. Here. Simply. And you can see him. And then I remembered Gauguin, and why he went where he did, and then it became clear where I needed to go. I don't know why it had taken me so long; it was so evident. . . . (Csáky 1994, 16)

This logic led Szederkényi to an old Gypsy man in a small village, who appeared perfect for the role.

On a small scale, Szederkényi reproduces the process of the imperialist self-construction of whiteness "on the backs of equally constructed Others" (Stam and Spence, 636). The fact that she thought of a Chinese character first betrays Orientalist reflexes, which are "second nature" to Hungarian intellectuals. Szederkényi sees a certain analogy between the Chinese and Gypsies, but this realization does not compel her to examine her own position, which is analogical to that of a European imperialist.[20] The only factor that decides in favor of a Roma character is his geographical closeness, which supposedly increases his "knowability." It is significant that Gauguin's modernist self-exile from European civilization to Tahiti serves as the vehicle for the analogy: the reference to modernist high culture automatically ensures political immunity. One is reminded, again, of hooks's claim that whiteness is a cultural value intimately bonded to the aesthetics of European high culture.[21]

If Gypsies exist predominantly as "images" in the cultural fabric (Hancock), it is evident that improving the alarming situation of the Romani is contingent on confronting harmful stereotypes. It is not so clear how to go about this, however. Hancock suggests that "in order for things to change, the Gypsy image must be deconstructed and replaced by a more accurate one—in the bureaucratic structures as well as in the textbooks" (Hancock 2001). But this corrective impulse faces the same danger that Cosby's corrective impulse faces in the case of media representations of African Americans. How does one draw the line between "accurate" and "positive" images? And how does one aim for accuracy in the case of such a diverse and dispersed group?

These are crucial questions, since the media has become a mirror in which white majority and Gypsy minority see each other. In the emerging discussion about ethnic representation in the media, the example of American multicultural representation recurs. "White" (and almost by definition, male) politicians, sociologists, journalists, and filmmakers seem to agree that the American way of "positive discrimination"—allowing images of Gypsies on the screen, and encouraging Romani cultural productions—is irrelevant to Hungarian circumstances, if not harmful (Turcsányi 2000). The arguments warn of the dangers of "mixing the aesthetic with the political"[22] and privileging skin color over talent. Most transparent of all, some think it is impossible for Gypsies to represent themselves in the media, since very few of them have learned the profession, and those who have lost their Romani identity in the process of necessary assimilation (Rádai, 20). In other words, Gypsies are to blame if they do not assimilate in order to learn media trades, but it is also their fault if they do assimilate and cease to be "authentic" Gypsies.[23]

Even in the liberal press, which claims to be more sympathetic to Roma concerns, descriptions of the Romani's situation often implicitly blame the victim. "Positive" articles—headed by titles such as "Gypsies Get Down to Work"—often simply reinforce negative stereotypes by presenting the "good," "civilized" Roma as the exception to the rule (Kerényi, 146).

The problem with striving for representational accuracy is that it perpetuates racial essentialism. While my purpose has been to make race visible as a category that has silently underlined and supported racism, I am aware that stopping at the point of reinstalling "race" would fix ethnic minorities in their subordinate positions. How does one separate race and racism without reproducing the latter's essentialism in the former? Race is an essentially racist category: it is a product of racism and, as such, it inevitably carries racist assumptions and structures. For this reason, Paul Gilroy calls for a rethinking of the politics of antiracist theorizing and antiracist activism. Gilroy claims that the usefulness of race as an analytical category has come to an end because of the profound transformations that have taken place in the last few decades in the way the body is understood, largely as a result of the emergence of molecular biology, digital processing, and other technologies (Gilroy 1998, 840):

> These new ways of seeing, understanding and relating to our selves point to the possibility that the time of "race" may be coming to a close. This possibility brings new dangers, but it also brings new hope to a situation in which, as Zygmunt Bauman has argued persuasively, a task-oriented relation to the corporeal constitutes the primal scene of postmodernity as an emergent sociological formation in the overdeveloped world. (840)

Gilroy is aware of the polemical nature of his argument, especially of the charge that renouncing "race" might be interpreted as a betrayal of the antiracist solidarities achieved precisely in the name of racial connections. However, as he points out, the taken-for-granted bond between antiracist activism and intellectual work on race has significantly changed in the last twenty years, not the least due to the intervention of corporate multiculturalism and its cultures of simulation, which have reevaluated racial difference on a commercial basis (842–43). Gilroy asks academics working in Ethnic and Racial Studies to reexamine their professional interests, the degree of their possible complicity in the reification of racial difference (842). The same questions can and should be asked of academics working in East European Studies, and of politicians involved in decisions concerning ethnicity and race in Eastern Europe. I consider the category of "race" to be of limited, temporary usefulness only. It is indispensable to foregrounding the racist violence of "innocent" ethnic and national representations, but it will always remain complicit in the processes that justify racist violence.

It seems that those forms of Romani self-representation that have had the most political impact are less concerned with racial essentialism and correct images, but, instead represent Gypsy "authenticity" in new, hybrid, transnational and multicultural forms. These forms foreground how "whiteness" and "the national" are naturalized in the aesthetics sanctioned by dominant culture. "Roma rap," for instance, initiated by the Gypsy group *Fekete Vonat* ("Black Train"), may be characterized as the Roma's own, ironic use of global media. Like the Irish working-class musicians of *The Commitments* (1991, d. Alan Parker), who play soul and call themselves "the blacks of Europe," *Fekete Vonat* draws on images and sounds associated with African Americans for self-representation. While members of the group do not disavow the stereotype that Romani have music in their veins, *Fekete Vonat*— and the Gypsy groups that have sprung up in their wake—defy canonized and commercialized "Gypsy music" by mixing various musical styles as well as languages, including Romani. Roma rap is at once part of global cultural expression and specific to the "local Harlem," the 8th district of Budapest (Fáy 1999, 24). Their lyrics, which embed racial politics in humor and irony, address white and Gypsy audiences alike. Members of *Fekete Vonat* say in an interview: "Our lyrics talk about our problems as Gypsies, and the problems of Gypsy people in general. This is one of the things that makes this music Roma rap. . . . We also try to attack everyday racism, and throw back in the gadjes'[24] face what they say about us, Roma" ("Roma rap," my translation).

Many Romani musicians have successfully entered the international music scene recently. Ironically, this has increased their popularity and respectability in Eastern Europe.[25] Roma rap is becoming part of the "world beat" which, Arjun Appadurai claims, is an excellent example of "fundamentally postnational and diasporic" cultural forms ("Patriotism," 426), and is a very different response to global media imperialism than the defensive refusal of globalization by the nationalistic Hungarian cultural elite. Roma rap resembles the cannibalistic, carnivalistic aesthetic of many third world groups, which "pick through capitalist leavings, and use them ironically as a strategy of resistance" (Shohat and Stam, 307–309).

Paris-based Romani filmmaker Tony Gatlif's film *Latcho Drom* (1993) is a similar attempt at subverting stereotypes without didacticism. *Latcho Drom*, which means "Safe Journey," is a film without dialogue. It traces the history of Romani migration from northern India through North Africa and Eastern Europe to Spain through musical vignettes, which feature many different Gypsy groups and musical styles against changing backdrops. It is an ironic history conveyed through music, which mocks narratives of origin designed to confer authenticity on people and places. The strength of Gypsy identity, according to Gatlif, is precisely the Gypsies' ability to survive across great diversity.

Many Gypsy intellectuals and scholars of Gypsy culture claim that the time of the Gypsies has arrived at the beginning of the millennium. One reason for this is exactly that Gypsies are not obsessed with national mythologies, with absolute collective roots. It is true that most Gypsies are not in a position to invent their own identities freely, either. Yet the transnational nature of Gypsy communities foreshadows a "new type of community," for which there is yet no vocabulary (Vajda and Kende, 2000). There is no proper terminology available, because

> [a]lthough many antistate movements revolve around images of homeland, of soil, of place, and of return from exile, these images reflect the poverty of their (and our) political languages rather than the hegemony of territorial nationalism. Put another way, no idiom has yet emerged to capture the collective interest of many groups in translocal solidarities, cross-border mobilizations, and postnational identities. Such interests are many and local, but they are still entrapped in the linguistic imaginary of the territorial state. (Appadurai, "Patriotism," 418)

Although, in the lack of new vocabulary, East European "territorial states" are currently trying to force the Romani into the vicious cycle of opposing ethnocentrism with ethnocentrism, such attempts have not been too successful. More and more Gypsy intellectuals emerge who are more likely to embrace antiessentialist and antinationalist paradigms (Vajda and Kende). Even if positing a common origin and emphasizing a common language will be necessary to come into representation and gain legitimacy within the current hegemony of the nation-state (Hancock), the Romani's outsider position and great linguistic and cultural diversity will constantly undermine the legitimacy of the nation-state as we know it. Most white Hungarians continue to despise, fear, and exclude from the nation real Roma, but romanticize them in movies that they hope to distribute on the global market. In this contradictory process, Hungarians undermine their own effort to protect the traditional boundaries of nation and ethnicity. Conversely, when some Roma reject identities imposed on them by dominant society— those of the victim, the criminal, and the romantic savage—and recreate their "authentic" culture in hybrid images and sounds, they affirm antiessentialist identities with the strategies of *mestizaje* and *creolité* in Caribbean and Latin American cinemas: strategies with which "marginalized groups try to find leaks in the systems of representation and turn them into floods" (Shohat and Stam, 316).

East European ethnocentrisms and nationalisms are permeated by such leaks. The geographical, political, and economic instability and inferiority of the region has nurtured a desperate insistence on primordialisms. The fact that the operation of racial and racist categories is invariably effaced at state and individual levels alike is a sign that the naturalness of these categories is highly unstable. In the current time of transformation, ethnic and racial representations are extremely vulnerable to contestations, to revelations that they perform, and not faithfully reflect, reality. My ultimate goal in this chapter has been to contest the often spontaneously unraveling biological essentialisms inherent in the discursive performances of white supremacy. They provide prime examples for Appadurai's claim that the invention of tradition and ethnicity becomes a slippery search for certainties, and is regularly frustrated by the fluidities of transnational communication ("Disjuncture," 325). The new global culture is not unequivocally beneficial, since it has also brought new refugee-flows and ethnocide. But for East European Roma, even if the state retains control over access to political rights and economic opportunities, global culture provides formerly unavailable cultural outlets for the expansion of suppressed hope, and nurtures fantasies that implicitly question the primacy of the national.[26] The introduction of new theoretical models will help reveal the extent to which the reigning old models are appropriated by intellectuals and the state in the service of a white, nationalistic majority. New models will hopefully begin to liberate such studies from the "shackles of highly localized, boundary-oriented, holistic, primordialist images of cultural form and substance" (335).

NOTES

1. See for instance Connelly, 1997; "From Bad"; Solimano and Mori 2000; Lawday 1991; Bade and Anderson 1997; and Bering-Jensen 1993.

2. The Habsburg Monarchy was rather parochial, uninterested in the acquisition of distant territories (Anderson, 107).

3. For a detailed discussion of cultural nationalism (as opposed to "political nationalism"), see Hutchinson 1987, especially 12–19 and 30–36.

4. I rely on Edward Said's distinction between "imperialism" and "colonialism." Said considers the two related terms with different emphases: Colonialism, "the implanting of settlements on distant territory," is almost always the consequence of the imperialism. "In our time, direct colonialism has largely ended; imperialism . . . lingers where it has always been, in a kind of general cultural sphere as well as in specific political, ideological, economic, and social practices" (*Culture*, 9).

5. Similar to its imperial model, East European white supremacy has sought proof of its power in unchanging mirrors of racial others. But the instability of Eastern Europe's geographical position has had to be counterbalanced by the idealization of Europe—the tower of civilization—on one side, and the projection of backward, exotic Asia on the other. The Hungarian language, similar to other East European languages, abundantly reflects this racialized geography: "European" is the synonym of "modern, civilized," while "Asian" connotes "primitive" and "uncivilized." See Iordanova's "Balkans," which reflects on a similar use of "Europe" in the Balkans.

6. Along a different division, women and femininity have represented the "love" of nation—or the nation in its most lovable, European form. Hate, however, has been transferred to racialized outsiders to the east and south, and within the nation (Eisenstein, *Hatreds*, 51–52).

7. The implication of East European nationalisms in the discourses of imperialism, colonialism, and racism is an almost entirely unexplored area for research. Such research would examine the "vast colonial intertext" and "widely disseminated set of discursive practices" in which colonialist representation is rooted (Stam and Spence, 636) in Eastern Europe. The communist era would be a treasure house of such research: not only had European civilization not ceased to be the object of desire and the only credible source of information about other cultures, but it had become particularly valued precisely because the connections with Europe were severely restricted and monitored by the state. At the same time, the state maintained a peaceful symbiosis between communist internationalism and Eurocentric nationalism.

8. "Convening in London in 1971, the first World Romany Congress condemned ethnic appellations traditionally applied to Gypsy groups, including czigany, Gypsy, gitano, and zigeuner, adopting instead "Roma" or "Rom" as a self-chosen ethnonym (Kurti, qtd. in Portuges n.d., 201). While this is an important step, it does not automatically erase the difficulty of naming without perpetuating prejudices. In Hungary, both "roma" and "cigány" are such prejudiced names. Romany groups use both as self-designation. See also Tanaka, and Hancock.

9. East European states offered the Romani only one option: to transform themselves into an obedient "national" or "ethnic" minority and copy the progressive model of their "Europeanized" mother-nations. The Romani's continuing refusal to assimilate to the white national majority amounts to a rejection of the claim that nation forming following the European model is the only enlightened progressive prospect for a group. For centuries, Gypsies have managed to maintain their smaller, non-national community affiliations within various nation-states and refused to adopt the monolithic racial and racist categories which dominant discourses had tried to impose on them.

10. Since 1989, news of atrocities committed against East European Roma proliferated: an innocent Romani woman was beaten to death in front of her children in Slovakia (Johnson 2000). A Czech city built a wall to separate Romani homes from Czech ones (Johnson). A Hungarian high school organized a segregated graduation ceremony for its Romani students (Kerényi 1999, 143). Daily examples of police brutality, prejudiced education, unlawful evictions, and various other forms of blatant discrimination abound.

11. In Hungary, as in most East European socialist states, the anti-Gypsy campaign started as early as the 1980s, when the socialist order was about to collapse and unemployment and inflation appeared to be increasingly menacing realities. The media, in service of the state, were instrumental in trying to rebuild a crumbling national unity by representing the Roma in terms of age-old negative stereotypes (Kerényi 142).

12. Recently, the Romanian Ministry of Foreign Affairs issued a memorandum, which advises all public officers to address all Romani as "Tigani," or Gypsies, despite the pejorative connotations of the word, and despite the fact that Gypsy organizations identify themselves by other nonpejorative names such as Rom, Romani, or Rromani. The government does not hide the fact that the motivation behind the memorandum is to prevent the confusion of Romanians with Rroma. "Romania's reputation" is at stake in the eyes of the world. See Tanaka.

13. As Catherine Portuges writes, hatred of Gypsies unites Eastern and Western Europe. See Portuges 212.

14. Werner Cohn, Wim Willems, and Judith Okely, for instance. See Hancock.

15. See some of the authorative books on the history of Hungarians and the Hungarian language. (Benkö and Imre 1972; Engel 1990; László 1981.)

16. The stereotype of the vagrant Gypsy still flourishes, even though only about 5 percent of the entire Gypsy population in Europe (estimated between 7 and 8.5 million) lead an itinerant life (Tanaka 2000).

17. Some of the films that have earned international recognition are *Time of the Gypsies* (1989, dir. Emir Kusturica); *Montenegro* (1981, dir. Dusan Makavejev); and *Latcho Drom* ("Safe Journey") (1993, dir. Tony Gatlif). Dina Iordanova provides a detailed account of postcommunist "Gypsy" films in her book, *Cinema of Flames* (2001, 213–34).

18. For instance, in the classic Hollywood film, *Golden Earrings* (Mitchell Leisen, 1947), Marlene Dietrich plays a seductive and wild, vagrant Hungarian-Gypsy woman, true to the exotic stereotype. Another well-known example is *The Wolf Man* (1941), which features (the Hungarian) Bela Lugosi, a Gypsy called "Bela," who turns into a werewolf. The ease with which the West collapses Hungarian and Gypsy cultures into one would shock most Hungarians.

19. For a representative analysis, see Müllner 1998.

20. Of course, this is not to say that modernist art is by definition imperialist. On this question see Said and Burgmer 2000, 7.

21. *Csajok* (*Bitches*, 1993), a film made in a German-Hungarian co-production by the Hungarian Ildikó Szabó, shows admirable sensitivity to its three female protagonists, but has no qualms about representing racialized characters in the most stereotypical light—predominantly for comic effect. The film portrays sometimes mercilessly naturalistic, at other times widely unrealistic, tragicomic moments from the lives of three women who try to escape from failed marriages. While most characters are on the verge of insanity, from the women's points of view, men appear especially driven by uncontrolled emotions. Most of the men are simultaneously violent and childish. Interestingly, this combination of features is frequently represented by racialized alter-egos that the men invent for themselves. Enikö's lover, for instance, imagines that he is an Indian chief, and he expects everyone to participate in his grossly exoticized, Hollywood-style fantasy. In a similarly oversimplified flash, we see a group of half-naked, "tribal" Africans drumming away in the small apartment of Juli's parents. We know so little about the inhabitants of the household that the Africans convey only a sense of irrationality. But the most revealing instance of representational violence is a long scene in which Barbara, a young actress, takes Enikö and Juli to a Gypsy celebration. It is hinted that Barbara herself is of Gypsy origin, because she knows her way around, and has romantic ties with the "Gypsy king," a tall and powerful man with a parodically long moustache and an excessively colorful shirt. While Enikö and Dorka drink and watch, Barbara, who is carried away by Gypsy romanticism and alcohol, begins a ritual, erotic dance with the man. The dancing ritual leads to a mating ritual, to which the film only alludes. In the next scene, Barbara awakens sober and in disbelief, runs home—to her drunken husband—and frantically cleanses herself in the bathtub, in disgust. It is unmistakable, and presented by the film with sympathy, that she has undergone a maturing process in which she, the actress living in her various roles, has been forced to separate dreams from reality. The "other Gypsy" that she saw through the cloud of alcohol was the material of dreams, while the reality is the racial contamination that she tries to get rid of.

22. This is a conspicuously hypocritical claim, since East European art of the last fifty years has been saturated with national politics. It is obvious that the minority politics of ethnicity is not considered of the same weight and value as the politics of the nation.

23. There are practically no Roma faces on television or among the producers of TV programs. "If a foreigner ignorant of East European matters were asked to watch Hungarian television—except for the news—for a while, he wouldn't have the slightest idea that there are Gypsies living in this country" (Gyurkovics, 23).

24. A Gypsy term for white people.

25. A review of an international musical festival, held in Budapest in August 2000, notes that most of the Hungarian participants were Roma. It also predicts that, similar to many of their predecessors, some of these Romani musicians will end up with contracts with well-known Western groups. Klezmatics. "Filmszakadásig." *Magyar Narancs*, 30 December 2000: 27.

26. "The critical point is that both sides of the coin of global culture today are products of the infinitely varied mutual contest of sameness and difference on a stage characterized by radical disjunctures between different sorts of global cultural flows and the uncertain landscapes created in and through these disjunctions" (Appadurai, "Disjuncture," 334).

REFERENCES

Alexander, Jacqui, and Sandra Mohanty, eds. 1997. *Feminist genealogies*. New York: Routledge.

Anderson, Benedict. 1992. *Imagined communities: Reflections on the origin and spread of nationalism*. London: Verso.

Appadurai, Arjun. 1993. Patriotism and its futures. *Public Culture* 5:411–29.

———. 1994. Disjuncture and difference in the global cultural economy. In *Colonial discourse and postcolonial theory*, ed. Patrick Williams and Laura Chrisman, 324–39. New York: Columbia University Press.

Bade, Klaus J., and Lieselotte Anderson. 1994. Immigration and social peace in united Germany. *Daedalus* 123, no. 1: 85–97.

Balibar, Etienne. 1991. The nation form: History and ideology. In *Race, Nation, Class*, ed. Etienne Balibar and Immanuel Wallerstein, 86–105. London: Verso.

Barany, Zoltan. 1998. Ethnic mobilization and the state: The Roma in Eastern Europe. *Ethnic and Racial Studies* 21, no. 2: 308–27.

Benkö, Loránd, and Samu Imre, eds. 1972. *The Hungarian language*. Paris: Mouton.

Bering-Jensen, Henrik. 1993. A flood of strangers in estranged lands: Neo-Nazi attacks on refugees and foreigners in Germany. *Insight on the News* 9, no. 1: 6–14.

Bori, Erzsébet. 1998. *Vászoncigányok* (Screen gypsies). *Filmvilág* 41, no. 10: 53.

Brinker-Gabler, ed. N.d. *Writing new identities*. N.p.

Cohen, Richard. 20–27 July 1998. Camille Cosby's complaint. *The Washington Post Weekly*, 26.

The Commitments. 1991. Alan Parker, director. Paramount.

Connelly, Joel. 14 January 1997. In Eastern Europe, new gains vie with old ways. *Seattle Post-Intelligencer*, A5.

Cosby, Camille. 8 July 1998. America taught my son's killer to hate blacks. *USA Today*, 15A.

Csajok (*Bitches*). 1993. Ildikó Szabó, director. Hungary/Germany.

Csáky, M. Caliban. 1994. *Van* (There is). *Filmvilág* 37, no. 9: 15–19.

Csepeli, György. 1991. Competing patterns of national identity in postcommunist Hungary. *Media, Culture, and Society* 13: 325–39.

Dissanayake, Wimal. 1994. Introduction: Nationhood, history, and cinema: Reflections on the Asian scene. In *Colonialism and nationalism in Asian cinema*, ed. Wimal Dissanayake, ix–xxix. Bloomington: Indiana University Press.

Eisenstein, Zillah. 1996. *Hatreds: Racialized and sexualized conflicts in the twenty-first century*. New York: Routledge.

Engel, Pál. 1990. *Beilleszkedés Európába a kezdetektöl 1440-ig* (Europeanization, from the beginnings to 1440). Budapest: Háttér Kiadó.

Fáy, Miklós. 1999. Mit ér a vér, miszter fehér? (What is your blood worth, Mr. White?). *Filmvilág* 42, no. 1: 24.

Frankenberg, Ruth, ed. and Intro. 1997. Introduction: local whitenesses, localizing whiteness. In *Displaying whiteness: Essays in cultural criticism*, 1–33. Durham: Duke University Press.

Gates. Nathaniel, ed. 1997. *Cultural and literary concepts of race*. New York: Garland.

Gilroy, Paul. 1998. Race ends here. *Ethnic and Racial Studies* 21, no. 5: 838–47.

Golden Earrings. 1947. Mitchell Leisen, director.

Gyurkovics, Tamás. 1999. *Cigányok ideje* (The Time of the Gypsies). *Filmvilág* 42, no. 1: 22–24.

Hall, Stuart. 1997. New ethnicities. In *Cultural and literary concepts of race*, ed. Nathaniel E. Gates, 373–82. New York: Garland.

Hancock, Ian. 18 July 2001. The struggle for the control of identity. *http:// www.geocities.com/Paris/5121/identity.htm*.

hooks, bell. 1991. *Yearning: Race, gender, and cultural politics*. London: Turnaround.

Hungarians disguised as Roma. 4 July 2000. *Budapest Sun*, 4–5.

Hutchinson, John. 1987. *The dynamics of cultural nationalism*. London: Allen and Unwin.

Intellectuals support Zamoly Roma. 1 September 2000. *http://www.romapage.hu/eng/ hiren028.htm*.

Iordanova, Dina. 2000. Are the Balkans admissible? The discourse on Europe. *Balkanistica* 13: 1–35.

———. 2001. *Cinema of flames: Balkan film, culture, and the media*. London: BFI.

James, Beverly. 1995. The reception of American popular culture by Hungarians. *Journal of Popular Culture* 29, no. 2: 97–107.

Johnson, Eric. 25 August 2000. Beating death of Romany mars Slovakia's image. United Press International.

Kapitány, Gábor and Ágnes. 1995. Changing world-views in Hungary, 1945–1980. *Journal of Popular Culture* 29, no. 2: 33–43.

Kennedy, Michael D. 1994. An introduction to East European ideology and identity in transformation. In *Envisioning Eastern Europe: Postcommunist cultural studies*, ed. Michael D. Kennedy, 1–45. Ann Arbor: University of Michigan Press.

Kerényi, György. 1999. Roma in the Hungarian media. *Media Studies Journal* 13, no. 3: 140–47.

Kiossev, Aleksandar. 2000. Megjegyzések az önkolonizáló kultúrákról (Notes about self-colonizing cultures). *Magyar Lettre Internationale* 37 (Summer): 7–10.

Klezmatics. 30 December 2000.*Filmszakadásig* (Until the film tears). *Magyar Narancs*, 27.

László, Gyula. 1981. *Ostörténetünk* (Our ancient history). Budapest: Tankönyvkiadó.

Latcho Drom. 1993. Tony Gatlif, director. France. 1993.

Lawday, David. 9 December 1991. No immigrants need apply. *U.S. News and World Report* 111, no. 24, 46–49.

McClintock, Anne. 1995. *Imperial leather: Race, gender, and sexuality in the colonial context*. London: Routledge.

Meddö (Barren). 1995. Tamás Almási, director. Hungary.

Montenegro. 1981. Dusan Makavejev, director. Sweden/UK.

Nichols, Bill, ed. 1976. *Movies and methods*. Berkeley: University of California Press.

Ó Tuathail, Gearóid. 1996. *Critical geopolitics*. Minneapolis: University of Minnesota Press.

Paramicha (Tale). 1993. Livia Szederkényi, director. Hungary.

Pók, Attila. 1998. Atonement and sacrifice: Scapegoats in modern Eastern and Central Europe. *East European Quarterly* 32, no. 4: 531–47.

Portuges, Catherine. Hidden subjects, secret identities: Figuring Jews, Gypsies, and gender in 1990s cinema of Eastern Europe. In *Writing new identities*, ed. Gisela Brinker-Gabler, 196–215. N.p., n.d.

Pynsent, Robert B., ed. 1996. *The literature of nationalism: Essays on East European identity*. Basingstoke: Macmillan and Company.

Rádai, Eszter. 1999. *Ugyanolyanok vagyunk mint te* (We are just like you). *Filmvilág* 42, no. 1: 18–22.

Ravetto, Kriss. 1998. Mytho-poetic cinema: Cinemas of disappearance. *Third Text* 43: 43–57.

Romani kris/Cigánytörvény (Gypsy law). 1997. Bence Gyöngyössy, director. Hungary.

Roma-filmek (Romani Films). 1999. *Filmvilág* 42, no. 1: 42.

Roma rap: avagy beindult a Fekete Vonat (Roma Rap, or the *Black Train* is on its Way). 3 July 2000. Amarodrom. *http://www.amarodrom.hu/archivum/98/vonat.html*.

Romany studies to be offered in Hungary. 25 August, 2000. *RFE/RL*. Budapest: N.p.

Said, Edward W. 1989. *Orientalism*. New York: Knopf.

———. 1993. *Culture and Imperialism*. New York: Knopf.

Said, Edward, and Christopher Burgmer. July 2000. *Bevezetés a posztkoloniális diskurzusba* (Introduction to Postcolonial Discourse). Trans. Zsolt Farkas. *Magyar Lettre Internationale* 28.

Salecl, Renata. 1994. *The spoils of freedom: Psychoanalysis and feminism after the fall of socialism*. London: Routledge.

Sherwood, Peter. 1996. A nation may be said to live in its language: Some socio-historical perspectives on attitudes to Hungarian. In *The literature of nationalism: Essays on East European identity*, ed. Robert B. Pynsent, 27–39. Basingstoke: Macmillan and Company.

Shohat, Ella. 1997. Post-third-worldist culture: Gender, nation, and the cinema. In *Feminist genealogies*, ed. Jacqui Alexander and Sandra Mohanty, 183–209. New York: Routledge.

Shohat, Ella, and Robert Stam. 1994. *Unthinking Eurocentrism: Multiculturalism and the media*. New York: Routledge.

Solimano, Nicola, and Tiziana Mori. June 2000. A Roma ghetto in Florence. *UNESCO Courier*, 40.

Stam, Robert, and Louise Spence. 1976. Colonialism, racism, and representation: An introduction. In *Movies and Methods*, ed. Bill Nichols, 632–49. Berkeley: University of California Press.

Stam, Robert. 1997. *Tropical multiculturalism: A comparative history of race in Brazilian cinema and culture.* Durham: Duke University Press.

Tanaka, Jennifer. 11 June 2000. Roma in Romania: Struggle for self-identification. *Patrin Web Journal. http://www.geocities.com/Paris/5121/rroma.htm.*

Time of the Gypsies. 1989. Emir Kusturica, director. UK/Italy/Yugoslavia.

Tismaneanu, Vladimir. 1994 Fantasies of salvation: Varieties of nationalism in postcommunist Eastern Europe. In *Postcommunist cultural studies,* ed. Michael D. Kennedy, 102–24. Ann Arbor: University of Michigan Press.

Turcsányi, Sándor. 17 July 2000. *Kell a romantika: Romani kris—Cigánytörvény* (We need romanticism: *Romani kris*—Gypsy law). *Amarodrom. http:// www.amarodrom.hu/archívum/98/romani.html.*

Vajda, Róza, and Kende Ágnes. 17 July 2000. *A gázsók minding megtalálják a maguk rossz cigányát* (The Gadjo will always find their own bad gypsy). *Amarodrom. http://www.amarodrom.hu/archívum/98/thomas.html.*

Városlakók (Urbanites). 1997. András Salamon, director. Hungary.

Wolf Man, The. 1941. George Waggner, director. Paramount.

Žižek, Slavoj. 1998. A leftist plea for 'Eurocentrism.' *Critical Inquiry* 24, no. 4: 988–1009.

Žižek, Slavoj, and Dorothea Schuler. 18 August 2000. *Ez van, ezt kell szeretni?* (This is it, we'd better like it?). Trans. Éva Karádi. *Magyar Lettre Internationale* 28. *http://c.3.hu/scripta/scripta0/lettre28/02zizek.htm.*

FIVE

VAMPIRIC DECOLONIZATION:

FANON, "TERRORISM," AND

MUDROOROO'S VAMPIRE TRILOGY

GERRY TURCOTTE

INTRODUCTION

LONG BEFORE THE FACT of Australia was ever confirmed by explorers and car-
tographers it had already been imagined as a grotesque space, a land peopled
by monsters.[1] The idea of its existence was disputed, was even heretical for
a time, and with the advent of the transportation of convicts its darkness
seemed confirmed. The Antipodes was a world of reversals, the dark subcon-
scious of Britain. It was, for all intents and purposes, Gothic *par excellence*,
the dungeon of the world. It is perhaps for this reason that the Gothic as a
mode has been a consistent presence in Australia since European settlement.
Certainly the fact that settlement began in the eighteenth and nineteenth
centuries, during the rise of the Gothic as a sensationalist and resonantly
influential form, contributes to its impact on the literatures of Australia.

There are other reasons for its appeal. It is certainly possible to argue
that the generic qualities of the Gothic mode lend themselves to articulating
the colonial experience inasmuch as each emerges out of a condition of
deracination and uncertainty, of the familiar transposed into unfamiliar space,
and then forcibly "naturalized." It is this very quality which Freud identified
as the condition of the uncanny, where the home becomes unhomely—
where the *heimlich* becomes *unheimlich*—and yet remains sufficiently familiar

to disorient and disempower.[2] All migrations represent a dislocation of sorts, but Australia posed particularly vexing questions for its European immigrants. Nature, it seemed to many, was out of kilter. To cite the familiar clichés: Its trees shed their bark, swans were black rather than white, and the seasons were reversed. And while these features represented a physical perversion, it was widely considered to be metonymic of an attendant spiritual dis/ease. This sense of spiritual malaise is often communicated through the Gothic mode, that is, through a literary form that emphasizes the horror, uncertainty, and desperation of the human experience, and represents the solitariness of that experience through characters trapped in a hostile environment, or pursued by an unspecified or unidentifiable danger. From its inception the Gothic has dealt with fears and themes that are endemic in the colonial experience: isolation, entrapment, fear of pursuit, and fear of the unknown. The Gothic, moreover, is itself a hybrid form—a mode delineated by borrowings and conflations, by fragmentation and incompletion, by a rejection of set values and yet a dependence on establishment. In this sense it is ideal to articulate the colonial condition.

From the beginning, Gothic texts have used "alien" spaces to mark or chart alienation, and to test their protagonists' attitudes, principles, and fears. Where that alien space may once have been, to the English, say, Paris or Transylvania, the New World soon became the ultimate signifier of extreme deprivation. Where once a character may have been taken to the wilds of Italy (for example, Emily in *The Mysteries of Udolpho*), the colonies would become the register for all that was darkest and most obscene. Similarly, the notion of the monstrous would find a ready figure in which to be metaphorized—the Indigenous peoples of the New Worlds—peoples simultaneously primordial and newly discovered; peoples unknown and yet always already imagined and delineated.

For many Australian writers, then, the Gothic offered a useful mechanism through which to speak the New World contradictions. It allowed for a familiar representational gesture—where the unfamiliar could be accounted for through a Gothic style that in part provided a language to speak it. If the Indigenous proved terrifying, then the Gothic could offer a ready-made discursive structure to represent the unrepresentable (or at least to account for the elusiveness of the sign).

If it is true that the Gothic was deemed useful for helping to establish a local Australian voice, it also functioned as a silencing discourse for some, in particular Aboriginal peoples. It is not surprising that Aboriginal writers have tended to avoid the Gothic mode until very recently, since it has generally represented for them a disabling, rather than an enabling, discourse. As has already been suggested, the Aboriginal peoples were themselves constructed as the monstrous figures haunting the Australian landscape, specters more frightening than any European demon, because they represented a physical threat to settlers and to theories of enlightenment that expressed a faith in the indomitable civilizing influence of whiteness.

Concomitantly, Aborigines posed a threat to the very fiction of *terra nullius*, the obscene construction in British law that made Australia "a land owned by no one," and therefore a place that could be claimed for the Crown (a conceit only recently overturned by the Australian High Court through the Native Title Act of 1993, more popularly known as the "Mabo" decision). The Aboriginal presence in itself unsettled—to use the full measure of the pun—the course of Empire.[3] In that respect, colonial policy dictated that Aborigines had to be obliterated or absorbed through assimilation policies. It is strange indeed, given the voraciousness of the European appetite, that it should be the Aborigines who were constructed as savage, monstrous, and insatiable. And yet, it is a feature of master narratives to incorporate that which is feared, by way of addressing, at least in part, something profoundly disturbing to the national psyche. Increasingly, however, racialized writers have begun to utilize the Gothic mode and to deploy its uncanny structures in the service of a decolonization practice. None have done so in a more sustained and explicitly politicized way than Colin Johnson/ Mudrooroo, one of Australia's most prolific and controversial figures. Johnson/ Mudrooroo was born in 1938 in Western Australia. After a troubled youth in which he was removed by Welfare into foster care, and then later imprisoned in Fremantle Gaol, he emerged to become the first published Aboriginal novelist. His novel *Wild Cat Falling* appeared in 1960. Some twenty-eight years later, and as one of Aboriginal Australia's most vocal writers and intellectuals, Johnson chose to change his name to Mudrooroo Narogin in protest of the Australian Bicentennial celebrations. Eventually he would adopt the single monicker, Mudrooroo, a Nyoongah word meaning the paperbark tree.

In 1996, journalist Victoria Laurie published a controversial article asserting that Mudrooroo was in fact not Aboriginal at all, but a child of a white mother and an African American father, facts that have since been debated by numerous Aboriginal and non-Aboriginal scholars. Uncertainty continues to circulate around the level of Mudrooroo's own duplicity in the matter of his identity, the question of Mudrooroo's socialization as an Aboriginal man, and the high esteem many Indigenous scholars still hold for his work despite the current controversy. Perhaps not surprisingly, Mudrooroo himself has refused to comment publicly. His works have been withdrawn from many university subjects, he was forced to leave his position in academe, and has since returned to India where he lived for many years as a Buddhist monk.[4]

In the meantime, his work continues to challenge and trouble, asking questions about hybridity, whiteness, and the complicity of master narratives in the perpetuation of the colonizing enterprise. It will be the task of the remainder of this chapter to examine the way Mudrooroo has turned to the

Gothic mode, in particular via Frantz Fanon's notion of decolonization, vampires, and terrorism, to rewrite and resist oppressive narratives. This study will conclude by gesturing toward the issue of Mudrooroo's identity crisis and the impact of this debate on his theories and work.

MUDROOROO'S VAMPIRES

In an earlier paper on Mudrooroo's tendency toward the Gothic mode, I examined the way Aboriginality itself was figured by master narratives as a macabre construct, a monstrous representation of the other that forever located Indigenous peoples in an antiquated, perverse space that they were never meant to escape. My focus was on the way minority writers have resisted such interpellations into categories of containment, precisely by returning to foundational European narratives and divesting them of meaning (or at least, to produce such a promiscuity of meaning that the fiction of their primacy and cohesiveness was inevitably revealed). Mudrooroo is arguably one of the most challenging writers to do this.[5] A not uncontroversial figure whose prolific output has frequently interrogated canonical structures, Mudrooroo has, both throughout his writing career, but in particular in his most recent trilogy of novels, specifically rewritten established texts of empire, and cannibalized the monstrous images of Indigenous peoples put forward by such texts. Indeed, he has gothicized the very notion of the invasion of Australia, and has referred to the British as *num*—literally ghosts—who haunt Aboriginal land.

In *The Undying, Underground*, and *The Promised Land*—sequels of a sort to his much-praised *Master of the Ghost Dreaming*[6]—Mudrooroo focuses specifically on the notion of vampirism, literally feeding off *Dracula* (among a plethora of intertexts) to comment on the way Indigenous identity, mythology, spirituality, and values have been fed on by European invaders, but also to suggest how Indigenous writers might conceivably bite back.

Mudrooroo devours the vampire legend, but not by way of attempting fictionally to erase the European presence. He is never content to write utopic fantasies that eradicate the political realities that impact on Indigenous communities. Instead, he interweaves the concept of European vampirism with Aboriginal Dreamtime stories and culture in order to comment directly on the very real impact of colonization/ contamination on the Aboriginal people of Australia. For Mudrooroo, vampires and ghosts are textual metaphors, representing colonizing predators, which he uses to transform hegemonic accounts of Indigenous peoples. European narratives, which literally (pre)figured the Indigenous as absent or insubstantial via the notion of *terra nullius*, are in turn potentially refuted by the very existence of his own "ghostly" characters.

If Gillian Beer is correct when she suggests that the "usurpation of space by the immaterial . . . is one of the deepest terrors released by the ghost story" (Beer 1978, 260), then Mudrooroo's spectral imaginings are indeed horror stories of the most potent kind. If they are terrifying, however, it is because they haunt both ways. In Mudrooroo's tales, ghosts are always doubled in function. Certainly they signal the haunting of Indigenous Australia by Whites (or *num*), and they figure the power and spiritual strength of an Indigenous past (another kind of spirit), that will fight on into the future. But they also record the ongoing history of possession and consumption of Aboriginal peoples by the bloodlust of invading forces. In this sense, then, as Graham Huggan has argued, ghosts "are double agents: they are working for the 'other' side" (Huggan 1998, 129).

Ghosts, like vampires, represent the liminal space that separates structured and safe notions of reality from a noumenal, insubstantial realm that shadows and haunts the everyday. They are incarnations of the repressed. Both ghosts and vampires are also simultaneously insubstantial and material—able to disappear at will, to dematerialize, but also to manifest themselves, usually in/through another. In this sense, then, they are also cannibals, incorporating the other. They are literally the past in the present, and frequently, they foretell the future. The "disruptive properties of ghosts" (129) as Huggan puts it, suggest why such vampiric imaginings provide an ideal medium for Mudrooroo's revisionist histories.

In the context of decolonization politics, the vampire who exists between worlds, this specter that threatens the solidity of borders and the reality of a dominant imaginary, has much in common with other potentially destabilizing figures, such as terrorists, counterrevolutionaries, and of course writers (who can be all of these things). Indeed, Mudrooroo brings these beings together through the metaphor of the vampire to suggest a commensurability of experience and purpose.

In order to trace the way that Mudrooroo works through this vampiric figuration, in what I will hereafter refer to as the vampire trilogy, I want to consider one crucial point of entry into the vampiric that establishes a genealogy entirely in keeping with Mudrooroo's revisionist narratives. In other words, rather than locate the vampiric purely within the European frame, I would like to approach this through an important critical influence on Mudrooroo, the writings of Frantz Fanon, and in particular a superb article on Fanon's writings on violence and decolonization written by Samira Kawash.

FANON'S VAMPIRES

Fanon, according to Kawash, identifies two different types of violence that frame the colonial reality:

> [I]nstrumental violence and absolute violence are two ways in which violence emerges into and operates on a reality that is always constituted and conceived discursively. It is characteristic of Fanon's

text that every scene of violence oscillates between these two dis-cursive attractors, the instrumental and the absolute. Instrumental violence in Fanon's text is the violence of revolt and of reversal, the violence whereby the colonized challenge and attempt to upend the domination that has oppressed them. At the same time, another violence (perhaps alongside or unleashed by instrumental acts of violence) emerges as the world-shattering violence of decolonization. Decolonization destroys both colonizer and colonized; in its wake, something altogether different and unknown, a "new humanity" will rise up. (235)

It would be difficult to measure to what extent Mudrooroo is consciously invoking Fanon's specific model of violence in his own works. It is certain, however, that Mudrooroo has read Fanon carefully, and draws extensively on Fanon's work to explicate and contextualize Aboriginal literature. In *Writing from the Fringe* Mudrooroo refers to Fanon's *The Wretched of the Earth*, and to his description of the three levels of development in the literature of a colonized people (Mudrooroo 1990, 29). Mudrooroo speaks scathingly of works produced under the first two models: that is, works designed to show that Indigenous writers have successfully assimilated white forms, and works written from a position outside of Indigenous culture (29), comments that now take on an "uncanny" and ironic feel in terms of the identity questions which now circulate around him (and which I will address later in the chapter).

Mudrooroo is particularly taken with the third level, "the fighting phase in which there is an upsurge in literary production" with books that try to avoid "the encircling majority" and that refuse to "be dark imitations of the metropolitan culture" (Mudrooroo 1990, 29). While it is dangerous to link notions of textual violence with "actual" violence, the metaphoric connec-tion between a textual terrorism and actual decolonization is one drawn by Mudrooroo throughout his creative and academic work. I do not mean by this that Mudrooroo promotes an armed uprising by Aboriginal peoples, but that he insists on recognizing the very real discursive power of colonization and that he celebrates a textual response to hegemonic controls as part of an overall revitalization of Indigenous cultures. In this way, Fanon's model is a useful frame text.

The distinction that Fanon arguably produces between instrumental and absolute violence is reproduced in some measure through the complex structures of Mudrooroo's vampire trilogy, which comes into existence after the milder, more positive *Master of the Ghost Dreaming* where reversals as resistance abound. In the trilogy, a grimmer prognosis emerges, one that focuses on the ends of civilizations—Aboriginal and European. Through the metaphor of the vampire, Mudrooroo invokes the uncanny individual—the person who is both familiar and unfamiliar, both human and inhuman, both individual and communal, both black and white, simultaneously. And it would be possible, given the questioning of Mudrooroo's status as an Aboriginal man, to add Aboriginal/not-Aboriginal to this dichotomous structure. As Gelder and Jacobs have argued, the question of "simultaneity is important to stress since, in Freud's terms, it is not simply the unfamiliar in itself which generates the anxiety of the uncanny; it is specifically the combination of the familiar and unfamiliar—the way the one seems always to inhabit the other" (Gelder 1998, 23). For Mudrooroo, it is precisely this simultaneity that generates terror and uncertainty, both in the divided individual and in the observer, struggling for the simplicity of categories of oneness and containment. Arguably, the vampire as metaphor offers the potential to validate this state of in-betweenness—to signal the potential for action, self-affirmation, even revenge which this position affords.

My argument here locates the vampire (writer) metaphorically as terrorist, but only once Mudrooroo has inverted the traditional vampiric figure. In its initial configuration in *The Undying*, the vampire is European culture, which descends upon and feeds off Indigenous peoples (neatly reversing the cannibalism stereotype). The Indigenous are thus infected, colonized, by the vampiric. Their "revolution"—their resistance either to death or full absorption—potentially marks an instance of reverse colonization. Mudrooroo deploys an Indigenous figure who does unto Europeans what Europeans did onto him. His vampire/ terrorist is both colonized and colonizing. More than this, he suggests the potential for the destruction of the dominant social order—he is the ultimate terrorist.

As Samira Kawash argues,

> [T]errorism is a spectre that haunts the social order and public safety . . . terrorism is ubiquitous and constant. The danger of terrorism, the violence of terrorism, is thus in excess of the effects of any particular "terrorist act." This is what we might call a "spectral violence," the measure of a violence that is never fully materialized, that is always in excess of its apparent material effects. . . . (Kawash 1999, 238)[7]

In this sense then, as Kawash goes on to argue, "[t]he terrorist is . . . structurally similar to the ghosts and vampires of the Victorian imagination, exemplary figures of the Freudian uncanny" (238–39).

As has been argued elsewhere, Freud's theorization of the uncanny is particularly useful for understanding colonial encounters with "new" worlds and with Indigenous peoples.[8] Indeed, the colonial enterprise frequently combines a discursive construction of an alien space as familiar, a figuration that is constantly ruptured by instances that contradict the fiction of familiarity. Hence, the homely repeatedly becomes unhomely—the secure becomes insecure.

According to Kawash, Lacan uses Freud's theory to understand/underline the way the uncanny can be a "disturbance to the bordering functions that separate inside and outside." Mladen Dolar, discussing Lacan's notion of *extimité*, argues that the "extimate is simultaneously the intimate kernel and the foreign body," itself an exemplary analogy for the figure of the vampire (qtd. in Kawash 1999, 239). For Mudrooroo, the experience of invasion, of contamination, produces precisely this horrific in-betweenness for his Indigenous vampire, as he becomes both Indigenous and non-Indigenous simultaneously. It is a particularly poignant rendering of the Indigenous figure between worlds who is a threat to both the European and his own people.[9] And it is a human category crisis made agonizingly complex in the context of Mudrooroo's own identity crisis, and debates about his "belonging."

In his very genetic composition, the in-between figure promises to impale/empale his own people—while simultaneously threatening the putatively inviolate category of whiteness. More to the point, what Mudrooroo's clever refigurations demonstrate is that the very idea of an isolated and pure whiteness has always been an impossibility—a pigment of the white imagination. If Kawash is correct in maintaining that, for Fanon, "on the other side" of the irruption of absolute violence is the "possibility of a 'new humanity' " (240), then it is possible to read Mudrooroo's strangely (and initially) upbeat, and undeniably "contaminated" figure, in a similarly "positive" sense, as suggesting a new world order, and another way forward. For Kawash, this new order is understandable via structures that avoid metaphors of "progress" (themselves offensive figurations frequently applied to Indigenous lives by imperial forces), and instead present "not a transition to the future, but rather a 'leap into the open air of history' " (240).

Mudrooroo follows Fanon quite closely in writing out a discursive model of decolonization. If, as Fanon suggests, "it is the settler who has brought the native into existence and who perpetuates his existence," and similarly, if "the settler owes the fact of his very existence . . . to the colonial system" (Fanon 1952, 36), it is possible to see the female vampire Amelia (who first appears in *The Undying*) as acting out this relationship. What begins as mere reversal of dreamings in *Ghost* becomes in the later trilogy an attempt to explode the relationship entirely. For Fanon, decolonization will produce a new type of being, one removed from the cultural instrumentalities of the colonialist project. The solution to Amelia's infection of George, which contaminates his Aboriginal Dreaming, is not to seek some pre-contact, and hence resistant, antiquity. Instead, it is to become something other—something that cannot be contained by discursive structures established by, and hence arguably in the service of, colonialism.

It seems to me that this notion of something other, figured via the vampiric, may have emerged as a result of Mudrooroo's reading of Fanon, even though, as we learn in *The Mudrooroo/Müller Project*, Mudrooroo was at one stage in his life steeped in Victorian Gothic novels.[10] While Mudrooroo's vampire trilogy may operate on one level as a rewriting, even a satire, of eighteenth- and nineteenth-century Gothic fiction, to read it as merely a reversal is to miss its radical commentary on discursive decolonization, a narrative that owes much to Fanon. For Fanon, the notion of decolonization "is not the violence of the colonized that threatens bodies or properties; decolonization is rather the excessive violence that threatens reality as a whole. While the violence of reversal can be identified in terms of its material manifestations, the absolute violence of decolonization can only be 'symbolic violence,' violence that threatens the symbolic order, violence that bursts through history" (Kawash 1999, 243). Decolonization potentially disrupts the very boundaries between the real and the unreal, the historical and the ahistorical. Perhaps this is why Mudrooroo insists on speaking of a Maban reality, an alternate reality that cannot be contained by traditional humanist constructs of the real. As he puts it,

> [M]aban reality is political in that it seeks to establish an Indigenous reality which is counter to the dominant natural reality of the invaders, a so-called natural reality which permeates just about every genre of endeavour and constructs narratives such as history which serve to establish and maintain nothing but the dominant position of those in power. . . . What this means is that any ways of constructing an alternative history are driven from the "real" and into the fictional or into fantasy or into the dark areas of occultism. (Mudrooroo 1997, 100)

His brutal initial attacks on Sally Morgan can be read according to this explanation. For Mudrooroo, Morgan's My Place was weak precisely because it "did not shout" at its white readership; in fact, he felt it "mirrored their concerns as to their place in Australia" (Mudrooroo 1997, 195). Where the text was strong was in its "Gothic" elements, where it embraced "a different reality" (93). For Mudrooroo, the vampire is appealing: he or she has no reflection; he or she cannot be reflected, and hence cannot reflect—cannot mirror—the concerns of the dominant classes. And it foregrounds invader anxieties about their own (il)legitimate belonging.

The vampire, in my reading of Mudrooroo, is a nonrepresentational figure, just as it was for Fanon. As Kawash has argued, the spectral figure that haunts Fanon's The Wretched of the Earth

> is a vampire, dreamed up by one of his patients who fears the vampire's predations. . . . The terror of the vampire marks the violence of "deposing," a violence that cannot be represented within the normal modes of representation but which nonetheless signals a dangerous gap in reality, that is to say, a gap dangerous to the continuing existence of colonial reality. (Kawash 1999, 245)

What is particularly fascinating in this account of Fanon's vampires is the way Mudrooroo, deliberately or otherwise, has produced a series of texts that initially enact Fanon's more radical theorizations on decolonization. Fanon's influential studies describe the way colonial subjects are made "archaic," fixed, by a colonial history that insists that the colonized object be read as part of the landscape, as therefore inhuman, and thus as nonexistent. It is this existential crisis that marks the colonized as the "living dead," but it is an existence that possesses the settler as well, who is "haunted by the persistence of the native as living being . . . who nonetheless cannot appear as such. The 'empty' landscape perceived by the colonizer is shadowed by an uncanny double, a landscape traversed by the 'non-existent' colonized" (Kawash 1999, 253). Again, for those familiar with the construction of Australia as *terra nullius*, this (dis)figuration becomes particularly haunting. For Mudrooroo, the parallels are clear. Indigenous Australians have been made insubstantial—ghosts haunting their own land—by invader discourses.[11]

It is not surprising then that Mudrooroo would turn to the ambiguous figure of the vampire to represent the state of Indigeneity in Australia today. Indeed, he must have been moved by one of Fanon's patients who literalized his feelings of existence and nonexistence by claiming that he was haunted by nightmares of a vampire that sucked him dry. As Fanon writes, "[T]he patient talked of his blood being spilt. . . . He implored us to stop the haemorrhage and not to let him be 'sucked by a vampire' within the very precincts of the hospital" (Fanon 1963, 210). As Kawash argues: "[T]he distinctiveness of this patient's fantasy must not be overlooked" (Kawash 1999, 247). The fact that the nightmare is represented as a vampire "becomes the effect of a reality that simultaneously denies, defines, and contains the colonized . . . the corresponding name for its corporeal manifestation might be *living death*" (247).

For Mudrooroo, as for Fanon, the vampire is an ambiguous register since it is neither one thing nor another. It stands between. Like Plato's Pharmakon, it is both infection and cure. Mudrooroo mobilizes first the figure of a female vampire, Amelia, herself a "contaminated" rendition of the figure of Elisa Fraser,[12] and then the central Aboriginal character George, who is "infected" by Amelia's bite. It is interesting to note that in Fanon's study, the vampire that haunts his patient is also figured as female, "a settler woman whom the patient himself has killed" (Kawash 1999, 248). The vampire is a metaphor for the invading colonial power, and for the "fate" of the Indigenous colonized. But it is also more than this. The vampire—and this is true of Mudrooroo's vampire George—is a sign of the incompleteness of the colonial paradigm. As Kawash puts it:

> Where the colonial system claims to be "all," the persistence of the vampire exposes this "all" to something else, a being neither living (as the colonizer) nor dead (as the landscape or the colonized bodies

filling that landscape). The vampire marks the "not-all" of colonial reality. (249–50)

Kawash goes on to argue that the figure of the vampire produces the most terrifying threat to colonial stability: "The vampire is an inextricable element of the relation that brings settler and native into being. It is in this sense that we might conclude that the vampire terrorizes reality; the vampire is a terrorist" (254).

Mudrooroo's vampiric inversion can best be understood through this sequence of theorizations on vampirism. His vampire trilogy demonstrates a passion for revising European narratives, and for exposing the heinous practices of colonizing discourses. These are satirized in a range of ways. In *Underground* Mudrooroo replicates the offensive practice of the British invaders of naming the Indigenous people they encountered with Greek and Roman names, so that one of the characters, for example, is known as Hercules. He retells well-known foundational narratives, such as the Eliza Fraser story, or popular fictions, such as *Dracula*, in order to cannibalize and divest these stories of meaning. *The Promised Land* begins in England with the slightly pornographic rendering of the story of Lucy and Mina (literalizing the account that Stoker could only hint at), which is then realigned with the early George Augustus Robinson narrative, and a return of the soft-porn figure of Amelia.

But what is equally of interest is the way Mudrooroo mobilizes the figure of George to haunt the landscape, to terrorize non-Maban reality. The main character in the latest trilogy is a young Aboriginal man who is bitten by a European female vampire, and the result of this bite is to make him an in-between figure—a man of mixed blood—neither in one world nor the other. Throughout the texts George struggles, in fact, between competing dreamings, Aboriginal and European. It is a poignant metaphor for the figure of many Aborigines in Australia. Given the recent scandals about Mudrooroo's heritage, and claims that he is part African American rather than part Aboriginal, moreover, the notion of blurred bloodlines takes on a particular importance.

Perhaps this is why Mudrooroo's narratives about colonized spaces are filled with doppelgängers. There are two Georges who haunt the vampire trilogy, both impostors of sorts, neither one thing nor another. There is the "mixed-blood" George, and the British George Augustus Robinson. Mudrooroo's oeuvre is itself haunted by this latter figure. As Maureen Clark has pointed out, Robinson becomes the specter that Mudrooroo is least able to exorcise. He first appears as the bloodless parole officer in *Wild Cat Falling*, and he resurfaces in *Dr Wooreddy*, in *Master of the Ghost Dreaming,* and throughout the vampire trilogy itself.[13] Indeed, we discover in *Underground* that he is George's real father—the absent, ever-present father. In one sense, they are one and the same, of course, although entirely different beings as well—simultaneously. The vampire George is both the colonized and the colonizer, just as he is both prey and hunter, the site of the brutalized and the brutalizing. He is, in this sense, a quintessential vampire who bears always the marks of his/her maker, and what he/she was before. But he is also both and neither.

For Clark, the haunting represented by the figure of Robinson is a signal of a potentially insidious and deliberate act of imposture on Mudrooroo's behalf, a gesture of impersonation that he may well have been engaged in since the time of his first publication. However Mudrooroo's fraught identity is read, the vampire trilogy offers a remarkable opportunity for Mudrooroo to script yet another potential space for himself to inhabit, via the figure of the vampire hybrid, the model of undecidability and disruption. The vampire is always already both original (the person prior to infection) and unoriginal (the infected)—an embodiment perhaps of the very questionability of authenticity debates that seek an origin for a source that cannot be traced.[14]

Mudrooroo, in the course of numerous contradictory (and perhaps demonstrably false) public statements about his heritage,[15] has assumed a vampiric persona, at the same time, ironically, as he gradually rejects the hybridized figure as an empowered symbol of Aboriginal agency. He has remained "intact," in a certain sense, but has maintained this cohesion through remarkable destabilizations, becoming a range of characters, foregrounding his hybridization by way of disrupting any possibility of stable, containable identity narratives. In terms of minority discourse, Mudrooroo's racialized— if not Aboriginal—identity (he remains "a subject created by racism")[16] refutes and refuses the "containability narratives" that dominant culture so often insists on, imposes, and of course produces. Similarly, in his texts (of which he himself is one),[17] there is a continual rewriting at work which resists stability in all its forms; hence the wildcat trilogy and the *Master of the Ghost Dreaming* quartet (which itself continues and rewrites the earlier *Dr Wooreddy*).[18] His novels rephrase, contradict, and resist each other and any facile critical containment that would attend them. As Wendy Pearson puts it, "[E]ach novel in the *Master of the Ghost Dreaming* series reinvents itself, disrupting the possibility of a singular linear reading and suggesting a variety of potential modes of hybridized Aboriginality which can be read against each novel's reiterated yet individual response and resistance to discourses of authenticity" (199).[19]

CONCLUSION

How Mudrooroo's oeuvre will be judged in the future remains to be seen. The assertions that Mudrooroo is not Aboriginal will no doubt heavily impact on the weight given to his works as "Aboriginal," though of course they will always speak as hybrid texts—works by a person of color—about decolonization politics. However he is judged on the question of imposture and performativity—and despite calls by some Aboriginal groups to have his books destroyed[20]—Mudrooroo's texts will remain powerful figurations of the dilemma of hybridity in the context of the fiction of cohesive nationalist identity formations. His writings, for all their misogynistic, judgmental and angry inflections, speak more pointedly about the violence of colonization than virtually any other contemporary Australian text. And the power of these texts is located precisely in the way Mudrooroo deploys the Gothic mode, to turn it against its traditional range and values, and yet also to enact the mode's own wonderfully promiscuous changeability. As Pearson asks, is the master of the ghost dreaming "on an extratextual level, a reference to Mudrooroo himself, who has mastered the European art of the novel in order to tell precisely those stories which have been suppressed, ignored or appropriated by non-Aboriginal writers (exactly the position to which Mudrooroo ironically finds himself condemned)?" (200).

Mudrooroo's work has always probed the impossibility (the undesirability) of reconciliative narratives, insisting on the need not to compromise, which he sees as a type of relinquishment. As Pearson puts it, "The possibility of reconciliation hinges on the larger resolution of society's desperate commitment to the very ideological binarisms that the immortal figure itself brings into question" (200). Mudrooroo's turn to the vampire as a symbol of the unquashable, forever unresolvable, nature of the postcolonial hybrid, is a powerful and poignant gesture of both resistance and self-awareness. The figure of the African Wadawaka may well become increasingly dominant and important in the trilogy; and in *The Promised Land* Mudrooroo appears to deliver a harsh blow against Aboriginal agency, with the vampire figure, George, reduced to a lapdog for most of the novel. One could certainly read this last gesture as Mudrooroo's impassioned and angry response to what he no doubt feels is his abandonment by Aboriginal Australia. But despite these revisions, the figure of the vampire in the "contaminated world" of the trilogy mobilizes a fragile, contradictory space into which Mudrooroo's oeuvre might exist, and a space perhaps for his own controversial self to operate within—a space that is never fixed, always fluid, and unrepentantly hybrid. Again, whatever judgment is eventually brought to bear on the "validity" and "authenticity" of his works, there can be no question that this reinvention is a masterful stroke, a work of amazing sang froid, and surely still a work in progress.

NOTES

1. This chapter is part of a larger research project on the Gothic and minority discourses. It emerges in part from a long-standing study of the Gothic in Australia. The introduction appeared as Turcotte, "Australian," 10–19. The present chapter focuses on Mudrooroo's use of vampirism, and his debt to Fanon. For a more sustained reading of his use of the Gothic in *The Undying*, see Turcotte, "Mudrooroo's," 111–22. I'm grateful to my many students in my Fantasy & Popular Fiction subject for

long-ranging discussions of Mudrooroo's Gothic fiction, and in particular to two of my PhD students, Maureen Clark and Wendy Pearson, for their insightful work on Mudrooroo, referred to elsewhere in this paper.

2. See Freud, 368–407. The idea of the uncanny as a mechanism for understanding colonial and postcolonial structures has been addressed in a number of studies. It was a major focus of my doctoral thesis, *Peripheral Fear: Australian and Canadian Gothic Fiction* (University of Sydney) in 1991. This idea was further examined in a series of articles exploring the Gothic in nineteenth- and twentieth-century Australian literature. See Turcotte "Speaking"; "Footnotes"; and "Dark." It was also a focus of "The Gothic in Australia," a thirty-five-minute radio feature for ABC Radio's *Books and Writing*, 24 July 1992. More recently, Ken Gelder and Jane Jacobs have developed this idea in an excellent study on "sacredness and identity in a postcolonial nation." See Gelder and Jacobs.

3. For more extended readings of this particular issue see Penny van Toorn, 87–97. See also Gelder and Jacobs. As they put it: "Freud's 'uncanny' might well be applied directly to those emergent . . . procedures for determining rights over land. In this moment of decolonisation, what is 'ours' is also potentially, or even always already, 'theirs': the one is becoming the other, the familiar is becoming strange" (23).

4. For a detailed account of this story see Clark, 48–62. See also Laurie, "Identity" for the original article that started the more public debate.

5. See Turcotte, "Mudrooroo's," 333–46. For an extended version of the article see Turcotte, "Re-mastering."

6. See Mudrooroo, *Undying; Underground; The Promised Land;* and *Master.*

7. It seems almost pointless to add that this model has been given a particular clarity for Western audiences by the events of September 11, 2001.

8. See Turcotte, "Australian" and Gelder and Jacobs.

9. For my analysis of collaborations between Indigenous and non-Indigenous writers in *The Mudrooroo/Müller Project* and *The Book of Jessica,* and the way these issues of "double agency" are negotiated, see Turcotte, "Collaborating."

10. See Mudrooroo, "Aboriginalising," 22.

11. See Gelder and Jacobs, 135–36.

12. For my reading of the Eliza Fraser/Amelia Fraser figure see Turcotte, "Re-mastering" and "Mudrooroo's." For a more general account of the Eliza Fraser myth, see Schaffer; and Turcotte, "Fraser's."

13. See Clark, 48–62 for a detailed discussion of Mudrooroo's use of G. A. Robinson.

14. Many critics will no doubt argue, however, that this clever metaphorization is merely self-serving, a disingenuous gesture by which Mudrooroo can attempt to avoid being "judged" for his arguable duplicity. See Clark on this issue of accountability, and also Mudrooroo's defenders, such as Fischer and Shoemaker. For a general, and recent, discussion of authenticity issues see Huggan, *Postcolonial,* although interestingly, Huggan discusses Mudrooroo's views of Morgan yet chooses not to engage in the identity issues surrounding Mudrooroo himself.

15. See Clark for details regarding such comments.

16. See Goldie, 107.

17. Although perhaps, initially, not of his own making. He speaks, for example, of having been "textualized" by Mark Durack. See Mudrooroo, "Tell."

18. See Mudrooroo, *Doctor.*

19. See Pearson.

20. See, for example, Robert Eddington's insistence that Mudrooroo's works be "mashed," in Jopson, 5.

REFERENCES

Beer, Gillian. 1978. Ghosts. *Essays in Criticism* 28, no. 3: 259–64.

Clark, Maureen. 2001. Unmasking Mudrooroo. *Kunapipi: Journal of Post-Colonial Writing* 23, no. 2: 48–62.

Fanon, Frantz. 1967(1952). *Black skin white masks.* Trans. Charles Lam Markmann. New York: Grove Weidenfeld.

———. 1963. *The wretched of the Earth.* Pref. Jean-Paul Sartre. Trans. Constance Farrington. New York: Grove.

Fischer, Gerhard. 2000. Mis-taken identity: Mudrooroo and Gordon Matthews. In *Race, colour, and identity in Australia and New Zealand,* ed. John Docker and Gerhard Fischer, 95–112. Sydney: New South Wales University Press.

———, ed. 1993. *The Mudrooroo/Müller project: A theatrical casebook.* Sydney: New South Wales University Press.

Freud, Sigmund. 1956. (1917). The uncanny. In *Collected papers: Papers on metapsychology, papers on applied psycho-analysis,* Vol. 4, trans. Joan Rivière, 368–407. London: Hogarth.

Gelder, Ken. 1994. *Reading the vampire.* London: Routledge.

Gelder, Ken, and Jane M. Jacobs. 1998. *Uncanny Australia: Sacredness and identity in a postcolonial nation.* Melbourne: Melbourne University Press.

Goldie, Terry. Who is Mudrooroo? In *Compr(om)ising post/colonialisms: Challenging narratives and practices,* ed. Ratcliffe and Turcotte, 105–13. Sydney: Dangaroo.

Huggan, Graham. 2001. *The post-colonial exotic: Marketing the margins.* London: Routledge.

———. 1998. Ghost stories, bone flutes, cannibal countermemory. In *Cannibalism and the colonial world,* ed. Francis Barker, Peter Hulme, and Margaret Iversen, 126–41. Cambridge: Cambridge University Press.

Jopson, Debra. 1997. Destroy books: black group. *Sydney Morning Herald.* 25 March 1997, 5.

Kawash, Samira. 1999. "Terrorists and vampires: Fanon's spectral violence of decolonization. In *Frantz Fanon: Critical perspectives,* ed. Anthony C. Alessandrini, 235–57. London: Routledge.

Laurie, Victoria. 1996. Identity crisis. *The Australian Magazine.* 20–21 July 1996, 28–32.

Mudrooroo. 2000. *The promised land.* Sydney: Angus and Robertson.

———. 1999. *Underground.* Sydney: Angus and Robertson.

———. 1998. *The undying.* Sydney: Angus and Robertson.

———. 1997. *Milli Milli Wangka: The indigenous literature of Australia.* Melbourne: Hyland House.

———. 1997. Tell them you're Indian. In *Race matters,* ed. Gillian Cowlishaw and Barry Morris, 259–68. Canberra: Aboriginal Studies Press.

———. The Aboriginalising of Heiner Müller. In Fischer 19–31.

———. 1991. *Master of the ghost dreaming.* Sydney: Angus and Robertson.

———. 1990. *Writing from the fringe: A study of modern Aboriginal literature.* Melbourne: Hyland House.

————. 1983. *Doctor Wooreddy's prescription for enduring the ending of the world.* Melbourne: Hyland House.

Oboe, Annalisa, ed. 2003. *Mongrel signatures: Reflections on the work of Mudrooroo.* Amsterdam: Rodopi.

Pearson, Wendy. "I, the undying": The vampire of subjectivity and the Aboriginal "I" in Mudrooroo's The undying. In *Mongrel signatures,* ed. Annalisa Oboe, 185–202. Amsterdam: Rodopi.

Ratcliffe, Greg, and Gerry Turcotte, eds. 2001. *Compr(om)ising postcolonialisms: Challenging narratives and practices.* Sydney: Dangaroo.

Schaffer, Kay. 1995. *In the wake of first contact: The Eliza Fraser stories.* Melbourne: Cambridge University Press.

Shoemaker, Adam. Mudrooroo and the shackle of authenticity. In *Mongrel signatures,* ed. Annalisa Oboe. Amsterdam: Rodopi.

————. 1993. *Mudrooroo: A critical study.* Sydney: Angus and Robertson.

Turcotte, Gerry. Re-mastering the ghosts: Mudrooroo and gothic refigurations. In *Mongrel signatures,* ed. Annalisa Oboe, 129–51. Amsterdam: Rodopi.

————. 2002. Mudrooroo's gothic inter/mission statement. In *Missions of interdependence: A literary directory,* ed. Gerhard Stilz, 333–46. Amsterdam: Rodopi.

————. 2001. Collaborating with ghosts: Dis/possession in the book of Jessica and the Mudrooroo/Müller project. In *Siting the other: Re-visions of marginality in Australian and English-Canadian drama,* ed. Marc Maufort and Franca Bellarsi, 175–92. Amsterdam: Rodopi.

————. 1998. Australian gothic. *A handbook to gothic literature,* ed. Marie Mulvey Roberts, 10–19. London: Macmillan.

————. 1996. Mrs Fraser's ravenous appetite: The taste for cannibalism in captivity narratives. In *Crossing the lines: Formations of Australian culture,* ed. C. Guerin, P. Butterss and A. Nettlebeck, 165–74. Adelaide: Association for the Study of Australian Literature.

————. Footnotes to an Australian gothic script: The gothic in Australia. *Antipodes* 7, no. 2 (December 1993): 127–34.

————. How dark is my valley? Canadian and Australian gothic. *Scarp* 22 (May 1993): 26–32.

————. The gothic in Australia. 35-minute feature for ABC Radio. *Books and Writing.* 24 July 1992.

————. 1992–93. "Speaking the formula of abjection": Hybrids and gothic discourses in Louis Nowra's novels. *Westerly* 3 (September 1991): 102–13.

Van Toorn, Penny. The terrors of *Terra Nullius*: Gothicising and de-gothicising aboriginality. *World Literature Written in English* 32, no. 2 and 33, no. 1: 87–97.

SIX

"WHITE TALK":

WHITE SOUTH AFRICANS AND THE

MANAGEMENT OF DIASPORIC WHITENESS

MELISSA STEYN

IN THE EXTREMITY of its intergroup dynamics, South Africa has always been instructive to those with an international perspective on the issue of inter-racial and intercultural relations.[1] The history of settlement and conquest and the subsequent cultural stratification within the society bears similarities to most of the territories that were part of Europe's expansion across the globe. Yet in its particularities, the South African "mix," governed by en-trenched minority white supremacy, was notorious across the globe as epito-mizing racial oppression and segregationist extremism.

Since April 1994, with the first democratic election, the country has been rearticulating its intergroup relations through a process of reconcilia-tion and nation building. This process inevitably involves a substantial reframing of social identities, among other complex collective psychological adjustments being made by all the groups within the country.

How white South Africans are negotiating this adjustment makes for fascinating research. The buttresses that held white identity in place in the old South Africa have collapsed, and new frames of understanding have to be found. The political and social pressures within the country militate against "whiteness," and push to deconstruct the taken-for-granted privileges of being at the center of power. Here again, there are both parallels and divergences from whiteness in contexts such as Euro-America, where whiteness is also

119

being challenged, but not with the same intensity, and where many of the assumptions of whiteness remain unthreatened.

This chapter discusses the particularities of a whiteness that can be called diasporic whiteness. It explores an interesting intersection between what are usually theorized as two diametrically opposed identity positionalities: the "center" of mainstream racial identity construction, whiteness, and its relationally marginalized counterpart, diaspora. The context, then, provides an interesting example of how multiple, and even conflicting, aspects of identity compete for our single bodies.[2] The chapter introduces a discursive repertoire that I call "White Talk." This is a set of discursive practices that attempts to manage the intersectional positionality of white South Africans to their greatest advantage, given the changes in their position within the society.

WHITENESS: AT THE CENTER

A growing body of literature that has come to be known as "whiteness studies" or "white studies" dedicates itself to subverting the power of whiteness. The first work in the field emerged in the early 1990s. Since then, it has taken the academic world by storm. Fishkin ascribes the credit for having put whiteness on the academic agenda to Toni Morrison's *Playing in the Dark: Whiteness and the Literary Imagination.*[3] Morrison points out the asymmetry in how the impact of racism is portrayed in American literature: while African Americans are depicted as "different" as a consequence of being racialized, the effects on the psyches of those who perpetuate racism are never exposed. They are simply seen as "normal." Subsequent to this groundbreaking work, there has been a deluge of literature examining the construction of whiteness from a broad range of disciplines. The last two years have seen the advent of "readers," such as *Critical White Studies* by Richard Delgado, and *Off White* by Michelle Fine, which indicates that a field has "arrived"; enough has been written for certain works to have become staple fare for graduate reading.

Taking whiteness as an object of study is seen as a critical move in race studies. It involves redirecting the academic gaze: from "racism," the way in which the center constructs the margins, to the way in which the center constructs itself. Dyer explains how concentrating on the racialization of the margins has functioned to keep attention fixed on "others" as the problem needing explanation, and needing to come in line with the center. The center, by this dynamic, constructs itself as the norm, the still, unproblematic point of reference:

> Looking with such passion and single-mindedness at non-dominant groups has had the effect of reproducing the sense of the oddness, differentness, exceptionality of these groups, the feeling that they are departures from the norm. Meanwhile the norm has carried on

as if it is the natural, inevitable, ordinary way of being human.
(Dyer 1988, 44)

Reframing the racial problem in terms of whiteness has been a very
powerful critical move. An analogous strategy has occurred in some feminist
studies. In *The Man Question*, Kathy Ferguson shifts attention away from the
way in which women have been socialized to the construction of masculinity
as the issue that needs explanation. Yet another example of how critical
scholars are increasingly interrogating the norm is Monique Wittig's *The
Straight Mind*, which analyzes how heterosexuality constructs itself to retain
the marginalization of homosexuality.

What, then, is whiteness? I believe it is best understood as an ideologically supported social positionality that has accrued to people of European
descent as a consequence of the economic and political advantage gained
during and subsequent to European colonial expansion. The position was
originally facilitated by the construction of "race," which acted as a marker
of entitlement to this position. The phenotypes, especially skin color, around
which the notion of "race" was organized, acted as a useful means of natu-
ralizing what in fact were political and economic relationships, supporting
the fiction that the inequalities structured into the relationships were the
result of endogenous, probably genetic, inequalities between "races." Whiteness is the shared social space in which the psychological, cultural, political,
and economic dimensions of this privileged positionality are normalized, and
rendered unremarkable.

Viewing whiteness as a social positionality allows for multifaceted study.
Scholars have looked at the strategies that peoples thus positioned have used
to ensure their advantage. Critical race theorists, such as Delgado and Fine,
have done a great deal of this work. Walter Allen has looked at economic and
legal strategies that have systematically advanced "white" interests; Nakayama
and Krizek have used a rhetorical perspective to expose strategies that whites
in the United States of America use to maintain their central position.

Other scholars have examined the ideological underpinnings of whiteness, particularly the intersection of race and class. From a historical perspective, scholars such as David Roediger and Noel Ignatiev have been central to
tracing the historical processes by which the "white" working class population
in the United States was able to insert itself advantageously into the economy,
through identifying as "white," rather than as workers. In her groundbreaking
analysis *White Women, Race Matters*, Ruth Frankenberg makes the important
point that "whiteness" has definite cultural content, in that certain assumptions, belief systems, and value structures tend to characterize the "white"
social space. One area of focus is identity, and the self-(mis)understandings
that develop within, and are constitutive of, "whiteness." An example of this
work is Martin et al., who examine the labels "white" people in the United

States use to self-identify. All the critical work in this field shares the fundamental goal of rendering whiteness visible, thereby pulling its teeth and deny-
ing it the capacity to distort societies without detection.

Of course, the world of whiteness is far from homogenous. Interesting
studies seek to particularize groupings and positionalities within this broad
social category. For example, Bonnett's work on whiteness in Europe particularizes whiteness in contexts other than the United States. Wray and
Newitz have looked at the particular position of poor whites, who are
marginalized from mainstream whiteness. Vron Ware and Frankenberg have
looked at ambivalences in the way white women are positioned. An important trend in recent work is the attempt to theorize ways in which a
resistant, rearticulated whiteness can be a socially useful identity, building
antiracist alliances with people of all groupings who seek to further the
cause of social justice and democracy.[4]

The particular historical and political configuration in South Africa
has meant that whites have never experienced their whiteness and the advantage it afforded them as invisible—one of the key components in the way
whiteness is theorized in the metropolitan heart of whiteness. Throughout
the apartheid era white South Africans knew they were racialized, and some
of their earliest memories recount differences in how they were positioned
relative to "others."[5] What *was* taken for granted, however, was the "naturalness" of being thus privileged. White South Africans held on to many of
the colonial assumptions that helped to underwrite the social construction of
whiteness with particular tenacity. Perhaps one reason white South Africans
embraced this narrative so ardently is that whiteness here has never been as
secure as in countries where Europe's settlers gained demographic, as well
as political and economic power.

What has happened in South Africa is particularly interesting because
we have seen here a sudden and fairly decisive de-centering of whiteness
within the society, from a position where white advantage was legally entrenched, to where it is actively disciplined. Whites have lost political power.
They largely maintain economic power, and because Western cultures are
held in esteem as the believed key to internationalism, they still hold cultural power. The de-centering of white power is therefore unequal in terms
of social capital; their position is certainly not that of marginalization.

Nevertheless, the pressure within the new society is toward dismantling, and indeed deconstructing, old social relations. In such circumstances,
being "white" is replete with dissonance. Whites need to find new narratives
to explain who they are, what they are doing in Africa, and what their
relationship is to the indigenous people and to the continent. Some of the
narratives attempt to recycle the old "Master Narrative" in such a way that
it may still do the job of preserving privileged positionality, despite the new
dispensation. All of the narratives have to position themselves in relation to
past constructions of whiteness. All of the narratives have to make sense of,

and provide a stance toward, the subjective experience of losing aspects of a highly privileged positionality.[6]

This change in the positioning of South African whiteness sets it apart from whiteness in the centers from which whiteness is generally theorized. It also brings to the fore the diasporic dimension of this particular site of whiteness. The next section therefore briefly turns to the notion of diaspora, in order to chart some of this paradoxical white terrain.

DIASPORA: AT THE MARGINS

Dispersion and migration have always been part of human history (Ahmad 1995; Goldberg, Kotkin 1995) and cultures and nations have always been hybrid (Werbner and Modood 1997; Hall 2000).[7] Yet almost all contemporary diasporas have been brought about by modern colonial and imperial history (with notable exceptions, such as the Jewish and Roman peoples). Edward Said has said that one of the achievements of modern imperialism has been to redistribute populations in such a way that Europe and its "others" now live side by side across the length and breadth of the globe. The West and the rest are irreversibly intertwined; all have been influenced by, and structured into, relations established by European expansion. This is true of the original colonial expansion, but it is also, as postcolonial critics have argued, true of the reverse migration of previously colonized people into the cosmopolitan centers.[8] Whiteness and blackness were co-constructed, so were Europe and its others. There has been a psychological enmeshment between the colonizer and the colonized.[9] Imaginations were shaped within the "dialectics of empire and emancipation" (Nederveen and Parekh 1995, 14). Enmeshment is carried through in the social and political spheres. As O'Callaghan argues, the "others" ceased to exist when European expansion created a world in which the "others" were created (O'Callaghan 1995, 42).

Having said this, however, there is a need to recognize that an important consequence of the way in which the dispersals have been brought about is that they fit into patterns of stratification within a deeply unequal global system. All dispersed people are not in the same relation to the distribution of the globe's assets. Through the modern era, patterns of population diffusion followed the movements of colonial settlers moving outward from the European center. Given the differentials in power, the people thus transplanted were in control of the places where they settled, in charge of the people amongst whom they settled. Usually, however, when we think of diaspora, we think of those who have been dispossessed; those displaced through slavery, through forced, involuntary, limited choice migration: exiles, refugees, migrant workers, those who have had to leave home as a consequence of economic imperatives to make their living in a new environment—trying their hands at small-scale trade, undertaking domestic and farm labor—people who have very little bargaining power in the countries where they end up, and are politically, socially, economically, and culturally vulnerable.

Diaspora, then, has usually been understood to consist of those who are dislocated from their own centers of identification, and usually have very limited power in relation to the centers that impact immediately upon their lives. These are people whose identities are grounded in founding narratives that originate away from the context in which their lives are lived out, but who have enduring ethnic identities, real or ascribed, that link them to those contexts. Diasporic people are bonded though shared structures of feelings, such as their suffering, which gives a sense of being caught up in a common history, despite being scattered.[10] Probably the most salient point usually made in relation to diasporic identity, though, is the prevalence of hybridity—multiple, fluid identities—what Gilroy has called "restless (dis)continuity."

In our contemporary, globalizing times, the flows of diaspora are still stratified, but the picture is probably even more complicated, and cannot be viewed in monological terms. Hall argues that the reconfigured social forces and relations across the globe since World War II have, at the very time of globalization, brought about different and new forms of the local and the multicultural, which emerge

> at many sites, one of the most significant being that planned and unplanned, compelled and so-called "free" migration, which has brought the margins to the centre, the multi-cultural disseminated "particular" to the heart of the metropolitan western city. (Hall, 217)

For example, another layer, perhaps a "middle tier" of diasporic people, are elites from their homelands, such as India and Nigeria, who leave home and become dispersed through choice and opportunity. This "untimely appearance of the margins in the centre" (Hall, 217) consists of global players—skilled professionals, employees of multinational companies, and internationally competitive intellectuals. This is the positionality from which a great deal of postcolonial theory is given voice, a point perhaps not fully acknowledged in the growing body of literature that valorizes hybridity. As Friedman points out, the truly marginalized of this world have no truck with the type of antiessentialist theory coming from this relatively privileged positionality, as it leaves them with less political leverage than more essentialized, primordial identities. Hall emphasizes, however, that even invocations of "traditional" identities in contemporary multicultural context are not

> [a] simple revival of archaic ethnicities, though such elements persist. Older traces are combined with new, emergent, forms of "ethnicity" which are often a product of uneven globalization and failed modernization. (Hall, 214)

The attribute of hybridity suggested in the above quotation is usually theorized as integral to the diasporic condition. As a social concept, the notion of hybridity has undergone a sea change as the postcolonial ethos has reworked the terrain of colonial knowledge systems. Earlier, the colonial imagination, as Young has shown, was preoccupied with notions of degrees of "falling away" from the "pure" white norm. The hybrid was associated with all the negative consequences of transgression of racial boundaries. The abomination of the hybrid could act a disciplinary strategy for maintaining the purity of the in-group. Increasingly, however, in the time of the "posts," the notion has gained status as a signifier which is paradoxically "celebrated as powerfully disruptive and yet theorized as commonplace and pervasive" (Werbner 1997, 1). This paradox is perhaps not as contradictory as it seems; both of these rhetorical strategies can fit into a progressive, antiessentialist agenda. On the one hand, to disrupt the oppressive effects of essentialism requires recognizing the logical and psychological impossibility of the notion of purity where it is not readily discerned, just as acknowledging the genetic variation within racial groups disrupts the notion of homogenous racial groupings. These are the *reductio ad absurdum* counters to arguments for distinct, bounded, homogenous social groupings—racial, ethnic, cultural, or other. On the other hand, celebrating the hybrid where it *is* easily recognized is to applaud and encourage the disruptive, the transgressive, and to turn conventional racist discourse upside down. The theorization of diaspora as a troubling, resistant, and interruptive presence, exerting its influence from the margins, generally fits into the latter category. By this turn in the "post" literatures, diaspora has become a liberatory position, unseating the centers of power.

What is important for the argument of this chapter, however, is that while diasporas are not uniformly dispossessed, nor are they necessarily the wellspring of emanicipatory energy some postmodern theorists would have us believe.[11] Those who have a leg in two different continents can be privileged in one context, and marginalized in another. The identity politics of dispersed groups can hinge on maximizing their positions by playing these dimensions off against each other. White South Africans occupy such an uneven positionality. While decentered in the local context, their whiteness links them to the centers of international power: economically, culturally, politically, socially. The next section of the chapter explores this positionality more closely, arguing that it is a source of some quite diehard social behavior.

DIASPORIC WHITENESS: DISRUPTING THE DICHOTOMIES?

White South Africans inhabit a complicated, intersectional positionality, which can be traced back to the formation of modern South Africa within the history of colonial conquest. O'Callaghan indicates that settler societies differed from earlier movements of people:

European settlers remained part of the former exporting country both in terms of tracing ancestry and of being brokers in the extraction and exportation of surplus. (O'Callaghan, 26)

In the South African context this meant that a sense of identification with others "like them" in heritage was maintained, and also a strong economic bond with the West was cultivated, operating from a dominant position within the local context. These connections became part of the mechanisms of control over the disenfranchised African majority. As "brokers" for the Western capitalist project, white South Africans were able to maintain an excellent first world lifestyle and see that as the "norm": white people elsewhere formed the reference group in comparison with whom they set their expectations.

Since the change of government, however, white South Africans have a more ambivalent relationship to the power of the state and, through the enfranchisement of the majority African population and the establishment of constitutional rights that guarantee dignity, freedom, and equality to all citizens, a dramatically different relationship to those whose labor they previously exploited. More acutely than ever before, then, they confront the diasporic dimension in their positionality: a small minority in the country, separated from their cultural heartlands, their whiteness seems genuinely at risk.

Positioned at the intersections of the African and the European, South African whiteness has the quality of shifting layeredness that is so characteristic of diaspora. Part of this is manifested in what Werbner has called the "reaching out to the valued other." White South Africans draw toward white people elsewhere: "home" is where other whites are. In typically diasporic manner whiteness in South Africa retains and nurtures a sense of its bonds with the centers of whiteness, such as Euro-America and Australasia. Moreover, the characteristic groundedness in shared sentiments is apparent. It is not suffering, as in the case of the many other diasporic peoples, that bonds these people to whites elsewhere. Rather, Eurocentric expectations of privilege relative to "others," which comes to be experienced as the norm, forms the common, uniting structure of feelings.

As a dispersed, but privileged, grouping, this diasporic experience is qualitatively different from that of diasporic peoples who are oppressed by colonial, imperial and neocolonial dynamics. One main difference lies in the degree of choice available to white South Africans. They may move internationally with relative ease, through business and leisure travel; they may relocate. They have a great deal of choice in claiming a symbolic ethnicity, to use Waters's term: just how much "Africanness" or "Europeanness" they wish to take on, is a matter of their own taste. To a large extent they control the symbolic resources of the country, and can still dominate the flow of discursive influences that define how issues are interpreted. This is hybridity very much on their own terms: white South Africans can invoke, or deny, the tensions of living at the intersections at will.

Both the vulnerabilities and the strengths of being thus situated are managed by "White Talk." "White Talk's" main function is to manipulate the contradictions of diasporic whiteness, in order to maximize the advantage of whites in the new South Africa. "White Talk" holds in tension the privileges that usually accompany mainstream racial identity, with the displacement and de-centeredness of a diasporic people. It plays this field so as to obscure what is disadvantageous to reveal, and to display what is disadvantageous to conceal. These discursive strategies are "white" in that they are concerned with preserving privilege, with maintaining, as far as possible, the status quo inherited from the era of institutionalized unequal power distribution, and with slowing down the rate of change toward a more substantively democratic, multicultural society within the country. These discourses are "white," moreover, in that they preserve this centered position through employing exclusionary tactics and strategies, and in that they are structured in negative sentiment toward the "other." Yet, through the shift in power in the immediate context, "White Talk" has to deal with enormous emotional dissonance. It carries the emotional load of whiteness evicted from paradise, whiteness on the edge, of being off-center in a manner that runs counter to the entire premise on which whiteness is based.

In the next section, I outline some characteristics of "White Talk." The list by no means exhaustively delineates the discursive strategies employed to manage this positionality. Nor is the intention to imply that all white South Africans speak only in "white talk." Nevertheless, this is a pervasive discursive repertoire, which shapes, and is shaped by, diasporic whiteness in this context.

"WHITE TALK": SOME CHARACTERISTICS

"WHITE TALK" ADOPTS A STRATEGIC ANTIESSENTIALISM

To create its hybridity South African whiteness appropriates Africanness expediently. This borrowing is careful nevertheless to leave its real power centers intact. It presents itself as open to mixing and matching cultural repertoires, and in doing so is able to exercise a measure of control over the processes of change by being just African enough to gain legitimacy in the new order. This means that claims to entitlement can be preserved. Audaciously, it is even able to present itself as the place from which change is emanating. The most obvious example of this is the "white" brand of political discourse that represents white people as being best able to "take charge" of societal transformation, in the interests of Africans. The ideologies of European superiority are strong enough to ensure a certain amount of "buy-in" from some African people. While not openly expressed, whiteness is still mobilized as a signifier of clean governance, reliability, and competence. In this way, the very people who were responsible for oppression of the black majority, now present themselves the only ones who can "deliver" real changes to black people's quality of life. ("We need to restore good governance. Fight back!" the electorate is urged.)

"WHITE TALK" USES ITS DIASPORIC LINK TO MAINSTREAM WHITENESS

Whiteness in South Africa relies heavily on its connection to the centers of whiteness, invoking Eurocentric norms as the legitimating field that underwrites its power moves. An obvious example of this is the unproblematized insistence that only English is appropriate as the language of business, or as the lingua franca for the nation in a country where 49 percent of the population struggles to understand English, whereas 70 percent understand Zulu, for example.[12] ("The one thing I stand by is that we can't employ anyone who can't write decent English. It's the international language," a director of an advertising company insisted to me. He was talking about employing someone for a position of graphic artist.)

Other examples are tried-and-tested tropes of progress and development, foregrounding technology, which people who advocate for "other" interests find difficult to counter. This link also provides a hedge for the subjective experience of losing control of the local context. A common response to this loss is withdrawal: withdrawal into private business, into pockets of white suburbia, into anomie and apathy, and into the ultimate withdrawal, emigration to countries where whiteness is more secure. (By claiming that "[t]his new government is chasing away those that produce," a guest on a radio talk show puts the "white" spin on emigration.)

The credibility that comes with being perceived as "of the same kind" by the international community is also not lost on this diasporic community. The sympathies of people overseas need to be secured, as an acquaintance, a mother of two whose family was emigrating well knew. For a year prior to their departure she collected every newspaper article on crime, mismanagement, and inefficiency in an album to illustrate to her children, and those abroad, why they had left their country of origin.

"WHITE TALK" PRIVILEGES THE GLOBAL OVER THE LOCAL

In order to bolster its position, and counter the minority status of white people in the new South Africa, whiteness in this context draws heavily on discourses of globalization and internationalism. The access it has to the broader global community through ethnic and racial affiliation is used to attenuate its connection to local situation, as well as to emphasize the "weakness" of being without those links. "White talk" tends to be more in touch with, and sympathetic to, sentiment in, particularly, the West regarding issues, than to the responses of African people at home. Dominant Western definitions of issues are preferred, even if these have imperial overtones, and this is regarded as "greater objectivity" and the avoidance of vested interests. ("We can all agree that preserving the environment for tourism is the top priority for our town," a white town councillor comments at a local government meeting of a coastal town. "What about our people living in the squatter camps in shacks? We want resources allocated there—surely giving them a better life should be our top priority?" a black councillor rejoins.)

"WHITE TALK" REFUSES THE PAST

As with all positionalities constructed from privilege, whiteness in South Africa is characterized by *ignore-ance*.[13] This is the sum total of thousands of more, and less, conscious decisions not to know that were made to get on with life without rocking the "white" boat during the apartheid era of institutionalized whiteness. Of course, the previous dispensation formally structured this ignore-ance into the system through media censorship and deliberate misinformation. Whites in the new South Africa are now confronted with previously repressed stories about the past, told by "others." The Truth and Reconciliation Commission exposed what many choose not to know: that which was done in the name of securing their whiteness. "White Talk" establishes enough *personal* innocence to provide levels of psychological comfort in dealing with questions of the past. ("I didn't vote for the Nationalist government. I didn't support Apartheid." The former apartheid supporter has become an extinct species.)

Issues of collective responsibility remain out of focus: how the steady, systematic and compounding accrual of privileges and assets was premised upon "others" being positioned outside of the advantaged group, and largely outside of conscious awareness. In general, the past is either not acknowledged at all, or it is minimized. Certainly, the effects of the past that *still structure the present* are vigorously repressed in this discursive repertoire.

"WHITE TALK" OPPORTUNISTICALLY EMPLOYS REACTIONARY DISCOURSES THAT DRIFT ACROSS THE ATLANTIC

Whiteness in South Africa has received a great boon in the form of the conservative turn that has taken place in (especially American) Western politics. The structures of feeling that link this diasporic whiteness with whiteness elsewhere makes for easy cross-dissemination of discourses that are, *mutatis mutandis*, working well to preserve privilege elsewhere. Borrowed discursive strategies abound in "White Talk": privileging the individual as the primary social unit; trashing discourses that run counter to the conservative grain as fascist "political correctness" on the part of the loony Left; adopting premature and power-evasive "color blindness." Throughout, the tendency is to stem the tide of national priorities being recast in the direction of redress. An example is advocacy of "small government." ("Government should be outsourced," the stranger sitting next to me on a recent international flight gave me as his formula for rescuing South Africa's economy.)

"WHITE TALK" LINKS TO ESTABLISHED INSTITUTIONAL PRACTICES

An important way in which whiteness holds onto its still dominant economic and cultural position within the society is through mobilizing established links into the institutional life of the country's infrastructure. Good schooling, the banking system, the press, private health care are all still infused with white interests, values, and customs. This is presented as incidental, or co-incidental; the inherited power interests are downplayed, so that the continuance of such articulations is represented as innocent and inevitable, and in everybody's interests. ("The black parents want their children to get their education in English. It's not something we're forcing on them," an educationalist assures the audience in a lecture on sociolinguistics.)[14]

The "right" way, the tried-and–tested way, cannot but be ideologically linked to the white way, and "White Talk" makes it difficult to extricate the socially genuinely valuable from purely sectarian interest.

"WHITE TALK" PRIVILEGES DISCOURSES OF BUSINESS

Private enterprise, "the market," "what's good for business" is presented as being more advantageous to the society than courses of action advanced by discourses of social justice, social context, and morality or ethics. Business should be left unchallenged as if it operates outside of the sphere of morality, responding to market forces which seem to find their levels in some free-floating, autonomous manner, unconnected to sectarian interests, but linked nonetheless to a "market sentiment" that is not recognized as the expression of conversations, decisions, judgments of people who are situated contextually, driven by motivations that are anything but neutral. ("Business will never allow me to get a special deal because my grandparents were badly done by. All they want to know is can I do the job. To hark back on the past is the way of the loser," my traveling companion assures me. "I've arranged to be paid in dollars, and I advise all the international business people I interact with overseas to steer clear of the SA economy.")

"WHITE TALK" IS LINGUISTICALLY PLASTIC

Like all dominant discourses, "White Talk" is a skilled shape-shifter. Linguistically, this can be seen in the manner in which the languages of inclusivity and nonracialism, of being progressive, are used to perpetuate inherited, exclusive racial privilege. "Race" is rearticulated through other signifiers.

Some of the idiom of "White Talk" is thus encoded, as when references to the "New South Africa" (wink, wink) are indirect ways of referring to perceived confirmation of "black" incompetence and corruption, anticipated by old white South Africa. "White Talk" tends therefore to dwell on certain themes: crime and violence, corruption, dropping standards, affirmative action, and Africans' ingratitude. (Someone in my neighborhood who was recently the victim of crime registers his indignation in the local newspaper: "For years I've been putting cartoons onto the Internet for all to enjoy. And this is what I get in return," he writes.)

"WHITE TALK" UTILIZES INTERNATIONAL SENTIMENT OF AFRO-PESSIMISM

By far the most important trope in "White Talk" is Africa. The denigration of the African continent and its people, so central to, and well suited for, the colonial and imperial projects of the West, are still the stock-in-trade of "White Talk." ("Africa will fall further and further behind. The gap between the haves and have-nots globally is just widening all the time. Then this idiot of a president talks about an African Renaissance. We should be differentiating ourselves from the rest of this basket case of Africa. See when Nelson Mandela dies how the Rand will plummet." The person next to me on the airplane continues to suffocate me.)

"White Talk" feeds into and draws on that strand of international sympathy that writes off Africa. In doing this, white South Africans are propelled toward the international white center; the social distance between them and those who share this ideology of African hopelessness decreases.

"WHITE TALK" RECONSTRUCTS WHITENESS AS VICTIMIZED POSITIONALITY

In order to prevent further eroding of its power and privilege base, whiteness in South Africa constructs itself as the victimized in the new dispensation, using the country's demographics as its major rationale. ("There is no future for a white man in this country," I am further edified during the flight.)

This is similar to the way in which whiteness constructs itself elsewhere where the assumptions of entitlement are firmly in place, but the privilege is perceived as threatened. Being placed on a more equal footing is presented as marginalization; the binaries that underpin whiteness are seen to be simply reversed. Whites, it is averred, are now in the "the same" position now as black people were in the past under apartheid.

"WHITE TALK" ASSISTS, LEGITIMIZES, RATIONALIZES DENIAL

Richard Rorty has argued that if human beings are to develop an inclusive culture of human rights, it is education of the emotions, which he calls "sentimental education," that is needed. Many South African leaders have commented on the fact that one cannot legislate a change of heart. Interestingly, "White Talk" provides many mechanisms for denial and defense, protecting white South Africans from feeling the very emotions that are needed in order to move through, and out of, the assumptions of exclusivity that underpin whiteness. ("I am not going to be apologetic because I am white," a woman at a workshop asserts.)

The premature moratorium on "white guilt" circumvents a necessary process of self-examination and heightening of conscience. Some acknowledgment of guilt is both functional and appropriate in the South African context, and far from paralyzing. On the contrary, my data indicate that whites who are shifting their paradigm from preserving privilege for some to taking responsibility for promoting development of all have grappled with, or at least have not evaded, these uncomfortable feelings.

CONCLUSION

The above analysis illustrates an irony in the way in which this discursive repertoire operates. "White Talk" reaches into its diasporic dimensions in order to maintain, and regain, its centeredness, the power of whiteness.

After three hundred years of living in Africa, there is no doubt that whiteness in South Africa *has* produced a complex, hybrid identity position. This hybridity is generally unconscious, the type of hybridity that Werbner discusses as a major impetus for cultural creativity. Whites in South Africa have lost some aspects of mainstream Euro-American whiteness. They have moved in a different direction. They have acquired other characteristics through living shoulder to shoulder with Africans. Undoubtedly, white South Africans *do* live in a cultural *mest-iche*, as many find when they travel to Europe and feel alien. Indeed, some of the techniques of "White Talk" that insist on the connection to the whitest part of their hybrid cultural inheritance are reminiscent of the syndrome of "trying for white" in old apartheid South Africa—attempting to remain most closely associated with the international seats of wealth, privilege, and status.

A rhetorical space has opened up for white South Africans that has as its extremes identification with Afro-pessimism at the one end, and optimistic discourses about an African Renaissance at the other. At this stage, the identity construction of white South Africans is highly contested, and very fluid. Which narratives of whiteness gain dominance will be the function of many interlocking variables: economic, political, and other. As well as determining in which subjective realities whites will end up dwelling locally, the shaking-down process is also of interest to the theorization of whiteness internationally. The extent to which "White Talk" tenaciously hangs in here, in spite of changed political dynamics, will reveal a great deal about the tenacity of racial solidarity, and of how protean the solidarity can be in its strategies and tactics. As such, it may be a sad reminder of how those committed to social justice need to remain constantly vigilant, and of the continuing need to build self-reflexivity amongst white people.[15] To the extent, however, that "White Talk" gives way over time to discourses that embrace the African hue in the hybrid, diasporic whites in Africa, and that take on the project of building a compassionate and prosperous country for all its citizens, the voice of whiteness in South Africa may yet become part of a liberating strain in the history of "race."

NOTES

1. Earlier versions of this chapter were presented at the conference on *International Perspectives on Race, Ethnicity, and Intercultural Relations,* University of Mississippi, 20–22 April 2001; and at the Conference on *The Burden of Race: Whiteness and Blackness in Modern South Africa,* The University of the Witwatersrand, Johannesburg, 5–9 July 2001.

2. See Appiah.

3. See Fishkin, 428–66.

4. See Bonnett 1998; Giroux.

5. See Steyn, *Whiteness.*

6. See Steyn, *Whiteness.*

7. For more thorough exposition of these general arguments, see Ahmad; Goldberg; Kotkin; Werbner; Hall.

8. See Hall.

9. For a more detailed analysis of this type of psychoanalytic approach to colonial relations, see Bhabha; Memmi.

10. For more thorough discussions of this phenomenon among diasporic peoples in different contexts, see Gilroy; Werbner.

11. See Henderson;, Barkin.

12. See Pansalb.

13. See Frye.

14. Research by the Pan South African Language Board (2001) indicates that in fact only 12 percent of people interviewed favored English as the medium for instruction. See Pan.

15. On this point, see Bonnett 1997.

REFERENCES

Ahmad, Aijiz. 1995. The politics of literary postcoloniality. *Race and Class* 36, no. 3: 1–20.

Allen, Theodore W. 1994. *The invention of the white race: Racial oppression and social control.* London: Verso.

Appiah, Kwame Anthony, and Henry Louis Gates Jr., eds. 1995. *Identities.* Chicago: University of Chicago Press.

Barkan, Elizar, and Marie-Denise Shelton, eds. 1998. *Borders, exiles, and diasporas.* Stanford: Stanford University Press.

Bhabha, Homi K. 1994. *The location of culture.* London: Routledge.

Bonnett, Alistair. 1997. Constructions of whiteness in European and American anti-racism. In *Debating cultural hybridity: Multi-cultural identities and the politics of anti-racism*, ed. Pnina Werbner and Tariq Modood, 73–102. London: Zed.

———. 1998. How the British working class became white: The symbolic (re)formation of racialized capitalism. *Journal of Historical Sociology* 11, no. 3: 316–40.

Delgado, Richard, and Jean Stefancic. 1997. *Critical white studies: Looking behind the mirror*. Philadelphia: Temple University Press.

Dyer, Richard. 1988. White. *Screen* 29: 44–65.

Ferguson, Kathy. 1993. *The man question: Visions of subjectivity in feminist theory*. Berkeley: University of California Press.

Fine, Michelle, et al. 1997. *Off white: Readings on race, power, and society*. New York: Routledge.

Fishkin, Shelley Fisher. 1995. Interrogating "whiteness," complicating "blackness": Remapping American culture. *American Quarterly* 14, no. 3: 428–66.

Frankenberg, Ruth. 1993. *White women, race matters: The social construction of whiteness*. Minneapolis: Minnesota University Press.

Friedman, Jonathan. 1997. Global crises, the struggle for cultural identity and intellectual porkbarrelling: Cosmopolitans versus locals, ethnics, and nationals in an era of de-homogenisation. In *Debating cultural hybridity: Multi-cultural identities and the politics of anti-racism*, ed. Pnina Werbner, and Tariq Modood, 70–89. London: Zed.

Frye, Marilyn. 1993. *The politics of reality: Essays in feminist theory*. New York: Crossing Press.

Gilroy, Paul. 1993. *The black Atlantic: Modernity and double consciousness*. Cambridge: Harvard University Press.

Giroux, Henry A. 1997. *Channel surfing: Race talk and the destruction of youth*. New York: St. Martin's Press.

Gordon, Avery F., and Christopher Newfield. 1995. White philosophy. In *Identities*, ed. Appiah and Gates, 209–41. Chicago: University of Chicago Press.

Henderson, Mae G., ed. and Intro. 1995. *Borders, boundaries, and frames: Cultural criticism and cultural studies*. New York: Routledge.

Hesse, Barnor, ed. 2000. *Un/settled multiculturalisms: Diasporas, entanglements, transruptions*. London: Zed.

Ignatiev, Noel. 1995. *How the Irish became white*. New York: Routledge.

———. 1997. Treason to whiteness is loyalty to humanity. In *Critical white studies: Looking behind the mirror*. ed. Richard and Jean Stefancic. Philadelphia: Temple University Press.

Kincheloe, Joe L., et al., eds. 1998. *White reign: Deploying whiteness in America*. New York: St. Martin's Press.

Kotkin, Joel. 1995. *Tribes: How race, religion, and identity determine success in the new global economy*. New York: Random House.

Memmi, Albert. 1965. *The colonizer and the colonized*. Trans. Howard Greenfield. Intro. Jean-Paul Sartre. New York: Orion.

Morrison, Toni. 1992. *Playing in the dark: Whiteness and the literary imagination*. Cambridge: Harvard University Press.

Nakayama, Thomas K., and R. L. Krizek. 1995. Whiteness: A strategic rhetoric. *Quarterly Journal of Speech* 81, no. 3: 291–310.

Nederveen Pieterse, Jan, and Bhikhu Parekh, eds. 1995. *The decolonization of imagination: Culture, knowledge, and power.* London: Zed.

———. 1995. shifting imaginaries: Decolonization, internal decolonization, postcoloniality. In *The decolonization of imagination: culture, knowledge, and power,* ed. Jan Pieterse Nederveen and Bhikhu Parekh. London: Zed.

O'Callaghan, Marion. 1995. Continuities in imagination. In *The decolonization of imagination: Culture, knowledge, and power,* ed. Jan Pieterse Nederveen and Bhikhu Parekh. London: Zed.

Pan South African Language Board Home Page. 15 June 2002 *.http://www.pansalb. org.za.*

Papastergiadis, Nikos. 1997. Tracing hybridity in theory. In *Debating cultural hybridity: Multi-cultural identities and the politics of anti-racism,* ed. Pnina Werbner and Tariq Modood, 257–81. London: Zed.

Roediger, David R. 1991. *The wages of whiteness: Race and the making of the American working class.* London: Verso.

———. 1994. *Towards the abolition of whiteness: Essays on race, politics, and American working class history.* New York: Verso.

Rorty, Richard. 1993. Human rights, rationality, and sentimentality. In *On human rights: The oxford amnesty lectures, 1993,* ed. Stephen Shute and Susan Hurley. New York: Basic.

Steyn, Melissa E. 2001. *Whiteness just isn't what it used to be: White identity in the new South Africa.* Albany: State University of New York Press.

Ware, Vron. 1992. *Beyond the pale: White women, racism, and history.* London: Verso.

Waters, Mary C. 1990. *Ethnic options: Choosing identities in America.* Berkeley: University of California Press.

Werbner, Pnina. 1997. Introduction: The dialectics of cultural hybridity. In *Debating cultural hybridity: Multi-cultural identities and the politics of anti-racism,* ed. Pnina Werbner and Tariq Modood, 1–29. London: Zed.

Werbner, Pnina, and Tariq Modood, eds. 1997. *Debating cultural hybridity: Multicultural identities and the politics of anti-racism.* London: Zed.

Williams, Patrick, and Laura Chrisman, eds. and Intro. 1994. *Colonial discourse and post-colonial theory: A reader.* New York: Columbia University Press.

Wittig, Monique. 1992. *The straight mind and other essays.* Boston: Beacon Press.

Wray, Matthew, and Annalee Newitz. 1997. *White trash: Race and class in America.* New York: Routledge.

Young, Robert J. C. 1995. *Colonial desire: Hybridity in theory, culture, and race.* London: Routledge.

SEVEN

THE COLOR OF SCHIZOPHRENIA

CHERYL TEMPLE HERR

THIS CHAPTER INTERVENES in emergent cross-cultural discussions about mental illness: it calls for replacing the confrontational politics of psychiatry versus antipsychiatry with a proactive linking across both disciplines and former colonies of discourses about mental illness. The question of "colonial madness"[1]—an unusually high incidence of diagnosed psychosis among colonial and previously colonized populations—has been studied in medical literature since the 1880s, and in more popular formats since the 1950s, but information about this topic remains largely uncoordinated across the postcolonial geography. From Algeria to South Africa to India to Trinidad to Ireland, individuals labeled psychotic continue to experience intense shame, a social affect that can surely be lessened by an awareness of the global nature not just of schizophrenia but also of the reasons for the high incidence of diagnosis among postcolonials.

Vincent Kenny exemplifies a diagnostician who is able to make these links. His 1985 essay, "The Postcolonial Personality," although specific to Ireland, resonates strongly with reports of colonized people around the globe. At the same time, scientists around the world work hard to demonstrate and sharpen the infallibility of their diagnoses by way of universalizing diagnostic tools and, as a byproduct of their disciplinary norms, suppressing the rhetoric pertinent to patients' cultural differences. I argue that the whiteness of Irishness can teach us about the nature of worldwide stigmatization/ racialization processes and the contours of a form of clinical insanity that is both global and postcolonial.

THE EMPIRE WRITES BACK

The concept of colonially induced mental illness took political, anticolonial shape in the works of Martinique-born Frantz Fanon during the 1950s and 1960s. In *The Wretched of the Earth* (1961), this revolutionary black psychiatrist wrote with fierce passion about the Algerian war of liberation and its toll in behavioral and thought disorders. Famously, Fanon claimed that "[b]ecause it is a systematic negation of the other person and a furious determination to deny the other person all attributes of humanity, colonialism forces the people it dominates to ask themselves the question constantly: 'In reality, who am I?'" (Fanon 250). More recently, Richard Price has questioned the high incidence of "madness" in the postcolonial Caribbean, arguing that insanity, which he regards as culturally produced, still constitutes a "mirror" of colonial protocols (Price 1998, 158).

Fanon's work is often compared with that of Albert Memmi, a Tunisian Jew whose *The Colonizer and the Colonized* (1957) studies the psychology of the colonial experience. This is the case in Henry Louis Gates's widely circulated 1991 essay, "Critical Fanonism." Gates emphasizes cultural scholars' enthusiastic and multifarious embrace of Fanon's sometimes contradictory writings. Framing his discussion of Homi Bhabha's reading of Fanon, Gates concludes, "Fanon's current fascination for us has something to do with the convergence of the problematic of colonialism with that of subject formation" (Gates 1991, 458). Gates also makes much of Memmi's insistence on the eternal tension between the individual and society, psychoanalysis and Marxism, indicating that "all political appropriations of the psychoanalytic" are marked by that chiasmic relation (Gates 467). Gates's final insight bears repeating more than a decade after it was published: "[W]e, too, just as much as Fanon, may be fated to rehearse the agonisms of a culture that may never earn the title of *post*colonial" (Gates, 470).

One way in which this politicized writing about mental illness has been seized upon by cultural studies theorists is in response to Dominican-born Jean Rhys's *Wide Sargasso Sea* (1966). Rhys's portrayal of Antoinette shows the recoding of the Jamaican Creole woman of high passions, resistant to English decorum, into the generic madwoman in the attic, Charlotte Bronte's Bertha in *Jane Eyre*. It is unclear whether Antoinette has been predisposed to mental disorder because of her mother's genetic code or whether both women are deranged by their violent experiences with colonial patriarchy. Certainly, Antoinette now occupies an iconic place in postcolonial discourses; her story seems to provide evidence for the ascribed bias in diagnoses of madness within a shattered Caribbean everyday. Gayatri Spivak's imprimatur has sealed this designation and Antoinette's allegorical status: "I must read this as an allegory of the general epistemic violence of imperialism, the construction of a self-immolating colonial subject for the glorification of the social mission of the colonizer" (Spivak 1986, 270). It is no surprise that in the carceral scenario of *Jane Eyre* Antoinette-Bertha's only option is to burn down the edifice that entraps her or to suffer endlessly from isolation and shame.

There is an overwhelming amount of good sense in the works of Fanon, Memmi, Price, and Rhys, but all of it would be described today by medical establishments as interpretive (to various degrees, from insiderly observation of psychiatric patients to outright literary fabrication) rather than whatever we might mean by the term *scientific*. Within the scientific community, Fanon is regarded with the silence surrounding any American doctor who questions AMA regulations. This disciplinary exclusion, understandable as it is by contemporary requirements regarding experimental verifiability, totalizes the exclusion of Fanon's insights into the impact of colonization on the minds and bodies of the oppressed. The same problem has faced the infamous figures of the antipsychiatry movement in its many guises, including Thomas Szasz, R. D. Laing, and Deleuze/Guattari. Their adversarial relationship to a medical establishment keen to hook schizophrenic symptoms such as hallucinations and auditory delusions to structural problems in the brain of the afflicted has resulted in a popular bias against their collective insights and toward a theory of neurobiological causation.

In contrast, the contemporary medical study of schizophrenia emphasizes neurobiology, neurochemistry, and genetics. Neural research has located abnormalities in both the frontal system (governing thought and volition) and the temporolimbic system (controlling perception, memory, and language). Neurochemical studies target hyperactivity in the dopamine system of the brain, that part that acts as a "chemical messenger" and "governs . . . personality" (Andreasen 1984, 222–23). A variety of *in vivo* brain imaging techniques are receiving a great deal of attention in the contemporary search for a definitive classification of the subtypes of schizophrenia: CT scans provide evidence of structural brain abnormality—specifically for ventricular enlargement and cortical atrophy; RCBF (regional cerebral blood flow) measurement has enabled researchers to detect diminished blood flow to frontal lobes in schizophrenic patients; PET (positron emission tomography)-scans locate distinctive patterns of neurotransmitter functions and glucose metabolism as well as measure metabolic activity in different regions of the brain. In genetic research, studies have linked schizophrenia to markers on chromosome 5 (Kendler 1989, 559). and the Human Genome Initiative continues to provide information about the possible genetic components of at least certain aspects of this disorder or set of disorders.

Certainly, *in vivo* neuroimaging holds out the comfort of cure or at least of amelioration; these diagnostic modalities also work to lessen the stigma and shame associated with mental illness. In effect, they redirect our attention from the dodgy concept of mind to the photographable certainties of the brain.

AFRO-CARIBBEAN INSTANCES

However, the relations between brain scans and cultural processes of racialization remain, as yet, almost unaddressed by scientists. In October 1999, echoing findings from the mid-nineties onward, the BBC's "Black Britain" program popularized findings that "[b]lack men are 10 times more likely than white men to be diagnosed as schizophrenic."[2] Dr. Kwame McKenzie, who practices psychiatry in London and teaches at the Royal Free and University College Medical School, explained that the African Caribbean community is being let down at several stages of health care.[3] Kwame's view is supported by the study of F. W. Hickling, who found that "of 29 African and African-Caribbean patients diagnosed with schizophrenia, the diagnoses of the British and Jamaican psychiatrists agreed in 16 instances (55%) and disagreed in 13 (45%)" (Hickling, McKenzie, and Murray 1999, 283). It follows that, as the UK's National Schizophrenia Fellowship (NSF) claims, "[i]n Britain, you are between three and six times more likely to be diagnosed with schizophrenia if you are from the African-Caribbean population . . . you are up to 12 times more likely to be diagnosed with schizophrenia if you are second-generation" in the UK.

The NSF admits that causes may exceed the usual genetic theories of transmission. The organization notes that rather than target genetic vulnerability, there may be "environmental factors" to blame—factors "more common in the black community than among whites." Poverty, the stress of racism, and diagnostic tools insensitive to cultural difference are all said to be under investigation in "the controversial area."[4] At the same time, 2001 saw reports coming out of Australian research that a key factor in developing the disease may be a lack of sunlight, with its accompanying decrease in Vitamin D availability. The Queensland Centre of Schizophrenia Research contends that a mother's lack of sunshine can cause her baby to become mentally ill; by the same token, city life, especially for "dark-skinned migrants" to northern countries, constitutes a risk factor (Queensland 2002).

Writing in *The Guardian*, James Meikle reports that the incidence of schizophrenia "among black people" may result from a failure to live with others from one's ethnic background. Between 1987 and 1997, London's Institute of Psychiatry studied mental health in Camberwell (South London) and discovered that "the lower the proportion of non-whites in an area, the higher the rate of schizophrenia." Researchers implied that without appropriate social support, the Afro-Caribbean population suffered from mentally damaging racism (Meikle 2002, 7). The Centre for Caribbean Medical Research at King's College, London, summarizes recent findings and adds that "the high rate of schizophrenia in British African-Caribbeans provides a valuable opportunity to test contemporary theories about the aetiology of schizophrenia."[5]

The only thing that is clear here is that being Afro-Caribbean in the UK has many potential drawbacks. It would seem that the question just

under the surface of these collected statements is to what extent does re-
sidual imperialism play a synergistic role together with other indicators for
mental disorder and/or for a set of symptoms intelligible as schizophrenia?
We might also ask, how does the splintering of self and community result in
a shameful fiction of othering created between patient and doctor? Does
schizophrenia bear witness to the traumatic experiences of an entire society?
Why and how does first world science continue to recolonize postcolonial
migrants into the second generation and possibly beyond?

AN IRISH PROBLEM

The comparison of Afro-Caribbean Briton to white Briton shaping the studies
cited above is put in a new light when we introduce evidence that the Irish
suffer from a startlingly high incidence of schizophrenia. According to the
World Health Organization, the global incidence in the general population of
this most severe and intractable form of psychosis is 1 percent. For at least the
past 120 years (the time period covered by the scientific literature) a much
higher incidence of schizophrenia has been detected in the British Isles, first
in Ireland and among Irish migrants in Britain, and only much more recently
among Afro-Caribbean migrants to the U.K.

   Below, I try to excavate socially induced schizophrenic symptoms from
the forms of disease that are usually accounted for by reference to genetics,
viruses, or other aspects of biology. I also connect this information with a
literary-cultural perspective on schizophrenic expression. Taking on board
the possibility that the higher incidence has been systematically produced to
some degree by the colonial system, my inquiry exerts pressure on these
instances of racist quasi-diagnosis of mental illness in Ireland. Recognizing
the racist component in the construction of schizophrenia—itself a category
encompassing many causations and expressive differences—sheds light on
the construction of whiteness-as-blackness in the complicated cultural field
of Britain and Ireland. It also forces us to coordinate information from several sources: references in Irish literature to schizophrenia, statistics about
the incidence of mental illness in Ireland, medical discussions of the causes
and diagnosis of schizophrenia, ethnographic depiction of life in western
Ireland, inquiries into colonial and postcolonial Irish life, literary and cultural theory, and studies of the differences between the Irish language and
English. This variety of discursive takes on schizophrenia in Ireland enables
us to get at an occluded racism toward which they variously gesture.

   To begin with the literary view, in Ireland as in the Caribbean, we
find a robust body of writing depicting mental illness, one that resonates
with popular beliefs in Ireland about the island's tendency to breed
schizophrenics. As early as 1731, when Jonathan Swift provided funds for
the first mental hospital in Ireland, he wryly captured this body of ideas on
his tombstone:

> He gave what little wealth he had
> To build a house for fools and mad
> To show by one satiric touch,
> No nation needed it so much.

By the early years of the twentieth century, the madhouse was a standard feature of the Irish imaginary, whether urban or rural. Consider John Synge's Widow Quinn, convincing old Mahon that he is mad to think that the quasi-heroic Christy is his son. Mahon decides to take himself to the hospital in Mayo: "There'll be a welcome before me, I tell you, and I a terrible and fearful case, the way that there I was one time, screeching in a straitened coat, with seven doctors writing out my sayings in a printed book" (Synge 1990, 154). The lunatic asylum, ever-present and ever-consuming of relatives and neighbors, sometimes all too conveniently, was a fearful reality for everyone in the Irish world throughout the history of British colonization.

Fifty years after Synge's play, Seamus Deane encountered Crazy Joe, about whom he writes in *Reading in the Dark* (1997). Crazy Joe "was regularly consigned for periods to Gransha, the local asylum" (Deane, 195). The figure of the local schizophrenic, like the "local asylum," recurs often in Irish reminiscences, fictions, and films—perhaps most famously in Neil Jordan's film of Patrick McCabe's *The Butcher Boy* (1986). He or she is the wise fool in every imaginary Irish town (and many real ones), a functional mad person, angrily resisting social mores and slyly indicating the aggressive British regime that subtends most Irish institutions.

This lived reality underwrites Padraig Rooney's 1993 poem, "Mantle."

> Once, as a young teacher, for homework,
> I assigned words to be put in sentences
> to show their meaning. This one word,
> *mantle*, was in a story we were doing.
> Most got it right, they'd looked it up,
> but one boy wrote about his aunt
> "who was odd and went into the mental."
> I marked it wrong, never found out more
> but told the story for years, in staffrooms,
> honing it, reining back the punchline.
> Until today, in two minds, I too looked it up,
> *mantle*, its myriad shifting meanings. . . . (Rooney, 9)

At once everywhere and hushed up, the apparent Irish tendency to mental disorder has been a widespread social burden, the sort of "cloak" of which Rooney writes, both abject and "incandescent."

So it is that in 1992, when I presented a talk on this topic at the James Joyce Summer School, the director, Augustine Martin, told me that in Ire-

land the discussion of schizophrenia with outsiders has always been taboo—
"radioactive" was his word—because "every family has an uncle up at
Grangegorman."[6] Only at the end of the twentieth century did caretaking
discourse about mental illness become more open, more channeled through
Internet-accessible support services from Schizophrenia Ireland's Lucia Foundation (named after James Joyce's schizophrenic daughter) and less a question of shame-ridden silences.

INCIDENCE AND CAUSATION

A few observations by a prominent Irish psychiatrist can help to establish
the magnitude of this social problem. Ivor Browne, emeritus head of the
Department of Psychiatry at University College, Dublin, reports that the
main mental institution in Dublin, St. Brendan's Hospital, which opened in
1814, by 1900 housed 2,254 patients, a figure that by 1903 had ballooned by
40 percent. Browne notes,

> By 1900 the nation as a whole could boast of five psychiatric beds
> per 1000 of population. With further population decline and demo-
> graphic changes leading to greater dependency, particularly in
> Western areas, these numbers were to rise still higher until by 1958
> the figure stood ... in certain Western areas of the country ... as
> high as 13 per 1000; that is, more than one in every hundred per-
> sons was resident in a mental hospital. (Browne, interview by au-
> thor, 5 April 1995)

In 1961 and again in 1968, the World Health Organization statistical sector
reported that the Irish had the highest "hospitalization treatment rate for
mental illness in the world" (Scheper-Hughes 1979, 3).

For this reason, Ireland has produced a good deal of research on schizophrenia. The most prominent twentieth-century researcher in Ireland into
the causes of schizophrenia was Dermot Walsh, Chief of the Mental Health
Section of the Health Research Board in Dublin. In a 1974 study, Walsh
found half of all mental patients in Ireland suffering from what was regarded
as well-documented schizophrenia. Hospitalization and non-hospitalization
rates in 1973 in three Irish counties were 3.5 times higher than in South
London. And "Walsh estimate[s] the lifetime expectancy for hospitalization
for schizophrenia in Ireland as 4%"—with the highest figures in the rural,
traditional western part of the island. This is "approximately four times the
American rate" (Torrey 1980, 984). It is significant that E. F. Torrey, a prominent statistician in this field, in a 1987 British Journal of Psychology article,
cited Ireland as showing more than three times the schizophrenia incidence
of London, New Haven, or Sri Lanka (Torrey 1984, 966).

Wanting to understand the nature of an equation that traversed modern Irish literature and history, I conducted a Med-Line and Hist-Line search of the medical literature from the 1880s to the present, and pored over dozens of articles in several languages that attempted to describe, categorize, and speculate about schizophrenia in general and the Irish incidence of schizophrenia in particular.[7] Looking on from the perspective of medical diagnosticians positions us in waters muddier and more turbulent than those that flow through *Finnegan's Wake*. In the medico-cultural literature schizophrenia has been correlated with many variables—from large-scale historical events such as the rise of civilization, the industrial revolution, social crisis, or demographic shiftings to more individual possible causes such as contracting a viral infection or developing coeliac disease, having a schizophrenic relative, suffering brain damage at birth, being born of an older mother, being single, and experiencing constant ambiguity in the parental discourse. None of those correlations has been robust enough to constitute in the eyes of the majority of researchers a true and sufficient cause. So it is that Nancy Andreasen and many other contemporary researchers now view schizophrenia as "probably a heterogeneous group of diseases, some of which are caused by one factor and some by another" (Andreasen 1984, 222).[8]

Nonetheless, medical discourse often reads as though there were a single cause, a single condition. Moreover, probably no one in the medical community proper doubts that a genetic factor is predisposing. In the extensive medical writings on the condition *in Ireland,* many Irish-specific causes have been hypothesized and jettisoned. Several studies have specifically ruled out such things as diagnostic differences between Ireland and elsewhere, the results of syphilis misdiagnosed as schizophrenia, inbreeding, intestinal disease, poor diet, social stress, and mass emigration. And yet there seems to be something in the Irish situation that combines with a genetic or other physical predisposition to mark the body in the distinctive ways characteristic of schizophrenia—with passivity and loss of volition; with overexcited, incongruous, or flattened affect; with dreamlike and lethargic posing; with staring facial grimaces; and with other disturbances in bodily movements and repose.[9] It has been repeatedly (though not unproblematically) documented that the Irish schizophrenic population is highest in the west of Ireland—specifically in rural areas where the Irish language is or was spoken, particularly in those regions long associated with poverty and a declining population, the condition afflicting especially unmarried Catholic males or Catholics born of older mothers.

On the anthropological side, one of the most controversial ethnographies ever written takes this apparent prevalence of schizophrenia in the Irish countryside as its almost uninterrogated starting point. Nancy Scheper-Hughes became notorious for her 1979 book, *Saints, Scholars, and Schizophrenics: Mental Illness in Rural Ireland*—ironically, the winner of the 1981 Margaret Mead Award. Critics of Scheper-Hughes, such as indigenous novelist Eilis Dillon, assert that she radically misunderstood the interactive norms of the community; she phrased many of her putative "findings" crudely; without sufficient understanding of local traditions, she took as truth the reality that villagers *allowed* her to see; and she dramatically overgeneralized from individual instances, apparently unaware of the not only-but also contradictions in which Irish culture is skilled (Dillon, interview by author, April 1992).

For example, Scheper-Hughes accepts without question the judgments of psychiatrists at a nearby clinic in Kerry that even rudimentary attempts at psychotherapy would be counterindicated for people who come from a "primitive," that is, Irish, background. On the one hand dismissing the village's sense of itself as Gaeltacht, on the other she sees the Irish language as a blunt instrument, unemotional and insensitive, this regardless of comments at the outset of her study in which, relative to Anglo-Irish, she backhandedly praises Irish speech: "[C]ommunicating with the Irish is tricky for the plodding, literal-minded Saxon, and in many an initial encounter I would think myself to be following a linear path of conversation, only to find myself lost on a forked road, waylaid by shortcuts and switchbacks, and invariably led up a blind alley or cul-de-sac. In short, I was being *had*, Irish style. Well, no matter. Reputation of the Irish aside, I'd also been had in the past by Mexican and Brazilian peasants (and more than once found myself on the wrong bus en route to nowhere), and I had eventually learned to crack *their* code" (Scheper-Hughes, 11–12).

Later, I will return to the Irish language and its possible role in diagnostic situations. For now, it is enough to note the resonance of Scheper-Hughes's attitudes with those observed in other extra-Irish researchers by Vincent Kenny, Director of the Institute of Constructivist Psychology (Rome and Ireland). Echoing Gregory Bateson and R. D. Laing, Kenny notes that in Ireland

> medicine and psychology have been dominated by a British training machine embodied in the Irish universities, and monitored by the relevant British institutions; eg, the *Royal* College of Physicians / General Practitioners / Psychiatry / etc. All training has tended to be positivistic following the typical British "empiricist" mode. . . . From 1979 to 1986 I was the psychological trainer for the Irish College of General Practitioners, and most of my time was spent in trying to undo the personally damaging effects of the medical training system on the G.P.s and to liberate their own humanity to operate in their clinical practices. When we were ritually "examined" by the visitors from the Royal C. of G. P., the English would usually complain that these Irish doctors were spending too much time with their patients (ie, more than the British 6-minute average!). It was fairly obvious that the British model of doctor-patient

languaging could work very well only if the patient-as-person was virtually "ignorable"—as in when a patient is comatose, or their problem is clear and precise.

But this British model "simply was not good enough" and "broke down" when it came to the "significance of a given symptom for a given patient" (Kenny, letter to author, 1 October 1991).

For all of this medical, scientific, and anthropological study and debate, the important question remains, *If Ireland does have more schizophrenics than other Western countries, why is this the case?*

THE IRISH LANGUAGE

Australian professor of psychiatry and social anthropologist Robert J. Barrett has studied assessment interviews, how those interviews were documented in medical records, the "transformations that occurred from spoken dialogue to written record" (Barrett, Barrett, and Good 1995, 2), and the discourse among one hospital's practitioners about its patients. He is concerned with the changes that the institutional experience, centered in its practices of speaking and writing, produces in the client. The constitution of schizophrenia, which has changed over the decades and from institution to institution, receives attention in his groundbreaking book *The Psychiatric Team and the Social Definition of Schizophrenia*, in which Barrett emphasizes:

> There are important differences between this approach and that of labelling theory, which asserts that the hospital merely imposes a false and stigmatizing identity upon the patient. By contrast, I argue that the psychiatric hospital is a site where common-sense ideas about mental illness are concentrated and refined. Many of these ideas have currency within the broader community and are shared by patients and their families. Worked up into scientific concepts of schizophrenia they take on a distinctive objectivity and distance. When patients, during the course of their treatment, learn that they are suffering from schizophrenia, their experience of illness and of themselves is transformed. This book traces these transformations. . . . For clinicians it is a severe illness that is difficult to treat and has a poor prognosis. Within the field of biomedical research it is a poorly understood syndrome at the basis of which is a brain disorder with genetic, cognitive, and neurophysiological aspects. To the antipsychiatrist it is a myth—an invention of psychiatry and of the hospital as joint agents of social control. At a common-sense level, it is madness. . . . These competing definitions point to fundamental ambiguities in the way reason, autonomy, and the person are defined in our culture. . . . It impoverishes schizophrenia to reduce it to one

version or another. On empirical grounds it is more accurate to assert that schizophrenia is all these things; and that in order to understand it we must grasp it as a multiple reality (Barrett, Barrett, and Good, 3).

Barrett points out that we cannot merely dismiss the "medical model" by putting forward contradictory evidence. He also distinguishes his study from that of cross-cultural psychiatry, which attends to the various ways in which schizophrenia is experienced in social groups. While emphasizing everyday interactions between patients and clinicians, Barrett also notes that recent decades have seen some rapprochement between positivist medical science (which aims to avoid cultural biases by working through structured interview mechanisms) and ethnographic investigation. Barrett characterizes the style of resulting reports as technical, abstract, and given to the passive voice—all an effort to move "the patient and clinician out of focus in order to bring a decontextualized disorder into focus" (4). In contrast, the aim of ethnography is to bring the immediate circumstances into focus. Barrett seizes on interpretative work performed at every stage of the formal and informal encounters among *everyone* associated with the patient.

Barrett's emphasis on the language of doctor-patient interactions has contextual implications for interpreting the tangled schizophrenic heritage in Ireland. Consider that for English speakers untrained in the Irish language, Gaelic is a peculiarly unreadable tongue. From the perspective of English, the Irish language is orthographically puzzling and opaquely unpronounceable. Indigenous scholars of Irish studies have long drawn amusement from the attempts of outsiders to speak Irish words as though they followed Irish sound-sense. I would not be alone in arguing that the syntax of the Irish language affects how native Irish speakers have historically processed information. I propose that we consider these syntactic issues when we think about the ways in which schizophrenia classically expresses itself and the nature of the medical interrogations that have eventuated in diagnosis.

Most diagnoses of schizophrenia have been based not on brain scans or even family history, but rather on personal interviews. Today, there are several diagnostic packages available to regulate such an interview. Consider a report in the 1989 *Schizophrenic Bulletin* about a diagnostic tool that has been praised precisely because its construction and initial deployment involved doctors from various sites in the United States and the west of Ireland. The resulting instrument, the "Structured Interviews for Schizotypy" (SIS), promotes itself as explicitly context-sensitive. This instrument provides clues about how and why interviews with Irish speakers might have gone astray in the past, based as the instrument is in a communal medical tradition.

First, a sense of how the SIS works. As an instance of its context-sensitivity, the authors note that in earlier tests "to assess 'facial' flat affect, . . . the interviewer simply would ask the respondent: 'Do people often

say that your face looks like a blank screen? Or that you have a 'poker face'?"
(Kendler 1989, 561). Walsh and his fellow researchers have created their
instrument to take into consideration that in some cases people have actual
facial disfigurements; the belief of many schizophrenics that something terrible
has happened to their bodies will not necessarily be registered as positive in
the cases of otherwise disturbed people who actually do have poker faces.
Other diagnostic questions probe one's relations to the world at large: "At one
time or another, when in public, many people have had the feeling they are
being watched. How often have you had such an experience?" "Why do you
think you are being looked at?" "How about the feeling of being laughed at
when you are in public?" "How often do thoughts come into your mind that
feel as if they don't belong?" (14–15). Throughout the lengthy questionnaire,
the patient is tested not only for the paranoia and delusions that hallmark
many schizophrenic disorders but also on a style of engagement.

That noted, a chief cognitive problem in schizophrenia is that it involves difficulty in abstract thinking, and the medical establishment concurs
that this aspect of the condition does not dramatically change with neuro-
leptic drug treatment (Rochester, Sherry, and Martin 1979, 79). Hence, a
schizophrenic who is asked to generalize and to whom the question is posed,
"To what aim do you refer," might respond, "I do not refer; fur is . . . fur is
a cover for the animal kingdom." The trajectory of the dialogue is short-
circuited by the patient's concretizing of the question. It is thus of great
interest that throughout the twentieth century, both Irish and British writers
have gone on record as seeing the Irish and the Irish language as incapable
of generalization or of abstract thinking. The pre-Celtic-Tiger cliché has it
that the Irish writer strongly prefers concrete particularity to higher-order
statements. Irish authors who have written about Irishness,[10] even while
displaying a considerable ability to abstract, have often regarded the immediate situation and its concrete particulars as their proper and most comfortable domain. A cultural bias toward specificity would have to be factored
into any assessment of this exchange, but notably, the SIS lacks any such
overt mechanism.

Like Barrett, I was impressed that of the many medical articles that I
read, none recorded either the typical or the atypical responses of a schizophrenic individual. In such reports, the words of the schizophrenic are suppressed. Most of the medical literature exemplifies how often doctors rely on
their own oral culture for transmitting among themselves what the schizophrenic is like. Notably, in the publications attending to Ireland and Irish
patients, I have found no vivid descriptions of patients and little consideration of the specificities of what this or that individual patient says. It is thus
difficult to picture what any given individual Irish patient is or was like
under testing. However, it takes no great leap of the imagination to conclude
that this suppression of the Irish interviewee is homologous with the near
erasure of the Irish language from common usage. Not only did English

imperialism make one of its major goals the effacement of the Irish language, but psychiatric testing mechanisms appear to be particularly insensitive to the specificities of Anglo-Irish or Hiberno-English or, indeed, to the self-image of Gaelic culture. That said, what if clinicians were taught to look for perceptual and cognitive difference at the level of syntax? Even when Irish lost its primary-language status, the underlying syntax of linguistic and enworlded relations clearly remained relatively intact.

Hence, it is important that many schizophrenics speak repetitively and display an echolalia that depends "extensively on lexical cohesion" (Rochester, Sherry, and Martin, 80). In fact, schizophrenics often use some form of iteration in place of yes and no responses to questions, and the SIS tests for this affect. A key point for me is that the Irish language technically lacks words for yes and no. A strict translation into English of the answer to "Is that a table," would be "Be table it" (*Is tabla é*). There is modulated repetition rather than affirmation or negation, a phenomenon that Augustine Martin underscored when we discussed Ireland and schizophrenia. Of course, there are many constructions, in practice, by which to indicate negative and positive responses in the Irish language. And it is clear to any English speaker that Hiberno-English conversation draws its fundamental shape from the relays and interweavings of modified repetition. In addition, Irish linguist Terence Dolan, when presented with the above argument, rapidly compiled several pages of Hiberno-English locutions that would be misunderstood by English speakers. A host of potential opacities between Irish-inflected speech and English, normally glossed over in ordinary interchanges, would rise forcibly to the surface for an Irish speaker/thinker undergoing a medical interview.

It is not surprising, then, that the west of Ireland has historically occasioned the most controversy in medical circles for its high rates of schizophrenia. Two or three generations ago, before most of the population spoke English as a first language, the Irish-speaking area known as the Gaeltacht was a site of alternative syntax and hence of alternative perception and strategies of verbal interaction. Returning to the peculiarity of traditional Irish in lacking a word for the negative, we can instance James Joyce's 1907 article about some notorious murders in 1882 in the western town of Maamtrasna. With his penchant for coincidence, Joyce was undoubtedly both charmed and cautioned by the fate of the man wrongly charged with the crime, an Irish speaker named Myles Joyce.

In the situation as Joyce describes it, England is the interrogator, and Ireland is the guilty, misunderstood victim. Referring to the interpreter used at the trial, Joyce records that when the magistrate questioned Myles Joyce about the details of his behavior on the night of the murder, "The old man . . . began to talk, to protest, to shout, almost beside himself with the anguish of being unable to understand or to make himself understood, weeping in anger and terror" (Joyce 1959, 197). To communicate this response, the interpreter merely remarked, " 'He says no, 'your worship' " (197). That "no" is one thing that he could not say was quite apparent to Joyce the writer, and he nominates Myles Joyce, his own retrospective namesake, as an emblem of the Irish nation rendered "deaf and dumb" (198).

Finnegan's Wake I.4 deals with the Myles Joyce murders in the midst of portraying the multiple assaults on HCE and his status as accuser and accused. The Mayo man, Festy King, defends himself in Irish, and, reversing the fate of Myles Joyce, gets away with it, speaking in his "royal Irish vocabulary" (Joyce 1939, 86.1), dripping in recollection of the archaic Prankquean with her own riddling language, and taking his place with the other "noncommunicables" (87.19). A look at Brendan O Hehir's guide to the presence of the Irish language in *Finnegan's Wake* verifies that these Gaeltacht-resonant pages are full of Irish words, buried in an imperializing quasi-English but producing a disturbance, sure enough: "King . . . murdered all the English that he knew" (Joyce 1939, 93.1–2).[11]

Meanwhile, Jacques Derrida has famously located ten categories or modalities of the word *yes* in Joyce, a kind of implosion of the Irish language's lack of the direct affirmative.[12] Part of what produces this pervasive feature of *Wake*-speak is the underlying pressure of the Irish language to negotiate some sort of refusal and undoing that are not precisely negations but that constitute a positive knowing in itself. Joyce himself feared the western Irish hinterland and its people even as he defended them. And it is easily argued that the language that Joyce develops for *Finnegan's Wake* dramatizes not an obvious dualism or split personality but rather the ways in which withdrawal from engagement, florid delusion, institutional repression, and canny clinging to the concrete specifics of life provide a syntax for understanding the politics of confusing messages within an oppressive colonial subworld. *Finnegan's Wake* acts out on a grand cultural scale, on the stage of high modernism, this Irish plight—the institutional impact and social cost of discursive, syntactic, expressive dispossession.

The presence of Irish on every page of *Finnegan's Wake* is not just a way of insisting that we see that the language is *there* but also a way of invoking the administratively occluded system within which those words, now schizoid, make all kinds of sense. And the effect is to suspend the reader in a palpably overdetermined realm where colonial and postcolonial history is traversed by the disjunctures of modernization. Hence, what a steady overview of the literature on schizophrenia strongly suggests is that Ireland has had an unanticipated number of what Joyce would call "schizophrenetic" speakers (*Finnegan's*, 123). This is not to say that no one in Ireland has actually suffered from disorders of the mind and body that elsewhere in the world are diagnosed as some form of schizophrenia. It is rather to draw attention to the conversational subtleties and contextual pressures that might have contributed to an inflated sense of how prevalent schizophrenia has been on the island of Ireland. It is also to refuse to allow the fictional version of the malady to efface the fact that schizophrenia clearly has multiple causes and that it is often unclear precisely what is being diagnosed.

Throughout the world, schizophrenia-as-disorder appears to require biology as well as contextual pressures to be made, in certain circumstances and individuals, to speak—in a language that, throughout the world, is structured very much like the collision of the Irish language with an interrogative English language. A cultural studies view of the medical literature, open to the possibility that Fanon might be taken seriously, would have to connect the Irish schizophrenic heritage with the plight of a disturbed Afro-Caribbean male living today in London. In this view, the mulitiplicity that is called schizophrenia is clearly a disease of adaptation and one that refuses to adapt to contextual changes. It marks a failure of cross-cultural semiotics as well as a remaking of the prevailing semiotic field. It is a disorder that routinely affects 1 percent of the world's population but has also repeatedly surfaced as an aspect of the colonial encounter. Both dark-skinned Afro-Caribbean migrants to Britain and white Irish people living in the British Isles have physically and psychically expressed their legacy of oppression in congruent ways. Such cross-cultural linkages must be the starting point for future discussion of mental illness in the postcolonial world.

In this chapter, I have drawn on a substantial literature in psychiatry, cultural studies, cultural psychology, and cross-cultural ethnopsychiatry. While surveying these fields in relation to the specificity of schizophrenic diagnoses, I have found persistent questions. Is the concept of mental disorder culturally relative? If so, to what extent? How do the interactions between clinicians and patients shape mental illness in given cases? How do race and ethnicity affect diagnostic procedures and treatments for mental illness in various countries? In a fragmentary fashion, these several disciplines have explored the varying lifeworlds of schizophrenics in the context of socially specific constructions of selfhood, the relevance of folk descriptions of mental deviance from the norm, the role of migration in psychopathology, the impact of modernity/ postmodernity on perceptions of mental illness, the politics of schizophrenia in terms of both medical institutions and public health funding, and the development of instruments for transcultural diagnosis. The study (whether scientific or literary, positivistic or impressionistic) of mental illness describes a contradictory field rife with searching, speculation, unverifiability, and imprecision. The notable, and noted, incidence of schizophrenia in widely separated former colonies enables us to foreground the relations of racialization constructing the colonial confrontation and rendering the weaker party multifactoriogenetically defective and socioeconomically invalid. From the perspective of European imperialism, the high incidence of perceived psychosis in Ireland and the Caribbean demands a response as complex as the overdetermination of that psychosis. In a world still struggling to become fully postcolonial, that response must aim for a world-historical comparative interpretation.

NOTES

I am grateful to Anna Spyra for bibliographical suggestions on Caribbean madness.

1. See Fisher.

2. See "Black."

3. Along with five of his colleagues, Dr. McKenzie published an essay in 2001 in the *British Journal of Psychiatry* that compared "the outcome and treatment of psychosis in people of Caribbean origin living in the UK and British Whites." See McKenzie, 160.

4. See Queensland.

5. See Centre.

6. Grangegorman is a large asylum in Dublin.

7. In this task, I had assistance from my research assistant at that time, Jonathan Highfield.

8. In 1994 when I asked Andreasen about the Irish incidence, she inclined toward a viral causation.

9. See Schwartz.

10. See for example O Faolain and Dunn. O Faolain's description of the Irish in the early twentieth century bears comparison with Fanon's recitation of colonizers' clichés about the colonized.

11. See O Hehir, 56–66.

12. See Derrida.

REFERENCES

Andreasen, Nancy C. 1984. *The broken brain: The biological revolution in psychiatry.* New York: Harper and Row.

————. 1988. *Schizophrenia.* Current Concepts series. Kalamazoo: Upjohn.

Andreasen, Nancy, and William T. Carpenter. 1993. Diagnosis and classification of schizophrenia. *Schizophrenia Bulletin* 19:199–214.

Barrett, Robert J., Rob Barrett, Byron J. Good. 1995. *The psychiatric team and the social definition of schizophrenia: An anthropological study of person and illness.* Cambridge: Cambridge University Press.

Black men failed by mental health system. 13 October 1999. BBC News. *http://news.bbc.co.uk/go/em/fr/-/1/hi/health/464989.stm.*

Browne, Dr. Ivor. 5 April 1991. Interview by author. Dublin. Centre for Caribbean Medical Research. 15 June 2002. Psychosis. www.kcl.ac.uk/depsta/ccm/CCM_research.html.

Deane, Seamus. 1998. *Reading in the dark.* New York: Vintage Books.

Derrida, Jacques. 1987. *Ulysse gramophone: Deux mots pour Joyce.* Paris: Editions Galilée.

Deleuze, Gilles, and Félix Guattari. 1983. *Anti-Oedipus: Capitalism and schizophrenia.* Trans. Robert Hurley, Mark Seem, and Helen R. Lane. Minneapolis: University of Minnesota Press.

Dillon, Eilis. April 1992. Interview by author. Dublin.

Dunn, Breda. 1990. *An intelligent visitor's guide to the Irish.* Dublin: Mercier.

Fanon, Frantz. [1952] 1963. *The wretched of the Earth.* Trans. Constance Farrington. Reprint. New York: Grove Weidenfeld.

Fisher, Lawrence E. 1985. *Colonial madness: Mental health in the Barbadian social order.* New Brunswick: Rutgers University Press.

Gates, Henry Louis, Jr. 1991 Critical Fanonism. *Critical Inquiry* (Spring): 457–70.

Hickling, F. W., K. McKenzie, R. Mullen, and R. Murray. 1999. A Jamaican psychiatrist evaluates diagnoses at a London psychiatric hospital. *British Journal of Psychiatry* 175: 283–85.

Joyce, James. [1939] 1965. *Finnegan's wake*. Reprint. New York: Penguin Books.

———. 1959. *James Joyce: The critical writings*. Ed. Ellsworth Mason and Richard Ellmann. New York: Viking Press.

Kendler, Kenneth S. September 1989. The Structured Interview for Schizotypy (SIS).

Kendler, Kenneth S., Jeffrey A. Lieberman, and Dermot Walsh. 1989 "The Structured Interview for Schizotypy (SIS): A preliminary report." *Schizophrenia Bulletin* 15:14–15.

Kenny, Vincent. 2 October 1991, Letter to author. Rome.

———. 1985. The Post-colonial personality. *The Crane Bag* 9: 70–78.

Laing, R. D. 1967. *The politics of experience and the bird of paradise*. London: Penguin.

McCabe, Patrick. 1992. *The butcher boy*. London: Fromm.

McKenzie, K., C. Samele, E. Van Horn, T. Tattan, J. Van Os, Robin Murray. 2001. Comparison of the outcome and treatment of psychosis in people of Caribbean origin living in the UK and British whites. *British Journal of Psychiatry* 178: 160–65.

Meikle, James. 10 January 2002. Schizophrenia link to lack of ethnic community. *The Guardian*. 7 Dec. 2001. *http://society.guardian.co.uk*.

O Faolain, Sean. 1969. *The Irish*. New York: Penguin Books.

O Hehir, Brendan. 1967. *A Gaelic lexicon for Finnegans Wake*. Berkeley: University of California Press.

Price, Richard. 1998. *The convict and the colonel*. Boston: Beacon Press.

Queensland Centre of Schizophrenia Research, The. 15 June 2002. Schizophrenia. *http://www.at-ease.nsf.org.uk/schizophrenia*.

Rhys, Jean. 1966. *Wide Sargasso sea*. New York and London: Norton Press.

Rochester, Sherry, and J. R. Martin. 1979. *Crazy talk: A study of the discourse of schizophrenic speakers*. New York: Plenum.

Rooney, Padraig. 1993. 24 April 1993. Mantle. *Irish Times*. Weekend 9.

Scheper-Hughes, Nancy. 1979. *Saints, scholars, and schizophrenics: Mental illness in rural Ireland*. Berkeley: University of California Press.

Schizophrenia "Linked to lack of sun," 20 July 2001. http://news.bbc.co.uk/1/hi/health/1446968.stm.

Schwartz, S. 1982. Is there a schizophrenic language? *Behavioral and Brain Sciences* 5: 579–629.

Spivak, Gayatri Chakravorty. 1986. Three women's texts and a critique of imperialism. In *"Race," writing, and difference*, ed. Henry Louis Gates Jr., 262–80. Chicago: University of Chicago Press.

Synge, J. M. 1990. *The playboy of the western world*. In *Irish drama 1900–1980*, ed. Colin D. Owens and Joan N. Radner. Washington, DC: Catholic University of America Press.

Torrey, E. F. 1980. *Schizophrenia and civilization*. New York: Jason Aronson.

Torrey, E. F., M. McGuire, A. O'Hare, D. Walsh, and M. P. Spellman. 1984. Endemic psychosis in western Ireland. *American Journal of Psychiatry* 141: 966–70.

Walsh, D. 1976. Two and two make five—Multifactoriogenesis in mental illness in Ireland. *Irish Medical Journal* 69: 417–22.

EIGHT

THE GAZE OF THE WHITE WOLF:
PSYCHOANALYSIS, WHITENESS,
AND COLONIAL TRAUMA

ALFRED J. LÓPEZ

PSYCHOANALYSIS AND WHITENESS

GIVEN THAT PSYCHOANALYSIS has at times appeared as a metanarrative that would bring itself to bear on a subject composed of more or less universal components and impacted by the same transcendental forces regardless of gender, ethnicity, etc., it has come under attack by contemporary theorists of race, gender, and culture. Notable recent critiques include Gayatri Spivak's dismissal of Freud and psychoanalysis in her *Critique of Postcolonial Reason*, in which she questions "the ethico-political agenda of psychoanalysis as a collective taxonomic descriptive in cultural critique" (Spivak 1996, 107) and Jacques Derrida's "Geopsychoanalysis: 'and the rest of the world,'" which takes psychoanalysis to task for its aspirations to the status of a universal narrative with global efficacy and the colonial impulse that lies latent in such a desire (Derrida 1998, 66–67). Yet it is nevertheless true that the praxis of psychoanalysis remains uniquely at the service of its object, in the sense that the method is always and self-reflexively informed by the spectral unconscious content that it episodically but only partially and contingently uncovers. This constant sliding-away (*glissement*) of the object is precisely what makes psychoanalysis ideally suited to a theory and praxis of trauma, and colonial and postcolonial trauma in particular. Given its fundamental acknowledgment of the fluidity of the object, and of the radical difference that constitutes each individual analysand in their personal histories, experiences, inherited tendencies, and so on, psychoanalysis thus emerges in its self-reflexivity as a discourse that could potentially more fully address the process of social, political, and psychological reconstruction that remains in the aftermath of colonialism. Part of this process will require a careful analysis of the impact of race on the colonized in the form of colonial imperatives and regulations. And a crucial component of this analysis must in turn include a focus on whiteness as a colonial cultural imperative calculated in every instance to instill in the colonized an internalized sense of their own inferiority and the inevitability of white European rule.

In the United States, whiteness studies has emerged within the last ten years as a field that critiques relations between race and power within an American studies setting. Scholars such as Richard Dyer, Ross Chambers, and Noel Ignatiev have taken a cue from Henry Louis Gates's poststructuralist portrayal of race generally as a kind of malignant fiction,[1] and have sought to bring greater scrutiny to bear on whiteness as a tacit norm in Western society.[2] Although the aims of white critiques can vary widely—some critics wishing to do away with race as a category entirely, other merely to render whiteness visible as one racial category among others—they nevertheless share the aims of critiquing the privilege and power associated with whiteness, and exposing the ways in which whiteness has historically used its normative power to suppress and marginalize its others.[3] Despite such efforts, however, whiteness continues to retain much of its status and desirability, if not its overt colonial-era power.

Although the stated goal of whiteness studies, following Dyer, is to render whiteness "visible,"[4] much white critique has shifted attention away from race as a visual signifier of difference and privilege and toward an analysis of whiteness as a *cultural* imperative. Two significant consequences follow from this critical moment of recognition that whiteness is more than skin deep: that (1) for the purposes of social privilege there are *gradations* of whiteness, which is to say that some people or groups are culturally "whiter" than others; and (2) "white" skin alone does not make one white. One need only consider the "racial" distinctions that have historically been made among otherwise "white-looking" peoples (Latin American, Irish or other non-English British, European Jews of whatever nationality), and the fact that these distinctions implicitly stand in opposition to the spurious ideal of a "pure" (Euro-Aryan) whiteness, to see at once how and in whose favor hierarchies of whiteness have operated.

Very little of Freud's work directly addresses any explicitly colonial, or even intercultural or interracial, context. Throughout his work Freud strives to present his psychoanalytic theories in the role of the objective scientist-physician, in keeping with the dominant positivist scientific discourse of his day. Paradoxically, this very positivism claimed to have determined objectively—*scientifically*—the physical inferiority and moral degeneracy of the Jews and the superiority of the white (Aryan) race.[5] In fact, Freud's own relative obscurity during the Wolfman's analysis stands out all the more starkly in contrast with the fame and admiration enjoyed during this time by another Jew: the suicide Otto Weininger, celebrated in Viennese intellectual circles for his deeply misogynistic and anti-Semitic diatribe *Sex and Character*.[6] This unresolved tension between the blatant anti-Semitism of the medical establishment of the time and Freud's desire to present himself, as Frank Sulloway tersely puts it, as a "biologist of the mind,"[7] and his new discipline as a science of the mind, never culminates in any explicit manifesto or critique of racism or cultural imperialism.[8]

Applying Freud's own psychoanalytic tools, however, one could argue that his reluctance to tackle such personally resonant subjects only signifies the repression of his own cultural difference from—and tangled relation to—normative (in this case German) whiteness. But we also know that repression is by Freud's own definition never complete, never final. Repression, to borrow Freud's term, is distinguished by the *Nachtraglichkeit* (deferred action)—or in other words, what the subject represses in one form inevitably turns up in another, what is repressed here returns with a vengeance there.

Thus, following the Freudian logic of repression, Freud's awareness of the hostility of the science of his day to his own Jewish identity must necessarily have left a mark, however latent, on his work. As Sander Gilman explains this point, "one of the definitions of the Jew that [Freud] would have internalized was a racial one, and it was a definition that, whether he consciously sought it or not, shaped the argument of psychoanalysis" (Gilman 1993, 3). As a Jew, and one aware of his categorization as a racial other by the white German mainstream, what might Freud's manifest silence on issues of race mean?

It is instructive in this context to note that Freud also displays a certain reticence to tackling the theory of countertransference, as the relative dearth of direct discussion or exposition of it in his work will confirm.[9] Because we have no substantial exposition from Freud himself regarding countertransference, we must resort to a close analysis of the major case histories themselves for an *exegesis*, in the sense of a demonstration or performance, of just how countertransference functions in Freud's work. Given that "From the History of an Infantile Neurosis" is arguably Freud's most important case,[10] it would be a logical place to begin reading for the countertransference and the particular forms it takes for Freud. And as we will see, one crucial—but neglected—dimension of the transference between Freud and the Wolfman centers on not only cultural but also *racial* difference, as each man would have understood it in the context of the times. One a Germanized Jewish intellectual, the other a once-wealthy Russian émigré, neither Freud nor his patient were quite white by Aryan standards, and both were second-class citizens according to the racial logic of the time. To put it

simply, much of what fuels the transference—and countertransference—in
the Wolfman case is precisely each man's awareness of his own qualified,
marginalized relation to whiteness.

COUNTERTRANSFERENCE IN "THE WOLFMAN"

A full reading of Freud's case history of the Wolfman is beyond the scope of
this chapter.[11] However, we need go no farther than Freud's analysis of the
Wolfman's anxiety-dream, from which the analyst (re)constructs the patient's
primal scene, to see how the case provides an instructive example of a psychoanalytic praxis that strives throughout to defend its claims to a universal
scientific efficacy while maintaining a self-reflexive awareness of itself as it
interacts with—and acts upon—its object.

But the Wolfman case study contains other lessons for a specifically
cross-cultural and even a *postcolonial* psychoanalysis. Although it does not
itself portray a colonial relation in the narrow sense, the study does reveal
a transference that turns on the analysand's—and to some extent, the
analyst's—relation to normative hegemonic whiteness. Additionally, although
postcolonial studies have until very recently focused primarily on the
Anglophone literatures of the Caribbean, Africa, and India (the recent ex-
plosion in Irish postcolonial studies notwithstanding), the turn toward a
more global literary studies has meant that scholars are beginning to explore
the benefits and potential pitfalls of bringing postcolonial theoretical approaches to a broader range of literatures and cultures. Particularly relevant
to the present context are Anikó Imre's assertion that "[p]ostcolonial thinking would become more inclusive by taking into consideration . . . Eastern
European nationalisms" (Imre 1995, 406) and David Chioni Moore's
postcolonial analysis of Russia and recent Soviet republics.[12] Further, the
analysis takes place within the larger historical context of pre–World War I
Russia and Germany as rival imperial powers (Young 2001, 165); the former
is in crisis with the imminent demise of the Tsarist government and on the
cusp of a new, arguably equally imperial, Soviet phase, while the latter stands
at the end of its ascendance as an imperial power and the verge of a precipitous, if temporary, fall.[13] In fact, an increasing climate of racial intolerance
and rise in the fever pitch of racialized discourses of national "purity" clearly
mark the period immediately preceding the war. Hamilton and Herwig describe the "war euphoria" and rhetoric of national (read "racial") "rejuvena-
tion" that "gripped the European capitals" in August 1914, at the start of the
war (Hamilton 2003, 33). Racism drove much of this "war euphoria, fueled
by a social Darwinist view of war as a necessary vehicle by which to defend
the racial purity of nations. For Germany and Austria-Hungary, this meant
holding the racial line against the "lesser Balkan peoples," a racial category
which included Russians (Hamilton, 117).[14] Nor is this by any stretch a new
or revisionist historical view. In a widely-read study published at the height

of the war, R. W. Seton-Watson argues for "the Slav Question" as *the* central issue of day and an indispensable point of entry for understanding the origins of the war (Seton-Watson 1968, 9). Seton-Watson goes on to describe the German-Magyar bond as a mutual agreement (formalized in the Compromise of Ausgleich in 1867) to share power in Central Europe by in effect shutting out the remaining ten "races" in the region (32–35), and points to "pan-German aspirations" (171) as the imperialist project underlying much of the push toward war. Russia's July 1914 mobilization only provided the immediate impetus for war already driven by a racist ideology of Aryan supremacy.[15] Thus, whiteness, not as skin color but as a *cultural imperative*, was very much in the Viennese air while Freud and the Wolfman met for their daily sessions, and were reaching their height (for the moment at least) precisely at the end of the analysis, as the Wolfman himself explains in his memoir: "The end of my analysis with Professor Freud coincided with the assassination of the Austrian Crown Prince . . . and his wife . . . this fateful 28th of June 1914." Race, and the dangers posed to Jews and Russians alike by an ever more powerful ideology of white supremacy, could hardly *not* have been on both men's minds, whatever the analyst's claims or aspirations to a positivist or scientific neutrality.

As we shall see in the Wolfman case, the positioning of the subjects in relation to both Western scientific discourses and European (German) whiteness as a cultural imperative illustrates what Imre calls "the effaced colonial relationship between Eastern Europeans and western intellectuals" (406). Although Freud does not divulge the specific professional background of the patient, we know that he is a well-educated young man from a wealthy family. Freud reveals his national identity only at the very end of the study. As for Freud himself, we could hardly hope to find a more iconic representative of Imre's "western intellectual."

Happily, more thorough biographical information is available on the Wolfman, aka Sergius Konstantinovich, and his notoriously guarded psychoanalyst. This additional information, I would argue, reveals a dimension of the analysis—more specifically, a dimension of the transference itself—that neither Freud nor his famous patient ever cared to address at any length. Freud's struggles during his early years of establishing a successful practice in late-nineteenth-century Vienna are well known and documented, and turn-of-the-century Vienna has long been characterized as a place filled with young talent hobbled by a hidebound social, professional, and political order.[16] The fact and significance of his Jewishness—and even the possibility that some of the young doctor's difficulties may have been the direct and indirect result of anti-Semitism— seldom receive much mention. In otherwise excellent portrayals of turn-of-the-century Vienna, both William Everdell and Frederic Morton blame the young Freud's struggles in the early days on Vienna's paradoxical status as a city that generated so many great young innovators only to stifle them. Freud, according to this view, suffers a sort of benign neglect at the hands of the conservative Viennese medical and scientific establishment.[17] Morton goes so far as to aver that Freud possessed a very "unViennese personality,"[18] and

> could not control those essentials in his behavior that prevented
> fashionable success in his field or for that matter in any other field
> in Vienna. . . . The stage instinct of the Viennese, the flair that
> commanded attention by seducing it, escaped Freud entirely. He
> could not even affect a popular consultation-room manner. (Morton
> 1979, 139)

In fact, Freud's most "unViennese" trait—that which permanently barred from professional and social ascendancy in turn-of-the-century Vienna—was the indelible mark of his Jewishness. As Gilman points out, Freud's Vienna was an intensely anti-Semitic place, where "[b]eing Jewish meant being marked as different" (Gilman 12). Thus, Freud's understanding of his own Jewishness would necessarily have been informed by the anti-Semitic rhetoric of the day, which portrayed the Jew, however acculturated, as a racial other. For Freud, then, "[b]eing Jewish meant being a member of a race" (Gilman, 6). For white Vienna, to be "Viennese" may or may not have meant having "stage instinct" or flair or "surface charm" (Morton, 139). But it certainly meant being white. And both Freud and white Vienna—and the Wolfman—knew that he was not.

Although the Wolfman seldom mentions Freud in the context of his Jewishness in either his memoir or interviews, the few references he does make indicate that he is at least aware of the fact. Certainly the Wolfman would have been aware of psychoanalysis's reputation as a "Jewish science," and of the pejorative implication of that phrase. Freud grew increasingly aware of the possibility of psychoanalysis's failing to reach a broader audience precisely because of its close association with Jews, which is one reason he sought to cast Jung as the Aryan inheritor of Freud's psychoanalytic mantle.[19] Psychoanalysis as a treatment for mental disorders was in fact so far from the mainstream in the Wolfman's day that he considers it "quite remarkable" that he learned of Freud from a doctor who "was probably the only person in Odessa who knew of the existence of Freud and psychoanalysis" (Wolfman, 79). Freud's famous patient also marvels at Freud's having opened to him "a completely new world . . . known to only a few people in those days" (Wolfman, 83). And the Wolfman's ethnic identity as a young Russian man from a wealthy Russian Orthodox family would certainly have marked him as different from the vast majority of Freud's patients and colleagues, who were Jewish. Both professionals and the population at large would have been aware, as was early Freudian Victor Tausk, of "the nearly exclusive involvement of Jews in the progress of psychoanalysis" (qtd. in Gilman 1993, 53). Given the Wolfman's own marginalized position vis-à-vis German whiteness by virtue of being Russian (i.e., a Slav), we can already see how such mate-rial can enter the narrative frame of analysis and be transferred onto the person of the analyst. Given the atmosphere of anti-Semitism and growing war hysteria that served as the background for the Wolfman's analysis, it should not surprise anyone to find that the Jewish analyst and Russian analysand share a transference based on each one's awareness of the other's marginal relation to normative German whiteness. The questions now is how to *read* the progress of that transference in the case study itself.

THE DREAM OF THE WHITE WOLF

Let us begin with the patient's description of the anxiety-dream:

> I dreamt that it was night and that I was lying in my bed. (My bed stood with its foot towards the window; in front of the window there was a row of old walnut trees. I know it was winter when I had the dream, and night-time.) Suddenly the window opened of its own accord, and I was terrified to see that some white wolves were sitting on the big walnut tree in front of the window. There were six or seven of them. *The wolves were quite white,* and looked more like foxes or sheep-dogs, for they had big tails like foxes and they had their ears pricked like dogs when they are attending to some-thing. In great terror, evidently of being eaten up by the wolves, I screamed and woke up. (Freud [1918] 1974, 29)

Freud emphasizes that although the patient related this dream early on in the analysis, its interpretation "dragged on over several years" and became clear "only during the last months of analysis, and only then thanks to spontaneous work on the patient's part" (33). For Freud, the anxiety-dream "reproduces the unknown material of the scene in some distorted form," thus constituting the manifest version of a latent, unknown but traumatic content (34).

The general outline of the rest of Freud's interpretation of the anxiety-dream, and the relation of the dream to the larger trajectory of the patient's analysis, is well known and at any rate too intricate for me to do it justice here.[20] For now suffice it to say that the dream metonymically links the primal scene, of the patient's parents having sex *more ferarum* (from behind), with the patient's own repressed desire for his father. The dreamer realizes the memory of the scene "which was able to show him what sexual satisfac-tion from his father was like; and the result was terror, *horror of the fulfillment of the wish,* and consequently a flight from his father to his less dangerous nurse" (36).

More relevant to my purposes here is the fact that Freud ventures only brief, somewhat contradictory remarks on the cross-cultural dimension of the

Wolfman case, and these only toward the end of the study. In the conclusion of the case history, Freud lists the patient's cultural difference—which he obliquely calls "a national character which was foreign to ours"—among the difficulties that "made the task of feeling one's way into his mind a laborious one" (104). Freud's lament here, however, apparently contradicts his earlier statement in the text that the patient's admiration for all things German, and disdain for his native cultural and scientific products, held advantages for the transference. This earlier remark, divulged in the context of a German tutor whom the patient loved as a father-surrogate (68–69), marks the first mention of the patient's national or cultural difference. Freud does not elaborate, and in fact does not mention the matter again until he finally and flatly states the patient's nationality in the final chapter, and even then only in a footnote at the very end of the narrative: "It will have been easy to guess from my account that the patient was a Russian" (121 n.1). This brief mention, and the fact that Freud makes very little of it in the case history despite his admission that the cross-cultural nature of the analysis "was incidentally of great advantage during the treatment" (69), begs the question of why Freud doesn't introduce more of this element of the analysis into the case history. One reason might be Freud's own assumptions about the universal applicability of psychoanalytic concepts across national origins, cultural or religious identifications, and so on. Another possibility, however, is Freud's own failure to recognize the patient's marginal relation to European whiteness—and more specifically to German culture and nationality as paragons of this whiteness. Gilman presents a third possibility: that Freud actually works in his writings to exclude as much as possible any mention or consideration of race in an effort to avoid as much as possible the stigma of psychoanalysis as a "Jewish science." I would add only that beyond protecting his discipline, Freud acts largely out of an awareness of his own precarious position in relation to German whiteness and "white" Viennese science. According to Gilman many of Freud's best-known theories " all fit into the models of 'universalization' of attributes and 'projection' of these attributes onto other categories of difference" (Gilman 1993a, 7).[21] One effect of such a strategy, however, is the exclusion from the analysis of a crucial part of the transference and countertransference.

Whatever Freud's own qualms about his own marginal position vis-à-vis German Euro-whiteness, his view of the patient's relative ethnicity compared to normative whiteness as a "great advantage to the transference" belies the fact that the patient implicitly suffered from an inferiority complex with regard to German culture, one possibly triggered by his attachment to a German tutor as a father-surrogate. It is worth citing the relevant passage in its entirety:

> It was as an after-effect of [the patient's] affection for the tutor, who left him soon afterwards, that in his later life he preferred German

things (as, for instance, physicians, sanatoriums, women) to those belonging to *his* native country (representing his father)—a fact which was incidentally of great advantage during the treatment. (Freud [1918] 1974, 69).

This attachment of the patient's, as well as the fact that this complex emerges "as an after-effect of his affection" for the German tutor—an affection that the patient then obviously transfers onto Freud himself—and the homoerotic dimension of all the patient's father-surrogate object choices strongly suggests that we read the symptom in a particular way. First, the patient has come to associate normative whiteness, in the form of German culture, with masculinity, and his own national culture—in relation to his now-sick father and his own passive-homosexual urges—with femininity. Second, and perhaps more illustrative of Freud's conspicuous omission of this part of the analysis from the history, Freud is himself loath to discuss his patient's transference toward him—and thus his own implication in the homoerotic countertransference—although he is apparently not above using it to his advantage ("a fact which was incidentally of great advantage to the transference during the treatment"). This latter point is consistent with Freud's general reticence to discussing countertransference.[22]

The larger problem, however, is that Freud's apparent strategy belies (1) his own homophobia and conflation of masculinity with Euro-whiteness; (2) his assumption of his own culture's "masculine" superiority over his patient's; and most damningly (3) his suppression of his own fears and complexes toward his own relation of marginality and inadequacy as an ethnic Jew to normative, masculine Euro-whiteness. Clearly, Freud identifies with Euro-German culture in a way that belies and subsumes his own background as a Moravian Jew who began his career in a very anti-Semitic nineteenth-century Vienna. This despite Freud's well-documented awareness of himself as a Jew, and his various public demonstrations of this awareness.[23] Although it would be beyond the scope of the present essay, an oppositional counterinterpretation of Freud's dream self-analyses in, for example, *The Interpretation of Dreams*, would offer a way to begin to read Freud's ambivalent imaginary relation to his own Europeanness and whiteness.[24]

More plausible within the scope of this chapter, however, would be a detailed reading of whiteness as a point of transference and countertransference within the Wolfman case study. More specifically, such a reading would examine the ways in which Freud himself avoids entering into a sustained consideration of whiteness as an overdetermining factor in his patient's illness. We may begin with the Wolfman's narration of the anxiety-dream itself, and more specifically with the obvious element of staging in the dream: the window as a frame or stage within which the "action" (which is not an action, since nothing in the dream moves) occurs, and its opening as the drawing-back of a curtain. In any case, the dream-staging presents both a

barrier to signification and its facilitation: the window functions as a demar-
cating line to distinguish the dream "there" and dreamer "here," and it opens
"of its own accord" to reveal the dream symbols and commence the dream
(Freud [1918] 1974, 29). The patient's first descriptor for the wolves that
then appear sitting in a walnut tree thus framed in the window is that they
are white—in fact "*quite white*, and looked more like foxes or sheep-dogs, for
they had tails like foxes and they had their ears pricked like dogs when they
are attending to something" (29; emphasis added). So already within the
patient's recollection here is whiteness *watching* the dreamer, and the dreamer's
anxiety at finding himself under the intent gaze (and implicit menace, and
judgment) of that whiteness.

Freud soon addresses this element of the dream with the question,
"Why were the wolves white?" (30). Freud then explains that the patient
associates whiteness with the sheep his father used to take him to see, and
an epidemic that killed many of them. Thus, the dream presents whiteness
within an immediate context of passivity and death, both in relation and
proximity to the father. The insistence of the color white—what Lacan
might call its "agency"[25]—returns as Freud considers "why [there were] six or
seven wolves" in the dream (31). The number points to a fairy tale entitled
"The Wolf and the Seven Little Goats," in which "the number seven occurs,
and also the number six" (31). The wolf eats up six of the seven little goats,
with the last escaping by hiding in a grandfather clock. Yet the color white
enters here too, "for the wolf had his paw made white at the baker's after the
little goats had recognized him on his first visit by his gray paw" (31). Both
fairy tales that figure in the dream analysis (the other one is "Little Red
Riding Hood") feature images of eating up, the wolf's belly being cut open,
the death of the wolf, and the tree. This second appearance of whiteness,
this time in the form of the wolf's paw *masquerading* as white, corresponds
again to the patient's apparent dread of whiteness and his regard of it as a
menace. This time, however, whiteness is no longer sitting quietly in judgment, as its move to "eat up" the children would seem to indicate it has
already made up its mind as to what to do with them. Freud doesn't pursue
this strand of the analysis. But the recurrence of whiteness in the dream,
however displaced onto the patient's family romance or overdetermined
with it, is consistent with Freud's earlier explanation of the patient's screen-
memories by way of an analogy with the nation's myth of origins:

> Here, then, was the explanation of the phantasies whose existence
> had already been divined. *They were meant to efface the memory of an*
> *event which later on seemed offensive to the patient's masculine self-*
> *esteem, and they reached this end by putting an imaginary and desirable*
> *converse in the place of the historical truth.* . . . These phantasies, there-
> fore, corresponded exactly to the legends by means of which a
> nation that has become great and proud tries to conceal the

insignificance and failure of its beginnings. (Freud [1918] 1974, 20; emphasis added)

The national "myth of origins" analogy is as remarkable for its sudden emergence in the Wolfman case study as for its equally abrupt disappearance; Freud never returns to the analogy. The only hypothesis Freud ever offers for the insistence of whiteness in the anxiety-dream comes in a footnote in which he speculates that the patient's parents may have worn white underclothes to bed (37 n.4). The entire summary of the dream that follows in a long footnote isn't necessary for me to rehearse here. More significant for present purposes is Freud's interpretation within that summary of the significance of the color white—and what that interpretation leaves out:

> [The wolves] were quite white. This feature is unessential in itself, but is strongly emphasized in the dreamer's narrative. It owes its intensity to a copious fusion of elements from all the strata of the material, and it combines unimportant details from the other sources of the dream with a fragment of the primal scene which is more significant. The last part of its determination goes back to the white of his parents' bedclothes and underclothes, and to this is added the white of the flocks of sheep, and of the sheepdogs, as an allusion to his sexual inquiries among animals, and the white in the fairy tale of "The Seven Little Goats," in which the mother is recognized by the white of her hand. ("History" 43 n.2)

At no point, either here or in Freud's subsequent discussion of the case history, does the analyst make any association between whiteness, the patient's ethnicity, and his affinity for all things German. Indeed, the overdetermination of these factors seems to escape Freud entirely. While the presence of white underclothes as part of the traumatic scene is certainly possible, and could serve as an associative link in the elaboration of the dream analysis as part of the overdetermined chain of signification, it is in itself insufficient as an explanation of the emphasis on whiteness in the dream. Given all of this, Freud's failure to further pursue this strand of the analysis, especially in a case study as painstakingly developed as this one, must strike us as peculiar given that both the screen-memory of the white wolves and the patient's affinity for German culture as manifested in his choice of father-surrogates, culminating in the transference onto Freud, collectively point to the possibility of the whiteness of the wolves as a screen not (or at least not only) for the primal scene that Freud constructs but the patient's own troubled relation to normative European (as represented by German) whiteness.

Indeed, in this context an exercise as simple as following the Wolfman's transference along the series of father-surrogates suggests an overdetermination of object-cathexes that includes the patient's troubled relation to whiteness as a key factor in his choice of objects. The commingling of piety and sexual impulses in the patient, for example, lead him to "fear God" and thus enter into a complicated dialectic of clinging to the old father and rejecting the new (God-as-father). Nevertheless, Freud points out, this new hostility toward God "had its prototype in a hostile impulse against his father, which had come into existence under the influence of the anxiety-dream, and it was at bottom only a revival of that impulse" (66). In fact, Freud directly associates the coexistence or overdetermination of this new stage alongside the old with the patient's sudden discovery of his father's illness:

> He had not seen his father for many months, when one day his mother said she was going to take the children with her to the town and show them something that would very much please them. She then took them to a sanatorium, where they saw their father again; he looked ill, and the boy felt very sorry for him. ("History" 67)

Thus, the patient begins to associate his father "with all the cripples, beggars, and poor people" he has come to loathe; and thus begins the series of transferential moves away from the biological father and onto the string of father-surrogates which includes a Latin teacher named Wolf (!), the German tutor, and finally Freud himself (39–40).[26] We should note in this context that the wolf figure in the stories never appears weak or ill, but as a wily, threatening, and predatory animal. Further, in Russian folk tales and legends the figure of the wolf is often associated with sorcerers and forest spirits; it is a common Russian folk belief that the wolf is a favorite of the *leshii*, or forest-master, who sometimes appears in the form of a white wolf (Ivanits 1989, 68).[27] Russian folk beliefs often also associate sorcerers with certain physical characteristics. Consider this description of a sorcerer by folklorists Boris and Iurii Sokolov in 1908–1909, a time roughly contemporaneous with the Wolfman case:

> [H]e was an old man of about sixty with a permanent frown and angry eyes that gazed out from thick brows. . . . [He] kept thick books from which, the peasants believed, he told fortunes. He spoke slowly and imposingly, communicating for the most part in riddles and hints and thus imparting an aura of mystery to his person. The Sokolovs considered him a clever rogue who gained considerable profit from the fear and respect that he inspired. (Ivanits 98)

In Linda Ivanits's useful study of Russian folk beliefs, she explains that such descriptions of sorcerers are quite common, and almost all such descriptions "mention the sorcerer's bushy eyebrows, his penetrating, or sometimes, furtive ('wolfish') glance, and his tendency to be aloof and secretive" (Ivanits, 98). Given that Freud himself was "an old man of about sixty" during the time of the Wolfman's analysis, we may plausibly wonder to what extent Freud's own appearance and general demeanor may have contributed to his patient's association of him with the wolf-figure, and thus to the transference. Certainly the analyst's physical resemblance to the figure of the Russian sorcerer, who is himself associated with the wolf, would have struck the patient, if only unconsciously. Additionally, Freud's reputation among his defenders as an aloof, erudite (see "thick books" above), powerful healer—and among his detractors as a "clever rogue" who knows how to inspire "fear and respect"—could only further strengthen the patient's association with the Russian folk sorcerer.[28] Finally, aside from the "grandfather clock" anecdote Freud tells to demonstrate the patient's transference toward himself as a father-surrogate, we can read at least one latent sign—we might call it a Freudian paraprax or "slip"—in Freud's reference to the analyst's "prick[ing] his ears" (Freud [1918] 1974, 89) at the addition of new material from the patient; this statement very directly echoes the patient's own description of the wolves in the anxiety-dream "with their ears pricked" (29).[29]

More easily glimpsed within the Wolfman narrative, however, is the patient's displacement of his affection away from his Russian father, first onto another white Wolf, then on to more explicitly German figures of masculine authority (the tutor, then the analyst). Thus, we may read the entire succession of father-surrogates as one in which the patient transfers his affection away from an ailing, failing figure of Russian whiteness and onto the healthier paragons of normative German whiteness. This transference would be strengthened between the initial phase of analysis and the second postwar session by the facts of the patient's family fortune having been lost in the war, and Freud's relative rise in fortunes as a prominent and successful scholar and analyst during the same period.[30] The Wolfman's transference toward Freud continued almost to the end of the patient's life, and certainly outlasted the analyst's own; in a late interview, psychoanalysis' most famous patient blames Freud for his having lost the family fortune: "I blame him for not having allowed me to travel to Russia. You see, that intestinal business came through psychoanalysis. I lost my fortune. . . . He should not have kept me back" (Obholzer [1980] 1982, 49).[31]

I would argue that the Wolfman's reproaches and even hostility toward Freud in later years paradoxically confirm both the enduring strength of the transference and the Wolfman's awareness of it. Such a reading would also make sense libidinally, as the patient would almost certainly associate health with virility; if his Russian father is no longer able to give him the passive sexual satisfaction he craves, he has found more virile German father-surrogates who can. This latter point is implicit in Freud's mention of the patient's association of him with the predatory wolf in "The Seven Little Goats."[32] The Wolfman's lingering transference toward Freud as a father figure also emerges in Ruth Mack Brunswick's discussion of the case, when she describes him as having been "shocked at Freud's appearance" after the analyst had surgery on his mouth (Gardiner 1971, 268). The Wolfman's hostility toward Freud erupts during his analysis with Mack Brunswick, in the immediate aftermath of his having seen Freud in an ailing state; and his neurotic symptoms also return during this period.[33] Clearly, this behavior is consistent with the Wolfman's lifelong pattern of displacing affection away from ailing father figures and onto stronger, more virile ones. The Wolfman's later dreams about Freud, especially one described by Mack Brunswick in which the analyst appears as castrated father figure, confirms both the continuing effect of the transference and its latent cross-cultural component:

> The patient's father, in the dream a professor, resembling, however, a begging musician known to the patient, sits at a table and warns the others present not to talk about financial matters before the patient, because of his tendency to speculate. His father's nose is long and hooked, causing the patient to wonder at its change. (Gardiner 286)

The Wolfman's dream-portrayal of Freud here—an old "professor" in the guise of a beggar, sporting a "long and hooked nose" (!)—confirm all at once the patient's lingering attachment for the father figure, his resentment and horror at the latter's declining health, and his awareness of the father/analyst's Jewishness. The Wolfman cannot displace his affection onto the new analyst, because as a woman she is an inappropriate choice for a father figure. Thus, along with his "rage" toward Freud comes a growing "contempt" toward Mack Brunswick; he dreams of her as "an old gypsy woman," another racially encoded piece of the transference (Gardiner, 283). ("Gypsies," as Mack Brunswick explains, "are notorious liars.") Finally, Freud's own discussion of the Wolfman's history of father-surrogates coincides with his first hint of the patient's nationality (i.e., that he is not German), which the analyst does not explicitly divulge until the study's final footnote. This coincidence suggests an association between symptom and cultural unconscious that Freud neither confirms nor denies, but simply neglects—a curious omission in an otherwise elaborate, painstakingly constructed narrative.

The Wolfman's dream of "riding on a horse . . . pursued by a gigantic caterpillar" (Freud [1918] 1974, 69–70) provides further evidence of Freud's neglect—or evasion—of the significance of whiteness for his patient's case. That the dream lends itself to a more culturally nuanced interpretation than Freud himself ascribes to it becomes evident in the recurrence of elements from previous dreams. First, the patient himself recognizes the dream as "an allusion to an earlier one from the period before the tutor," in which the Devil, dressed in black and standing "in the upright attitude with which the wolf [as appeared in a children's book illustration] . . . had terrified him so much" is pointing at a giant snail, which Freud identifies as "a perfect female sexual symbol" (69–70). The patient avers—and Freud agrees—that the dream portrays the patient's desire for a teacher to "give him the last pieces of information" missing from his knowledge of sexual intercourse (70). The fact, however, that this dream occurs immediately before the patient's "replacement" of his ailing Russian father with the German tutor, and that he comes to associate Freud himself with the wolf, would indicate that the patient has already begun to overdetermine—and thus associate—authority, sexual knowledge and prowess, the figure of the analyst himself, and normative German whiteness. The fact that this association occurs despite the patient's manifest knowledge of Freud's Jewishness, and even of psychoanalysis as a "Jewish science," underscores the power of the transference that Freud so carefully cultivates.

A waking experience the patient has while horseback riding on the family estate provides further links in the associative chain of whiteness: (1) the patient rides past "a peasant who was lying asleep with his little boy beside him," who then awakes and angrily chases the dreamer away; and (2) his recollection on the grounds of "trees that were *quite white*, spun all over by caterpillars" (70; emphasis added). Freud's interpretation, while largely plausible, fails to fully address the whiteness of the trees:

> We can see that he took flight from the realization of the phantasy of the son lying with his father, and that he brought in the white trees in order to make an allusion to the anxiety dream of the white wolves on the walnut tree. It was thus a direct outbreak of dread of the feminine attitude towards men against which he at first protected himself by his religious sublimation and was soon to protect himself still more effectively by the military one. (70)

For Freud, both the waking incident and dream point solely to the patient's increasingly frantic attempts to sublimate his passive-feminine attitudes beneath a more masculine current, via first religion, then the military (which begs the question, if only in passing, of whether all such repressive religious and/or military regimes—Nazism, the Taliban, and so on—always already repress a latent homoerotic current). But given the associative links and overdeterminations I have already pointed out, we may begin to identify in both the case and Freud's interpretation a conflation of masculine sexuality with normative Euro-whiteness—an element with which Freud himself is complicit as part of the transference and countertransference, and which, to the extent that he thinks of it at all, he evidently does not consider problematic. (As Freud does not at all mention this association of normative whiteness with normative heterosexuality, there is no reason to think that he does.) As the analysis unfolds, Freud comes to associate the Wolfman's later somatic symptoms with hysteria, thus further feminizing the patient and rendering more (but not completely) explicit the association between sexuality, repression, and whiteness that I have been attempting to delineate.[34]

Thus, to the extent that the analyst shares the patient's cultural associations as they pass into the libidinal realm, these associations and assumptions go generally unchallenged in the analysis. Given the centrality of the Wolfman case, both within the Freudian oeuvre as his most celebrated case study and willy-nilly as a theoretical text for psychoanalytic training and study, one may plausibly wonder to what extent the racial and cultural blindness displayed in the case study have become part of the legacy of psychoanalysis in its analysis of its ethnic and cultural others.

As Freud himself points out toward the end of the Wolfman case, in his discussion of the patient's "dangerous" homosexuality, "[t]he process of repression left behind it *a trace* which cannot be overlooked" (Freud [1918] 1974, 112). This is precisely the way in which the process of association, along with its corresponding elements in the dream-work, functions in psychoanalysis. Repression is never complete or totally successful—it always leaves a trace, some element, however small or apparently insignificant, which will become part of the next deferred stage of formation of symptoms. Thus, in psychoanalysis' own narrative the analyst/scholar simply learns to follow the symptom along the chain of signification, as it manifests at different points and under different signs. We might think here of the popular science fiction plot of texts such as Robert Heinlein's *The Puppet Masters* or Ira Levin's *The Stepford Wives*, or John Carpenter's films *The Thing* and *They Live!*, in which the alien possession of humans leaves no apparent (read "manifest") trace but is always detectable by the discerning eye.[35] In the colonial context this idea becomes useful for formulations such as Homi Bhabha's conception of the postcolonial subject of color as "*not quite . . . not white* (Bhabha, 89) or the more poignant example of Fanon's black man who *almost* transforms himself into a perfect white Frenchman.[36] In these and other cases of colonial or neocolonial hegemony, the governing or normative discourse institutes in the conquered an identification with, and often a desire to emulate, the dominant culture. But although many of the colonized may come to identify at least partially with the dominant power, and some completely, none ever fully receive such unqualified identification or recognition from those of the cultural elite. Such subjects remain hopelessly split, irremediably mediated by the dominant culture but never fully admitted to it. Such science fiction plots, I would argue, latently portray the paranoia of purity of the dominant culture; as it maintains a specious image of itself as pure and fears contamination or penetration of its ranks from without, it looks for ever-smaller signs and ever-finer distinctions between itself and the invading entity (which is always already inside). This dynamic of white purity and paranoia reaches an identifiable crisis point in recent mainstream films such as *American Beauty, Pleasantville, Election, Eyes Wide Shut,* and even *The Truman Show;* in each case the normative American society—which for the purposes of the plot appears hyper-normal, almost unreal in its utter homogeneity—is besieged by what the films initially portray as an outside threat but emerges over the course of the film as internal tensions already existing within the characters.[37] Given the specific cultural logics of nationalism and racial purity that everywhere surround, even envelop the period of the Wolfman's analysis with Freud—the so-called "Social Darwinism" informing national rhetoric and even government policies immediately before the war, the ideology of race surrounding German, Jewish (both Western and Eastern), and Slavic identities—Freud's remarkable self-reflexivity in the case study is conspicuously absent *only in regard to the patient's ethnicity as a Russian in relation to normative German Euro-whiteness*, an element that—because of its uncomfortable proximity to his own countertransferential issues with the topic—receives scant mention and no real analytical attention within the case study.[38]

The final footnote of the Wolfman case study, which as I have indicated contains Freud's final disclosure of the patient's Russian nationality, strongly suggests the analyst's own avoidance of the countertransference, more specifically of the implications of the patient's relation to German Euro-whiteness for his own status as an acculturated Western Jew. Freud's curious placement of the note at the very end of the study already lends it a paradoxical position that suggests a certain ambivalence, as a location both marginal (as footnotes are generally considered to be) and central (as the final sentences of the text, appended as they are as a footnote to the final sentence of the main text) to the text's final assertion of its own meaning. It is thus possible and even compelling to read the study's final footnote as a supplement, in the Derridean sense, to the main text's conclusion; that is, its apparently elliptical or secondary status in relation to the main text's ending belies its centrality to an alternative reading of the case study—one that focuses on the ethnic or racial element that Freud's own interpretation ignores.[39]

Freud's tactful (and perhaps tactical) neglect of the countertransference of whiteness emerges most strongly in light of his awareness of the patient's attachment to him as a representative of all things German: "[The patient] then came to Vienna and reported that immediately after the end of the treatment *he had been seized with a longing to tear himself from my influence*" (121–22 n.1; emphasis added). Given the very nationalistic nature of the then-imminent war, could the patient's resistance constitute a latent realization of his own identity as a marginalized subject in relation to German whiteness, thus marking his desire to break away as an act of either self-disgust or self-assertion (or as is so often the case in psychoanalysis, both)? After the patient's confession, Freud reports, further therapy followed with the end of eliminating "a piece of the transference which had not hitherto been overcome" (122 n.1). After this matter-of-fact statement come the astonishing final two sentences of the footnote and study:

> Since then the patient has felt normal and has behaved unexceptionably, in spite of the war having robbed him of his home, his

possessions, and all his family relationships. It may be that his very misery, by gratifying his sense of guilt, contributed to the consolidation of his recovery. (122 n.1)

We know that the Wolfman suffered much during the years immediately following Freud's analysis. As Muriel Gardiner explains, Freud's most famous patient "lost his home and his fortune, and became a stateless émigré in Austria" (vi). In addition to his lifelong struggles with his obsessional neuroses in their various forms, Freud's once-affluent patient "was occupied just keeping himself alive and had little direct interest in world events" (Gardiner, vi). Yet what *else* might Freud's final, rather cryptic sentence mean? Had the patient's relation to German whiteness changed from what it had been before the war, before Germany suffered defeat and humiliation at the hands of the other Western European powers, and before it was forced to surrender both its colonial possessions and territory it had taken from Russia during the war?[40] What, in short, had German whiteness as a normative cultural imperative suffered in the patient's eyes, in terms of post-Versailles damage to its imperial prestige? Finally, of what did that "piece of the transference which had not been hitherto overcome" consist? Did at least part of its "overcoming" necessitate the analyst's implicit reinforcement of the preeminence of German culture, and his own status of authority as representative of it?

These and other questions must unfortunately remain unanswered, because of the minimal amount of space that Freud grants to this most intriguing—and I suspect for the Wolfman, crucial—dimension of the analysis. Yet given what we have already learned about the transference and the role of German Euro-whiteness within it, can it be mere happenstance that Freud, who is explicitly aware of his role as the latest in the patient's chain of father-surrogates, reveals the patient's nationality in the same final paragraph in which he so pointedly reasserts his lasting authority—or that of psychoanalysis, which in this context amounts to the same thing—over him? Any responsible exploration of this question must consider the Wolfman's abandonment of his ailing Russian father, and the danger Freud must have intuited of the patient's likewise abandoning Freud himself as a representative of a now defeated, ailing nation (and an increasingly discredited one, given the rise of anti-Semitism and the growing association of psychoanalysis with Jewishness). It would not be implausible to read Freud's response to the radical change in the transference as the analyst's recognition of the need to reassert himself and his German culture as a still viable, powerful force in the patient's life. Freud, in short, would preserve the homoerotic love of the patient's so-called positive transference[41] in order to avoid symbolically suffering the biological father's fate and the patient's transferring his affection and allegiance to a new father-surrogate. By forestalling the patient's shift in cultural affinity from Germany to one of the war's victors—say, England or France—Freud can ensure the continuing efficacy of the analysis and its enduring influence over the patient. Thus, the footnote's paradoxical status as supplement to the main text's conclusion: The very success of the analysis *depends on Freud's ability to imprint the hegemony of German Euro-whiteness on the patient in a lasting manner.* Or to return to the later Freud, the possibility of the certainty of a terminable analysis relies paradoxically on the uncertainty of the *interminable*, indeed unending task of maintaining white European (in this instance German) cultural hegemony.[42] And as a crowning paradox, Freud must undertake all of this in the name of a whiteness from whose material privileges he himself is excluded, as the analyst was himself keenly aware. As Sander Gilman demonstrates, Freud very early on internalized a racialist model of his self-identity as a Jew, a fact he confessed most pointedly in a 1927 letter to George Sylvester Viereck: "[My] language . . . is German. I considered myself German intellectually, until I noticed the growth of anti-Semitic prejudices in Germany and German Austria. Since that time, I prefer to call myself a Jew" (Viereck 1930, 30).

A POSTCOLONIAL PSYCHOANALYSIS?

Such aporias as the one Freud encounters in both the Wolfman and his late essays reveal psychoanalysis in its function as a contingent universal grounded in an interminable calculation of the other's difference—a contingency that not even Freud himself at the end of his long life and career, as we have seen, could unequivocally claim to have solved.[43] Near the end of the Wolfman study, Freud himself asserts

> that everything cannot be learnt from a single case and that everything cannot be decided by it; we must content ourselves with exploiting whatever it may happen to show most clearly. There are in any case *narrow limits* to what a psychoanalysis is called upon to explain. (105)

At such moments psychoanalysis would step back from the position of a would-be master narrative, and remain within the realm of processes or situations or conditions that "do not require to be explained but merely to be described" (105). Such a psychoanalysis—of description rather than prescription—is most appropriate for the postcolonial ethos of listening I have argued for elsewhere—that is, a discourse that would learn to listen to its others and their needs, rather than impose upon those others universalized dogmas and schematics inherited from an often oppressive and violently dominating Western scientific and philosophical tradition.[44]

Psychoanalysis can succeed at this task, however, only to the extent that it can check its own tendencies toward universalization, and its complicities with the systematic imposition of Western cultural paradigms on the rest of the world that still poses as a universal humanism. The point is not, as some would argue, that such universals might prove valid and even beneficial in the "right" hands, or that the problem has been a more or less inappropriate or ill-advised application of them. The point is rather to ask what lies *within the discourse* that always already lends itself to such misuses and abuses, whether of deed or omission—that is, what in the system makes them possible in the first place. If such elements within the human health sciences are in fact irreducible to the system—essential, universal elements, in other words—how have these elements historically been deployed in the service of empire and racial hegemony? In what form and to what extent do such elements exist within psychoanalysis, and how is the latter better situated than, say, psychiatry to undergo this necessary and constant self-critique? How might psychoanalysis be likewise better situated to engage cultural difference, and how exactly would such difference be deployed within a revisionist postcolonial analysis? And finally, is it possible for such a postcolonial psychoanalysis to succeed at engaging otherness without losing its own structural preconditions—in other words, without surrendering the transcendental theory of the subject that gives it its contradictory coherence?

In beginning to address these and related questions, I would argue that the entire point of a postcolonial psychoanalytic theory and practice must be to delineate, demarcate, and signify respect for heterogeneity and difference whenever it encounters them. Its task must be to recover particular and historically specific symptomatologies of cultures during and after empire according to certain generalizable, but always contingent, structural concepts that would in turn inform a psychoanalytic reading of that culture—but without subsuming the heterogeneity and difference of cultures to psychoanalysis' universalizing tendencies. Such a project means rethinking not only the applicability of general psychoanalytic concepts in different cultural contexts (whether such developmental theories as the Oedipus complex hold up as universally true across cultural boundaries, for instance), but remaining always on guard against the uncritical generalization of those concepts and constantly questioning whether and how the machinery of psychoanalysis can operate in the service of oppression.[45] It also means remembering that even if, as many have argued, the concept of race—and in particular, the white race—has no literal referent,[46] the fantasy of white supremacy has unquestionably persisted, if not prevailed.

NOTES

1. For arguably the most famous example of this theoretical approach, see Gates, 2–15.

2. See Dyer, especially 1–4; Chambers; and Ignatiev, respectively.

3. In this context, the recent arguments in the United States by conservative thinkers for a more "race-blind" society must be viewed with suspicion, as a cynical attempt to deploy the language of equality as a ruse to return whiteness to its place

as unacknowledged, invisible norm. For a recent and widely read example of this sort of argument, see D'Souza.

4. See Dyer, 41–44.

5. For book-length studies of turn-of-the-century positivist theories of race, their contribution to anti-Semitism, and the effect of both discourses on Freudian psychoanalysis, see Gilman *Freud* and *Case*.

6. Weininger's stated thesis in the book is to demonstrate the moral inferiority of both women and Jews, whom he lumps together based on a particularly racist blend of biology and a "positivist" quasi-sociological approach to observing and interpreting gender roles. See Hyams.

7. See Sulloway.

8. In fact, Freud received considerable criticism from his Jewish contemporaries for his portrayal of Moses as an Egyptian murdered by his own people in *Moses and Monotheism*. It was charged that Freud's book attacked the Jewish community precisely at a time (1938) when European Jewry was already besieged by anti-Semitism. Freud himself denied any accusation that his work undermined the Jewish faith or communities. See Freud 1970, 162–63.

9. Lacan, for one, theorizes the problem of countertransference much more thoroughly—and self-reflexively—than Freud ever did. See especially *Seminar XI*, 123–34 and 230–43.

10. Notable Freudians who hold this belief include Philip Rieff, editor of *The Collected Papers of Sigmund Freud*; Ernest Jones, Freud's first major biographer; and Muriel Gardiner, editor of the Wolfman's memoirs. See Rieff, x; Jones 1, 202–203, and Gardiner, vii, respectively.

11. Freud himself never published the full details of the case, as was his custom. Freud explains early in the narrative that he has "abstained from writing a complete history of [the patient's] illness, of his treatment, and of his recovery, because I recognized that such a task was technically impracticable and socially impermissible" ("History," 8).

12. Although the latter's *PMLA* article focuses mostly on the "post-" in "post-Soviet" (and thus former Soviet republics) within a postcolonial frame, he does also persuasively discuss Russian colonialism in its pre-Bolshevik incarnation. See Moore.

13. At the end of World War I, Germany was to surrender its overseas colonies as part of the Treaty of Versailles, with victors Britain and France competing for the lion's share of the colonial spoils. Germany would, of course, return one last time in an attempt to turn Europe itself into a German imperium. See Young, 2, 31.

14. See also Hamilton, 26–27, 102–104.

15. For a more thorough discussion of how institutionalized Magyar racism and Pan-German imperialist aspirations contributed to the German-Austrian drive toward war, see Seton-Watson, 37–47 and 171–87, respectively.

16. For biographies that address this early phase of Freud's life and professional struggles, see Jones; and Gay, *Godless* and *Freud*. For broader studies of Vienna at the turn of the twentieth century and Freud's and psychoanalysis' place within it, see Morton and Everdell.

17. See Morton, 27–30 and 138–40; and Everdell, 13–29 and 127–41.

18. This is how Morton lists the entry in his index, under "Freud": "his unViennese personality"! See Morton, 335.

19. See Gilman, *Freud*, 30–31.

20. To give a brief and wholly inadequate summary, Freud interprets the dream as representation by its opposite: the window opening = "My eyes suddenly open," the wolves' stillness and intent staring = the patient's own staring and stillness and their "most violent motion": "That is to say, he suddenly woke up, and saw in front of him a scene of violent movement at which he looked with strained attention" ("History," 34–35). Next, "The tree was a Christmas tree," which provides an additional explanation of the patient's anxiety and its cause (i.e., the anticipation of presents). "But instead of presents they had turned into—wolves, and the dream ended by his being overcome by fear of being eaten by the wolf (probably his father), and by his flying for refuge to his nurse" (35). The satisfaction is paradoxically the source of the anxiety as well, the former being the patient's masochistic longing for sexual satisfaction from his father, the traces of which the dream exhumes in distorted (but not sufficiently distorted) form. The dreamer realizes the memory of the scene, "which was able to show him what sexual satisfaction from his father was like; and the result was terror, horror of the fulfillment of the wish, and consequently a flight from his father to his less dangerous nurse" (36). Although the dream distorts much of the material that informs it, it nevertheless "preserve[s] the essential connection between his unsatisfied love, his rage, and Christmas" (36). Additionally, no small part of this horror is the dreamer's realization of the single most necessary condition of this satisfaction: he must be castrated like his mother, in order to receive the sexual satisfaction from his father that she obviously does.

21. See also Gilman, *Jewish*.

22. See Lacan, *Seminar XI*, 123–34 and 230–43.

23. See Gilman, *Freud*, 29–36.

24. I am thinking particularly of the "Uncle with the yellow beard" dream in *The Interpretation of Dreams*, which receives one of the longer expositions in that book. One plausible "against the grain" reading of that dream is of a subject (Freud) who wishes simultaneously for his Jewish colleagues to be punished for their offenses (usury, lechery, etc.) and for himself to remain "unblemished" by their Jewishness. See *Interpretation*, 136–45.

25. The reference is to the seminal essay "The Agency of the Letter in the Unconscious," in which the word *agency* carries the further meaning of "insistence." See Lacan, *Ecrits*, 146–78.

26. The fetish of breathing out forcefully at the sight of "beggars, cripples, or ugly, old, or wretched-looking people," which the patient also deployed to combat evil spirits that he had "heard and read about," also relates to the sick father. Thus, the application of the "breathing" compulsion to such people begins right after this visit with his sick, old father. Freud also finds the patient's "breathing" fetish to be overdetermined with the primal scene, in that by performing it he "was also copying his father in the positive sense, for the heavy breathing was an imitation of the noise which he had heard coming from his father during the coitus"—or so Freud thinks: in a note, the analyst immediately qualifies his claim ("Assuming the reality of the primal scene"). Nevertheless, Freud asserts, "[the patient] had derived the Holy Ghost [of the breathing exercises] from this manifestation of male-sensual excitement. Repression had turned this breathing into an evil spirit, which had another genealogy as well: namely, the malaria from which he had been suffering at the time of the primal scene." So that here again we see (1) the coexistence of naughtiness and piety that mark the rest of the symptoms at this stage, and (2) Freud hedging his bets even

as he argues for them, in the form of the marginalized qualifications in the notes. See "History," 66–67.

27. For a comprehensive collection of Russian folk tales, see Haney.

28. Of course, this type of ad hominem attack on psychoanalysis via its founder persists today, a fact to which so many anti-Freud books will attest (see Crews; Sulloway; Webster, to cite only the best known). One of the most notorious of these attacks, however, is Stanley Fish's unsubstantiated paraphrase of the Wolfman's alleged statement that Freud was "a Jewish swindler [who] wants to use me from behind and shit on my head." See Fish, 156.

29. Given what we already know about the patient's latent homosexuality and wish for passive sexual satisfaction from his father, which he transfers accordingly onto the father-surrogates, I trust that I need not comment further on the verb "pricked."

30. The Wolfman's memoir provides ample evidence of his declining fortunes during and after World War I, and Ruth Mack Brunswick's "Supplement" to Freud's case history also discusses this period of the Wolfman's life. See Gardiner, 90–115 and 266–68, respectively.

31. The Wolfman's comment comes in response to this remark from the interviewer: "I sometimes get the impression that you bore Freud ill will for not continuing to play the role of the father until the end of his life." See Obholzer, 49.

32. I am referring to what Freud calls a "transitory symptom" during the "first sittings" of the analysis:

> [T]here was a large grandfather clock opposite the patient, who lay upon a couch facing away from me. I was struck by the fact that from time to time he turned his face towards me, looked at me in a very friendly way as though to propitiate me, and then turned his look away from me to the clock. I thought at the time that he was in this way showing his eagerness for the end of the hour. A long time afterwards the patient reminded me of this piece of dumb show, and gave me an explanation of it; for he recalled that the youngest of the seven little goats hid himself in the case of the grandfather clock while his six brothers were eaten up by the wolf. So what he had meant was: "Be kind to me! Must I be frightened of you? Are you going to eat me up? Shall I hide myself from you in the clock-case like the youngest little goat?" ("History," 40)

33. See Gardiner, 282–89.

34. In his discussion of the patient's intestinal problems, Freud identifies these as representing "the small trait of hysteria which is regularly to be found at the root of an obsessional neurosis." This association of the somatic symptom with the traditionally female disorder of hysteria, combined with Freud's assertion of his own authority to effect a recovery in the face of the patient's resistant "doubt," underline the analyst's role in the transference as the confident, empowered father-surrogate overcoming the feminized patient's hysterical weaknesses.

It is worth noting an interesting paradox here, however, namely that the symptom in this instance initially appears in the patient's childhood as its opposite: incontinence, as "an expression of defiance" against his English governess. This contingency perhaps signifies a more complex relation between the patient's imaginary relation to

German whiteness and its English variant. This relation must unfortunately remain a speculative one, as Freud's case study does not offer very much material from which to build a reading of it. See "History," 74–77. For more on the origins of Freud's definition of hysteria, including the "founding" case study of Anna O., see also Breuer and Freud, 1–47, 253–305.

35. See Heinlein; Levin.

36. Practically all of Fanon's *Black Skin White Masks* addresses this idea in one way or another, but see especially 17–40 and 109–40.

37. These observations could serve as a useful point of departure for a broader critique of whiteness in Hollywood films, which regrettably lies beyond the scope of the present essay. Such a critique would necessarily require its own separate development, which it will receive as a chapter within a larger study I am planning on Hollywood, whiteness, and the transference. Apropos of *Eyes Wide Shut*—a film based on a short novel by Arthur Schnitzler, a contemporary of Freud's in late nineteenth-century Vienna—it is perhaps worth mentioning here in passing, that certain moments in Stanley Kubrick's film retains traces of this nineteenth-century racial paranoia from the novel. I am thinking here primarily of two scenes: the fancy ball at the beginning of the film in which the suave, and according to one website "dangerously charming"—and obviously a Slav—Sandor Szavost (Sky Dumont), attempts to seduce the protagonist's wife Alice (Nicole Kidman); and a later scene in which the protagonist Dr. Bill Harford (Tom Cruise) visits a costume shop and discovers that its owner, Milich (Rade Sherbedgia), who is clearly a Gypsy (Romani), is involved in prostituting his own pre-teenage daughter.

38. For a historical explanation of how the social Darwinist debate of the time informed racial thinking leading up to World War I, especially Germany's, see Hamilton and Herwig, 26–27 and 162–64. For a more detailed discussion of racial hierarchies among European Jews themselves, especially between the Westernized intellectual classes and their stigmatized Eastern Slavic counterparts, see Gilman, *Freud*, 9–10, 51–62.

39. See Derrida, *Writing*, 289–90.

40. See Young, 2, 31.

41. Lacan addresses this question of transference as an affect, more specifically as what he calls "a sort of false love," in Book XI of the Seminar. See Lacan, *Seminar XI*, 123–25.

42. As I mention briefly above, Russia suffered its own humiliation during World War I, primarily at the hands of the Germans. This part of the history perhaps helps explain the patient's inability to break away entirely from his subservience to German Euro-whiteness.

43. It is one of the more remarkable paradoxes of the Wolfman study that in it Freud introduces the technique of declaring to the patient an a priori termination of the analysis "at a particular fixed date, no matter how far it had advanced" ("History," 11), a tactic that he revisits early in "Analysis Terminable and Interminable." See "Analysis," 217.

44. See López, 65–84, 209–10.

45. For some excellent examples of the kind of approach I am suggesting, see Fuss, 141–65; Lane; Seshadri-Crooks; and Sullivan.

46. This argument goes at least as far back as Henry Louis Gates's influential collection *"Race," Writing, and Difference*, in which he and other contributors argue

that race is a fiction. In the context of whiteness studies, perhaps the most well-known formulation of the fictive quality of whiteness comes from Richard Dyer, who explains whiteness as a system of representations. See Gates, 1–20; Dyer, 1–40.

REFERENCES

Bhabha, Homi K. 1994. *The location of culture*. London: Routledge.

Breuer, Josef, and Sigmund Freud. [1886] 1974. *Studies in hysteria*. Vol. 2 of *The standard edition*, ed. and trans. James Strachey. Reprint. London: Hogarth.

Chambers, Ross. 1997. "The unexamined." In *Whiteness: A critical reader*, ed. Mike Hill, 187–203. New York: New York University Press.

Crews, Frederick, et al. 1995. *The nemory wars: Freud's legacy in dispute*. *New York Review*.

Derrida, Jacques. [1981] 1998. Geopsychoanalysis: ". . . and the rest of the world." Trans. Donald Nicholson-Smith. In *The psychoanalysis of race*, ed. Christopher Lane, 65–90. New York: Columbia University Press.

———. [1967] 1978. *Writing and difference*. Trans., intro., and notes Alan Bass. Reprint. Chicago: University of Chicago Press.

D'Souza, Dinesh. 1995. *The end of racism*. New York: Free Press.

Dyer, Richard. 1997. *White*. London: Routledge.

Everdell, William R. 1997. *The first moderns: Profiles in the origins of twentieth-century thought*. Chicago: University of Chicago Press.

Fanon, Frantz. [1952] 1967. *Black skin white masks*. Trans. Charles Lam Markmann. Reprint. New York: Grove Weidenfeld.

Fish, Stanley. 1987. Withholding the missing portion: Power, meaning, and persuasion in Freud's *The Wolf-man*." In *The linguistics of writing: Arguments between language and literature*, ed. and intro. Nigel Fabb and Derek Attridge, eds. Alan Durant and Colin MacCabe, 154–72. New York: Methuen.

Forrester, John. 1997. *Dispatches from the Freud wars: Psychoanalysis and its passions*. Cambridge: Harvard University Press.

Freud, Sigmund. [1937] 1974. Analysis terminable and interminable. In Vol. 23 of *The standard edition of the complete psychological works of Sigmund Freud*, ed. and trans. James Strachey, 209–53. Reprint. London: Hogarth.

———. [1918] 1974. From the history of an infantile neurosis. In Vol. 17 of *The standard edition*, ed. and trans. James Strachey, 7–122. Reprint. London: Hogarth.

———. [1900] 1974. *The interpretation of dreams*. Vol. 4 and 5 of *The standard edition*, ed. and trans. James Strachey. Reprint. London: Hogarth.

———. [1900] 1974. *Introductory lectures on psycho-analysis*. Vol. 15 and 16 of *The standard edition*, ed. and trans. James Strachey. Reprint. London: Hogarth.

———. 1970. *The letters of Sigmund Freud and Arnold Zweig*. Ed. Ernst L. Freud. Trans. Elaine Robson-Scott and William Robson Scott. New York: Harcourt.

———. [1938] 1974. Some elementary lessons in psycho-analysis. In Vol. 23 of *The standard edition*, ed. and trans. James Strachey, 279–86. Reprint. London: Hogarth.

Fuss, Diana. 1995. *Identification papers*. New York: Routledge.

Gardiner, Muriel, ed., notes, and intro. 1971. *The Wolf-man by the Wolf-man*. New York: Basic.

Gates Jr., Henry Louis, ed. 1986. *"Race," writing, and difference*. Chicago: University of Chicago Press.

Gay, Peter. 1987. *A godless Jew: Freud, atheism, and the making of psychoanalysis*. New Haven: Yale University Press.

———. 1988. *Freud: A life for our time*. New York: Norton.

Gilman, Sander L. 1993. *The case of Sigmund Freud: Medicine and identity at the fin de siècle*. Baltimore: Johns Hopkins University Press.

———. 1993a. *Freud, race, and gender*. Princeton: Princeton University Press.

———. 1986. *Jewish self-hatred: Anti Semitism and the hidden language of the Jews*. Baltimore: Johns Hopkins University Press.

Hamilton, Richard F., and Holger H. Herwig, eds. 2003. *The origins of World War I*. Cambridge: Cambridge University Press.

Haney, Jack V. 1999. *The complete Russian Folktale*. Armonk, NY: M. E. Sharpe.

Hegel, G. W. F. [1807] 1977. *The phenomenology of spirit*. Trans. J. V. Miller. Reprint. Oxford: Oxford University Press.

Heinlein, Robert A. 1951. *The puppet masters*. Garden City, NY: Doubleday.

Hyams, Barbara, and Nancy A. Harrowitz. 1995. A critical introduction to the history of Weininger reception. In *Jews and gender: Responses to Otto Weininger*, ed. Nancy A. Harrowitz and Barbara Hyams, 3–20. Philadephia: Temple University Press.

Ignatiev, Noel. 1995. *How the Irish became white*. London: Routledge.

Imre, Anikó. 1995. White man white masks: Mephisto meets Venus. *Screen* 40 no. 4 (Winter), 405–22.

Ivanits, Linda J. 1989. *Russian folk belief*. Foreward Felix J. Oinas. Design and Ills. Sophie Schiller. Armonk, NY: M. E. Sharpe.

Jones, Ernest. 1953–1957. *The life and work of Sigmund Freud*. 3 vols. New York: Basic.

Lacan, Jacques. 1977. *Ecrits: A selection*. Trans. Alan Sheridan. New York: W. W. Norton.

———. 1991. *The seminar of Jacques Lacan, Book I: Freud's papers on technique, 1953–1954*. Trans. and notes John Forrester. Ed. Jacques-Alain Miller. New York: W. W. Norton.

———. [1964] 1981. *The seminar of Jacques Lacan, Book XI: The four fundamental concepts of psychoanalysis*. Trans. Alan Sheridan. Ed. Jacques-Alain Miller. Reprint. New York: W. W. Norton.

Lane, Christopher, ed. 1998. *The psychoanalysis of race*. New York: Columbia University Press.

Levin, Ira. 1972. *The stepford wives: A novel*. New York: Random House.

López, Alfred J. 2001. *Posts and pasts: A theory of postcolonialism*. Albany: State University of New York Press.

Moore, David Chioni. 2001. Is the "Post-" in postcolonial the "post-" in post-Soviet? Toward a global postcolonial critique." *PMLA: Publication of the Modern Language Association of America* 116, no. 1 (January): 111–28.

Morrison, Toni. 1992. *Playing in the dark: Whiteness and the literary imagination*. Cambridge: Harvard University Press.

Morton, Frederic. 1979. *A nervous splendor: Vienna 1888/1889*. New York: Penguin.

Obholzer, Karen. [1980] 1982. *The Wolfman: Conversations with Freud's patient—sixty years later*. Trans. Michael Shaw. Reprint. New York: Continuum.

Rieff, Philip, ed. and intro. 1996. *Three case histories*. New York: Touchstone.

Seshadri-Crooks, Kalpana. 1994. The primitive as analyst: Postcolonial feminism's access to psychoanalysis." *Cultural Critique* 28: 175–218.

Seton-Watson, R. W. [1916] 1968. *German, Slav, and Magyar: A study in the origins of the Great War.* Reprint. New York: Howard Fertig.

Spivak, Gayatri Chakravorty. 1999. *A critique of postcolonial reason: Toward a history of the vanishing present.* Cambridge: Harvard University Press.

Sullivan, Megan. 1999. Reading the island: British psychoanalytic discourse and the "problem" of Ireland. *Literature and Psychology* 45, no. 3: 63–75.

Sulloway, Frank J. [1979] 1992. *Freud, biologist of the mind: Beyond the psychoanalytic legend.* Reprint. Cambridge: Harvard University Press.

Viereck, George Sylvester. 1930. *Glimpses of the great.* New York: Macauley.

Webster, Richard. 1995. *Why Freud was wrong: Sin, science, and psychoanalysis.* New York: Basic.

Young, Robert J. C. 2001. *Postcolonialism: An historical introduction.* London: Blackwell.

NINE

"MOTLEY'S THE ONLY WEAR:"

HYBRIDITY, HOMELANDS,

AND CONRAD'S HARLEQUIN

Frances B. Singh

IN 2000, I WAS ON SABBATICAL, writing about a woman who was born in Czarist Russia. She grew up stateless in China, learned English at the age of twenty, and first came to the United States in the 1930s on a Chinese diplomatic passport issued by the then occupying Japanese regime. Desirous of becoming an American citizen, she pressured Senator Fulbright to get her reclassified as Russian. The Russian quota had hardly been touched since the Communists had come to power in 1917, but there were many bureaucratic hurdles that had to be cleared before she could be reclassified. Her determination paid off, though; she became a naturalized U. S. citizen in the 1940s. This woman was my mother.

As I reflected on the transnational, multilayered cultural life she led, and the levels of belonging in the various cultures and communities she moved among, it seemed to me that displacement, replacement, and (re)membering potentially provide a blueprint for race relations neither based on an innate concept of cultural or racial superiority, nor characterized by hate and violence (Gandhi 1998, 124–29). For people such as my mother, whose identities bear traces of and have been shaped by all the places they have found themselves in, all the frontiers they have crossed, "motley's the only wear" (As You Like It, II. vii. 37). Such people, for whom identity is not an immutable essence but a matter of becoming and being open, also

183

potentially provide a model of how race and communal relations can be transformed (Rushdie 1991, 124–25; Hall 1994, 394).

The call of the personal pulled me into the magnetic field that is Conrad's *Heart of Darkness*. I found myself professionally attracted to someone called a "fabulous . . . insoluble problem" (*Heart* 1988, 54). These are Marlow's words for the displaced, replaced, border-crossing figure known generically as "the Russian" because he was born in Russia or "the Harlequin" because his clothing is a hand-stitched patchwork of colors and materials. Yet exactly because he has no special connection to his homeland, is comfortable in Africa, is multilingual, and has spent time on ships whose crews were historically motley, substantially international,[1] I saw him as a spokesperson for the "motley" point of view. Additionally, because he is so different from all the other white males in the novella—sartorially, cognitively, morally, philosophically, politically, socially—and appears so abruptly, I also thought of him as a kind of narrative eruption, perhaps a force signaling the breaking through into consciousness of an overriding ethical imperative (Harpham 1996, 51–52). For, as this chapter will show, he not only posits but enacts an ethical political alternative to the imperial status quo upheld in *Heart of Darkness*.

There is another transnational, hybrid figure in *Heart of Darkness*. This is Kurtz. His mother was half-English, his father half-French. Partly educated in England, he had partially completed writing a report for the International Society for the Suppression of Savage Customs when he went over the edge. Reflecting on his hybridity, Marlow says, "all Europe contributed to the making of Kurtz" (50), meaning that he was a product in which all of Europe was implicated. Obviously, by putting the Harlequin into the text, Conrad is setting up a contrast between these two characters composed of many parts. What Kurtz comes to stand for is only too clear. His words, summed up in the phrase, "Exterminate all the brutes" (*Heart*, 51), commit him to a single-minded program of racial genocide. Equally significant, his absolute control over the local tribes suggests that he held them, as A. E. Scrivener, a missionary writing only four years after the publication of *Heart of Darkness*, would say of the Belgians in relation to the Congolese who gathered rubber for them, in a "state of terrorism . . . and virtual slavery"(qtd. in Twain [1905] 1970, 42).

But the Harlequin is not at all like Kurtz. By virtue of the antithesis between the Harlequin and Kurtz, the Harlequin can be understood as illuminating an alternative way for a European to be and become in Africa, one not involving exploitation, slavery, extermination, terrorism, and loss of humanity. If Kurtz shows amalgamation or hybridity negatively (Young 1995, 18), the Harlequin presents an image of hybridity regained and a new human self in the making. The Harlequin presages the overturning of that "state of terrorism . . . and virtual slavery" that imperial and personal greed had produced and embodies an alternative to it in the form of a relationship based "on simple fellowship and honourable reciprocity of services." This phrase comes from a section of the "Author's Note" to Conrad's quasi-memoir, A Personal Record, where he describes the characteristics of the Polish mindset in glowing terms. "Simple fellowship and honorable reciprocity," he writes, growing out of "a special regard for the rights of the underprivileged of this earth" are the "dominant characteristic[s]" of the Polish mentality, and he adds that these beliefs shaped "the mental and moral atmosphere" in which he grew up (Conrad 1924, ix). In the same passage, he also points out that the Polish mentality was a hybrid: It had "received its training from Italy and France, [and] had always remained . . . in sympathy with the most liberal currents of European thought" (ix). Said called the Harlequin "semi-crazed" (Said 1993, 23). However, the fact that the Harlequin embodies "simple fellowship and honourable reciprocity of services," two characteristics of the Polish mentality that Conrad affirmed and praised in A Personal Record, suggests that what he stands for is to be taken both seriously and positively.

In 1835 Thomas Macaulay outlined before Parliament how he would reform Indian education so that a class of miscegenated persons would be created, "Indian in blood and colour, but English in taste, in opinions, in morals, and in intellect" (Minute, par. 30). In 1899, it seems that Conrad teased some of the implications out of this concept of a class formed of miscegenated persons through the character of the Harlequin.[2] Conrad's Harlequin can, thus, be seen as the prototype of a new line or race, white in color but egalitarian, open-minded, and brotherly in opinions, morals, and intellect. My thesis is that in Heart of Darkness, Conrad, no doubt naively or crudely, was attempting to reimagine, rewrite, or even right the history of the European scramble for Africa through the Russian Harlequin.

I was particularly attracted to the Harlequin because from my postcolonial, postnational perspective, it seemed that a figure dressed "in motley" (Heart, 54) appeared much more a solution than a problem, particularly when that figure had also served on ships. Crew members' survival may depend on their ability to put their differences aside and pull together as a team. Conrad, that ex-salt himself, personally experienced the life-saving properties of collaboration. In 1882, he sailed on the Palestine from Falmouth to Bangkok. Near Mintok, the boat caught fire, and the crew escaped to the lifeboats. More than twelve hours later, they all reached port safely. The crew from the Palestine was literally a motley one. It consisted of five men from Cornwall, an Irishman, an Australian, a black man from the Antilles, a Dutchman, a Norwegian, and a Pole, Conrad himself (Nadjer 1983, 77–78). Yet Conrad chose to repress the motley, international, and interracial aspect of the crew when he used the incident in his short story "Youth" to dramatize the disciplined unity of sailors under duress. In the story, all the sailors were from Liverpool, and he wrote that they survived because they shared a common racial heritage: "I don't say positively that the crew of a French or German merchantman wouldn't have done it, but . . . there was a completeness in it, something solid like a principle, and masterful like an instinct . . . that gift of good or evil that makes racial difference . . ." ("Youth," 170). At the same time, he hints at an idea which transcends this narrow racist point of view. Conrad also writes that it is service at sea that brings out the "right stuff" (167) in men. In the final analysis, then, Conrad seems to be suggesting that the highest race one can belong to is not the English race but the transnational, miscegenated Sailor Race, which men belong to after a period of perilous training and collaborative service. It is a race whose highest moral principle is that all must pull together for the common good. Having been built on the principles of "simple fellowship and honourable reciprocity of services," it is open to all.

In 1700, Daniel Defoe wrote "The True-Born Englishman," a poem that satirized the true-born Englishman's pretension to racial purity. He pointed out that on account of all the peoples who came to and settled in the British Isles—Gauls, Greeks, Lombards, Saxons, Danes, Norwegians, Scots, Picts, Irish, Norman, Dutch—the "true-born Englishman" was "derived from all the nation's under heaven" (Defoe 1841, 14). An Englishman was a "heterogeneous thing" (19); the English "a mongrel half-bred race" (19). Defoe took pleasure in calling himself a true-born Englishman. Conrad the true-naturalized Englishman, who consistently maintained that while he wrote from an English point of view, he was himself not an Englishman (Nadjer 1983, 295), took the opposite position in "Youth." He eliminated heterogeneity from the story. Behind that decision is both the convert's desire to express the superiority of his adopted country and the theory of racialist nationalism prevalent in the nineteenth century. The sailors in "Youth" survived because they were all and only English, of one race, of one nation. In this story, Conrad is so uncomfortable with diversity as a principle that he could not accept that other races had that same gift of solidity or steadiness that had ensured his own survival. Nor could he accept that the English people themselves were hybrid, a crew as motley as the sailors on board the historical *Palestine*. Thus, he paradoxically paid the motley, international, interracial crew of the real *Palestine* the highest compliment a racist could give. He transformed them into the top of the line, all-white, racially and nationally homogenous English crew of the fictional *Judea*.

In 1899, some months before *Heart of Darkness* was published, a fully illustrated second edition of Henry M. Stanley's two-volume *Through the Dark Continent* appeared. One of the illustrations depicts a white man directing the rescue of a black man. The white man is dressed in breeches, a jacket cinched with a belt, and a hat (Stanley 2:233). This nineteenth-century authorized representation of the white man exercising power and showing his superiority is a pervasive one. Conrad, familiar from his youth with the writings of such nineteenth-century African explorers as Mungo Park, John Hanning Speke, David Livingstone, and Henry M. Stanley, would have seen this depiction countless times (Conrad 1926, 14–16; Torgovnick 1990, 26).

But here in the figure of the Harlequin was a challenge to that uniformed representation of the white male explorer in Africa. Not only did his dress not conform to what the nineteenth-century "white man" wore in Africa so as to exercise power and demonstrate superiority over scantily clad black natives, but its very sartorial difference challenged the authorized, essentializing representation of colonial man.

No wonder Marlow finds the Harlequin a "problem," which he handles by conceptualizing him as a fabulous creature that, in defiance of the laws of time and space, seems to have absconded from a troupe of mimes only to materialize suddenly in central Africa. By having Marlow see him as not quite real, Conrad defuses the danger that the Harlequin presents to the West's racist way of relating to Africa and Africans. Through Marlow, Conrad suggests he's a joke, an aberration, a singular phenomenon not to be taken seriously.

How are we to respond to this suggestion? There are two ways, I think, one literary, one political, though the literary way has political overtones as well. By literary, I refer to the mode of writing called magical realism, which is characterized by the fusion of the real and the fantastic in reality. This hybrid mode allows for the presence of—the eruption of—the fabulous, which serves to offer an alternative to nightmarish political and social realities. Though magical realism is associated with South American writers of the late twentieth century, such as Gabriel Garcia Marquez and Isabel Allende, the fabulous Harlequin who appears as the opposite to all the hearts of darkness in *Heart of Darkness* seems to be an early example of a character composed in this mode. He offers, in the style of magical realism, the hope of another kind of social and political reality, one based on equality, regard for others, simple fellowship, honorable reciprocity, service, and collaboration, which, since it doesn't exist in reality, must necessarily appear fabulous or fantastic (Taussig 1984, 492).

The second way is strictly polemical and political. After the attack on the World Trade Center, postcolonialism's hope that postnationalism will usher in a time of nonviolence and global unity is being sorely tested and seriously questioned. For example, on September 22, 2001, Edward Rothstein wrote in *The New York Times* that postcolonialism is an "ethically perverse" idea (A17). Rothstein argues cogently for his point of view, but if we wish to believe in the hope that postcolonialism holds out, it behooves us not to accept the suggestion that the Harlequin is a hollow man, a piece of theatrical fantasy. For as Conrad himself implied, through the contrast between Kurtz and the Harlequin, the alternative to the latter is the death-dealing terrorism of a Kurtz.

The Harlequin is a border crosser whose life is a series of beginnings and becomings. He is not only open to encounters with the others on the other side of the frontier, but takes it as his mission in life to seek out frontiers to cross. When Marlow encounters him, he had been "wandering about that river for nearly two years alone" (*Heart*, 54); he last glimpses him setting off into the jungle in a canoe accompanied by three Africans. Yet he is not interested in personal gain or establishing colonies on behalf of a European nation. He claims to have plenty of friends among the local people, speaks some of the local languages, and realizes that he is dependent on the local people. He does not see Africa as an impenetrable mystery nor does he conceptualize Africa as a place where whites catch a disease called lack of restraint in lust gratification. In the figure of the Harlequin we have a fully functional white person, healthy, able to look after himself, physically, socially, and culturally comfortable in this new environment, and not in a position of power: in a nutshell, totally incongruent, totally "other." Yet the very fact that he exists opens up the possibility that there were other ways for a white man to comport himself in Africa and relate to the local peoples besides the terrorizing practices of a fictional Kurtz or the real Belgian traders, whose lust for ivory and rubber resulted in the deaths and mutilations of millions of Congolese.

About five years before Conrad went to the Congo and fifteen years before he wrote *Heart of Darkness*, Mark Twain's Huck Finn lit out for new territory in order to avoid being "sivilized" (Twain 1907, 46). In *The Adventures of Huckleberry Finn*, Twain consistently spells "civilize" and "civilized" with an initial "s" so as to emphasize Huck's resistance to authority and authorized representations. However, the sibilantly hissing "s" also suggests that civilization is the real snake from which it is better to distance oneself. Such an understanding is a challenge to the traditional relationship between Western civilization and the snake. The writings of the nineteenth-century explorers, white men preparing the way for the "missionary and the trader—those twin pioneers of civilization" (du Chaillu [1871] 1971, xi) to develop darkest Africa provide many instances of the clash between civilization, figured as a white man in the regulation breeches and cinched jacket, and a snake, huge, threatening, black, native to the environment, and clearly blocking civilization's path. An illustration from Paul du Chaillu's 1871 *Explorations and Adventures in Equatorial Africa* entitled "Crossing the Mangrove Swamp, With The Tide Out" makes this point clearly. The picture depicts a confrontation between a huge black snake coiled around the branches of a tree, its forked tongue jutting out like a twin bolt of lightning about to strike, and a gun in hand, sartorially correct du Chaillu.[3] Similarly, Marlow plays upon the convention of the evil snake's power by comparing the Congo River to "an immense snake uncoiled, with its head in the sea, its body at rest curving afar over a vast country, and its tail lost in the depths of the land" (*Heart*, 12) and saying that this metaphorical snake had him mesmerized. Judging by what happens to the white men who live along the banks of the Congo or ply its waters in *Heart of Darkness*, this snake is extremely dangerous to the mental and physical well-being of the bringers of Western civilization. However, like Huck Finn, the Harlequin sees Western civilization as that which one must reject. A pure spirit, he turns his back on civilization and lights out for new territory in order to stay free of the modern snakes of "sivilization," as embodied in the ivory traders come to retrieve Kurtz. Though Huck is a far more iconoclastic figure than the Harlequin, it seems that Conrad is using the Harlequin to make the same critique about civilization as Twain did through Huck, albeit in a considerably weaker, more compromised way. Of course, as a result of taking this position on Western civilization, the Harlequin will be perceived as politically incorrect by the upholders of civilization and its conventions: not quite right, and maybe, as I will show, not quite white, either.

The Harlequin tells Marlow that when he went deeper into the interior, he used his gun for one purpose only: to bag game for the local peoples. In using firepower only to solve a village's food problem, he distinguishes himself from other explorers of the period, men such as Frederick Selous and John Petherick who, while not averse to shooting a hippo or two for the locals, used their firepower primarily to terrify the local people into providing them with ivory or porterage services (McLynn 1992, 177–79). The Harlequin, on the other hand, practices an ethics of service, which is also evident in his nursing of Kurtz. In addition, by telling Marlow that one screech from a ship's whistle is worth an infinite number of rifles, he counsels a nonviolent approach to making contact with the local peoples. The advice shows his concern with the manner of culture contact. It is a concern not at all shared by any of the other white males in the text who, by such acts as indiscriminate firing of rifles into the bush, lend their support to Kurtz's program of extermination.

It is also significant that in the manuscript of *Heart of Darkness*, the Harlequin is color-blind with respect to Africans. He doesn't see them as "black" but as "simple" people, the same adjective Conrad used in his laudatory description of the Polish mentality in *A Personal Record*. "Simple" is also how the Harlequin describes himself.[4] Thus, the Harlequin identifies himself with the Africans through this adjectival bonding. Furthermore, the Harlequin plays the race card *against* the Europeans come to take Kurtz away. For him, the Europeans are "these whites" (*Heart*, 62), and he disassociates himself from them. Clearly, the Harlequin sees in the whiteness of the Europeans their distinguishing immorality. In this respect, he is unlike Conrad, who, as Achebe noted, seems to be pathologically incapable of not calling attention to Africans being black (Achebe 1988, 258). In the manuscript of *Heart of Darkness* the Harlequin only says as he is departing, "I have a canoe and three fellows" (*Heart*, 62). When the novella was printed, Conrad imposed his own "problem," his fixation with the color of Africans, on the Harlequin by adding the word *black* between "three" and "fellows." However, he left intact the Harlequin's empathetic blackness and white racism, and his own belief in "simple fellowship and honourable reciprocity of services."

In other words, in spite of Conrad's attempt to make the Harlequin reflect his own racial prejudices against Africans—prejudices that were not uniquely his, but social, and that underlay Victorian social science—he didn't do a complete job (Raskin 1967, 38–39; Johnson 1997, 115–20; Young 1995, 93–178). The Harlequin comes across as a figure representing a point of view so ahead of its time that he seems to be a character out of magical realism for whom the boundaries of time and space are porous. *Heart of Darkness'* final assessment of the Harlequin is that he is "an insoluble problem." Yet his ways of relating to the local people suggest that he is an imaginative solution offering a model of race and communal relations based not on the Victorian idea of the moral and mental inferiority of Africans compared to Europeans, but rather on how they could work together in partnership and on what they had in common.

"Never trust the artist. Trust the tale," said D. H. Lawrence in *Studies in Classic American Literature* (1964, 2); and by following this maxim, we can come to see that Conrad laid the groundwork for a less hegemonic understanding of race and communal relations (Said 1993, 26). However many reality-discrediting adjectives Marlow throws at the Harlequin, the fact is that the Harlequin is not presented as a delusion or the product of malarial delirium. It may be that by having him just vanish into the night, Conrad's judgment of the paradigm of racial equality and harmony that he stands for was that it was insubstantial and unrealistic, doomed to fail. However, the idea that the Harlequin embodies cannot be dissolved quite so easily by a novelist's trick.

Narrative's power lies in its independence from its creator's mind, its ability to throw up ideas for new stories. It was in a text that Conrad never wrote, but in which he personally had a walk-on role, that the idea embodied in the Harlequin became influential in the early twentieth century. In 1890, while Conrad was waiting for his steamboat to be made ready for its upriver journey, he met and enjoyed the company of the quite fabulous, improbable, unbelievable, bewildering, yet quite real Roger Casement. Later framed for homosexuality and hanged for treason, the Anglo-Irish Casement was a larger-than-life character, tall, handsome, musical, a storyteller with a voice nobody forgot, and a passion for fighting on behalf of the oppressed. Conrad highlighted the extraordinary elements of his character in his description of Casement, in a letter to his friend R. B. Cunninghame-Grahame. Looking back in 1903 on his Congo experience, he wrote that Casement had walked into the "unspeakable wilderness" with nothing more than a stick for a weapon, accompanied only by two dogs and a bearer. Casement walked out some months later, a little leaner, a little browner, carrying the stick, accompanied by the same two dogs and the same bearer, "quietly serene as though he had been for a stroll in a park" (Watts 1969, 149).

Casement spent most of the last two decades of the nineteenth century in the Congo, from where he lodged protests against colonial exploitation, injustice, and brutality. Marlow's words describing the Harlequin reflect quite accurately the attitude of the Belgian authorities to Casement. They found the behavior of a man who protested high railway fares by walking the two-hundred-plus miles from Matadi to Leopoldville baffling (Hochschild 1999, 199) or, to use one of Conrad's phrases for the Harlequin, "altogether bewildering" (*Heart*, 54). A report from one of Casement's first employers, the head of a Baptist mission, states that "he was too good, too generous, to ready to give away" to the native peoples (qtd. in Hochschild, 196). Aware that Casement had, to use Conrad's phrase from *A Personal Record*, "a special regard for the rights of the underprivileged of this earth," the British Government commissioned him to investigate the accounts of atrocities being perpetrated by the Belgians in their pursuit of rubber and write up the findings in the form of an official report. In 1903, Casement rented a steamboat and traveled upstream. To get to the interior villages he walked, accompanied only by his bulldog and a cook. The information he collected, and the depositions and pictures he took, confirmed that the Belgian authorities had been cutting off the hands, feet, and genitalia of local people in order to force them into gathering rubber. The report was published at the end of 1903. Although the British Foreign Office toned down the report, it was nonetheless one of the important instruments that pushed the Belgian Parliament in 1913 to take responsibility for the administration of the Congo and institute some reforms. Thus, depending on whether you were a supporter of colonialism and racism, or engaged in the struggle against this twinned evil, you either saw Casement as an insoluble problem—or, as I see the Harlequin, an imaginative solution, one for whom Africa was not the "unspeakable wilderness," but a place in which one could move about in a "quietly serene" way, as if one were walking through a European park.

Heart of Darkness was commissioned for a special issue of the politically conservative *Blackwoods Magazine* (Firchow 2000, 98). Could it just be that by presenting the not stupid, not ignorant, but pro-imperialist white male readership of *Blackwoods* with a different kind of white person in the figure of the Harlequin, one who didn't fit the box labeled "white male racist colonizer," Conrad had in mind the "improbable, inexplicable, and altogether bewildering" (*Heart*, 54) Roger Casement whose work helped put an end to the atrocities of Belgian imperialism? In spite of himself, was Conrad of the right party without knowing it? Was Conrad in *Heart of Darkness* a spokesperson for the "motley" point of view? Given that Conrad always affirmed that the unconscious spoke the truth about man, nobody might be less surprised than Conrad himself at such an assertion.

When Marlow calls Kurtz's companion at the Inner Station a "harlequin" and comments on his motley clothing, he also calls up the long and vibrant theatrical tradition in which a fool appeared in motley to indicate his difference from the dominant culture. The clothing suggested both that he was a walking critique of that dominant culture, and that he had the necessary imagination to construct alternative organizational possibilities. He had other ways to be, other ways to understand or put the world together

(Helder 1975, 363; Samad 2002). If the fool is a convention through which social criticism is offered, then the Harlequin's placement in this Forest of Arden raises a variant on that infamous question: "What is a girl like you doing in a place like this?" We need to ask ourselves why, in a text that condemns the excesses of colonial rule but not colonial rule as such, Conrad deliberately placed a figure whose incongruity vis-à-vis the status quo threatens that very norm.

Contemporary postcolonial criticism does not refer explicitly to the fool tradition, but its related notions of hybridity and mimicry build on it. Homi Bhabha understands hybridity as a process by which a monolithic sign of colonial authority develops a second identity when it is made to disclose the trace of another presence. The eruption of the Other deprives the imposed imperialist culture of its authoritative, authorizing function because instead of having a single essential meaning, it is now revealed to be an unstable amalgam: a two-in-one kind of thing, or hybrid. Because it is two, it can no longer essentialize. Mimicry in postcolonial discourse refers to the production of an Other who is almost, but not quite the same as the White Master. This Other that is produced is a threat to the status quo. In this sense, mimicry is the political arm of hybridity. Mockingly, it asks the rhetorical question: Who's in control now? Its existence made known, the presence of this Other, who is not quite the same as the Master, causes the authoritativeness of the signs of Western cultural superiority—books, weapons, marerial goods—to be called into question (Bhabha 1994, 85–118).

The Harlequin produces the positive effects associated with hybridity as well as with mimicry. The Western imperial powers established their superiority over the other races of the world with that foundational book, the Bible, in one hand, a loaded gun in the other, and porters carrying boxes and boxes of material goods. On the macro level, there is the example of H. M. Stanley's expedition. In 1874, Stanley left for Africa equipped with a yawl, a gig, and a barge, which latter apparatus could be broken down in as many as ten sections, pontoons, guns, ammunition, rope, saddles, religious tracts, medical stores, provisions, scientific instruments, stationery, canteens, watches, pipes, knives, silk banners, a number of dogs, and many more items. In Zanzibar, he inspected "bales of unbleached cottons, striped and coloured fabrics, handkerchiefs and red caps, bags of blue, green, red, white, and amber-coloured beads, small and large, round and oval, and coils upon coils of thick brass wire," which were then "packaged in portable bales, sacks, or packages" (Stanley [1899] 1988, I, 24). By the time he left Zanzibar, the total weight of his possessions—goods, cloth, beads, wire, stores, medicine, bedding, clothes, tents, ammunition, boat, oars, instruments and stationery, photographic apparatus—was a little over 18,000 pounds, roughly divided into loads of sixty pounds each. Three hundred porters carried these loads (I, 50). On the individual level, the late-nineteenth-century hunter and ivory trader Samuel White Baker's personal armory included No. 10 guns, a Ceylon

No. 12 double rifle, a Fletcher 24, a double-barreled breach loader accurate at three hundred yards, and elephant guns so powerful that their recoil could kill their firers (McLynn, 178).

The Harlequin, on the other hand, lights out lightly for new territory. He carries with him a book on the finer points of seamanship, a text singularly useless in his geographical position, some hundreds of miles upstream from Boma, where the mouth of the Congo empties into the Atlantic. Further, as Marlow informs us, the book's margins are filled with notes in Cyrillic, which he, Marlow, cannot read. Marlow takes his inability to read Russian as a sign of the incomprehensibility of the African environment, but this writing back from the margins to the center is also a sign of knowledge and power outside the authoritative text. The fact that it is beyond Marlow's horizon of comprehension (Gilliam 1980, 39–40) opens up the possibility that there are more ways to think about heaven and earth—earth, especially, in this case—than Marlow's philosophy knows. The Harlequin is also equipped with a bunch of Martini-Henry cartridges, singularly useless as he does not have the matching rifle in which to load them, and nothing that isn't carried on his person. Marlow last sees him walking toward the canoe that carries him out of the text with the red pocket bulging with cartridges and the blue one occupied by Towson's book on seamanship.

Although the Harlequin is dressed in some of the same colors identified earlier in the novella with the colonial powers that had seized pieces of Africa for themselves, his difference from them should be quite clear. So too should be the answer to the question I implied earlier: What is a character like him doing in a place like this? In dressing in motley, a figure composed of diverse parts, a hybrid or amalgamation, the Harlequin represents the opposite of what those colors on the map stand for: the division of Africa into parts. Simply by existing in sartorial motley-ness, he questions the signs by which the Western colonial powers—England, France, and Belgium principally, but also Spain, Portugal, and Germany—divided and ruled Africa.

When Marlow says that "all Europe contributed to the making of Kurtz," Conrad forces us to recognize that all of Europe was implicated in imperialism as it had come to be practiced at the end of the nineteenth century in Africa. However, because Russia was in Europe but, as I will explain, not of Europe, the Russian Harlequin is a means by which Conrad was able to offer an alternative to imperialism and white domination. This alternative, which allows for the presence of whites in a nonwhite area, is based on a set of relationships not characterized by possessiveness and greed, condescension, terrorism, hatred, and genocidal thoughts toward indigenous populations.

Until he became an English citizen in 1884, Conrad was a Russian national because his own country, Poland, had been divvied up among Russia, the Austro-Hungarian Empire, and Prussia. The Russian authorities imprisoned his father for his involvement in anti-czarist movements. Conrad and his parents spent four years in exile in Russia; the poor conditions under

which they lived led to his parents' early deaths. Despite spending his forma-
tive years in the Russian part of Poland and staying in contact with family
members who lived there, he denied any knowledge, reading, writing, or
speaking, of Russian. The presence of Cyrillic script in the margins of the
book that Marlow finds on his way to Kurtz in *Heart of Darkness* is, for him,
yet another sign that in Africa he, Marlow, is "cut off from the comprehension of his surroundings" (37); it is a code or cipher he cannot crack.

Conrad had no love for Russia. In "Autocracy and War," he called
Russia "the negation of everything worth living for" and "a bottomless abyss
that has swallowed up every hope of mercy, every aspiration towards personal
dignity, toward freedom, towards knowledge, every ennobling desire of the
heart, every redeeming whisper of conscience" (Conrad 1938, 100). Conrad's
representation of Russia is in line with the conventional representation of
Russia in late-nineteenth-century England (Lunn 1898, 509). Nonetheless,
because Poland was a part of Russia, Russia was also the mouthpiece for the
Polish mindset. And as Conrad had said in *A Personal Record*, that mentality
was characterized by "simple fellowship and honourable reciprocity of services." In other words, in spite of Conrad's hatred of Russia, Russia also stood
for, as it had absorbed, an alternative way of relating to subjugated peoples—
the Polish way (Harpham, 6).

Conrad's feelings toward individual Russians were not always incandes-
cently hateful. He appreciated the work of Turgenev and Tolstoy, and noted
individual acts of kindness performed by Russians toward his family (Conrad
1924, 123; Lewitter 1984, 663). Conrad could feel pity for the Russians
masses too, whom he described in "Autocracy and War" as "benighted, starved
souls" (89); but of Dostoveysky's *The Brothers Karamazov* he wrote, "it sounds
to me like some fierce mouthings from prehistoric ages" (Garnett 1924, 240).
The statement shows that for him, at least one Russian fell into the category
of the subhuman or bestial. In fact, as his comment on *The Brothers Karamazov*
makes clear, for Conrad there was not much difference between a Russian and
an African. Both were incomprehensible, both were prehistoric, both lacked
language. They were both savages. A Russian was a de facto black. Marlow
described his voyage up the Congo as "travelling back to the earliest beginnings of the world" (*Heart*, 35). Conrad's reading of *The Brothers Karamazov*
is its literary equivalent. For Conrad, Russia was only geographically in Europe.
He would have agreed with the saying of the Russophobes of the late nineteenth century: "Scratch a Russian and find a Tartar" (Lunn, 510).

In 1835, when Macaulay presented his *Minute*, he adduced the case of
Russia to support his argument for giving Indians an English education.
Macauley pointed out that Russia emerged from a state of barbarity and
ignorance when it changed its educational curriculum. By teaching the
Muscovite "those foreign languages in which the greatest mass of informa-
tion had been laid up and thus putting all that information within his reach,"
(*Minute*, par. 6) he finally became a European, a civilized person, and Russia

took its place among European civilized communities. Now, Macaulay says, there is in Russia "a large educated class . . . in no wise inferior to the most accomplished men who adorn the best circles of Paris and London" (par. 6). Macaulay wanted to create a class of people that would be Indian in blood and color, but Western in taste, opinions, morals, and outlook. For him, "barbarous" (par. 6) Russia offered the proof that it was possible to create such a class of people that would be different, yet not out of place in London and Paris.

The Anglophilic, English-speaking and reading, technically knowledgeable Russian Harlequin is proof that at least one member of that hybrid class got created; Conrad and his family—all educated people comfortable in French, some of whom knew English and German as well, and all of them Russian citizens—are others. Perhaps one reason that Marlow cannot dismiss the Russian Harlequin as a figment of his imagination is because of his English, or more generally Western, component. Nonetheless, the fact is that the Harlequin is a mimic man, not quite white in the way the rest of Europe was. Despite his fluency in English and dedication to the technical information contained in Towson's book, the position that he takes vis-à-vis Africa and Africans is not the one espoused by the European powers: that is his non-Western, "Russian" side talking.[5] He is a shade off, not quite white. He is "fabulous" rather than real or respectable.

Unquestionably, writing more than seventy years after Macaulay, Conrad did not agree that Russia had made the transition from non-Western backwardness into European modernity. At best, if the Harlequin's facial physiognomy is taken as a symbol of Conrad's attitude toward the nameless folk of Russia, they were not so much benighted or spiritually starved as childish people. However, in order to offer a critique of European imperialism from within the European context, he was forced to give the Harlequin a Russian identity. It was the only country in Europe that could be considered European in that it had had citizens (like himself) who were not out of place in the drawing rooms of London and Paris and yet was still perceived as barbaric and nonwhite. Consequently, for Conrad, it was the only European country from which the critiquing voice of the nonwhite Other could issue in speech comprehensible to the other significant European imperial powers (Harpham, 52). The consequence is that in *Heart of Darkness*, which appears only a year after "Youth," Conrad takes a significant step away from the position espoused in the short story, namely that only the English race or nation had in them that special "right stuff" (167).

This is not to say that Russia was not an imperialist or racist country. It was, and it was a signatory to the Act of Berlin ratified at the 1885 Berlin Conference called by Leopold II of Belgium. Per the articles of this treaty, Leopold's control over the Congo was recognized, France and Portugal were given land near the mouth of the Congo, and all the signatories were given navigation and trading privileges so that commerce, civilization, and

Christianity could come as a package deal into central Africa (Packenham 1991, 254). However, Russia never developed even a commercial toehold in Africa. Russia may have been "the negation of everything worth living for," but it was never tainted by an exploitative connection to Africa. Indeed, the only time Russia had any contact at all with Africa in the late nineteenth century was in 1895, when it opposed the expansion of a fellow signatory to the Berlin Act, Italy, into Ethiopia.

In the late essay "Geography and Some Explorers" Conrad describes the explorations of Captain Cook and others as "free from any desire of trade or loot . . . free from any taint of that sort" (Conrad 1926, 10). Because Russia never became a player for land or commerce on the African continent, the Russian Harlequin can be seen legitimately as the last of that line of pure and simple Galahads for two reasons. First, the other European powers had become corrupted from their no-holds-barred scrambling for the resources of Africa. Second, if the Russians were the only Europeans who were white enough to be invited to the Berlin Conference but-not-quite-white enough, as Macaulay's thumbnail sketch of Russian history suggests, then through the figure of the Harlequin Conrad could hint at a rewriting of the relationship between Europe and Africa. A relationship grounded in terrorism and domination could be replaced by some sort of fellowship of equals.

Additionally, by making the Harlequin a sailor, he allowed for a common denominator between himself and the character. "Brotherly," the Harlequin says, when Marlow offers him some tobacco, "where's a sailor that does not smoke" (*Heart*, 54), and Marlow does not dispute the relationship. At that moment, Marlow's creator Conrad is neither Polish nor English, the Harlequin is not a Russian—they shed these warring ethnicities and find common ground as members of the transnational, miscegenated Sailor Race, in which all pull together for the common good. As mentioned earlier, in "Youth," Conrad wrote that the sailors had survived because they were all English. But he had also written that it was the sea that catalyzed that "right stuff" in them. In the final analysis, in Conrad's pecking order, the highest race one could belong to was not one that certain people were born into, but the international, motley Sailor Race, potentially open to all whose "right stuff" could be tried and tested by the sea, and not found wanting. If Conrad could find once in his life a way to not let his antipathy to all things Russian blinker his response toward the Harlequin and stress the brotherhood of Marlow and the Harlequin in the Sailor Race rather than their mutual estrangement in the polity of nations, then *Heart of Darkness* holds out the hope, in spite of our personal hatreds and ethnocentricities and the Kurtzes of the world, that the relationship between Europe and Africa, or America and those who see it as an aggressor nation, can also be refounded along the principles of the Sailor Race.

I am well aware that in presenting the Harlequin as a fabulous and unreal character Conrad's vision is ultimately in line with late-nineteenth and early-twentieth-century thought. The fact is that he couldn't imagine a world in which Africa could be independent, or give an African the role of the Harlequin. Identifying a Russian as black and finding something decent in one of that tribe is not the same as saying that an African has the same capacities as a white. The fireman and the helmsman, both of whom have acquired a certain amount of Western knowledge, are compared to animals and treated as parodies of human beings, whereas the Harlequin is allowed the dignity of vanishing into the night. On the other hand, the Harlequin is not associated with the two ways by which the other Europeans in the text relate to Africa and Africans: as a site of either commercial exploitation or racial genocide. By making him a Cyrillic-writing Russian and tagging Russians as savages and black, Conrad actually sets him up as the mimic man, the one who is able to challenge authority exactly because he is "not quite/ not white/ not write." By showing the Harlequin putting his life into the hands of Africans, Conrad does moot the suggestion that if a white gives up his claim to being in charge, and is willing to develop a relationship based upon equality, openness, friendship, and trust, then Africa and its peoples no longer appear as a "problem" and there can be a place for a white person in Africa. He points toward this "righter" writing of history, but to go farther than this was beyond his scope. As he once said, he was only "a wretched novelist" (Watts, 148). That is why the Harlequin vanishes from the text, and the thought that hybridity and postnationalism can produce an ethical system (Gandhi, 137) remains an idea for us to flesh out and implement.

Interestingly, the point of view figured by the Harlequin prefigures one taken by Mahatma Gandhi in the twenties and early thirties. In his writings and at conferences held in England to discuss the future of India, he conceptualized Indian independence, not as separation, but as a partnership between the two nations predicated on equality—"such as can exist between two equals" (qtd. in Singh 1985, 267). By means of this partnership of equality, ill will between Hindus and Muslims, and Indians in general and the English, would be transformed into affection and friendship: there would be a place for all in a communally harmonious, undivided India. The possibility envisioned by Gandhi was, as the subsequent turn of events in the history of the Indian independence movement proved, mooted too early for it to be taken seriously. Neither the British nor the other leaders of the Indian independence movement went along with Gandhi's idea of a partnership of equality leading to affection and friendship and a communally harmonious India. In the post- or transnational world we seem to be living in, however, where so many people are, like the Harlequin, men and women of patches, a composite of all the places they have lived in who "belong" to many places simultaneously, the possibility presented by the Harlequin may now be a little more real, a little less imaginary than it was at the turn of the twentieth century. Judging by the fierceness of Edward Rothstein's attack on it in the pages of *The New York Times* (2001, A17), "motley's the only wear" is a leading and strong intellectual position, only too alive and well and living in our world.

Some days after the attack on the World Trade Center, Union Square Park at Fourteenth Street began to be used as a memorial. In an article that appeared in *The New York Times* on September 19, 2001, Michael Kimmelman makes the point that the park is functioning as it is supposed to, in that it is bringing "strangers together on common ground, people who otherwise might never have met, people who would not have bothered to notice one another on the subway or street" (E5). In other words, Union Square is serving as a site where Conrad's "unspeakable" is being transformed into Casement's "park," where hatred is being transformed into affection, with relationships reforged under the sign of equality. Of course, it is only a co-incidence, but Union Square Park is also the only park in New York City with a statue of Gandhi, frail and bowed, but striding forward.

NOTES

1. In the late essay "Well-Done" Conrad remarks that almost a third of the crews of the British ships he sailed on consisted of foreigners, and that the same situation prevailed in the merchant marines of other European nations (179–81). Nadjer mentions that Conrad underestimated the national and ethnic diversity of the seamen. According to him, on the ships Conrad sailed on, 30 to 60 percent of the crew was not English (82).

2. I am not suggesting by means of this parallel between Macaulay's *Minute* and the *Heart of Darkness* that Conrad was familiar with the earlier text, only that both Macaulay and Conrad helped evolve an idea, the possibility that a miscegenated class of people or new race could be created.

3. Interestingly, du Chaillu's text gives an opposite reading to the episode. Du Chaillu, who lists the nine snakes that he collected in the Appendix, calls the snake a "poor animal," and says the snake was as scared of them as they were of him (146). Are we to believe the words or the picture? Lawrence's dictum to trust the tale rather than the teller doesn't apply in this case, as du Chaillu's commentary alternated between sensationalism and accuracy or fairness (McCook 1996, 185–95; Goodall, par. 17).

4. "Simple" is almost always used as a positive attribute in Conrad's writings. It appears eleven times in *Heart of Darkness*. The Harlequin uses it three times to refer to the local people and twice to refer to himself. See www.concordance.com/cgi-bin/globalwordsearch.pl for a listing of the occurrences in the Conrad corpus.

5. In 1881, Conrad's uncle Tadeusz Brobowski wrote him a letter in which he stated that Russia's culture is "purely Eastern," though it was "accused" of being a mixture of Eastern and Western (Nadjer, 72).

REFERENCES

Achebe, Chinua. 1988. An image of Africa: Racism in Conrad's *Heart of Darkness*. In *Joseph Conrad, Heart of Darkness*, 3rd ed., ed. Robert Kimbrough, 251–62. New York: W. W. Norton.

Bhabhi, Homi K. 1994. *The location of culture*. London: Routledge.

Concordance to Heart of Darkness—Joseph Conrad. [1998] 27 July 2002. http://www.concordance.com/cgi-bin/methr.pl/.

Conrad, Joseph. 1938. Autocracy and war. In *Notes on life and letters*, 83–114. New York: Doubleday.

———. 1926. Geography and some explorers. In *Last essays*, 1–21. Garden City, NY: Doubleday.

———. 1988. *Heart of darkness.* Ed. Robert Kimbrough. New York: W. W. Norton.

———. 1924. *A personal record.* Garden City, NY: Doubleday.

———. 1938. Well-done. In *Notes on life and letters*, 179–93. New York: Doubleday.

———. 1991. Youth. In *Complete short fiction of Joseph Conrad,* ed. Samuel Hynes, 1:152–80. New York: Ecco.

Defoe, Daniel. 1841. The true-born Englishman. In *The novels and miscellaneous works of Daniel Defoe*, 20:1–46. Oxford: Talboys.

du Chaillu, Paul B. [1871] 1971. *Explorations and adventures in Equatorial Africa.* Reprint. New York: Johnson Reprint Corporation.

Firchow, Peter Edgerly. 2000. *Envisioning Africa: Racism and imperialism in Conrad's Heart of Darkness.* Lexington: University of Kentucky Press.

Gandhi, Leela. 1998. *Postcolonial theory: A critical introduction.* New York: Columbia University Press.

Garnett, Edward, ed. 1924. *Letters from Joseph Conrad, 1895–1924.* Indianapolis: Bobbs-Merrill.

Gilliam, Harriet. 1980. Undeciphered hieroglyphs: The paleography of Conrad's Russian characters. *Conradiana* 12: 37–50.

Hall, Stuart. 1994. Cultural identity and diaspora. In *Colonial discourse and postcolonial theory: A reader,* ed. Patrick Williams and Laura Chrisman, 392–403. New York: Columbia University Press.

Harpham, Geoffrey Galt. 1996. *One of us: The mastery of Joseph Conrad.* Chicago: University of Chicago Press.

Helder, Jack. 1975. Fool convention and Conrad's hollow harlequin. *Studies in Short Fiction* 12: 361–68.

Hochschild, Adam. 1999. *King Leopold's ghost: A story of Greek, terror, and heroism in colonial Africa.* New York: Houghton Mifflin.

Johnson, A. James. 1997. Victorian anthropology, racism, and Heart of Darkness. *Ariel* 28: 111–31.

Kimmelman, Michael. 19 September 2001. In a square, a sense of unity: A home-grown memorial brings strangers together. *New York Times*, E1.

Lawrence, D. H. 1964. *Studies in classic American literature.* New York: Viking.

Lewitter, L. R. 1984. Conrad, Dostoyevsky, and the Russo-Polish antagonism. *Modern Language Review* 79: 653–63.

Lunn, Edward. 1898. The progress of the Russian empire. *Gentleman's Magazine* 285 (November): 509–14.

Macaulay, Thomas. 1835. *Minute on Indian education.* www.geocities.com/bororissa/mac.html. 20 July 2002.

McCook, Stuart. 1996. "It may be truth, but it is not evidence: Paul du Chaillu and the legitimation of evidence in the field sciences. *Osiris* 11: 177–97.

McLynn, Frank. 1992. *Hearts of darkness: The European exploration of Africa.* New York: Carroll and Graf.

Nadjer, Zdzislaw. 1983. *Joseph Conrad: A chronicle*. New Brunswick: Rutgers University Press.

Packenham, Thomas. 1991. *The scramble for Africa: White man's conquest of the dark continent from 1876–1912*. New York: Avon Books.

Raskin, Jonah. 1967. *Heart of Darkness*: The manuscript revisions. *Review of English Studies* 18: 30–39.

Rothstein, Edward. 22 September 2001. Attacks on U. S. challenge the perspectives of postmodern true believers. *New York Times*, A17.

Rushdie, Salman. 1991. *Imaginary homelands: Essays and criticism, 1981–1991*. London: Granta.

Said, Edward W. 1993. *Culture and imperialism*. New York: Random House.

Samad, Daizal Rafeek. 20 July 2002. Enigmatic proportions: The harlequin in Conrad's *Heart of Darkness*. www.ucalgary.ca/UofC/eduweb/eng 1342/492/daizalcom.html.

Shakespeare, William. [1914] 2000. *As You Like It*. Ed. W. J. Craig. London: Oxford University Press. New York: Bartlebly.com. www.bartleby.com/70/index20.html.

Singh, Frances B. 1985. a passage to India, the independence movement, and independence. *Twentieth century literature* 31: 265–78.

Stanley, Henry M. [1899] 1988. *Through the dark continent*. 2 vols. Reprint. New York: Dover.

Taussig, Michael. 1984. Culture of terror—Space of death: Roger Casement's Putumayo report and the explanation of torture. *Comparative Study of Society and History* 26: 467–97.

Torgovnik, Marianna. 1990. *Gone primitive: Savage intellects, modern lives*. Chicago: University of Chicago Press.

Twain, Mark. 1907. *The adventures of Huckleberry Finn*. Reprint. New York and London: Harper.

———. [1905] 1970. *King Leopold's soliloquy*. Reprint. New York: International Publishers.

Watts, C. T., ed. 1969. *Joseph Conrad's letters to R. B. Cunninghame-Grahame*. Cambridge: Cambridge University Press.

Young, Robert. 1995. *Colonial desire: Hybridity in theory, culture, and race*. London: Routledge.

TEN

HYMNS FOR AND FROM

WHITE AUSTRALIA

CHRISTOPHER KELEN

Thou art of purer eyes than to behold evil, and canst not look on iniquity: wherefore lookest thou upon them that deal treacherously, and holdest thy tongue when the wicked devoureth the man that is more righteous than he?

—Habakkuk 1:13

HOW IS THE AUSTRALIAN SOUL stirred, officially and unofficially? What can we learn of that soul and its prisoners (to put a Foucauldian construction on things) from the songs that serve to stir patriotic sentiment among Australians?

Australia's official national anthem is a song entitled "Advance Australia Fair." It first succeeded "God Save the Queen" in that role in 1974 following a national opinion poll conducted by the Australian Bureau of Statistics for the then Labor government. Incoming Liberal prime minister, Malcolm Fraser, reinstated "God Save the Queen" in 1976, reserving "Advance Australia Fair" for some other than viceregal occasions. A referendum on the anthem issue was held in 1977 but no action was taken on its result until Labor was returned to power in 1983. "Advance Australia Fair" was adopted again as the national anthem (replacing "God Save the Queen") on April 19, 1984. It has remained in that role since, despite the great popularity of the unofficial national song, "Waltzing Matilda."[1]

"Advance Australia Fair" was politically corrected (not a phrase in use at the time) when reinstated as national anthem in 1984, with a view to giving the girls a fair go.[2] The original opening line of Peter Dodds McCormick's[3] ninteenth-century song was: "Australian sons let us rejoice/ For we are young and free." The complete "official" anthem (published in the *Commonwealth of Australia Gazette* of 19 April 1984) is now as follows:

Australians all let us rejoice
For we are young and free.
We'll golden soil and wealth for toil
Our home is girt by sea.

Our land abounds in nature's gifts
Of beauty rich and rare.
In history's page, let every stage
Advance Australia Fair.

In joyful strains then let us sing
Advance Australia Fair.

Beneath our radiant Southern Cross
We'll toil with hearts and hands
To make this Commonwealth of ours
Renowned of all the lands

For those who've come across the seas
We'll boundless plains to share.
With courage let us all combine
To Advance Australia Fair.
In joyful strains then let us sing
Advance Australia Fair.

The "correction" is noteworthy given the emphasis the song places on a self-conscious effort at nationhood. These lyrics situate a collective effort at being a nation in the "act" of being seen to be one. The claim is justified on two grounds: possession and intention. We have golden soil, wealth, youth, the ability to toil, freedom, a beautiful country possessed of nature's gifts, boundless plains. We make no particular claim to have done anything as yet but we have intentions, specifically to toil with hearts and hands to make our nation famous. The setting of the song then is temporally ambiguous: we have x and we're about to y.

The big questions one might ask this far into the song are naturally, "Who are we?" and "How did we get to be in a place that needs to be sung about by us in this way?" "What effect does it have on us or on others, that we sing this particular song about ourselves?"

The "we," I hope to show in this paper, is the white nation, under construction in Australia at the time of writing (1878), under construction at the time of the song's official revision (1984), and still under construction today, as I write.

INVISIBLE SPECTACLE

The original version of "Advance Australia Fair" (mildly suppressed by Australian governments since 1984)[4] places emphasis on Australia's nation making as world spectacle.

> While other nations of the globe
> Behold us from afar,
> We'll rise to high renown and shine
> Like our glorious southern star;
> From England, Scotia, Erin's Isle,
> Who come our lot to share,
> Let all combine with heart and hand
> To advance and etc. (McCormick 1974, 1–4)

A paradoxical investment is entailed in the symbolic means of Australia's construction as white nation. The white man is a spectacle embodying human progress. To be white is to be beheld aspiring. Whiteness, on the other hand, is invisible. It functions as norm only to the extent that it is overlooked as a quality of those who possess it. It's able to be overlooked because it's white people by and large who do the looking. Or at least an unmarked point of view and narrative style in Australia traditionally and systematically presuppose and privilege a white man's view of the world. The rewriting of "Advance Australia Fair" foregrounds this paradox in the investments of whiteness and of nation.

The idea of whiteness as unexamined norm has been extensively theorized over the last decade (Dyer 1997, passim; Chambers 1997, 197). The white man as spectacle is necessary in the colonial setting because, as Satya Mohanty writes, the white man must be seen in order "to command respect and fear in the subject race" (315). Spectacularizing the rule and authority of white men has been as essential in the project of Australian nationhood as it has been in the western genre in the United States. By contrast, the indigenes are traditionally not spectacular in themselves, although what they do to the white man and what the white man does to them, may be sensational, and so provide a proof of the white man's heroism.[5]

The invisibility conferred in (usually unmentioned) racial whiteness allows various interests and practices to remain unexamined.[6] Whiteness for Albert Murray, in his essay "White Norms, Black Deviation," allows white people "to avoid circumstances that would require confrontation" with their own contradictions (Murray 1973, 112). Whiteness can thus be seen not only as a property that goes unexamined, but also as a means of protecting one's identity (and its inherent contradictions) from examination. Whiteness, as transparent normative condition, rarely rates a mention. Whoever draws attention to such norms or contradictions risks being accused of seeing things that aren't there. The paradoxical investments of "Advance Australia Fair" are by no means unique. White identity for Richard Dyer "is founded on compelling paradoxes":

> A vividly corporeal cosmology that most values transcendence of the body; a notion of being at once a sort of race and the human race, an individual and a universal subject; a commitment to heterosexuality that, for whiteness to be affirmed, entails men fighting against sexual desires and women having none; a stress on the display of spirit while maintaining a position of invisibility; in short a need always to be everything and nothing, literally overwhelmingly present, and yet apparently absent, both alive and dead. (Dyer, 39)

Dyer's formula, "Other people are raced, we are just people" (1), finds expression in the Australian context in the use—since the seventies—of the adjective -cum- noun *ethnic*, meaning other than Australian of Anglo-Celtic descent. The unmarked category (white) is posited as normative because lacking ethnicity. Who lacks ethnicity becomes autochthonous, by virtue of a rhetoric that only works as long as it is not spelled out.

Now I think it's important to note that while "whiteness" as manifestation of cultural value has a long history, its near universal currency as unmarked category (Ø) is a relatively recent phenomenon. It's critical to track the development of whiteness alongside that of "nation," the other key abstraction here.

A postmodern global human rights rhetoric allows us to speak of individuals as racially unmarked in a way that would have been implausible in the nineteenth century, or even before World War II, in mainstream Western societies. Thanks to the value of whiteness as unmarked category, this rhetorical shift may, far from opening the range of humanity to all races and ethnicities, rather have the effect of rendering white subjectivity both invisible and universal (i.e., normative) in the one stroke. Whiteness confers unearned privileges on those who happen to be white (Dyer, 9). This systematic privileging does not apply only to individuals, but to nations as well. Paradoxically, then, it's the other races, and the other than white nations, who disappear from the picture (or who go unheard) where the white people can't be seen as such. It's perhaps easiest to recognize these effects in the world dominance of Hollywood cinema and its modes of representation, the ranges of possibility open to characters appearing as un-typed individuals.

In studying the official identity expressed in "Advance Australia Fair" we are not observing a merely historical phenomenon; it's the unanalyzed aspect of a postmodern condition that should interest us. A general difficulty in theorizing absence finds application in the work of understanding Australian identity, historicized and in the here-and-now.

The specific paradox in this case is that the country's emptying of its former cultural content has been accomplished by those who've progressively made themselves more invisible in the process. There was no "Australia" in this continent to conquer prior to the coming of white people. Nevertheless, the continent was invaded, and is still occupied, by forces that absolve themselves for responsibility in the process by absenting themselves from the action.

Apparently nothing (and no one) in particular has replaced the nothing that was here before things naturally became the way they're meant to be. And so naturally, no one has to be blamed.

How could *we* be blamed? *We* weren't there at the time. We millennial Australians are not the dispossessors of yore. Who are we then? How are we here? By what rights? What relationship have we now to those dispossessors, and to the dispossessed? The question will not be ruled irrelevant because the fact is—whether you think about these questions or not—we *are* here.

In this sense one can claim that the *terra nullius* epoch[7] is over now only because it's no longer necessary. Despite various fears of white decline (cf. Hage 1998, 179–232) there is no threat—Aboriginal or otherwise—to white dominance in Australia. Or at least, there is less threat now than there has ever been.

FEAST OF THE BACKWARD AND ABYSM

It's the depth of contradiction in the present and official version of "Advance Australia Fair" (its "look at me, I'm not here" quality) that leaves some of those who sing it a little uneasy afterward as to the question of what they've meant. But I think that depth of contradiction well expresses the Australian condition.

Nor is it the case one need dig far to unearth contradictions in the song. In terms of form, the song begins as if it were a hymn or a prayer, with the formula: "Let us (pray/sing?)," but without the locutionary force of an appeal to God (cf. "God Save the King/Queen"). It's a pseudo-hymn. Who is addressed? *We* are. The temporal setting of the hymn is substituted with the imminence of an imperative: "Let us rejoice." Rejoicing is something we should all do for a long list of reasons. That being the case, "let us sing." In "Advance Australia Fair" it is the imminent future to which voices attend in their act of unison.

Who is this "we" we can't see because we're so busy singing when we're not toiling, when we're not rejoicing? The invisibility of those singing is assured by their identity with themselves. Who in Australia in 1878 can sing a song in English praising Captain Cook for his nation-making role? In the second stanza of the original song:

> When gallant Cook from Albion sail'd,
> To trace wide oceans o'er,
> True British courage bore him on
> Till he landed on our shore.
> Then here he raised old England's flag,
> The standard of the brave;
> With all her faults we love her still,
> "Britannia rules the wave"
> In joyful, etc. (McCormick, 1–4)

It's British people who sing such praises. By doing so they participate in that story as establishing their rights and identity.

Notice the elision of the performativity of Cook's act in relation to those singing the original song. Chrono-*logically* it wasn't *our* shore when he landed on it. His act in landing—along with the right annexing phrases (on Possession Island and elsewhere)—dutifully recorded in a journal, transmitted down to us, as the historical record—made it *our* shore.[8] The clause "he landed on our shore" appears to make timeless the possession Cook effected. We attend to a vanishing spectacle, a spectacle into which we vanish in becoming ourselves. Today, more than ever, we are the spectacle vanishing in the text we sing. It's through that act of vanishing our authority comes to be unassailable. Notice the elision of Captain Cook from *our* song today.

Like the feast Ariel prepares for the court conspirators at the end of *The Tempest*, everything's gone the moment one tries to touch it.[9] But the disappearance in this case is only in the text. Australians, having disappeared themselves from the text, get to enjoy the real feast, the feast on what the land abounds in. Aboriginal people (or partly Aboriginal people) would be British precisely to the extent that they could do that. Imagine the Aboriginal man on his own fenced homestead, saluting his Union Jack. "You're a real white man," he might be told. But this figure—descended from the name-plated King Billy of the early nineteenth century—has always been an incongruous image in our story, in fact a figure of fun.

In *White Nation*, Ghassan Hage is able to write of whiteness as "an aspiration" in Australia still today. In his conception, whiteness in Australia is not predominantly an either/or concept. Rather there are degrees of whiteness, and likewise of its corollary, Australian-ness. Both are able to be accumulated up to a point (Hage, 20).

Australian-ness emerges not fully blown as national aspiration, but in stages from British sub-nationality. The only distance from a more British Britishness in the original version of "Advance Australia Fair" is established rather unconvincingly in the lines, "With all her faults we love her still/ 'Britannia rules the wave" (McCormick, 1–4). The song is not really about Britannia's faults. It's about the value of being invisibly British everywhere. The difference that's asserted is about placing the British soul under the southern cross.

Some nations are whiter than others. In the case of Australia, "Advance Australia Fair" in its original rendition was an effort to assert the whiteness of a new British possession. You could claim that this emphasis is gone from the song today because in the era of multiculturalism and reconciliation, the issues of race and nation have been (or at least are being) disentangled. But Australia's whiteness is now an accomplished fact. That these statements may both be true at once demonstrates that the song "works" to the extent that it keeps multiple audiences from asking the kinds of questions I'm asking here. An anthem should surely confirm those who sing it in a common identity. Its function isn't to pose a question along those lines or to cast doubt.

"Advance Australia Fair" really is eat your cake and have it too stuff: We white Australians want to be a young nation about to play on the world's stage but at the same time we want to pretend that what is ours has an eternal quality. We want to borrow the timeless land myth; we don't want to acknowledge the time before our coming.

A key difference between the original and the official anthem is that in the words we sing today we don't even want to acknowledge our coming. In the original version it's *as if* "we" were here before Cook. In the present official version, with Cook written out of the story altogether, it's as if there were—paradoxically—a timelessness to our presence still always under construction. Is there rhetorical precedent for this déjà vu sense of identity?

British imperialism had self-consciously chosen classical and especially Roman models for its authority. If, as Martin Bernal argues in *Black Athena*, that modeling has entailed a homeostatic reversal such that antiquity had to be whitened in order that it be fitting precedent for,[10] for instance, Britishness, then what's conjured up in that teleological reading of the classical world is the epic inevitability of Rome as predestined in Virgil's *Aeneid*. The British Empire needed an authorizing myth to outstrip. Camoens in *The Lusiads* had already made such a claim for the Portuguese: their empire was truly worldwide compared with Rome's. Britain was bent on morally outstripping the great Iberian empires of the New World. This kind of civilizing moral imperative did not diminish the acquisitiveness of British imperialism, any more than it diminished Rome's.

The fifth and last stanza of the original "Advance Australia Fair" was concerned with preventing others from coming. It describes what Australia would be defending itself from in the case of war:

> Should foreign foe e'er sight our coast,
> Or dare a foot to land,
> We'll rise to arms like sires of yore
> To guard our native strand;
> Britannia then shall surely know,
> Beyond wide ocean's roll,
> Her son's in fair Australia's land
> Still keep a British soul,
> In joyful strains and etc. (McCormick, 1–4)

In the old version we were ambiguously from somewhere and yet autochthonous, we were people with something to be afraid of, our courage though yet to be proven as "ours" could be relied on because of our British souls. Similar sentiment was widely expressed in the lyrics of many now obscure Australian anthem attempts of the fin-de-siècle Boer War/Federation period.

That today we no longer sing of defending the country becoming ours from anyone else who might like it to be theirs, merely indicates that we're more comfortable with the facts of possession.

There is a displacement in these fin-de-siècle fears, entailing the kind of role reversal confirmed by the place of Gallipoli in the national myth: the culture threatening black people (the white people of the frontier) became the people whose civilization was threatened by distant and appalling others. The need for identification outstrips any commitment to objectivity. In fact it's a double displacement that keeps minds off the unspeakable. Fear of the blacks was displaced through the nineteenth century by fear of the yellow peril, a fear kept strongly alive in Australia through World War II, and even beyond the Vietnam War, with the arrival of the first "boat people." This is the fear Pauline Hanson's One Nation Party worked to revive in the late 1990s. Gallipoli displaced this close and ongoing fear with something more characteristically British (a Near for a Far Eastern fear), and definitively over. Gallipoli replaced present fear with the memory of horror. The Ottoman Turks were the kind of foe you could associate—at least from a distance—with the Crusades. Having licked us in 1915, they had the decency to evaporate as a political entity a few years later when they themselves were beaten. Terrifying for the losses we sustained in engaging them, they provided Australia with a benign—because abstract—kind of threat, and nothing to worry about any more.

After Gallipoli, any ethical problem that might have been associated with having been there faded naturally into the distance. How much guilt can one attach to martyrdom? Along with actual distance, the Treaties had consigned everything of the Great War and before to another world "back then." But by then Gallipoli had already served the function of displacing from popular consciousness the ethical problems associated with being here, now.

UNEXAMINED ETHICS

The ethical basis for Australia-as-becoming-British nation, established in "Advance Australia Fair," is simply this: having stolen something very big (big enough to physically contain us) we now wish to aggressively claim this place as ours by rights, and to rattle our sabers at anyone else who thinks they're entitled to a share of the action.

Rhetorically the world empire in which Australia participates is made possible through a logical loop involving the invisibility conferred in having always been here, or having at least—like the gospel or Kant's categorical imperative or Virgil's Trojans-cum-Romans—always having been destined to be here. Having always been here was the rhetorical wish behind the (1871) creation of the Australian Natives' Association, a friendly association of native born white men, bent on the unification of Australia as one Commonwealth. In the case of the A.N.A., part of the white man's burden in Australia was (having taken the places that belonged to the native) to take the native's place. Calling oneself a native was a rhetorical means of writing the real natives out of the picture. As "natives" white Australians could be as invisible as they were permanent in Australia.

The apparent hypocrisy (of a theft after which a right is asserted)—and the doublethink of the displacement of black by white "natives"—is founded on a powerful conviction of racial superiority, of what the Americans called "manifest destiny" (the phrase coined by John L. O'Sullivan in 1845 to indicate the duty of the United States to occupy the territory we now think of as the United States). Through the A.N.A., the borrowing of a name effects the merging of dispossessors and dispossessed. What's created is a new man, here by rights (by right of birth) and so not responsible for the actions of the others who enable him to be here. The spectacular creation of this blatant racism is the Australian: the new man, who renders both colonist and indigene surplus, anachronism.

Because these race convictions are no longer saleable today, the world's white empire—the entrenched power of racially European interests throughout the world—needs to be invisible if it is to survive. The old rhetoric of a song such as "Advance Australia Fair" can be retained, however, for nostalgic purposes because it is no longer spectacular. We can't remember what we're singing.

In the new rendition of "Advance Australia Fair," fear has evaporated with history. We're here and we welcome others here:

> For those who've come across the seas
> We'll boundless plains to share.
> With courage let us all combine
> To Advance Australia Fair.

Note that it's the boundless plains we're prepared to share. Apparently the ocean views are already spoken for. The new version of the song is thus strategically inoffensive in the multicultural sense. Who can be offended by these words? We're singing about Australians, about anybody: anybody could be Australian. Investigating the rewriting of the song shows what was there then and is missing now. But in removing the elements that might have offended Australians of other than British descent, isn't the problem now solved? Then again, if anybody can belong to any nation, then what are nations for?

Richard Dyer writes in *White*: "There is no more powerful position than that of being 'just' human" (2). "Advance Australia Fair" is not just about any humans. It's not about humans in general; if it's about a kind of humanity then it refers to the kind whose tracks have been covered in inventing the colorless identity sung in the song: the identity of the Australian, a character who doesn't just *happen* to be mainly white.

The ideal—if not the practice—of racial equality is a fact simply accepted today. To argue against it is, from a mainstream viewpoint, to argue unpalatably. This was not true a century ago. The nineteenth-century British world scene was the site of considerable open ambivalence on the race issue. That ambivalence is expressed by the formation of a paradoxical entity such as the A.N.A., which despite the mild and humanitarian rhetoric (and the borrowing of Aboriginal words such as "*corroboree*") was undoubtedly a white supremacist organization: an organization bent on creating Australia as a white nation. The motto of the A.N.A. was "Advance Australia." This became the rallying call of the Federation movement. This remained the legend under the (old) coat of arms on the Australian sixpence until 1966.

The transformation of "Advance Australia Fair" neatly expresses the evolution of the race ethic; it's a song from which the signs of whiteness have been expunged. Along with them has gone a particular myth which had expressed a sentiment of racial superiority our ancestors had been too coy to name as such. The present generation—more coy than its forebears—distances itself from veiled racialist sentiment. But it has celebrated the primal events. The Bicentenary of the coming of the First Fleet on 26th January 1988 marks the most impressive imaginable achievement of a central goal of the A.N.A.: to have "Australia Day" (also known as "Invasion Day") instituted as a holiday in the calendar. The present generation occupies exactly the territory the A.N.A. intended by "Australia," if somewhat more thoroughly (being more numerous). The present generation sings the same refrain, is anxious to assert continuity over the *longue durée* of Australian history. The present generation goes on establishing the identity commenced as Australian by the A.N.A and by Peter Dodds McCormick.

How easily can we dispense with the continuities that we've chosen to define ourselves, or that we go on choosing—or go on failing to reject—for this purpose? Why were our ancestors coy about the racist rhetoric that placed them where they were? They were coy because they were on the way to being us.

We—like them—claim, in singing this song, to be the recipients of "nature's gifts." What the land "abounds in" serves as a convenient synecdoche for Australia as a whole. We have been given—and bountifully—what is in Australia.

Those who sing "Advance Australia Fair" want to have always been here, but in an ahistoric way. The past should be irrelevant to the way we are now. This consciousness of an identity of pretended eternal rights is only achieved by multiple erasure: of time before the historic, of our historic consciousness of time. It is achieved by means of the *terra nullius* myth, of which "Advance Australia Fair" is the perfect representative: the myth of a land empty prior to our coming.

ETHICS OF EXAMINATION

Ross Chambers's essay "The Unexamined" posits "blank whiteness" as in the "the category of the unexamined."

> It is as if the system encompassed two mythic (or incomparable) categories, blank whiteness and absolute blackness, each of which is held to lie outside the sphere of examinability. One is unexamined "norm," and the other is unknowable "other" (or extreme of otherness), and between them lies the pluralized area of the multiple categories that come under scrutiny, constituting the knowable others of whiteness as the domain of the examinable. (Chambers 1997, 193)

"Blank whiteness" is the unexamined category we've witnessed (in the act of disappearing) in the evolution of Australia's national anthem. The original song had spectacularized the making of a white nation where there had merely before been another dark continent, a continent dark in the senses of unknowable and pagan and inhabited by sable savage creatures yet to be (if they ever could be) brethren. This is the kind of unknowable other that doesn't bear examination, but rather needs to be displaced.

The right kind of displacement in a nineteenth-century British imperial sense would be in advancing an idea such as "Australia" where there had been nothing before: no law, no land tenure, no history, no material signs of civilization.

The spectacle of the white man's coming—the spectacle that the A.N.A. succeeded in having celebrated as Australia Day[11]—was naturalized in the sense that it came into the category of inevitable events. Inevitable events have the virtue that they can be slated as beyond the influence of moral suasion. There's no arguing with earthquakes or thunderbolts.

The continuity here is—in Chambers's terms—in the movement away from examinability. The reification of "Australia" is in the movement away from events or assertions that might be subject to scrutiny, and toward the brick wall reality of—in this case—who and how we are.

Blank whiteness, which veils not the view but the gaze, leaves us the spectacle of golden soil and southern cross. What "we" see is land abounding—our possession—spectacular plenitude, yet empty in that we are entitled a view. The panorama is of nature's gifts (of no one's theft). It reveals (but in prospect) "wealth for toil." What effect does this spectacularizing of the originary moment have on the possessor of the gaze? Who do we become in seeing our world this way?

The emptiness posited by "Advance Australia Fair" is deeply ironic. It represents a refusal of the ethical question that must lie under European presence in Australia. The land is empty because we emptied it. We have land to share because we took land. We only get to look generous (sharing the boundless plains) because of a theft for which we do not wish to acknowledge responsibility. We sing from an emptiness wrought on ourselves in the act of emptying; the emptying of the land and at once the popular consciousness: emptying it of the fact of the emptying. Emptying ourselves of truth is the reflective act of nation: the basis of the collectivity on which a polity is claimed.

If the gender problem is fixed and if it appears now that no one is excluded by virtue of ethnicity from the possibility of an Australian identity, the official 1984 update leaves untouched two serious problems with the song. The first of these concerns the ways in which it might be unsatisfactory from the point of view of indigenous Australians (i.e., their ongoing erasure through the shedding of the story that conspicuously hadn't included them to begin with). Linked with this is the serious ambiguity of the title and the chorus: specifically, the problem with the word *fair*.

The word-order inversion in the title/chorus is a kind of pseudo-archaism that tilts the song in the direction of the unintelligible. The title and the refrain are in this sense themselves unexaminable. The core sentiment of the song defies reading for the simple reason that it's not the way that anyone actually speaks. "Advance Australia Fair" is something we should all sing and should all combine to do. It's something history should do, too.

The refrain presents in a chronological reversal, the stages of a reification: To Advance Australia Fair is what history should be continuously allowed to do. It's also what we should all do (who could argue?), and what we should sing, no doubt for the purposes of self-inspiration, so as to advance Australia, so as to allow history's every page to advance Australia.

This rhetorical loop proves nothing more than that the anthem is a circular genre par excellence. What else could singing oneself be? In this case the progression entails a reversible synecdoche: History's page reveals the stage on which we are singing. How much courage could it take to combine for this purpose? The emptiness is catching. The "we" of the song—recipients of the "gifts"—have disappeared into the act of possession. Performing nation itself thus becomes quintessentially empty act. The irony is that while we sing that we're collectively "somebody" now (come of age), that act of singing is the act of possession that keeps us from actually appearing in any role other than singing ourselves; it keeps us from actually doing anything or being anybody. We remain in stuck in the loop of becoming ourselves.

Advance Australia Fair? Exhortation, serving suggestion, statement of fact? The inscrutable sign[12] of identity becomes a kind of rite of passage, which needs to be explained to children and migrants alike. Perfect form of mystification to express as collective sentiment the sentiment of collectivity; no one can definitively know what these words mean. The unknowable privileges a teachers' grasp of the archaic as originary lore: The teacher says it means "Let's all work together to make Australia a beautiful country, a great country" or "We should all be proud of Australia because it's such a great country, so we should pull together to make it even better." Fair enough. Who could object?

Learning the song that makes you Australian means learning not to ask certain awkward questions. It's an induction into an ambivalence. Australians are embarrassed by their facts of presence, by the unresolved ethics of their presence. Australians are *as* embarrassed with the idea of independence (from the various "empires" in which they have participated, and continue to participate) as they are not to simply be themselves. And so they sing this embarrassing song. It's not merely a matter of substituting tradition for intention. Tradition is, in this tune, emptied of intending: "Look at me, now! I just happen to be here."

THE BEAUTIFUL IS THE SYMBOL OF THE MORALLY GOOD

The central ambiguity in the title and refrain of "Advance Australia Fair" is such that when we sing the song we don't know whether we are describing how things are or how they should be. Are we singing to keep things the way they are or to make things the way they ought to be? Advance Australia because it is fair or so that it will be fair or for both reasons: to keep the fair fair? Of course this speculation begs the question about the meaning of the word *fair*. Of all the various dictionary entries for the word *fair* the three that seem to coalesce in this usage are: fair as in beautiful, fair as in just, and fair as in white.[13] I would argue that these three uses likewise coalesce in the use of *fair* in that typically Australian rejoinder "fair enough": characteristic expression of a country seriously worried, if pragmatic, for most of its European history about the risk of racial impurity—even from "other" Europeans. In the expression "fair enough" the issue of justness is foregrounded. In "Advance Australia Fair" the strangeness of the diction makes it more difficult to decide how the word *fair* should be read. The phrase/line is emphatic because of repetition, inside and outside of the song. "Advance Australia" was the slogan of the A.N.A., it was the rallying cry of the Federation movement more generally. It became the legend under the coat of arms. It got onto all the silver coinage in Australia by 1911. But, adding the epithet *fair*, the anthem tells us—inscrutably perhaps—how Australia is to be advanced. One could say that the epithet was unnecessary on the silver coins because they were already paler and more precious than (bronze) pennies.

Is it rather that the song asks a question as to how should Australia be advanced? Should it be advanced, for instance, by consumer confidence, by helping silver coins to circulate? But this form of the question implies an adverbial construction. An adverb in this position would imply process and therefore a future orientation toward the quality of that process: how (by what means or in what manner) Australia ought to be advanced. But if the "fair" of the chorus is really an adjective then the implication is that Australia is already a "fair" entity; in advancing Australia one advances its already attained quality of fairness.

In the third critique (published when the British settlement at Sydney was in its infancy), Kant writes: "[T]he beautiful is the symbol of the morally good" (Kant [1952], 547). Kant's views on race—although perhaps typical of the anthropology of his time—demonstrate a powerful conviction that the white race was superior to the other three races Kant imagined as encompassing the human types. Kant particularly viewed black people as inferior, unintelligent.[14] There's no doubt that for Kant the beauty and goodness he conceived coalesced best under a white skin (and no doubt, the appropriate civilized garment). My aim here is not to take Kant to task for being of his time and place. Rather, it's to show that big ticket thought items—such as the categorical imperative and Kant's commitment to rationality as transcending the particular—do, perhaps despite their content, actually have an origin. Today's human rights and rule of law rhetorics are fueled by a universalizing spirit that no longer wishes itself to be seen as imperial or chauvinistic. These rhetorics have an origin, hidden not merely in the manner of blank whiteness, but hidden behind blank whiteness, of the kind that the rewriting of "Advance Australia Fair" exemplifies.

Today we take racial prejudice as presenting a problem for the categorical imperative. How can one act only on a maxim one can will to become universal law while dealing unfairly—unequally—with other humans (i.e., the rest of the human universe)? Kant's universal rule seems to be contradicted by his own prejudices. But there was no contradiction along these lines for Kant. Acknowledging the ongoing validity of Kant's ethics means recognizing the continuity between an imperial mindset and today's individual universal rights rhetoric. It's not that we can't pick and choose (e.g., reject racism but accept universal law); it's that we're dishonest and disingenuous when we unpick the manner in which our own ethics are invested. To do so is to dehistoricize and so eternalize things now as being the way they always had to be. Benedict Anderson's work has pointed us in the direction of recognizing anthem as the anathema of historical methods.

Mediating between imperial mindset and today's individual universal rights/rule of law rhetoric is the modernity of nation: the mainly banal and unanalyzed great good that powers anthems. Continuity from the imperial to the national is fueled in Australia's case by the slipperiness of this word *fair*. Through that slipperiness a tradition of racism can be neither directly lauded nor completely discarded, but rather distanced and indulged for set purposes and as occasion demands.

The beautiful inhabit a just polity. A just polity is a white polity. This is the advance, in the song, that is happening, or has happened, in Australia. In fact this is the advance that the European word (Latin made English down here) constitutes for the continent formerly known to Europe as New Holland: Australia is becoming a white man's country. In Kantian terms, this particular people have become universal and normative (have transcended their particularity) just to the extent that they are invisible.

Here's how an unexaminable expression of identity functions. The whiteness this song promotes is concealed in the justness and the beauty it promotes in the process of concealing the theft undertaken by the invisible people—people invisible in their capacity as thieves—who are promoted as fair because beautiful because white. To begin on this train of thought is to risk exposing nothing more than one's own paranoia.

It's easy to see why governments have seen fit to suppress McCormick's original lyrics, preserved for the public (for instance at various websites) by people anxious to keep tradition or racial sentiment or historical consciousness alive. The comparison of the two versions draws attention to the reification of Australia as a (naturally, unmentionably) white nation, which both versions—appropriately for their times—work to conceal.

The song nevertheless remains an embarrassment because of the manner in which it draws attention to the contradiction between the spectacularizing of, and the invisibility of, whiteness as performing the becoming of nation. In this way "Advance Australia Fair" can be read as the clumsy move that shows the world what should be kept hidden.

Nor is it by any means the clumsiest expression of the contradiction between the altruism of national devotions and the self-interest that is best served when concealed therein. Take a stanza of "The Song of Australia" for example:[15]

> There is a land where treasures shine
> Deep in the dark, unfathomed mine
> For worshippers at mammon's shrine, at mammon's shrine:
> Where gold lies hid and rubies gleam,
> And fable wealth no more doth seem
> The idle fancy of a dream
> Australia! Australia! Australia!
>   (in Radic 1983, 84)

HOW FAIR IS FAIR?

What's been achieved in the deracializing, dehistoricizing cleanup of "Advance Australia Fair" is to take the whiteness farther than it had been from a condition of examinability. Ambiguity in the refrain has been a key to this process. It's being able to read in (epochally appropriate) different ways that keeps the anthem alive. The association of beauty with justice today outweighs the association of either of these with race. And yet the connotation of racial purity, as desirable national good, remains available to the song's reader where the genderedness (and the historicity) of the original has been dispensed with. Clearly, we would not have gone on singing a song titled "Keep Australia White."

"Advance Australia Fair" sings the great singular plurality "we." That identity-in-common is made spectacular, in the original, through a specific history, through the story of an exemplary individual. Of the original song, a child—or a migrant, or a tribal Aborigine—might ask, who was this Captain Cook? Where's Albion? What's British? Who's foreign? What's it all got to do with us? In the new version of the song the only individual—gallant Cook—has been omitted. The spectacle admits of no point of view. It's a case of: "Look at us! You can't see me!"

The original song is about historical consciousness. It may not express our consciousness of history, but it tells a story about how it is we're here. Rhetorically, the key is in the synecdoche expressed in the line "In history's page, let every stage." History is a book consisting of pages. One of these pages stands for the book. On each page a scene is presented, in which stage in the spectacular sense coincides with the notion of a phase or of epoch. Word and image, action and depiction, are parts of the ongoing cycle invoked by the turning of the pages of a book, the reading of which conjures images, the writing of which is nation making.

McCormick's song is specifically about the civilizing process, about the white man's burden, as it applied to this particular far-flung reach of empire. The advance of the title concerns the progress of civilization; it assigns to this process a very specific metaphor, that of a military movement. The progress of the white race over the continent is an advance. That Aborigines are given no specific role in this song becomes less mysterious in this light: it is not their country or nationality that is being described here; rather, the advance of *fair* Australia, an advance that takes place at the expense of an unmentionable nonpolity. The noninclusion of Aboriginal people in the Australian citizenry prior to the 1967 referendum shocks many today (Attwood, passim). And it shocks as unjust, unfair, unreasonable. That it did not seem so for long stretches of white Australia's memory indicates that a different logic was then in force. In the anthem today:

> Our land abounds in nature's gifts
> Of beauty rich and rare.
> In history's page, let every stage
> Advance Australia Fair.

History's page ought to advance Australia Fair. But all of the pages up to now have been torn out of the book. And so none of the questions asked above, of the old story, have any reference now. In the bland terms of Prime Minister Bob Hawke's press release of 19 April 1984, in which the new version of the song was proclaimed the national anthem: "We can all identify . . . with our distinctive national anthem, proud of our past history and working together on constructing a great future." The ethic here is proclaimed to be benign and inclusive. But anywhere in the world, a deception would be essential to so ambitious a goal as the forging of a common identity through generalized pride in a past-in-common.

The convergence of moral value or integrity with race, with language, with tribal membership, is certainly a widespread human phenomenon and one with plenty of Old Testament backing. That it is a sentiment unacceptable today in a world dominated by human rights consciousness indicates that the ethics of the last couple of decades have evolved radically from the ethics of those preceding them. There's a discontinuity here of the kind that necessitated or enabled the revision of "Advance Australia Fair." And still there's a powerful motive for keeping a continuity alive. Theirs was the song of a people in the process of becoming us. Our race ethics didn't spring fully armed from the soil. So there are egalitarian continuities as well as racist ones.

Through the nineteenth century it became increasingly difficult to sell an overt doctrine of racial superiority in the British world. The Evangelical faction of the Church of England had been responsible for the abolition of slave transportation (1807) and finally slave ownership (1833) throughout the British Empire. The sable brethren were worth saving because they too were all God's children. But we would mislead ourselves to think that British conviction of moral superiority on these grounds placed British colonial practices above those of Catholic Spaniards in South America, only to have the rescuers of mankind on a level with benighted heathens like the Australian Aborigines. It's Bernal's thesis that nineteenth-century empires, such as the British, rewrote the ancient world so as to whiten their antecedents and so bolster the race-based authority on which those empires ran.[16] If that thesis is correct then it's not difficult to see Peter Dodds McCormick's lyrics as part of the project. The difficulty in seeing that project or acknowledging its effects is, simply, a measure of its success.

Ongoing success of the project is revealed in the fact that the whitest parts of the world are able today to continually and straightforwardly lecture the rest about good governance and human rights and rule of law, without a hint of racism. The whiter they are the less raced they are, the more their moral authority on questions such as governance. It's in this manner manifest destiny lives on.

As to the event of Australians singing themselves into the "fair" future: three connotations—just, beautiful, white—conflate in an ambiguity where through repetition, through emphasis, and through the dignifying effect of an anthem setting, they come to imply each other. The unspoken terms of the song suffice to imply the conflation: The white person (now standing for *all* the people) toils to make the land beautiful and just. Whether this is an accomplished fact or an uphill battle, regardless of who is now included in this mission, there is no doubt that this notion of progress as "Australia-making" is owing to the coming of the white man. Importantly, this "man"— the hero of the story—is able to go unmentioned and unexamined, because he is invisibly (and indivisibly) white.

The trace of "type" in the old song, gallant Cook hailing from Albion, is gone from the words sung today. No need to offend the migrants (formerly the "new" Australians of the fifties and sixties). How should Australians interrogate their anthem on the question of race now that the race question has apparently been removed from contention (along with the gender question)?

Should the question be asked of this chorus then: If this is not blatant racism, is it something subtler? Is it a kind of deep-seated racism that survives the bowdlerizing of those for whom white supremacist rhetoric might be a little close to the bone? One can go farther: This polysemy, on which nothing can be pinned, is actually a closet racist's gift because it generates paranoia. It accumulates the force of an exclusion without resorting to any culpable act of exclusion as such. Is this racism at the inscrutable and unconscious core of the nation's sense of itself? Is this the taunting of those whom the nation defines itself as excluding? Is this song taunting them to sing themselves in, or else remain silently out, of the picture?

If the significance of this chorus is to say that Australia should go forward under the stewardship of the fair = inter alia white race, then it is not a question of a particular idea of progress being conveyed despite the erasure of a previous story. The erasure of a particular past, which we are too polite to mention, enables the new story. The other past is erased together with the others who inhabited it. In the world outside of the song, however, the others, whom we might be too polite to see, do still inhabit. They inhabit the new story, not as flies on the wall but as flies in the ointment.

"Advance Australia Fair," its evolution, its status, its popular reading, its taboo readings (e.g., this one), the suppression of its earlier version, the fact that what it says and fails to say is officially accepted by Australians to represent Australians: All these things are living reminders of where Australians come from, of the thinking that brought us, of what we possess and how we come to possess it. Fostering awareness of these is of great value to

Australians both in understanding ourselves and in deciding where we should go with that knowledge. The lyrics of "Advance Australia Fair"—and likewise their revision—demand to be examined.

CARRYING A SWAG

Woe to him that increaseth that which is *not his!*

—Habakkuk 2:6

Who does a country rightly belong to? How (by what rights) does it end up in its present hands (or under its current regime of possession)? The question of land rights is about how much of Australia ought to be under Aboriginal control. Why should any of Australia be under Aboriginal control? Would that be because there are places in Australia in which Aborigines have remained more interested than anyone else? In lieu of a treaty that never happened? To assuage white guilt, or simply to acknowledge prior ownership? Note that none of these questions or possible motives directly challenges the national sovereignty of Australia as such.

Prior possession is the central fact underlying all of these doubts and the prospect of restitution or of reconciliation. Those who argue that "possession" won't wash because pre-contact Aborigines didn't have such a concept might as well argue that it's alright to murder babies in their cots because babies don't know what murder is. There are no world ethical systems avowing hypocrisy as their foundation, nor will societies traditionally claiming to be Christian avert the moral force of Christ's dictum that we do unto others as we would have others do unto us.

Nevertheless, there remains for every new Europe (as for many other nation types) the question of the theft of country, and of the consequent presumption that what we now know as law is founded in crime, whether that crime is genocide or widespread murder or "merely" theft and dispossession.

In the case of Australia's official national anthem, we can say that these doubts are buried, disappeared. There's a reason for this. The edifice of nation risks cracking up if a potential gap in the moral consciousness is not papered over. Such doubts and risks and gaps and cracks are part of the postmodern condition of nation. Post-Holocaust, post-decolonization, the mainly white denizens of new Europes cannot stomach the idea that racial superiority gives them a right to the things that they have inherited as a result of their ancestors' convictions of racial superiority.

Nation survives with us from a time when the racial kind of superiority carried with it deep convictions of moral superiority. It's because of that "natural" connection—one not needing to be argued—that there was nothing hypocritical for the eighteenth- and nineteenth-century British mind in those possessing acts we now think of as dispossessing. They were establishing law, order, land tenure, the cultivation of crops, writing, progress (and so with hindsight, history) where none of these good things had been before.

An irony of "Advance Australia Fair" is that despite the effort at historical consciousness (in the original version) and its failure to focus on a present situation as having arisen (in both versions), the homeostatic effect of the song is to keep the present stuck; the means to that end is to keep us from seeing the present (Ong 1982, passim). "We have this and that: let's party now, toil later." The past enabling is missing from the picture for the simple reason that in order to feel proud of where and what we are, we need to gloss over what makes us and our present position possible.

"Waltzing Matilda" (a song dating from the 1890s), by contrast, is set in the epic past—not in one of Bakhtin's peak times (183–84)—but in a fragment of memory, apocryphal perhaps and yet authentic. It's set in the nowhere of bad times that corresponds with the depression and the shearers' strike of the 1890s. This is a story endlessly retold as if in the retelling some lost clue might be retrieved so that the story could finally make sense. But it won't make sense; it's meant to not make sense.

The code of "Waltzing Matilda" is for a restricted audience. But the situation is distinctively colonial: "coolibah" and "billabong" are strange names under the arrangement of the English language. The characters are unnamed types, the place is merely the site of the action: a mysterious theft, a strange death. This lyric has the oneiric logic of the Old Testament. That's how the ever-thus of an unarguable past is established as in the logic of a patriarch's prophetic dream. Details, even the main events may be missing. But this much is got right: The story of the nation's beginnings is about a confusion of crimes for which restitution has not been made.

The irony of the often folksy scholarship devoted to the song is that contention over the provenance of the lyrics and the tune has displaced the mystery that lies in the story the singing buries.[17] The song has been much studied; its words and their meaning have gone unexamined.

Australia's national song, "Waltzing Matilda," the ghost of an anthem one might call it, is unusual among patriotic songs, for being a ghost story. The tune is well known,[18] but for the benefit of those unfamiliar, here's the tale in brief.

An old tramp, carrying all his few belongings on his back, decides to camp in a dry creek bed. He makes a fire, brews some tea, and dances with his blankets, his various few implements, imagining music, imagining his bedroll is a female companion. Of course he's got an appetite and about then a sheep happens by and naturally he grabs it without thinking too hard on the *whose sheep* issue. Unluckily for him in all this vast wilderness to wander in, the sheep-owning farmer and a couple of cops at his beck and call just happen by when there are still some pieces of undevoured sheep in the tramp's possession. Waft of singed wool about. They challenge him and rather than face them, he searches out a puddle in the creek bed and drowns himself. If you go past this place today you can hear his ghost. You can hear his ghost singing as he dances with the bedroll. Singing the whole story over and over. Like a stuck record. Isn't that what a ghost is after all?

This is not the usual exhortation expected of the stuck record we call an anthem. It doesn't tell anyone to gird loins, fight foes, wave banners, or save anybody. If it's about a battle it's about a lost one, one in which no shots were exchanged. It's about a battle that did not take place. And after this nonevent the (forgotten) place in question is left to the sheep (their number one less), left to be haunted by a lonely ghost. Postmodern reflexivity before its time, what we sing and hum to unofficially say "Australia" signifies a tale that haunts itself. A man drowns himself rather than face authority. The tale itself constitutes a report of dubious provenance. It could be a cover-up. The witnesses are few, the testimony is vague. It's hard to see how the words could inspire anyone with hope or to any action other than an investigation of the truth. And yet the words of this song do now seem ironically prophetic in that it is ghosts that Australia now seeks to acknowledge in order to understand its own identity: ghosts of those lost under the wheels of an empire, stolen generations, generations of thieves, ghostly intentions such as no one will now avow.

The song purports to tell a tale the chorus of which doubtfully implicates the listener in, as it were, an accomplished fact: "You'll/Who'll come waltzing Matilda with me./?" Stanza by stanza the value of that refrain shifts, each time into a new bout of irony. After the first stanza it emphasizes the loneliness and lack of the swagman's lot. He has no one with whom to dance, no one with whom to travel: The swag is personalized and sexualized as "Matilda" for precisely this reason. It is an imaginary compensation. The bundle of blankets and pots, which travels with the swagman and with "whom" the swagman sleeps, stands ironically in the place of a domesticity (feminine touch) lost or never found. There is in any case something ironic underlying a question as to who (else) might dance with the partner whom the protagonist lacks.

And yet that lack and this hint of competition for the phantom partner in the dance both imply a kind of (feminized) motivating agency. Everything in this song is done in the name of the absent Matilda with whom everyone is invited to dance, with whom no one can really dance, but under cover of which euphemized desire each victim is tricked into (or at least notified of) a loss, ultimately of life.

To return to the contextual "turns" of the chorus, though, which are all about the absenting of one after another party from the story, the emptying of the landscape as it were. The swagman really will go awaltzing with the jumbuck: It is his intention to eat the evidence in stages. This "third party" sheep then is unlikely to derive the same pleasure as the swagman from the waltz being contemplated. There is nothing mutual in this waltz. It is something inflicted. And likewise the policemen or troopers of the next stanza are more likely than the swagman to take pleasure in the waltz (incarceration at the least) they are planning for him.

The questions aren't really questions; rather, sarcastic assertions, taunts. The squatter claims to be asking for the sheep to be identified, to be asking to whom the sheep belongs. But we know that the squatter knows it's his sheep, or at least acts on the basis of such a presumption. His question is an accusation. Likewise, from the squatter's point of view, the swagman's question in the refrain after the first stanza really indicates an individual miscreant contemplating a next mischief. The undirected questions of the finally repeated chorus implicate any listener in the pattern of accusation and victimization veiled under the euphemism of a "natural" and properly social meeting of the genders: something elegant, civilized: a waltz. But here, in the emptied land, the *terra nullius* of white man's lore, the dance is as denatured as everything else. There is no civil society, there are no women. Rights are notional at the edge of the law's domain. It is superiority in numbers and weaponry that undermines the nine-tenths of the law that is in the swagman's tuckerbag. The sheep will be made to dance. The swagman will dance (perhaps in the manner of the outgunned in westerns). In fact the courtship ritual (dance) mentioned throughout functions as a displaced misogyny:[19] Dancing is a kind of violence inflicted on an unwilling party.

A tale of poverty, desperation, and suicide seems an ironic investment for a lucky country. But every polity begins unluckily for those whom it succeeds and perhaps "Waltzing Matilda" is about laying ghosts to rest or at least keeping them at a safe distance (this one may be heard "as you pass by that billabong" in some versions).[20] Perhaps it is an allegory of the past to put behind us, of the bad old days in which all those with current investments must remain blameless. Our encounter with this dubious fellow, his evanescent and self-expiating crime, saves us from the revolt of the small in general. The swagman is an anonymous character whose crime can't quite be placed. In this sense his position is somewhat analogous to that of an unknown soldier. But there's a strange kind of metonymy at work here, where the *out*-law represents the nation. In the orginary mythology of the United States (as with many other ex-colonial polities, arising out of independence struggles) it makes sense for the new law to establish itself from the outside of—and in a life-and-death—struggle with the old. Nor does such a scenario lack classical precedent: Titans are unseated by Olympians.

In Australia's case there's something mythically unsatisfying in the continuity from colonies to nation. It's as if an event, a story, were lacking. Where then, credibly, to find a myth of origin that might serve in defining Australian-ness? Such a myth would paradoxically give voice to a grievance without disturbing the status quo. In "Waltzing Matilda" we have such a myth. This particular swagman's individual rebellion is obscure, would be unknown but for the song. And perfectly convenient, it makes the perpetrator victim. The people sing not of the worker's victory but of the defeat of the workless at his own hands.

Truth is under the tale that haunts us; it is in lacks and absences made homely. If this song and its evocations are allowed their central place in defining Australian-ness then this signification seems to be an essentially ironic one. It reveals an ironic nationhood: nation installed in the absence of the signs of nation. In Australia, "Waltzing Matilda," the national song presents as anti-allegory: the story of what did not happen. The techniques by which the song's ironic investments are established rest on allegorical re/framing, on imagining truths outside of and to which the story can refer: an audience of people addressed or questioned or advised, a sociolegal reality in which crimes such as theft have meaning. The swagman's theft is petty compared with the thefts on a grand scale that place him somewhere and give him something to steal.

AN ART OF THEFT

In the first book of The Republic Socrates suggests that the poets speak darkly of the nature of justice, and he ridicules the contention he ascribes to Homer that "justice is an art of theft" (299). The trail of precedent and principle, in which law, always after the event, seeks to reify itself, as the quasi-nature of things ever-thus, depends on what is outside and before a canonic pattern. It depends on a kind of boyish enthusiasm, such as might be attributed to gods, in which the signs by which we know rights and responsibilities are erased, as it were, just this once, and just so that they might be commenced. What kind of hubris would hold the gods responsible for the theft, murder, incest, and cannibalism that makes them (and us) possible? It is by sleight of hand, declaring a beginning exempt from its rules, that the law establishes the territory of its jurisdiction, and likewise the jurisdiction of its ghosts.

Is it subversion or superstition to give credence to those ghosts? Where signs absent themselves all plot collapses to this unity: amnesia that masks history's principal recurrence—of invasion, of theft. How much of the past is simply the story of crime becoming law, or the story of the masking of that process? History is the process of making signs absent; discursive activity in the guise of passive apprehension. No habitable corner has been exempt from this process, which seems mere description but is the institution of events. In the case of Australia the lines are clear. Where else has a sovereignty been so suddenly, so irrevocably, overturned and all its signs so easily erased? The nineteenth-century British soul could countenance this suddenness precisely on the pretext that there was no sovereignty before theirs.

If a crime lies at the center of the quintessential Australian story then where, one might ask, would that not be the case? And what kind of a defense is it to ask that question? We are here because of (and despite) crimes against humanity, crimes that allowed us to become, that allow us to continue. The question of guilt relates not to what we ourselves never did, but to our unavoidable lifelong complicity and collaboration against the truth, that collaboration that characterizes lives lived in the absence of any intention to act. This question of bad faith is notwithstanding the fact that others may have hearts as dark as ours, darker. To be situated by crimes past is an aspect of the human condition. It is the universal ethical in medias res. The immensity of the crime enabling our presence, the powerlessness of individuals in the face of it, the security of a collective amnesia (these in the forms of myth, religion, legislation)—all haunt the propensity to act.

The "Waltzing Matilda" story needs to be examined/reread precisely because the words in which it consists are regularly disappeared, because where they are recalled they are emptied of meaning and sung as merely conventional phrases, as formulae the purpose of which is to include and exclude listeners, but without being seen to do so.

THE LAST LAUGH

In Australia "Waltzing Matilda," the national not-an-anthem, sings of silences, is composed of absences. Without doubting the genuine torment of the swagman as disinherited stranger, we note that in the context of a story that sings the facts of presence (the words Australians sing to represent themselves) the blacks are the principal absence. In the frame of *terra nullius*, by falling below the terms of civilization, they fall out of the story altogether, into a reality that must be ahistoric if it is a reality at all. The swagman is then the ersatz victim of the permanent facts of law and possession. Dispossession likewise falls below the threshold of the story. There are other absences here: of women, of the fauna (quintessential agency below the threshold of, yet recipient of the effects of the human story). This is a one-tree story. Told in a four-horse town. Of a farm with one less sheep.

The sublimation of sexual appetites in a defeminized landscape, in the forms of a dance that is always something other than a dance, points to the light and dark issues at the heart of the law's and the nation's becoming. Here, in the primal scene, the blacks are already driven out of the story. A white man (a man so filthy he could be black) takes on their vagabond and thieving role, the role of one who will always haunt the borders of the civilized world. White women have yet to be enticed into the twilit world of the law still emerging. The blacks aren't there and women aren't there. Most particularly, black women (undoubtedly the most sexually exploited persons of the frontier) are not there. But the hunger and the anger of the primal scene remains to be replayed forever, never fully understood or accounted.

Brutality and death result from the confrontation of masculinities: the law's and that of the man outside of the law. Violence is what happens instead of a dance. Who's to blame? The woman's not there. Which woman?

She's got a name. But she won't dance. She doesn't come across. A woman's touch might have made all the difference. In *White* Richard Dyer writes of these problematics, contrasting the Western and the Southern genres of white myth as representing respectively a masculine image of success and a feminized idyll of failure (34–36). In Australia's case I think we can associate "Advance Australia Fair" with a white and masculine image of progress. "Waltzing Matilda," by contrast, presents a landscape as misogynist as it is bereft of women. It too is a feminized idyll of failure, one in which women can be blamed for their absence. Like Gallipoli, it's the stupid and heroic failure that allows the here-and-now its comforts.

The western (U.S.) and Australian bush myths of origin (as in "Waltzing Matilda") are equally interested in the emergence of the law from lawlessness. What's at stake on this frontier is not merely the border between civilization as it encroaches on its outside, but as well the border between myth and history, between hearsay and fact, between popular and official culture.

Ultimately the reader/singer of anthems chooses between (or mixes and matches) the generic dyad Bakhtin offers in the contrast between the epic and the novelistic (182): the story already fixed forever as opposed to the continuing story in which choices are made, and in which we might play a part, dialogically, in determining who we will be.

Concealing themselves in order to sing absences, in both "Advance Australia Fair" and "Waltzing Matilda," Australians absolve themselves of a role in their cause, of the primal crimes (murder and theft) by which they come to inhabit that which was never given: the land abounding, the home girt by sea.

The disinherited stranger—wraith spectacle of "Waltzing Matilda"[21]— is neither a poet, nor a black singing the country, knowing the country by song. The doomed wanderer of this lyric is someone so marginally articulate and mired in his own needs, so out of society, that he sings to his billy boiling and mounts no defense in the face of the law. How quickly that laughter of victorious survival (stuffing the jumbuck in the tuckerbag) dissolves into the echo of justice: the what-becomes-of-the-transgressor! How lightly this man takes on the weight of time for good! He saves the troopers the trouble of discharging their firearms or of hanging him from the tree under which he would have absented (and might have expiated) his crime of theft. All this with the ring of the *ever-thus*: the justness of justice.

In "Waltzing Matilda" what is sung is the survivor's, the victor's story, the myth by which the victor absolves himself of the terrible event in which the past of an inheritance is constituted. "God save the Queen" and "Advance Australia Fair"—corollaries in Australia's nation-ness—likewise and quite sensibly fail to air the grievance that would be heard in *the other side of the story*.

In each case what is absented in the reiteration of what Australians name *their song* is the truth of how it is *they are here*. The search for a context, the historicizing of a text and its reading positions allows us to begin to discover its and our investments, ironic or otherwise. In "Waltzing Matilda"—in the words, I would argue, that are closest to our hearts—we find triumphalism in the guise of the battler's story, rendered now in that incarnation in which he proverbially *tells no tale*. Here is the magnificent denial on which the nation founds itself.[22]

NOTES

1. This information is public record in Australia, as documented for instance in an undated leaflet, *Australia's National Anthem*, and in the 2002 *Parliamentary Handbook of the Commonwealth of Australia*.

2. The rewriting of the lyrics was done by the National Australia Day Committee, in consultation with two of the Boards (Music and Literature) of the Commonwealth Government's arts funding body, the Australia Council (*Australia's National Anthem* leaflet).

3. Peter Dodds McCormick was a Glasgow-born joiner who had emigrated to Australia in 1855, where he became active in the Sydney Presbyterian Church. His lesser known works include "The Bonnie Banks of Clyde." According to the *Oxford Companion to Australian Music* "Advance Australia Fair" was first performed at a Loyal Orange Lodge ceremony in Sydney on 12 July 1878 (15).

4. Government documents rarely acknowledge any alteration from the original lyrics. Where they do, the original lyrics are not shown.

5. Note that Keith Windschuttle's recently released first volume on the fabrication of Tasmania's Aboriginal history suggests that the "orthodox school" of Aboriginal historians have been involved for several decades now in spectacularizing ("beating up") Aboriginal participation in frontier conflict, by for instance turning murders into battles and criminals into guerilla leaders (passim).

6. This is a theme carefully elaborated in Ross Chambers's essay "The Unexamined." See Chambers.

7. The High Court of Australia's 1992 "Mabo decision" rejected the validity of the *terra nullius* doctrine for Australian common law. In other words, Australia was recognized by this decision as having been subject to the antecedent rights of indigenous peoples prior to white settlement. *Terra nullius* has since this time been popularly referred to as a "legal fiction."

8. In Cook's entry for Wednesday, 22 August 1770:

[T]he Eastern Coast from the Latitude of 38°South down to this place I am confident was never seen or viseted [sic] by any European before us . . . and Nothwithstand I had in the Name of His Majesty taken possession of several places upon this coast, I now once more hoisted the English Couleurs [sic] and in the Name of His Majesty King George the Third took possession of the whole Eastern Coast from the above Latitude down to this place by the name of New South Wales . . . (171)

9. The reference is to *The Tempest* IV.i. See Shakespeare.

10. See Bernal, passim.

11. It wasn't until 1946 that commonwealth and state governments agreed on the concurrent celebration of "Australia Day."

12. The "fair" of this song alludes to the now little known last stanza of James Thomson's eighteenth-century poem and song, "Rule Britannia":

> The Muses, still with freedom found,
> Shall to thy happy coast repair:
> Blest isle! with matchless beauty crowned,
> And manly hearts to guard the fair.

The second stanza of the "Advance Australia Fair" has already pointed us toward the British imperial hymn, by quoting from it directly: "Britannia rules the wave."

13. The currency of this last reading is borne out in a 1999 kit (produced by the Ethnic Communities Council of N.S.W.) aimed at curtailing racial hatred and promoting the benefits of ethnic diversity. It was titled *Advance Australia Fair, Dark or Any Shade in Between.*

14. See Kant, "Different."

15. Written by Caroline Carleton in 1859, "The Song of Australia" was a serious contender for national anthem status, having been offered as one of four choices to the public at the 1976 referendum. It received more than one-half million votes, as against almost three million for the winner, "Advance Australia Fair."

16. Cf. the description of the position of the white European in relation to the rest of humanity in Charles White's famous 1799 treatise on race:

> Ascending the line of gradation, we come at last to the white European;
> who being the most removed from the brute creation, may, on that account,
> be considered the most beautiful of the human race. (Dyer, 71)

White's account accords with Kant's equation of the beautiful and the good, both qualities "removed from the brute creation."

17. See especially Magoffin, *Waltzing* and *Swagman.*

18. Here are the best-known lyrics to the song, those of A. B. (Banjo) Paterson:

> Oh! there once was a swagman camped in a Billabong
> Under the shade of a coolibah tree;
> And he sang as he looked at his old billy boiling,
> "Who'll come a-waltzing Matilda with me?"

> Who'll come a-waltzing Matilda, my darling,
> Who'll come a waltzing Matilda with me?
> Waltzing Matilda and leading a water-bag—
> Who'll come a waltzing Matilda with me?

> Down came a jumbuck to drink at the water-hole
> Up jumped the swagman and grabbed him in glee;
> And he sang as he stowed him away in his tucker-bag,
> "You'll come a-waltzing Matilda with me."

Down came the squatter a-riding his thoroughbred;
Down came the policemen—one, two and three.
"Whose is the jumbuck you've got in your tucker-bag?
You'll come a-waltzing Matilda with me."

But the swagman, he up and he jumped in the waterhole,
Drowning himself by the coolibah tree;
And his ghost may be heard as it sings in the Billabong
"Who'll come a-waltzing Matilda with me?" (213)

19. Doubts as to the plausibility of a misogynist reading in the Australian popular (unofficial) culture context should be dispelled by the parody, "Shagging Matilda":

Once some jolly poofters camped by a brothel shop
Under the shade of a syphilis tree;
And their cocks were covered in pox
"Cause they shoved it up her sloppy box—
Who'll come a-shagging Matilda with me?

See Tate.
20. In the Marie Cowan version: "And his ghost may be heard as you pass by that billabong" (in Radic, 21). In the "Queensland" version: "And his ghost may be heard as it sings in the billabong" (in Radic, 19).
21. See Gerry Turcotte's essay on Mudrooroo's vampire novels, which appears in this volume.
22. Thanks to my mother, Sylvia Kelen, for help with research on this paper.

REFERENCES

Anderson, Benedict. 1992. *Imagined communities: Reflections on the origin and spread of nationalism*. London: Verso.
Attwood, Bain, and Andrew Markus. 1997. *The 1967 referendum, or When Aborigines didn't get the vote*. Canberra: Australian Institute of Aboriginal and Torres Strait Islander Studies.
Australia's National Anthem: Advance Australia Fair. Canberra: Australian Government Publishing Service. Undated leaflet. Current at time of writing.
Bakhtin, Mikhail. 1994. *The Bakhtin reader*. Ed. Pam Morris. London: Edward Arnold.
Bernal, Martin. 1987. *Black Athena: The Afro-Asiatic roots of classical civilisation. Volume 1: The fabrication of Ancient Greece 1785–1985*. London: Free Association.
Chambers, Ross. 1997. The unexamined. In *Whiteness: A critical reader*, ed. Mike Hill, 187–204. New York: New York University Press.
Commonwealth of Australia Gazette, No S142. 1984. Canberra: Australian Government Publishing Service.
Cook, James. 1999. *The Journals of Captain Cook*. Harmondsworth: Penguin.
Davey, Gwenda, and Graham Seal, eds. 1993. *The Oxford companion to Australian folklore*. Oxford: Oxford University Press.

Dyer, Richard. 1997. *White*. London: Routledge.

Ethnic Communities Council of N.S.W. 1999. *Advance Australia fair, dark, or any shade in between*. Waterloo: Ethnic Communities Council of New South Wales Inc.

Hage, Ghassan. 1998. *White nation*. Sydney: Pluto.

Hill, Mike, ed. 1997. *Whiteness: A critical reader*. New York: New York University Press.

Kant, Immanuel. 1952. *The critique of judgement* In Vol. 42 of *Great books of the Western world*. Chicago: Encyclopaedia Britannica.

———. 1977. On the different races of man. In *Race and enlightenment*, ed. Emmanuel Chuckwudi Eze, 38-48. Oxford: Blackwell.

Magoffin, Richard. 1995. *Waltzing Matilda: The ballad of the fair go*. Cooparoo, Queensland: Robert Brown.

———. 1998. *The swagman's story of "Waltzing Matilda"—A centenary tribute*. Kynuna, Queensland: Matilda Expo.

———. Waltzing Matilda Home Page. Kynuna, Queensland: Matilda Expo, current at time of writing.

McCormick, P. D. (Peter Dodds). 1974. Advance Australia Fair. Brisbane: W. H. Paling.

Murray, Albert. 1973. White norms, black deviation. In *The death of white sociology*, ed. Joyce A. Ladner, 96–113. New York: Vintage.

Ong, Walter J. 1982. *Orality and literacy: The technologizing of the word*. London: Routledge.

Parliamentary Handbook of the Commonwealth of Australia, 29th edition. 2002. Canberra: Australian Government Publishing Service.

Paterson, A. B. 1921. *The collected verse of A. B. Paterson*. Sydney: Angus and Robertson.

Plato. *The dialogues of Plato*. 1952. Trans. Benjamin Jowett. In *Great books of the Western world, Vol. 7*. Chicago: Encyclopaedia Britannica.

Radic, Thérèse. 1983. *A treasury of favourite Australian Songs*. South Yarra, Victoria: Currie O'Neil Ross.

Royal Commission into Aboriginal Deaths in Custody, National Report Volume 1. 1991. Canberra: Commonwealth of Australia.

Semmler, Clement. 1988. *The banjo of the bush: The life and times of A. B. Paterson*. St Lucia: University of Queensland Press.

Shakespeare, William. 1974. *The Riverside Shakespeare*. Ed. G. Blakemore Evans. Boston: Houghton Mifflin.

Tate, Brad. 1982. *The bastard from the bush: Obscene songs and ballads of Australian origin*. Kuranda, Queensland: Rams Skull Press.

Windschuttle, Keith. 2002. *The fabrication of Aboriginal history, Volume One: Van Diemen's Land 1803–1847*. Sydney: Macleay Press.

ELEVEN

THE TIMES OF WHITENESS;
OR, RACE BETWEEN THE
POSTMODERN AND THE POSTCOLONIAL

Ryan S. Trimm

FRANTZ FANON TELLS HIS IMAGINED INTERLOCUTOR in "The Fact of Blackness" that "you come too late, much too late. There will always be a world—a white world—between you and us . . . [t]he other's total inability to liquidate the past once and for all" (Fanon 1952, 122; ellipsis in original). Attempts to shore up identity or forge relationships find that it is race that mediates and defers, yet temporally stumbles itself. The relay of whiteness means that identity always arrives too late, for this sense of self depends on the deferral of the self/other dialectic. Fanon articulates this oppositional definition as a necessity, one that codes black and white skin: "For not only must the black man be black; he must be black in relation to the white man. . . . The black man has no ontological resistance in the eyes of the white man" (110). Blackness then defines itself not only in its own terms but also in opposition to an other, a white other that in turn defines itself against black otherness. Indeed, as Richard Dyer notes, it often seems as if the only way "to recognize white *qua* white, is when non-white (and above all black) people are also represented" (Dyer 1997, 13). As a result, racial identity depends on a perpetual deferral, a relay of appeals to others in an effort to ground a sense of self. It is this postponement that ensures that the racial present will continually be haunted by the irruption of the past. The result is an unstable temporality of identity.

Caryl Phillips's 1991 novel *Cambridge* charts how the instability of race intersects with national identity, a charting that is written back into the colonial past. Centered around competing accounts of a nineteenth-century murder on a small Caribbean island, the novel's two longest narratives are those of the slave who kills his overseer and the daughter of the plantation's absentee owner. It is these disputing accounts and styles that generate what I am reading here as the novel's postmodernism, for the emphasis on pitching historically silenced voices versus official history, and on refusing a single authoritative narrative, correspond with most of the usual suspects in the postmodern identification game: Master narratives are disrupted, the onto-logical certainty of this history is brought into question, the narratives dem-onstrate self-awareness of their writing of interstitial history, and so forth. At the same time, both of the narrating characters ironically identify themselves as English: the slave through an Equiano-like life that gives him an English education, and the daughter through a native-born status that distinguishes her from the colonials. As a result, the novel interrogates the relation be-tween gender, race, and national identity—this is *Cambridge*'s postcolonial dimension. The narratives of Emily and Cambridge frame this identity crisis most particularly around contingencies that undermine the full effectiveness of their claims to English identity. Emily's narrative both in theme and form embodies a fractured Englishness, for she at once embodies the strongest claim to being an English subject at the very moment in which she is prac-tically divested of her rights of citizenship. This split is cast into relief by the figure of Cambridge, the slave, whose own narrative of citizenship betrays an imperial refusal of his claim to be a legal subject. These narrative antago-nisms effectively articulate a divided English identity, for the purportedly universal qualities of Englishness are in fact rent by an unstable reliance on the mediation of gender and race; this divide reveals striking temporal rents in these conceptions of identity.

These divisions point toward a larger structural issue, one that surfaces in the very title of the novel. Cambridge, of course, is only one of many names given to or adopted by the once and future African slave: Olumide, Thomas, and David Henderson (the name he himself claims at the end of his account) are the others. The novel's title thus indicates a problem in naming and identity, and raises the specter that we perhaps have the wrong label, that we have misapprehended the slave formerly known as Olumide. In addition to this invocation of a tension common in slave narratives, the title seems to misdirect in another fashion. Contrary to whatever expecta-tions might be raised by the title *Cambridge*, we discover that Emily Cartwright occupies a much larger position in the novel: Her journal occupies approxi-mately two-thirds of the text (122 pages out of 184, versus only 34 pages for Cambridge) and in addition, she is the focal point for both the prologue and the epilogue.[1] These framing sections make no attempt to situate or evaluate the three texts that they enclose. The different narrative strands of the novel stand as a collage; however, the combination stresses the gaps between these different sources more than any greater unity they might fall into. We are then on guard to read for fissures and ironies in the intersection of these different narratives. The concluding effect is that *Cambridge* calls our attention to an uncertain center, a center that itself seems to have been displaced. As such, the novel demands a reading that would position it not only historically but also historiographically, would articulate not only what the novel suggests about history and particular histories, but also how that history relates to the present. If our current ideas of race were forged in the colonial crucible, then *Cambridge*, however set in the past, implicitly follows this chain into the present (Frankenberg 2001, 76). As Gail Low indicates, "In our own time, the legacy of Cambridge's particular dilemma can be seen in the problems facing citizenship and belonging in the modern civil state" (Low 1998, 126); that is, Cambridge's identification with Englishness and his expulsion by the white characters from this imagined community positions Phillips's text as an anachronistic version of the postcolonial novel of the metropole.[2]

Although such fluidity of time and identity is usually seen as a postmodernist trope, as Ato Quayson points out

> [t]his cannot be taken solely as a postmodernist question of the dissolution of the centrality of the West; it is a postcolonial one as well because the demographic changes in the West today cannot be howevert of outside the various histories of empire (and slavery, in the case of the United States) which stretch back into previous centuries. (Quayson 2000, 106)

Such an anachronism is by design, one in which the disturbance of chronology is done not merely in play but rather to articulate temporal relations. *Cambridge* itself must be read not only back to the past, but also how that past relates to and prefigures the present. The result is an unstable temporality that parallels the shifting strategies of identification deployed in the novel around the intersection of race, gender, and nation. This reading inscribes a "prophetic vision of the past," one in which colonial chromatic coding figures the interrupted imagining of the postimperial nation (Ashcroft 2001, 104). In doing so, the novel aligns itself with the mainly metropolitan project of what Barnor Hesse has called "postcolonial memory." Such historicism is not simply an act of reclamation but instead an ethical project grounded in tracing the present back into the past:

> The ethics of postcolonial memory concerns itself less with the historical "wrongs" of the colonial question than with interrupted

and incomplete forms of decolonization and their relation to contemporary social constructions of injustice/justice. In this precise sense, postcolonial memory in the West is not concerned with the (colonial) past through an obsession with the past, but through an engagement with the (liberal-democratic) present. . . . In postcolonial memory it is the memory of present predicaments that recalls the dislocations of the past. (Hesse 2002, 165)

These dislocations in *Cambridge* can only be accessed via the competing discourses that materialize them. Because there is no master code offered for how these narratives work together, they must be read against one another as competing frames. However, as Hesse's remarks suggests, this antagonism cannot be seen as a struggle based around a straightforward referentiality to a verifiable past, one that would authenticate a clear victor. Instead, the emphasis on a textualization of the relations of colonial past and postimperial present, one that problematizes a retrieval of the past, suggests that *Cambridge*'s postmodernism must itself be read as a move that traces the postimperial articulation of race, gender, and nationality backward into the colonial crucible.[3]

The temporal rents are all the more effective for being placed in a novel that foregrounds narrative simultaneity. The three separate narratives that compose *Cambridge* (Emily's journal, Cambridge's apologia, and the local historical account) largely parallel one another, only obliquely intersecting around discrepant accounts of a few key events leading to the death of Mr. Brown and Cambridge's subsequent summary imprisonment and execution.[4] That is to say, these narratives of course cover roughly the same time period, have roughly contemporaneous times of composition (Emily's journal is composed as events transpire, Cambridge's apologia is penned in his cell as he awaits execution, the local history seems to be written a few years after the fact), and arrive at the same place to recount the death of Mr. Brown. However, the overlap between these narratives is quite restricted: Emily and Cambridge are no better than walk-ons in each other's tales and Emily (whose story comprises two-thirds of the novel) merits no mention whatsoever in the local history. Because of their relative independence from one another, the net effect of these accounts is simultaneity, for these roughly contemporaneous perspectives in effect go through their narrative motions largely oblivious of one another's existence. This coevalness, however, is not of the same nature as that of Benedict Anderson's imagined community, a simultaneity that has as its model the complementary and parallel plotlines of the realist novel. Instead, the narratives in *Cambridge* are naturally separate accounts, accounts that intersect with the same incident, yet which are not equally weighted: Emily's version is twice again as long as both of the others put together, Cambridge's apologia is by far the most convincing to my students, and the third and sketchiest narrative, the local chronicle, would be the one most likely to be passed down, to be accepted as the "official" history of the violent events on the unnamed island. This weight aside, time in this postmodernist reading of the novel is spatialized: competing accounts, side by side, though with something less than a complementary relationship. In contrast, the postimperial temporality is a stuttering one, an interrupted chronology that betrays the lingering legacy of the colonial construction of race.

Of course, this multiple presentness of the past works through a type of double time: The past is articulated and performed by these spatialized narratives. It is through this national double time that Emily and Cambridge's claims to Englishness may be evaluated, claims that start to reveal temporal fissures produced around reaction to racial difference. Race here depends on an anxious play between its different levels of distinction, between its sense as belonging to a (national) class of people who share characteristics and its broader, pseudo-biological sense as a breed or species of people largely defined around skin color. There is also the further slip between historical conceptions of race that David Theo Goldberg terms the naturalist and the progressivist, racial ideations reflected in the accounts of Emily and Cambridge. The naturalist depends on an ideology of biological distinction and genetic superiority, the progressivist on a notion of racial difference dependent on perceptions of uneven development and the possibility of aiding presumed inferiors into a position of self-sufficiency (Goldberg 2002, 82). *Cambridge* demonstrates the slide between these versions of race in the way that they are invoked implicitly and explicitly in the (dis)establishment of the English identity of Emily and the titular character, a displacement that looks forward to the postimperial articulation of race.

As both Emily and Cambridge demonstrate, ideas of race tends to collapse in defining and determining Englishness, a collapse that is historically positioned by this "post" fiction to anticipate Paul Gilroy's assessment of contemporary Britain. In discussing the postimperial crises besetting the United Kingdom, he notes that race and its current articulation play a unique role in signing a unity among these identity exigencies. As a result, "[t]his crisis is thus *lived* through a sense of 'race'" (Gilroy 1993, 22–23). Indeed,

> [t]he politics of "race" in this country is fired by conceptions of national belonging and homogeneity which not only blur the distinction between "race" and nation, but rely on that very ambiguity for their effect. Phrases like "the Island Race" and the "the Bulldog Breed" vividly convey the manner in which this nation is represented in terms which are simultaneously biological and cultural. (Gilroy 1987, 45)

This imbrication of conflicting versions of race is reflected in the contrasting ways in which Emily and Cambridge are seen to represent Englishness, as well as the ways in which this representativeness is refused.

Emily experiences her entire journey as a threat to her sense of self, an unraveling of identity that puts stress on the uncertain relation of Englishness and whiteness. It is largely this anxiety that leads her to seize upon her national identity as she surveys the island society around her. Initially, it is in fact the white creoles that provoke her strongest reactions and invocations of England. Much of Emily's initial reaction to life on the island is colored by the scorn she pours on the less-than-fulfilling company of the creoles and émigrés represented by Brown, Rogers, and McDonald (Phillips, 30–31 and 48–57). She accepts Brown's assessment of the poor quality of the immigrant tradesmen without question (58–59) and regards island society, as represented by its newspapers, as something between a scandal and a litigious offense (47). Emily's responses to these breaches in propriety depend largely on their violations of her sense of decorum, one rooted in England. Such constant disapproval spurs Brown to rejoinder that "everything is not as it is in England," a comment that marks the authorizing source for Emily's censure (58). Her English identity at this point then seems to depend on not just the claim of blood, but more specifically of a proprietary sense of place, a sense of ownership derived through dint of birthplace. Such nationness is not only proprietary but also nontransferable—it is one that depends on a past mark of birthright. Englishness, in comparison with the creole society of Baytown, is a cultural heritage fully bestowed only on those who possess a claim, not just through a genealogical descent, but through a biological (i.e., birth) initiation into the restricted circle of nation.

Emily's primary complaint with white creole society—a culture characterized by scandalous newspapers, decadent excess, and moral degeneracy—is that is a chaotic one:

> Without rank and order any society, no matter how sophisticated, is doomed to admit the worst kind of anarchy. In this West Indian sphere there is amongst the white people too little attention paid to differences of class. A white skin would appear passport enough to a life of privilege, without due regard to the grade of individuals within the range of that standing. (72)

Whiteness then becomes the primary marker of identity in this society. Emily feels the loss of fine gradations of class, social, and economic standing for a Manichean divide of white and nonwhite. Indeed, this overarching whiteness might help explain why her appeals to her own advantages—her English birth, her status as daughter and representative of the plantation owner, and her social class—bear so little weight in island society, particularly with the less-than-polished Mr. Brown. These advantages must give way to the primary distinction of race on the island.

Over the course of Emily's sojourn on the island, this easy dichotomy starts to break down. The plantation owner's daughter notes that the poor whites on the island—the destitute former slave owners and indentured servants—are a troubling sight largely because of the way that they unsettle the racial economy of the island. As a result, they must be consigned to a new category:

> Naturally these poor white *creoles* form an entirely different class from those whites who have emigrated in search of financial gain, or whose government or domestic duties have torn them, albeit temporarily, from the bosom of the land of their birth. Alhowever outnumbered by their superiors, there are not a few of these pale-fleshed *niggers* enduring these lamentable conditions. (Phillips, 108)

To become a poor white distinguishes one from more prosperous whites because it signals a break from one's home. If the Englishman "always means England" when he thinks of home (49), then poverty means an inability to return and a resignation to remaining on an the island. What distinguishes poor from rich whites on the island is the fact that the break from England is no longer temporary but permanent, a permanence signaled by the fact that such whites are now fully creolized and seasoned—in essence, they are no longer truly Englishmen for there is no return home.[5] Such a break from Englishness threatens racial identity as well. Poor whites are in fact now "pale-fleshed *niggers*," distinct from the slaves and "black Samaritans" only by the color of their skin rather than some essentialized racial or national distinction. As Ruth Frankenberg notes, the limit case in the status of poor whites reflects the fact that "alhowever ostensibly marked by the clearly distinguishable behaviors or characteristics of self-designated selves . . . whiteness turns out on closer inspection to be more about the power to include and exclude groups and individuals than about the actual practices of those who are to be let in or kept out" (Frankenberg 1997, 13). This racialized social disgrace is precisely the fate that seems to have befallen Emily at the end of the novel, a fall marked by her habitation of the formerly deserted and derelict Hawthorn Cottage rather than the plantation house. However, Emily marks this change not as a loss but as a result of development and progression: No longer is England "a dependable garment that one simply slipped into or out of according to one's whim," but is now instead something outgrown, a "country-garb . . . no longer of a correct measure" (Phillips, 177). Emily grudgingly grants that she will probably return to England (thus signaling that her social slide has not yet occasioned the permanent break of the poor whites) but this voyage back is now a choice, a free assumption of a "home" (178). Nation has become a habit, a cultural fashion that can be modeled according to will and whim.[6]

As the case of Cambridge proves, however, this trope of nation as clothing is complicated if one lacks the prerequisite whiteness, if one possesses the wrong skin beneath. Englishness is tailored to depend on a prior racial distinction even as it offers itself culturally as a garb that might be universally assumed. This lesson, however, is imparted not so much within the slave's tale as through it. Cambridge himself views his English identity not as something he was born to, but as something he acquired through his study and application of religious and legal texts. He views this assumption of identity not so much as a reworking of these identificatory texts, but as a mastery of—and hence assimilation into—a body of tradition. Cambridge demonstrates this newfound sense of identity in his longing to return to "dear England" and his howeverts of himself as an "Englishman, albeit a little smudgy of complexion" (166, 147). This vision of national self as acquirable and transferable is obviously one that marks the qualities and characteristics of Englishness as potentially universal, for it can be extended to any regardless of birth and origin.

In fact, Cambridge's whole narrative is built around a plea that these signifiers be regarded as universally transferable, a plea that begins and ends his narrative: "Pardon the liberty I take in unburdening myself with these hasty lines, but thanks be to God for granting me powers of self-expression in the English language. I humbly beg that those of my dear England, Africans of my own complexion, and *creoles* of both aspects might bear with me" (133; see also 167). The very telling of the slave's tale then depends on his appropriation and performance of English language and religion. His tale might indeed be understood as a movement toward—and struggle to retain—these gifts, a narrative structure that colors even the presentation of Cambridge's early years. Although he begins his apologia by remembering his people as "unsullied" by greed, lying, and the other usual symptoms of European modernity and civilization, this memory depends on the standard signification slide of the noble savage (133). By the time he is on the second leg of his triangular travels (his journey from the Carolinas to England), he already finds that "Africa spoke only to me of a barbarity I had fortunately fled . . . spoke to me only of a history I had cast aside" (143, 147). This break is largely figured around David Henderson's steady inculcation of English values, an ingestion ultimately done for the aim of his missionary work: "It was God's wish that I should return to my old country with the character of a man in upper rank, and a superior *English* mind, inferior only to the Christian goodness in my heart" (155).[7] These ennoblings significantly remain at the level of the performative: the future Cambridge is not actually a man of upper rank, he merely possesses the same type of character. Such an emphasis on similarity and resemblance ominously echoes the aspersions cast on Cambridge's very masculinity and humanity by an inn master who sees only "something black in the form of a man" (150). As a result, Cambridge comes to depend on his command of the English language and his Christianity as markers of his identity and humanity: Again and again, Cambridge flourishes these markers in an attempt to forge his selfhood in the eyes of skeptical whites.[8]

Ironically, Cambridge's first introduction to these English values comes in the form of their violation: he finds the sexual predation by the crew of the slaver on their cargo a shame that brands humanity itself: "These white vulgarians disgraced not only their nation, but the very name of man" (138). This shameful behavior follows Cambridge's description of "English talk [as resembling] nothing more civilized than the manic chatter of baboons" and his recording of the fear that the flesh-eating English will cannibalize their captives (135). These descriptions do in fact reverse the brutish figuration used by Emily and others against the African slaves; however, the descriptions are not simple reversals. The actions of these slave traders mark them as savage, a brutishness that Cambridge extends to their language and table. English civility and Englishness are not so much features of an essential identity here as a part that one can cast off—or put on—based on one's (im)personation. However, the performance of this part is affected by the reaction of the audience. Even after becoming David Henderson, this stress on the form and performance of elements of Englishness signals that Cambridge's new identity is impacted on its acceptance by the whites around him. Otherwise, he runs the risk of being viewed as a minstrel putting on airs, much like the "notorious fop of Bristol," Clarence de Quincy, the former slave whose mockery of Cambridge fuels his anxiety about his acceptance as an Englishman (151).[9]

Given this need of a proper reception for effecting Englishness, among the worst-case reactions for Cambridge are those of Emily and the anonymous history writer. The plantation owner's daughter remarks that the former David Henderson "seemed determined to adopt a *lunatic* precision in his dealings with our English words, as the black imagined himself to be a part of our white race" (120); the local historian describes Cambridge as one whose mind has been "destroyed by fanciful notions of a Christian life of moral and domestic responsibility which he, in common with his fellow slaves, was congenitally unsuited to" (172–73).[10] These naturalist judgments that the slave's claim to English language and religion are "fanciful" and "lunatic" both appeal to a race as that which prevents his claim from being a valid one, for his skin permanently restricts him from speaking English precisely or practicing Christian doctrine. The fact that Cambridge is quite obviously doing both of these things can only be explained by some form of insanity, some mental disturbance that prevents him from appreciating the fact that he cannot do that which he is doing with great precision. The slave's speech violates the naturalist dichotomy of race, one in which "those classified or considered not white are reduced to silence—both incapable of speech and in the end of being spoken about" (Goldberg, 96). Cambridge's appropriation of the markers of English rationality and civility are then received as a violation and an inversion, a negation of the whiteness of these marks; his assumption of the markers of (in his eyes) civilization mark him instead as insane, as outside the bounds of human rationality. By casting the black performance of these signifiers as irrational, Emily and the local historian both acknowledge the success of this performance and ultimately resort to the argument that markers associated with Englishness may only be performed by those possessing "white" skins. The signifiers of this national identity then suddenly appear contingent, for their function depends on the one who deploys them: If their utterance is performed under the aegis of whiteness, then they signify English identity; however, their remark within the context of blackness signifies less—and more—than Englishness. This excess national identity proves so unstable a threat that it must be marked as beyond the conceiving of reason. Cambridge's deployment of the signifiers of Englishness proves to be a very uncertain game. Race acts, as Etienne Balibar has pointed out, as a supplement to national identity. In the face of class antagonisms and tensions, nationalism alone cannot quite succeed in sublating these struggles: "You need more nationalism. You need a nationalism which is, so to speak, more nationalistic than nationalism itself: what I would call . . . in the language of Derrida a *supplement* of nationalism *within* nationalism"; racism is this supplement (Balibar 1994, 203). Cambridge's failure to possess the whiteness that is held out as an essential component of Englishness condemns him to remain outside this imagined community. However, Balibar's formulation locates class as the final determinant tension; as Emily's remarks about creole society underscore, this is not the case on the island, for race underlies and disrupts all identities. Indeed, as the reactions to Cambridge's staging of Englishness demonstrate, this supplement can only stand as an originary one to national identity.

Both Cambridge and Emily thus largely view their Englishness as depending on a connection with the pedagogical time of the nation, as hinging on an idea of national identity that stresses the archaic and the traditional, whether the archaic nature of birth or the espousal of the tradition of the English book (Bhabha 1994, 145 and 110). Of course, it is their claim on this pedagogic sense of nation that is performative: Emily's sense of superiority to the islanders is drawn from her claim to the England of her father; more strikingly, Cambridge's English identity is based on having mastered the faith and education that "official" gatekeepers such as Mr. Rogers would have denied him. However, it is precisely because of the threat of a performative extension of legal and cultural English citizenship to a woman and an African slave that Cambridge and Emily are treated so harshly: Mr. Brown in particular takes great relish in manhandling them back to their proper station. This reaction certainly demonstrates practical limits to the performance of English identity, limits imposed by those challenged by its transference to one who would undermine racialized and gendered authority on the island.

For Emily, this undoing largely occurs because, once on the island, she finds that gender and race complicate her identity, by her status as a native-born Englishwoman and her role as daughter of an absentee owner. These factors all depend on others to truly define them, yet their distinction is never settled or stable. Emily experiences gender as the first to impact her sense of self; significantly, this experience is largely figured in racialized terms. Her arrival upon the unnamed island is also the occasion of her fully realizing her part in what Ruth Frankenberg has labeled the "tropo-logical family." This "family" charts out the ideological construction of assigned identities based on the intersection of race and gender in the colonial crucible.[11] Within this colonial clan, "White Woman's ambiguous and ambivalent status in this family of tropes is striking: she is, on the one hand, accorded privileges and status by this race/gender positioning, and, on the other hand, confined by it. In any case she is advantaged only conditionally on her acceptance of the terms of the contract" (Frankenberg 1997, 12). In fact Emily, upon leaving the ship, remarks that the relief she notices on the faces of the crew is in part because of her departure: "These men were clearly used to treating female creatures as little more than beings of an inferior nature whose task it was merely to render service and expect in return neither gratitude nor the simplest cheering word or smile" (Phillips, 20). This link between women and slaves is strengthened by its echo of the ruminative third-person voice of the opening frame, a voice that notes Emily recognizing the logic of "the rude mechanics of horse trading" behind her arranged marriage to Thomas Lockwood, one arranged so that her father might pay off his gambling debts (4). Noting Emily's status as a living commodity as she boards a ship plying the triangular-trade routes cannot help but mark her similarity to the cargo that composed the middle passage of this route, an identification common in writings of women abolitionists (Ware 2002, 69). In fact, this subordinate status is so prevalent as to undercut what Paul Sharrad calls her "surrogate male" role as offspring of the plantation's owner (Sharrad 1994, 202): again and again she is dismissed and manhandled by Mr. Brown, her father's employee.[12]

However, once ashore Emily herself is quick to distinguish herself racially from the slaves. She is brought onto dry land on the back of a slave (Phillips, 20) and this introduction to blackness as beast of burden sets up all the standard brutish metaphors that pepper her account of the island: the slaves "bray" (32), breed "like animals of the field" (36; see also 39), give birth to "black wolf cubs" (64), inhabit "nests" (67), possess "paws" instead of hands (111), and most memorably, are indistinguishable from primates:

> A number of pigs bolted into view, and after them a small parcel of monkeys. This took me by surprise. . . . However, on resettling my position, I discovered that what I had taken for monkeys were nothing other than negro children, naked as they were born, parading in a feral manner to which they were not only accustomed, but in which they felt comfortable. I expressed my general concern at the blackness of the native people and was corrected on one count and instructed on the other. (23–24)

This episode marks Emily's first full confrontation with blackness, a confrontation that goes a great way toward helping to construct her own sense of racial identity, for the scene concludes with her first lesson about race on the island. Warren Montag comments on an almost identical scene in Janet Schaw's *Journal of a Lady of Quality*, undoubtedly one of the historical sources for the character of Emily, and notes that this purported mistake of vision betrays a fracturing of Enlightenment universalism.[13] By letting her mistaken vision stand even after she recognizes that the children are in fact human, Schaw (and Emily) casts doubt on the humanity of the slaves even as she proclaims it. In so doing, she pauses at the divide of the human and nonhuman, and positions the slaves at this outer limit of the human.

By discovering the children to be a limit case of the human, Schaw/Emily reserves full humanity for whiteness:

> To be white is to be human, and to be human is to be white. In this way, the concept of whiteness is deprived of its purely racial character at the moment of its universalization, no longer conceivable as a particularistic survival haunting the discourse of universality but, rather, as the very form of human universality itself. . . . [this formulation] allows us to ask whether, since whiteness is not logically confined to the status of a particularism but can be conceived as one possible form of universalism, the category or attribute of whiteness has functioned historically in opposition to universalism. (Montag 1997, 285)

Examining arguments about the nature of humanity in Locke and Rosseau, Montag discovers that this formulation of humanity rests on the notion of humanness arising out of and distinguishing itself from the nonhuman. Rather than a clean break, this progressive evolution imagines the human to be found as an immanent ideal. Because this ideal is an ultimate goal, "the human norm, of course, is always glimpsed only negatively: It is what allows us to see the deficient and the abnormal without itself being seen" (291). The different groupings of humanity can thus be assessed according to differing "degrees of perfection." Thus, by marking the slave children as closer to zero on this measuring stick of the human, Schaw/Emily implicitly marks whiteness as being "unmarked": As Schaw/Emily feels no confusion about the human quality of whiteness, to be white is to have gone a considerable distance in attaining a fully expressed humanness. By figuring the slaves as animals in the passage above, Emily emphasizes their corporeal embodiment. As Richard Dyer has pointed out, this material reduction has the effect of restricting blackness to the body, while whiteness is "something else that is realised in and yet is not reducible to the corporeal or racial" (Dyer, 14–15). The end effect is that this corporeality limits the potential human dimension of blackness, while the body is merely the materialization of a white humanity. In such a view, whiteness is as human as one can get.

This striving for human perfectibility has the effect of temporalizing race, doing so in a manner that recalls Johannes Fabian's work on time and the other. By positioning blackness at the bottom of the scale of human perfectibility, Emily marks racial alterity as not fully perfected, as primitive in its humanness. This sense of blackness as nascently human is further picked up by Emily's infantalization of the slaves. Not only does she continually refer to them as "children of the sun," but she also finds that their lack of human development exercises a claim on white responsibility:

> If treated with care these children are as loyal as any creatures under the sun. They may differ from us in their disregard of marriage vows, and they clearly have difficulty in performing any duty without giving voice to melody, or relaxing without tripping the light fantastic with their toes, but they are in our charge and must be provided for. . . . This being the case, we must be bold enough to take on the responsibility that comes with ownership, and learn to care with even greater dutiful application. (72)

Emily's formulation of slave ownership as white man's burden thus depends on playing a parental role to these "children." Whiteness is implicitly assumed to be a mature humanness, a humanity that, not being stuck in an early stage of development, has reached the present. Indeed, this progressivist maturity is equated with humanity itself: "Whiteness is itself the human universal that no (other) race realizes. In theory, no (other) race is, or need be, inferior (it is only the contingent and the accidental that make them so). In fact, all (others) are inferior, having fallen short of the universal and therefore of humanity" (Montag, 292). Whiteness therefore is seen as essential realization, a fulfillment against which other identities appear as cut by limiting contingencies.

Curiously, the ultimate leveling of both characters appears in narrative limits, in gaps, evasions, and silences. Emily's pregnancy is marked in her account only through elliptical comments about her "lamentable condition" and the "shame" that Mr. McDonald experiences upon his examination of this condition (Phillips 127–28). Cambridge himself remarks vaguely on Emily's condition (167), but it is not until the stillbirth in the epilogue that the truth emerges. In terms of the death of Mr. Brown, Cambridge laconically describes the central event of the novel in passive terms: "He struck me once with his crop, and I took it from him, and in the resultant struggle the life left his body" (167). Emily's account avoids all detail save attributing responsibility to Cambridge (128), while the anonymous local historian also describes the actual incident in the passive voice ("A heavy blow from the skimmer stunned him [Brown] . . . and his murderer was left standing alone"

[173]). This historical narrative further loses authority through an obsessive interest in the folklore surrounding Brown's death, romantically lingering over the "dead man's jumby" and spooky tales of the barrenness of the place of the murder rather than the event itself (173–74).[14] Although there seems to be little question that Cambridge killed Mr. Brown (or that Emily was carrying Arnold's child), these crucial events take place offstage and more or less off the narrative register: all three tales become suspiciously evasive when this climax comes. This muted recounting of events parallels the novel's oblique recording of a major historical moment: the coming emancipation of the slaves. Emily remarks only that McDonald "like all white people in the region . . . now works with a threatening dark cloud above his head" (128). McDonald himself refers glancingly in the epilogue to "this emancipation thing" that might take a few years to take "a grip, if it ever does" (179).[15] These oblique allusions offer a momentous event in litotic tones, which position this historical "ditch" as a mere suggestion of a chronological horizon. The result is to keep the novel's emphasis squarely on the narrative trajectories recorded by Emily and Cambridge: a travelogue and an apologia. This emphasis squares with Ursula Heise's account of the temporal emphasis of postmodern fiction: "[P]ostmodernist novels focus on the moment or the narrative present at the expense of larger temporal developments" (62). This narrative present is fractured into three separate tales that do not quite add up to a complete whole, tales that thus present a past in fragments. As a result, this fractured colonial past points back to a present that can articulate how these shards relate to one another and to its own postcolonial moment.

To this postmodern historiographical reflection is then added a proleptic and anachronistic hint of the postimperial condition. As both Cambridge and Emily reflect prophetically, "[I]n contemporary Britain, statements about nation are invariably also statements about race" (Gilroy 1987, 57). This congruence is charted by Paul Gilroy in the contemporary British figuration of racial otherness as internal threat, an enemy within, one characterized by violence, crime, and a "swamping" fertility: The "superficially simple question 'what kind of people are we' summoned those very images and axioms and answered itself powerfully in the negative. . . . The black presence is thus constructed as a problem or threat against which a homogeneous, white, national 'we' could be unified" (48). This "whitewashed" nation is then defined as one of order and law, a reversed image to the purportedly criminal and alien presence that helps to reconstruct a postimperial national sense of self. In such a situation, "blackness appears as a kind of disqualification from membership of the national community: The same national community which will be celebrated and reproduced in the reformed pedagogy of national history" (Gilroy 1993, 64). This self-imagined community brands colonial immigrants as "unassimilated and unassimilable populations," in the words of the notorious Tory politician and race-baiter Enoch Powell (qtd. in Gilroy 1987, 43). Cambridge thus stands as a precursor to the generations following the landing of the *Empire Windrush* in that he too attempts to integrate himself into English society through the painstaking acquisition of the language and culture.[16] Like the post-*Windrush* generations, David Henderson's attempts to assimilate into British society meet with a great lack of success, a failure based on a notion that these new Britons can never inculcate the national character. As a result, "[b]lackness and Englishness are constructed as incompatible, mutually exclusive identities. To speak of the British or English people is to speak of the *white* people" (Gilroy 1993, 27).

In the figure of Cambridge, the rejection of these immigrants is figured as a literal expulsion from the social body, an expulsion performed by way of unsettling betrayals. In contrast, the island's colonizers regards their Englishness as largely untouched by the trans-Atlantic journey and increasing acclimatization to the unnamed isle:

> Mr. McDonald contrasted the use of the phrase "at home" when applied by the English expatriate, with its use by the French. For the former, he always meant England. . . . The English planters look upon these islands as colonies to which they are exiled for a certain period . . . but very few expect to die on these tropical estates. Those who have troubled to bestir themselves all look forward to spending their last years in the land of their birth. They never see, or inhale the fragrance of, a *creole* rose without letting their imaginations stray through the rich gardens of fair England. (Phillips, 50–51)[17]

As a result, Englishness is figured in ways similar to what Kathleen Paul has tracked in the apparently paradoxical notions of British citizenship displayed in the immediate postwar years: "Native" British citizens were encouraged to emigrate to the dominions in an attempt to strengthen ties to Australia, Canada, Rhodesia, and South Africa; Eastern European refugees were encouraged to immigrate to Britain; and emigrants from the Caribbean and south Asia, however already "officially" British subjects, were actively discouraged from setting foot in the Isles. Paul finds that the rationale behind these seemingly contradictory strategies depends on competing communities of Britishness, communities that operate together as largely concentric circles. In the center are those who had actually been born in Britain of British "stock." Their Britishness was viewed as innate and so strong as to never be expunged; thus, it was reasoned, their migration to the dominions could only have the effect of strengthening and literalizing the "family" ties that bound the settler dominions to the motherland. As a result, the lasting prestige and economic importance of keeping a strong and vital Commonwealth in the family would far offset any loss of man- or brainpower in their emigration. To help make up for this loss of labor, it was supposed that European refugees, largely because of their white skins, could be readily assimilated into British society although a number of these displaced persons had been on the opposing side in the world war. This circle of Britishness encompassed those who could be brought into the fold and assimilated into British stock. The outermost community of Britishness was composed of persons from the Commonwealth, persons who had in fact been legally granted the status of British subject in the 1948 British Nationality Act (itself an attempt to shore up the strength of the Commonwealth by extending "United Kingdom and Colonies" citizenship to all citizens of Commonwealth nations and territories). However, immigrants from the *Windrush* and subsequent waves of migration soon discovered that they were not welcome in a country purportedly suffering both a labor and population shortage; indeed, a wave of subsequent nationality acts attempted to limit and then halt migration from the former colonies.[18] The reasoning behind this chilly welcome was of course that "because they were black, colonials could not be so absorbed and were thus unfit for permanent settlement" (Paul 1997, 125). However legally British citizens, nonwhite colonials could never be truly part of the "family." These circles of Britishness revolve around competing—or perhaps complementary—temporalities: those of British stock will forever maintain that family identity; those possessing white skin can, over time, become assimilated into this family; those who are racially marked as nonwhite are forever barred from any assimilation that goes beyond mere legal formalities. If, as Vron Ware and Les Back argue, "the past is approached as a source of evidence for the differences among national, ethnic, or even racial collectives," then this naturalist familial claim to time passed attempts to restrict cultural transmission (Ware and Back 2002, 188). Whiteness is the quality that allows continuity of identity despite apparent changes of material circumstance or, alternatively, a subtle transformation of that identity. Failure to possess this quality serves as a permanent break that prevents one from ever changing this sense of self; it is an original sin of sorts that prevents its bearer from ever joining the happy family regardless of legal citizenship.

Ironically, it seems to be this very exclusion of African, Asian, and Caribbean immigrants from the heart of the nation that grounds the revitalized search for the lost essence that is Englishness. Vron Ware charts just this movement in her discussion of assertions of English identity, assertions that key on whiteness as a primary characteristic of this selfhood (Ware 2001). However, these identity appeals are made by disaffected white British teens, appeals that are self-consciously modeled after the identifying assertions of Britons of Caribbean descent. Englishness, then, only comes after Britishness and is in fact modeled on particular performances of British identity.[19] What Ware does not note, however, is the way in which the restriction of "English" for whites begins to give "British" a racial marker. This new distinction is borne out in a recent *New York Times* article by Yasmin Alibhai-Brown celebrating a new "Cool Britannia" that is resolutely multicultural and multiethnic. Here *Notting Hill* is striking not because of its cinematic white-washing, but rather beguiles because "it is where the soul of multiracial

Britain resides . . . because it is so un-English" (Alibhai-Brown 2002, 14). Indeed, English is now only a "simplistic 'pure' identity," merely one of a number of ethnic identities occasionally appealed to as authorizing the young to violence. Integration has remade the "Scepter'd Isle" such that curry is the favorite food of the nation and Zadie Smith's *White Teeth* the most representative novel of London. Ironically, this remaking of the island of village cricket and warm beer stems from a long-standing desire for "consuming multiculturalism"; in fact, Alibhai-Brown attributes the entire imperial enterprise to a "peculiarly irrepressible English need for the exotic." It is an English need for otherness that brings about a remaking of identity into Britishness, one oriented around a movement of "the Other of the imperial Self back 'home'" (Jacobs 1996, 71). Englishness is undone from within, an undoing that ironically precedes its own formulation. It founders on the temporal instability of race.

If the whiteness at the core of Englishness is an identity formation that has, according to David Roediger, no positive value, then its normalizing function as a default difference from racial alterity operates in a temporal schism of sorts (Roediger 1994, 13). Similarly, Phil Cohen labels race itself as "an empty category or degree zero of representation, an 'X marks the spot' that is not Y, a difference placed outside language and inside the body by a discursive operation that is necessarily subject to unconscious disavowal and repetition" (Cohen 1997, 246). Whiteness as negated signifier naturally depends on the stock deconstructive deferral of reference—its presence as a sign of racial identity based first on the prior exclusion of all other hues and tones. More strikingly, by establishing a putative absence of racial marking, whiteness establishes itself as a pure absence, a lack against which any positive mark of identity appears as a contingency. Absolute absence equals a vision of self whose performance and agency is unmarked—and unimpaired—by any trace that would mark that identity as situated— and hence limited—by gender, sexuality, class, etc. The operations of this ideology would certainly seem to account for the limitations that Emily and Cambridge experience in the performance of their Englishness. Such limitations seem to reveal that on the island, national and racial identity work very similarly to what Kathleen Paul has charted in the extension of postimperial Britishness after the arrival of the *Empire Windrush* in 1948. Similarly, David Henderson enacts a cultural Englishness, but his transformation into the black slave Cambridge renders this identification "comical" and "lunatic" in the eyes of Emily and Mr. Brown. Likewise, Mr. Brown's treatment of Emily abrogates her advantages of Englishness and ownership (well, near ownership) by dint of gender. Whiteness gestures toward some originary identity that positions all other identifying characteristics as epiphenomena experienced as a fall away from this origin. This purported lack of race thus functions as a disciplinary move to conceal and co-opt other identifying differences. As a result, whiteness rhetorically gestures to an identity out of time.

However, in *Cambridge* this time of whiteness remains in tension with a competing racial temporality. This tension becomes apparent in scenes such as the one in which Emily initially imagines black children to be "monkeys," a classic denial of coevalness. As critics such as Warren Montag have noted, such a specular move at once renders distinctions from whiteness as prehistorical or pre-evolutionary while offering a simultaneous and implicit assumption of whiteness as congruent with the human itself, an overlay that then dates and limits the humanity of whiteness in the moment of colonial contact. Because of this overlap between white and human, whiteness functions as a universal characteristic of humanity, positioning it as an eternal and ever-present attribute. Whiteness is here the continual present of the human, yet one whose universal humanity is forever bound by the colonial frame in which it was composed. This temporal divide of racial identity parallels a gap between the three accounts that compose the body of *Cambridge*. Together these narratives point toward larger questions of temporality in the novel—namely, whether its historiography functions in a postmodern or postcolonial register. On the one hand, the competing tales problematize the writing of the past by implicitly marking the selections and omissions of historical composition. By making the operations of the present in writing the past an integral part of the story, such a gesture hints that if all times are not one, they at least operate on the same schizophrenic plane. On the other hand, because the events surrounding Mr. Brown's death are never fully clarified, the past is marked as irrecuperable, as a traumatic break. Indeed, both Emily and Cambridge regard their travels and final arrival on the island as an identificatory break: The former David Henderson leaves Africa for the first time thinking that "[o]ur history was truly broken" and that "Africa spoke to me only of a history I had cast aside"; Emily steps onto the island thinking that she "was breaking the last remaining link with a past that I understood" (Phillips, 137, 22). The novel's historiography then fractures into an antinomy of the past's eternal presence through pastiche and the past's signification of irretrievable alterity. This tension helps extend the conflicting deployments of whiteness as universal presence or originary— and unreconstructable—absence. This gap manifests itself in the split between Cambridge's attempts to acquire the purportedly universal distinctions of the white English—language, religion, culture—and Emily's refusal to grant "true" whiteness and Englishness even to the creole whites on the island by dint of their birth on the unnamed Caribbean island. Whiteness falters between a rhetorically extensive present and a constricted past, between an attempt to assimilate disparate identities and a reflexive ambition to deny all identificatory marks as contingent.

NOTES

1. Evelyn O'Callaghan has raised a similar point about the ironies bound up in the novel's title (35).

2. I have in mind novels such as Salman Rushdie's *The Satanic Verses*, Hanif Kureishi's *The Buddha of Suburbia*, and Zadie Smith's *White Teeth*. Largely staged in the postimperial city, these novels chart the performances and pains of identity of the "new British."

3. As my emphasis on textuality here indicates, I am tracing in *Cambridge* a strategy similar to the "postcolonial archive" that Sandhya Shetty and Elizabeth Jane Bellamy locate in Gayatri Spivak. In short, the postcolonial archive might be best viewed as a palimpsestic gap instituted by imperialism. My use of this layering moves not back toward the irretrievable figure of the historical subaltern but rather forward to the dislocated presence of what Spivak has recently termed the Resident Alien. This figure belongs to an abstract territoriality that robs it of "the more salient abstractions of an everyday civility, a willing suspension of civil rights . . . this Resident Alien is a vestigial postcolonial figure" (48).

4. A number of critics identify the third narrative as a newspaper account of the death of Mr. Brown. However, the narrative's opening clearly positions it as taking place some time after the events in question: "In the year 18__, another murder was committed, the details of which are as follows" (171). This stress on a series of murders that can only be narrated from a position of retrospect helps to highlight the detached historical tone assumed in this tale. However, this apparent objectivity is undercut by the narrator's obsessive interest with gothic atmosphere and superstition. Even more importantly, the unnamed historical narrator errs numerous times in details supplied by the accounts of Emily and Cambridge, and Emily, who has been an important factor in our understanding of Mister Brown's death, goes completely unmentioned.

5. It should be noted that Emily seems to suggest that class on the island is itself an adversial dichotomy; this is in contrast to what David Cannadine has suggested is the dominant British model of class, the seamless hierarchical web (20). Cannadine argues that while the web model stresses a backward-looking view in need of preservation, the dichotomy rubric of class "is often concerned with how society *might be*" (174).

6. Even without the contrast of Cambridge, there are significant hints within Emily's own narrative as to the inadequacy of this conception of nation and race. Emily suggests that England is a gift that she might "give" Stella, "[s]omething that the two of them might share" (178). However, this overlooks not only the question of whether the gift is something that is truly desired, but also Emily's own warning that the gift of nation will not be equally shared: "I have been thinking seriously of taking her [Stella] back with me to England, but my fear is that she may be mocked as an exotic, as are the other blacks who congregate about the parish of St Giles and in divers parts of our kingdom" (78).

7. Cambridge's unstable identity, one reflected in the many names he acquires over the course of his peregrinations (Olumide, Thomas, David Henderson, Cambridge, and Hercules—Emily's own nickname for him), places a great strain on his narrating/narrative to add a structuring coherence to his many incarnations. Much of this is supplied by the pattern supplied by his Christianity and his identification with the English language.

8. See for example the scenes with the Warwickshire minister (153), Rogers (160), and Emily (165). Cambridge, however, continually stresses his claims to Christianity, England, and the English language itself in his apologia. It is this

identification that largely grounds Paul Sharrad's suggestion that Cambridge's steadfast affiliation with Englishness constitutes his "mental enslavement" (203). However, Cambridge's Englishness, as I suggest here, is ambivalent: although the slave of many names does buy into a large portion of the ideology undergirding the imperial project, he at the same time does turn this ideology against itself. This reversal is displayed in such examples as his abolition lectures, discourses that offer the thesis that "the air of our island is too pure for slavery to breathe in" (Phillips 1991, 148). Perhaps even more striking is the threat that characters such as Emily, Brown, and the local historian locate in Cambridge's assumption of Englishness, an assumption that portends a rewriting of this national identity.

9. I am not suggesting that the assumption of Englishness depends on being accepted as English. Rather, I am tracing in *Cambridge* the postimperial lesson that reading the performance of nationness simply as enactment overlooks the injuries inflicted by those who reject the performer's "right" to play the part. Similarly, the danger of putting too much stress on Cambridge as an ideological dupe is that such a reading undercuts the destabilizing effectiveness of his performance. With regards to the minstrelsy of Cambridge's Englishness, Malini Johar Schueller has usefully labeled a similar staging of these cultural markers as performing "whiteface."

10. Contrast Emily's negative appraisal of Cambridge's polished English with her initial reaction to Stella's "anguished" command of the language: "I had no desire to hear my mother-tongue mocked by the curious thick utterance of the Negro language, so she might abandon her comical jargon and adopt English" (29). Emily, of course, displays anxiety in the face of very markedly different styles of adaptation and co-option. Her reactions with Stella and Cambridge demonstrate that she regards both with linguistic anxiety—that both a "comical" mockery and a precise performance are versions of what Homi Bhabha has described as a sly civility. See Bhabha, 93–101.

11. Frankenberg traces the assignment of roles as based on racialized and gendered division of ideologically complimentary identities: "White Woman is frail, vulnerable, delicate, sexually pure but at times easily led 'astray.' White Man is strong, dominant, arbiter of truth, and self-designated protector of white womankind, defender of the nation/territory (and here defense of the nation and its honor often also entails defending White Woman's racial chastity). Man of Color . . . is sexually rapacious, sometimes seductive, usually predatory, especially toward White Woman; it is he, in fact, from whom White Woman must be protected by White Man. And, finally, Woman of Color . . . is also sexually eager, seductress, willing and able consort, especially for the White Man of this tropological family, personally unhygienic, overly fertile, but also usable for breeding" (Frankenberg 1997, 11–12).

12. See for example Phillips, 58, 74.

13. See also Schaw 78. Evelyn O'Callaghan has identified some other intertextual sources for Emily's narrative as Monk Lewis's *Journal of a West India Proprietor*, *Lady Nugent's Journal of her Residence in Jamaica*, and Mrs. Carmichael's *Domestic Manners and Social Conditions of the White, Coloured, and Negro Population of the West Indies*. One source for Cambridge's own tale is *The Interesting Narrative of the Life of Olaudah Equiano* (O'Callaghan 1993, 36–39). Paul Sharrad suggests that another might be Thomas Day's "The Dying Slave" (212).

14. It is perhaps one of *Cambridge*'s little jokes that, while Emily's account is in part derived from Monk Lewis's journal, it is the purportedly factual narrative of the local history that is most inflected with gothic strains.

15. These allusions suggest that the novel takes place around the time of the 1833 Parliamentary act abolishing slavery. The act took effect on July 31, 1834; it was originally stipulated that the slaves would remain as apprentices to the plantations that had formerly owned them for a period of four to six years. However, this system of an apprenticeship transition did not work and was abandoned in 1838, thus formally bringing slavery to an end. See Martin 95–98.

16. The *Empire Windrush* docked in Britain in June 1948 bearing almost five hundred Caribbean immigrants. Its arrival is viewed as the beginning of large-scale immigration from the "New Commonwealth" colonies and former colonies in the postwar era. See Paul 111–30.

17. In contrast, by the end of her narrative, Emily wonders if she can ever return to England: "I began to wonder if I should ever again adjust to the fare of England. Was I doomed to become an exotic for the rest of my days?" (114).

18. These legal emendations and erasures of the 1948 Nationality Act culminated in the passing of Margaret Thatcher's 1981 Nationality Act establishing three tiers for British nationality: "British citizenship, British Dependent Territories citizenship, and British Overseas Citizenship. British citizenship was largely acquired by former UKC citizens who themselves, or whose parents or grandparents, had been born, adopted, naturalized, or registered in the UK, and former UKC citizens who had been legally settled in the UK for five years" (Paul, 182). By this legalization of "family ties," the Act effectively ended any hope of immigration to the UK for most nonwhite citizens of former colonies while preserving the Britishness of whites residing in these newly independent nations. White Britishness is thus maintained because of the bond of common stock, a bond that can survive emigration and the passing of generations, while nonwhite Britishness was concluded to be at best a mere legal formality, for such putative Britons could never hope to adequately assimilate into the family of true British blood. This denial of "true" citizenship and belonging to nonwhites is perhaps best seen in the drama surrounding the refusal of immigration appeals in the 1997 return of Hong Kong. Ironically, by basing its denials on actual blood ties and parentage, Britain's refusal emphatically gave the lie to the ideology that had encouraged colonials subjects to look to Britain as the "motherland," with itself as the head of the "imperial family." For an illuminating discussion of the identity ramifications of the 1981 Act, see Baucom (7–40). Goulbourne and Solomos also offer extensive discussions of the racial politics of immigration in postimperial Britain.

19. Robert Young notes that the uneasy distinction between British and English in fact veils a founding violence: "Englishness is itself also uncertainly British, a cunning word of apparent political correctness invoked in order to mask the metonymic extension of English dominance over the other kingdoms with which England has constructed illicit acts of union" (3).

REFERENCES

Alibhai-Brown, Yasmin. 25 June 2000. A magic carpet of cultures in London. *New York Times on the Web*. http://www.nytimes.com/library/arts/062500 multicultural-london.html. April 17, 2002.

Anderson, Benedict. 1992. *Imagined communities: Reflections on the origin and spread of nationalism*. London: Verso.

Ashcroft, Bill. 2001. *Post-colonial transformation*. New York: Routledge.

Balibar, Etienne. 1994. *Masses, classes, ideas: Studies on politics and philosophy before and after Marx*. Trans. James Swenson. New York: Routledge.

Baucom, Ian. 1999. *Out of place: Englishness, empire, and the locations of identity*. Princeton: Princeton University Press.

Bhabha, Homi K. 1994. *The location of culture*. New York: Routledge.

Cannadine, David. 1999. *The rise and fall of class in Britain*. New York: Columbia University Press.

Cohen, Phil. 1997. Laboring under whiteness. In *Displacing whiteness: Essays in social and cultural criticism*, ed. Ruth Frankenberg. Durham: Duke University Press.

Dyer, Richard. 1997. *White*. New York: Routledge.

Fabian, Johannes. 1983. *Time and the other: How anthropology makes its object*. New York: Columbia University Press.

Fanon, Frantz. [1952] 1967. *Black skin white masks*. Trans. Charles Lam Markmann. Reprint. New York: Grove Weidenfeld.

Frankenberg, Ruth, ed. 1997. *Displacing whiteness: Essays in social and cultural criticsm*. Durham: Duke University Press.

————. 2001. The mirage of an unmarked whiteness. In *The making and unmaking of whiteness*, ed. Brigit Rasmussen, Eric Klingenberg, Irene J. Nexica, and Matt Wray, 72–96. Durham: Duke University Press.

Gilroy, Paul. 1987. *There ain't no black in the Union Jack*. Chicago: University of Chicago Press.

————. 1993. *Small acts: Thoughts on the politics of black cultures*. New York: Serpent's Tail.

Goldberg, David Theo. 2002. Racial rule. In Goldberg, 82–102.

Goldberg, David Theo, and Ato Quayson, eds. 2002. *Relocating postcolonialism*. Malden, MA: Blackwell.

Goulbourne, Harry. 1991. *Ethnicity and nationalism in post-imperial Britain*. New York: Cambridge University Press.

Heise, Ursula K. 1997. *Chronoschisms: Time, narrative, and postmodernism*. New York: Cambridge University Press.

Hesse, Barnor. 2002. Forgotten like a bad dream: Atlantic slavery and the ethics of postcolonial memory. In *Relocating postcolonialism*, ed. David Theo Goldberg and Ato Quayson, 143–73. Malden, MA: Blackwell.

Hill, Mike, ed. *Whiteness: A critical reader*. New York: New York University Press.

Jacobs, Jane M. 1996. *Edge of empire: Postcolonialism and the city*. New York: Routledge.

Kureishi, Hanif. 1990. *The buddha of suburbia*. London: Faber and Faber.

Low, Gail. 1998. "A chorus of common memory": Slavery and redemption in Caryl Phillip's *Cambridge* and *Crossing the River*. *Research in African Literatures* 29, no. 4: 122–40.

Martin, S. I. 1999. *Britain's slave trade*. London: Macmillan.

Montag, Warren. 1997. The universalization of whiteness: Racism and enlightenment. In *Whiteness: A critical reader*, ed. Mike Hill, 281–93. New York: New York University Press.

O'Callaghan, Eveylyn. 1993. Historical fiction and fictional history. *Journal of Commonwealth Literature* 29, no. 2: 34–47.

Paul, Kathleen. 1997. *Whitewashing Britain: Race and citizenship in the postwar era*. Ithaca: Cornell University Press.

Phillips, Caryl. 1991. *Cambridge: A novel.* New York: Vintage Books.

Quayson, Ato. 2000. Postcolonialism and postmodernism. In *A companion to postcolonial studies,* ed. Henry Schwarz and Sangetta Ray, 87–111. Malden, MA: Blackwell.

Brander Rasmussen, Birgit, Eric Klingenberg, Irene J. Nexica, and Matt Wray, eds. 2001. *The making and unmaking of whiteness.* Durham: Duke University Press.

Roediger, David R. 1994. *Towards the abolition of whiteness.* New York: Verso.

Rushdie, Salman. 1992. *The satanic verses.* Dover, DE: The Consortium.

Schueller, Malini Johar. 1999. Performing whiteness, performing blackness: Dorr's cultural capital and the critique of slavery. *Criticism* 41, no. 2: 233–56.

Schaw, Janet. 1927. *Journal of a lady of quality: Being the narrative of a journey from Scotland to the West Indies, North Carolina, and Portugal, in the years 1774 to 1776.* New Haven: Yale University Press.

Schwarz, Henry, and Sangetta Ray, eds. *A companion to postcolonial studies.* Malden, MA: Blackwell.

Sharrad, Paul. 1994. Speaking the unspeakable: London, *Cambridge,* and the Caribbean. In *De-scribing empire: Post-colonialism and textuality,* ed. Chris Tifin, and Alan Lawson, 201–17. New York: Routledge.

Shetty, Sandhya, and Elizabeth Jane Bellamy. 2000. Postcolonialism's archive fever. *diacritics* 30, no. 1: 25–48.

Smith, Zadie. 2000. *White teeth.* New York: Random House.

Solomos, John. 1989. *Race and racism in contemporary Britain.* London: Macmillan.

Spivak, Gayatri Chakravorty. 2002. Resident alien. In *Relocating postcolonialism,* ed. David Theo Goldberg and Ato Quayson, 47–65. Oxford: Blackwell.

Tifin, Chris, and Alan Lawson, eds. 1994. *De-scribing empire: Post-colonialism and textuality.* New York: Routledge.

Ware, Vron. 1992. *Beyond the pale: White women, racism, and history.* New York: Verso.

———. 2001. Perfidious Albion: Whiteness and the international imagination. In *The making and unmaking of whiteness,* ed. Brigit Rasmussen, Eric Klingenberg, Irene J. Nexica, Matt Wray, 184–213. Durham: Duke University Press.

Ware, Vron, and Les Back. 2002. *Out of whiteness: Color, politics, and culture.* Chicago: University of Chicago Press.

Young, Robert. 1995. *Colonial desire: Hybridity in theory, culture, and race.* New York: Routledge.

CONTRIBUTORS

John C. Hawley is Associate Professor of English at Santa Clara University. He has edited ten books, most recently *Encyclopedia of Postcolonial Studies* (Greenwood, 2001) and *Postcolonial, Queer* (SUNY, 2001). He is currently co-editing a book on globalization.

Cheryl Temple Herr is Professor of English and Cinema/Comparative Literature at the University of Iowa. She has published widely on James Joyce, Irish studies, cultural studies, and film. Her recent books include *Critical Regionalism and Cultural Studies* (UP of Florida, 1996) and *Ireland into Film: The Field* (Cork UP, 2002).

Anikó Imre teaches film and media studies at the University of Washington, and is a postdoctoral research fellow at the Amsterdam School for Cultural Analysis. She is currently completing a book about East and Central European identities and media globalization. Her writings about feminism, postcoloniality, and visual media have appeared in *Screen*, *Framework*, *Camera Obscura*, and a number of collected volumes.

Christopher Kelen is Assistant Professor in the English Department at the University of Macau, where he also edits the online journal *Writing Macao: Creative Text and Teaching*. Kelen is the author of five volumes of poetry, the most recent of which is *New Territories: A Foreigner's Pilgrimage Through Hong Kong*. Apart from his creative work, Kelen publishes in a range of theoretical areas including writing pedagogy, ethics, rhetoric, cultural and literary studies, and various intersections of these. Kelen's work-in-progress is a book-length work tentatively entitled *Anthem Quality: Nation and Song in Australia*.

Alfred J. López is an assistant professor in the Department of English at The University of Mississippi. He is the author of *Posts and Pasts: A Theory of Postcolonialism* (SUNY, 2001) and the recipient of a Bellagio Residential Fellowship from the Rockefeller Foundation. López is currently at work on his next book, a study of Cuban revolutionary writer José Martí.

Diane Roberts is Professor of English at The University of Alabama. She is the author of *Faulkner and Southern Womanhood* (U Georgia P, 1993) and *The Myth of Aunt Jemima* (Routledge, 1994), and a contributor to various magazines including *The Oxford American* and *The New Republic*. Roberts is also a journalist, writing for the *Atlanta Journal-Constitution* and *Orlando Sentinel* and working as a commentator for National Public Radio. Her new book *Dream State*, a history of Florida, is forthcoming from Simon and Schuster in October 2004.

Frances B. Singh is Professor of English at Hostos Community College/ CUNY. She has published several articles on Conrad and Forster, and has also published in the areas of radical pedagogy, ESL, and feminist studies.

Melissa Steyn is the Director of the Institute for Intercultural and Diversity Studies of Southern Africa and Senior Lecturer in the Department of Sociology at The University of Cape Town. She is the author of *Whiteness Just Isn't What It Used to Be: White Identity in a Changing South Africa* (SUNY, 2001).

Ryan S. Trimm is Assistant Professor in the Department of English at The University of Rhode Island. His essays have appeared in *Politics and Culture* and *Contemporary Literature*.

Gerry Turcotte is Head of the School of English Literatures, Philosophy, and Languages at the University of Wollongong. He is the author and editor of many publications including *Jack Davis: The Maker of History* (HarperCollins) and *Neighbourhood of Memory* (Dangaroo). His novel *Flying in Silence* was published in Canada and Australia and was shortlisted for The Age Book of the Year in 2001.

INDEX